BLOOD & GUTS

VIOLENCE IN SPORTS

DON ATYEO

PADDINGTON
PRESS LTD
NEW YORK & LONDON

Library of Congress Cataloging in Publication Data

Atyeo, Don.
  Blood & guts, violence in sports.

  Bibliography: p.
  Includes index.
  1. Violence in sports.   I. Title.
GV706.7.A89   796   78-23413
ISBN 0-448-22000-8 (U.S. and Canada only)
ISBN 0 7092 0000 5

Filmset in England by SX Composing Ltd.,
Rayleigh, Essex
Printed and bound in the United States
Designed by Sandra Shafee

IN THE UNITED STATES
PADDINGTON PRESS
Distributed by
GROSSET & DUNLAP

IN THE UNITED KINGDOM
PADDINGTON PRESS

IN CANADA
Distributed by
RANDOM HOUSE OF CANADA LTD.

IN SOUTHERN AFRICA
Distributed by
ERNEST STANTON (PUBLISHERS) (PTY.) LTD.

"Detested sport,
That owes its pleasure to another's pain."

William Cowper

ACKNOWLEDGMENTS

For Sue Ready, who truly made it possible.

Besides those surgeons, psychologists and sports figures who gave me their time so generously for interviews and whose names have already appeared within the text, there are a number of others who should not go unmentioned. In the United States, the hospitality of the Runyon family, Lucy Lasky and Joel, and Louis Clark and Penny Bevis proved as valuable as it was delightful. Paddington's New York researcher Kati Boland assisted unstintingly, as did Dr. Friedrich Unterharnscheidt, Mark Masson, Gez and Janice Cox, Ted Quedenfeld and the publicity directors of the NY Jets, the NY Rangers, the Philadelphia Flyers, Madison Square Garden and the LA Rams.

In Britain Ruth Hapgood, the *Sunday Times*'s Dudley Doust, the *Observer*'s Bobby Campbell, Dave Wetton of the Hunt Saboteurs, James Black of the BFSS, Caroline Humphries, Dr. Desmond Morris and Felix Dennis all provided welcome assistance and encouragement, as did Australians Ben Hills, Bev Will and Rolly Perry. Finally there is Diane Flanel, an editor of infinite help and uncommon patience.

The extract on pp. 323–326 is an edited transcription from the CBS special entitled *Evel Knievel's Death Defiers*, aired in the USA in early 1977.

NOTE: Professional sport is, of course, in a state of constant flux. Players trade positions and owners trade players with bewildering frequency. Since I concluded this book, many of those with whom I spoke have changed allegiances, or, like Joe Namath, have retired from the bench altogether. I have tried my best to keep the names updated, but inevitably by the time this book is published others will have changed their loyalties. The problem, regrettably, is unavoidable. In the long run, though, the individual player is relatively unimportant; it is the condition of contemporary sport which is fundamentally at issue here.

CONTENTS

4 THE BRAWL GAME   184
Ball Sports

Origins · Mob Ball · Rugby · Soccer · Australian Rules ·
American Gridiron · Ice Hockey

5 THE WINNING EDGE

Gridiron · Ice Hockey · Baseball · Tennis ·
Basketball · Soccer · Rugby · Cricket

6 SOLDIERS FOR SPORT   298
Soccer Hooliganism and Other Spectator Sports

INTRODUCTION

O n August 15, 1976, second-division Rugby Union player Colin Vaughan had just completed what he reckoned to be his last kick for the season when he was crashed to the ground from behind by a vicious late tackle. It was a particularly nasty piece of premeditated violence, made all the worse by the fact that the game was already decisively lost. At the time, nothing much was said; the match had all but ended and a free kick either way would not have altered the score. Rubbing the small of his aching back where he could still feel the imprint of his opponent's knees, Vaughan consoled himself with the thought that his teammates had also been fairly well battered.

That night Vaughan and his girlfriend went to an end-of-season party. At the beginning he felt fine, but gradually the pain in his back became worse and worse. By eleven o'clock he was in agony, with great bolts of pain searing through his body. When he began to urinate blood, his friends rushed him to the nearest hospital. The doctor who examined him suspected kidney damage, but the tests showed nothing wrong. Luckily the hospital decided to keep him overnight for further observation.

By morning Vaughan was crippled with pain, pain which he had never believed possible. All he could do was curl into a ball and rock backwards and forwards on his knees. Every three hours a nurse injected him with as much morphine as she dared risk, but it made little difference. The doctors, still convinced it was a kidney injury, continued their tests. Suddenly Vaughan's blood pressure dropped alarmingly and a large swelling appeared across his back.

At eleven o'clock that night Vaughan was anesthetized and wheeled into the operating theater. After removing one rib and breaking through two others, the surgeon reached Vaughan's liver. It was burst open like an overstuffed feather cushion. In the membrane which surrounded the damaged organ hung an enormous blood clot comprising more than a liter of blood. Vaughan was fortunate; if the membrane had ruptured, the blood would have flooded his stomach and he would have died almost immediately, drowned in his own blood. As it was, he was still only moments away from death. For the next five hours the surgeon worked to remove the clot, in the process carving off the top third of his liver.

It was a week before the doctors were certain that Vaughan would live, and another two weeks before he was removed from intensive care. For the next four months he was bedridden, so befuddled with drugs that he could barely speak. His lung collapsed, requiring another operation to drain the fluid. When he was finally strong enough to stand, he found that a walk around the house left him totally exhausted. He lost over thirty pounds. It was not until January of the next year that he began to function normally.

I met Vaughan not long after, quite by chance – the friend of a friend. By then I was something of a connoisseur of sporting violence, having spent the previous six months tracking bleeding fists and broken skulls across two continents. I had seen an ice hockey player open an opponent's face with his stick much as one would slice a ripe melon; watched Evel Knievel leap a shark tank and slide across the stadium floor into a Chicago hospital bed; inspected Joe Namath's ruined knees; watched as a pot-bellied hunter riddled an exotic sheep at point-blank range with a pistol. I would see lots more; sporting violence is not hard to find.

Compared to some of the human wrecks I had encountered during my travels, Vaughan seemed in remarkably good health. Admittedly cold days still sent spasms of pain shooting through his chest where his rib once was and even moderate exercise left him exhausted, but he was in infinitely better shape than, say, the former rugby international paralyzed from the neck down whom I interviewed, or the ex-pug I saw swaying on the ring apron shouting garbled advice to his fighters through a mouth running with spit and filled with marbles. Sport's casualties are also not that difficult to find.

Yet out of all this glaring pain and suffering, it was Vaughan's story which chilled me most. For the first time I realized that I was dealing with *human* injury as opposed to sporting injury. "When you're stopped in your tracks in a major way like I was," he told me, "suddenly you realize that for a game of football, that could have been it . . . you're dead . . . and you don't get a second chance. And suddenly it's not the other guy, the guy you don't like because he's on the other team or whatever. Suddenly it comes home to you that, *shit!*, it's *my* pain!"

It was not my liver that had been ruptured; in fact, I barely knew the man whose liver it was. Yet he was someone a good friend of mine knew well, someone who could not simply be dismissed at the end of the interview as just another statistic in sport's continuing body count, and for me that was enough to cut through the rosy glow which surrounds the great, throbbing, neon-lit business we call sport.

Sports columnist Jimmy Cannon once said that sport is the toy department of newspaper journalism – which, when you consider it, is a reasonably fair observation. Sport does not revive flagging economies, end wars (although it has helped in beginning one) or effect any major changes in the running of state (unless one includes such incidentals as the death of the French ambassador at the hands of the Austrian ambassador during a recent hunting trip in Yugoslavia). The fact remains, however, that we spend an inordinate amount of our time in the toy room; more, for most of us, than we spend in the living room. Sport consumes our weekends and our Monday nights, our evenings and our vacations. In short, sport is what we choose to do when given the choice. "Did you get the results of the All-Star game?" asked Richard Nixon of the moon-walk astronauts on their return to Earth, and how many of his fellow Americans considered it such a bizarre question?

The result of this collective immersion in what author Robert Lipsyte has labeled "Sportsworld" is that we have become so familiar with our toys that we can now barely recognize them for what they are. While many of our most precious games are undeniably thrilling, invigorating and occasionally even breathtakingly beautiful, they are also by the same token savage, cruel and ruthlessly violent. Yet we fail to see them that way.

The thing about sport is that it legitimizes violence, thereby laundering it acceptably clean. Incidents routinely occur in the name of sport which, if they were perpetrated under any other banner short of open warfare, would be roundly condemned as crimes against humanity. The mugger in the parking lot is a villain; the mugger on the playing field is a hero. The pain inflicted in sport is somehow not really pain at all; it is Tom and Jerry pain, cartoon agony which doesn't hurt. We can sit happily at the ringside watching a Chuck Wepner have his face split and torn by a Sonny Liston, yet if we were forced backstage to watch the doctor lace 120 stitches into that same face we would turn away in horror.

The blindness with which we view sports is extraordinary. "Actually, I don't really know why you are here," said the spokesman for the British Field Sports Society, Britain's hunting lobby. "Field sports aren't *violent*." This after we had spent the better part of the morning discussing hares being torn apart by greyhounds, stags having their throats slit, foxes dying under packs of hounds and hand-reared pheasants being blasted out of the sky. The morality of such practices may be up for grabs, but even to question that they are all calculated set pieces of extreme violence – let alone to deny it – seems ludicrous. Yet that is invariably what happens, particularly among those who actually participate in the violence. "Nah, it's not so violent," shrugged battle-scarred and toothless ice hockey star Bobby Clarke.

Yet many of our most popular sports are violent – often incredibly violent. Each year American sportsmen and sportswomen sustain a staggering toll of twenty million injuries serious enough to be treated by a doctor. Of these twenty million, six million leave lasting and permanent reminders, ranging from scars to paraplegia to death. If those twenty million injured were the annual casualties of some foreign war, there would be uproar. As victims of sport, we hardly even notice them. The sports which began life as war games – boxing, hunting, wrestling, football and so on – we have continued as war games, playing them in exactly the same manner as we fight our wars – to win by any means at our disposal, including tooth-and-nail violence. After continuing centuries of playing-field Armageddons, the line dividing sport and war has never been so blurred. The images are continually overlapping: the gang tackling of a quarterback becomes a "blitz," the players become "platoons"; the mining of Haiphong Harbor becomes "Operation Linebacker," the strategy of bombing Cambodia a "game plan."

"It's like football," said Nixon, outlining his Vietnam "game plan" to the press. "You run a play and it fails. Then you turn around and call the same play again because they aren't expecting it." "It's like war," thinks Woody Hayes, the most successful college football coach in America, as he studies his numerous military history books. Fed an endless stream of computer data from his spies in the stands, Woody is as much a twentieth-century general as the NATO chief marching his divisions through the Rhine Valley. When Air Force jets fly over the Super Bowl, the symbols dove-tail perfectly: war into sport; sport into war. It has taken many centuries to achieve – countless Armageddons to condition us into blindly accepting warfare as our major entertainment. But that is what has now come to pass.

It is only when sport rears up and kicks us personally in the teeth – as it did to Colin Vaughan – that we recoil. For three years Arnold Mandell, a noted Los Angeles psychiatrist, was closely involved with American football, including one season spent directly on the sideline as a staff member of the San Diego Chargers. The season that I spoke to him was the season he finally quit going to football matches. His reason was this:

> The last game I went to a spectator got very excited and fell out of a stand thirty feet and hit the ground. He was jerking about and I thought he might have broken his neck. I thought, how awful that this should happen, how terrible! And then I said to myself, hey, what's happening over there will happen seven times this afternoon. . . . The players, they are doing that to each other *all the time* . . . broken necks and broken legs and broken ribs and fractured this and fractured that and concussions and unconsciousness. But they are in uniform and psychologically segmented off. . . . They are not *humans*. And suddenly there's this guy with no uniform – soft! – and suddenly it's a *human being* that hits the ground and jerks around. All the while the

band played and the loudspeakers gave out their announcements and the teams went on about their business, and suddenly it was too naked. Suddenly that was the essence of everything, and I couldn't go back.

Such revelations in Sportsworld are rare. We find it extraordinarily difficult to see our sports as they really are. It is almost as difficult as admitting that they are what they are because that is the way we like them.

This book is an attempt to discover just how violent our sports really are, to trace how we have come to accept them so happily and to examine how they affect us. It should, of course, include all sports as in every game there is either violence or the potential for it. However, I have selected sports which I consider best embody our passion for sporting violence – combat sports (boxing, wrestling, the martial arts), killing sports (hunting, bullfighting), heavy-contact games (football, hockey) and risk sports (motor racing). With respect to this last category, there are many risk sports which I have purposely omitted; hang gliding and mountaineering, for instance, are two supremely dangerous sports which do not appear here. This is because they are accessible only to their participants and as such remain only risk sports. Motor racing, on the other hand, has packaged its risks and sold them to an audience – not so much as risks, but as the spectacle of violence.

Violence is a threadbare catch-all of a word and I am no doubt guilty of stretching it even thinner. I have used it primarily in the sense of successful aggression toward an object, an animal or another person. Unlike most press reports which see sporting violence only as an infringement of the rules, I have applied the word to both "legal" and "illegal" incidents. For the purposes of this book, Mean Joe Greene is guilty of using violence whether he hits his opponent with his fist or blocks him with his shoulder.

One last word on semantics: throughout the book I have described athletes and, to a lesser extent, fans almost solely in terms of the male gender – "sportsman." I did this not just because it is easier, or because females are a nonviolent species, but because violent sports are almost exclusively a male preserve. The football field and the hunting lodge are two of the last great bastions of male bonding. Indeed, overt masculinity – *machismo* – is one of the reasons why sport today is as violent as it is.

I should perhaps add that I did not set out to write an anti-sport book, although that is what parts of it have turned out to be. I still believe that there is a need in our societies for the pleasure and joy which sport can offer to both its participants and its spectators. One of the genuine tragedies of our frantic rush toward more and more violent sports is that we have succeeded in ruining some very fine games.

CALL OF THE WILD

1

N CREEK
NCH
NG

1 Call of the Wild
Hunting

The hunt started from the kitchen of Richard Grona's comfortable clapboard bungalow shortly before sunrise. It was an encouraging place for a hunter to begin a day's sport, exactly what one might reasonably expect from a man whose job it was to manage eleven hundred acres of rolling Texas scrubland devoted exclusively to the business of hunting. The walls of the bungalow were cluttered with framed photographs depicting dozens of satisfied customers surrounded by their trophies: overweight softgoods manufacturers from Philadelphia proudly propping up unseeing heads; steely-eyed corporate chiefs standing ramrod straight beside prize carcasses dangling from the scales; immaculate Country-and-Western stars flashing pearly smiles amid masses of horns and antlers. In the adjoining trophy room the mounted heads of a dozen different species peered down through glass eyes.

But despite all this visible reassurance as to the pleasures of hunting at Indian Creek Ranch, Perry, the young Houston lawyer who was Richard Grona's client this day, seemed decidedly ill at ease. As the others drank their coffee, he kept nervously fiddling with the six-gun already strapped to his thigh, pulling it out of its holster to check the chamber or the safety catch, or just to feel it in his hand. Although a confirmed and experienced hunter, often leaving the office early on Friday afternoons so as to devote the full weekend to the sport, the trouble was that until now the only quarry he had ever hunted had been singularly unthreatening – ducks and deer mainly. Today, however, he had elected to hunt and kill a wild, full-grown, full-blooded European Russian boar, and that, by Richard Grona's reckoning, was no mean feat.

"Boar," said Grona, addressing the small gathering over his coffee cup, "are some mean critters. Cut you? Oh, *man*, they'll cut you . . . every time they *hit* they'll cut you!" Of this last fact, Grona had absolutely no doubts. Some time back a cornered boar had turned on him with its tusks, severely slashing his head, leg and hand before he could kill it with his pistol. Two years later he still could not move his hand properly. "They sure know what they're doin' with those tusks," he continued, surveying the injured hand. "*Man* do they charge! When the dogs've got him at bay, boar'll fight *anythin*'!"

Rising from the table, Grona pulled a picture from the wall and passed it around; it was a large color photograph of a mutilated dog, its head almost severed from its body. "I had six guys come up here once to kill a boar and I showed 'em a movie where a boar killed a dog and they said, 'Well, we'll hunt deer first and talk about the boar later.' Then later, after they'd thought some more, they came to me and said, 'Lissen, we want no part of it. We'll kill a boar up in a tree stand or somethin', but you couldn't *pay* us to walk up where a dog's got one bayed."

Perhaps it was Perry's rather sickly grin that prompted the manager to retrace his steps somewhat. "But it sure is worth it once you got one," he continued reassuringly. "Before you arrived I had this colored guy down here after boar – first colored guy I've ever had – and he was *really* scared, runnin' through the brush after that ol' boar with just his pistol. But when it was all over he reckoned he wouldn't take a million dollars for it, nosir. I tell you, ever' one who gets a trophy room started just got to have that big ol' European boar head in it. Yessir, boar is a lotta sport, alright."

Perry's wife Donna still seemed rather less than convinced. She, too, was carrying a six-gun on her hip, although she hadn't been expecting to use it. Now, however, she was glad she had brought it. It was nice to have it, she said, "just in case."

Dawn broke as we were bouncing along the ranch's well-rutted tracks in Richard Grona's red pick-up truck. In the halflight, the passing landscape appeared as rather sparse and scruffy, almost barren in fact. Then, as the sun rose, the most extraordinary variety of wildlife appeared, black silhouettes against the brightening skyline. The sight was breathtaking: sleek deer blowing vapor into the chill morning air; groups of exotic long-haired goats; rams with enormous curling horns thicker than a man's wrist at the skull; herds of spike-horned antelope. It was just as the brochure had promised, a jumbled Garden of Eden bursting at the seams:

Roaming free are majestic Axis buck from India . . . Aoudad sheep graze on rocky crags above a herd of Japanese Sika deer . . . the eyes feast on a collection of Blackbuck Antelope from India . . . European Fallow buck . . . Catalina goat . . . Corsican ram and the Big Horn Merina . . . *a year-round hunting paradise!*

For once, promotion had matched the reality; it was far easier to imagine oneself somewhere in the Serengeti than a bare five miles off Interstate Highway 10 in the middle of Texas. The animals barely paused in their feeding as we drove by. Reared to the sound of four-wheel-drive vehicles, they seemed totally unconcerned by our approach. Like a herd of dairy cows, they appeared completely at ease in their enclosed environment.

"It's well stocked alright," said Grona proudly, letting his eye linger over the healthy herds. "Look at them. They're all fat, all in good shape." Some, perhaps, in too good a shape, for it was one of Grona's continuing headaches keeping clients from blasting away at the first head they saw: "You have to really be with the guy 'cos he'll see a medium-sized buck and think it's a monster, which it's not. That's somethin' we don't do is kill anything small. That's your best advertisin'. Some of these places they let the people walk up and kill a little Axis that looks big to them, but they've never seen one. Then they see a big one and that really hurts 'em – spend all that money, taxidermist and so on. We've got so much game here that we just drive slow and try and find the biggest horn."

Donna was appalled. "You mean," she said, gesturing at the animals grazing less than a stone's throw away, ". . . you mean you shoot them from here?" Grona chuckled nervously and gave her a sidelong look. "Naw," he said, "I usually stop about a hundred yards back up the road. That way it's more . . . sporting."

The two exceptions to this stand-still-and-be-shot rule were Perry's Russian boar and the white-tail deer, one of the few true Texan natives bred at Indian Creek. A perennial favorite with hunters, the white-tail bucks had by necessity become far wilier than their exotic neighbors, deserting their does and sticking to the gulches, keeping as low a profile as they possibly could in an area criss-crossed with wire fences. Grona pointed out one ravine in particular where he had spent the better part of the previous day trying to flush one of the remaining bucks out into the open. He had met with no success, leaving his client, a near-sighted young man dressed in the American hunter's traditional padded Day-Glo orange jacket, stranded at the top of the ridge without a shot. "They'll shoot you out of white-tail, give 'em a chance," said Grona ruefully. "Big ol' 14-point buck white-tail standin' out there, you can just about ask your price."

Which is what keeps Indian Creek in business; a price on every head. It was once a regular cattle ranch, but the owners soon discovered that killing animals for sport was far more profitable than raising them for the table. Now, every potential customer receives a printed brochure setting out what game is available and at what price, just like a Sears-Roebuck mail order catalogue:

Corsican Ram . . . $250. Mouflon Ram . . . $300. Sika Buck . . . $400. Blackbuck Antelope . . . $500. Aoudad Sheep . . . $750.

Perry's Russian boar was $400, cheap considering that it was harder to find and required a full pack of hounds to flush it out.

"This is the way huntin's going to be," Grona would tell me later. "I think it'll be common all over. You see, you get better stuff, and you're *guaranteed* somethin'. You could go off like they do now, payin' sixty-five, seventy dollars a day for four or five days and get absolutely nothin'. Now if you had come in here, you'd have killed somethin'. It's a guarantee hunt. We guide them three days and if they don't get one it's no charge. And that's what people like."

The pick-up passed through a gate and we drove down a steep ravine to a dry creek bed. Grona stopped and released his best dog, leaving the rest of the pack snuffling and whimpering in the back. We set off on foot, keeping close together on Grona's repeated instruction. The dog ran on ahead trying frantically to pick up a scent.

After a fruitless half hour we returned to the truck. It was, Grona assured us, only a temporary setback. Since they had turned feral some thirty-five years before – "This guy had 'em in a little ol' pen and they all broke out" – Russian boars have reached pest proportion in this part of the state. "When I first started, if you caught one hog a month you were doin' good; this year I done killed one hundred and thirty nine."

We returned to the top of the ridge and exchanged the pick-up for a Jeep as Grona released the entire dog pack into the scrub. They set off yelping and barking with us following as best we could along the ridge. Within a matter of minutes there was a great howling from the undergrowth and we turned and headed downhill. Suddenly a large gray boar broke cover and shot out across the track, the dogs snapping at its flanks. Within a few yards it had hit one of the wire fences; turning, it took off along the line until, inevitably, it was confronted by a cross fence. Cornered, it turned to face the pack, quivering with fear.

We drove to within about fifty yards of the pack. Perry nervously stood up in the back of the Jeep, unholstered his pistol, aimed with both hands and fired. The pig did not move. Again Perry fired and again the pig remained on its feet, blinking in terror at the dogs which surrounded it. "Damn!" said Perry. "Don't hit the dogs," said Grona.

The third shot tumbled the animal forward onto its chest. Immediately the dogs leaped on it, tearing at its sides and pulling the carcass this way and that. By the time we reached it, it was dead. Grona kicked away the frantic dogs as Perry crouched beside his kill, grinning proudly into Donna's camera. Later the carcass would be strung up by a rope outside the ranch house for more photographs. Its head would then be removed for mounting by one of nearby Kerriville's many taxidermists whose shops, bearing such names as Star of the North Taxidermy Inc., line Interstate Highway 10 like so many fried chicken stands. Kerriville is the self-proclaimed world capital of Exotic Game Ranching, surrounded by perhaps a dozen or more spreads along the lines of Indian Creek. The town's shops and cafes all display prominent signs proclaiming We Welcome Hunters. Kerriville obviously knows a good thing when it sees it.

Grona slung the dead pig into the back of the pick-up, rounded up the hounds and we set off back to the bungalow. As we topped one of the ridges we came upon another hunting party, this one led by Grona's son. A few yards off the track a portly middle-aged man in a bright orange jacket was inching his way towards a majestic Corsican ram, a revolver held out in front of him like a divining rod. Behind him crouched a woman in purple ski pants; she, too, was carrying a revolver on her hip. The ram, its grazing interrupted, stood staring curiously at the gaudy couple no more than fifty feet away. Then we had turned the bend and they were lost from view. All we heard was the shot.

Violent Genesis

Indian Creek Ranch and its neighbors – the Y.O., Texotic Wildlife Inc., the Ram-Arm Ranch, the Honey Creek Ranch . . . all told some twenty-eight or so in this part of Texas alone – are the latest expressions of a desire which has been propelling mankind since its beginnings. Less than twenty years ago, anthropology knew little of man's primeval ancestry much beyond a million years. Since then, however, knowledge about our earliest forebears has expanded dramatically. Beginning with Dr. Louis Leakey's discovery of small-brained proto-men in Tanzania's Olduvai Gorge, the range of hominid existence was progressively extended to over three million years. Then, in the summer of 1975, Leakey's wife, Dr. Mary Leakey, unearthed the remains of no less than eleven hominids – eight adults and three children – which were dated between 3.35 and 3.75 million years.

Mark Leakey's was a remarkable discovery. Not only did it push back further the horizons of man's beginnings, but it also shed fresh light on the survival patterns of proto-man. An examination of their dentition revealed that all of Dr. Leakey's hominids had been meat eaters. All were apparently capable of fashioning stone tools and weapons, examples of which were discovered close to the remains. For most anthropologists the conclusions were inescapable. For almost four million years, and probably much longer (a hominid jaw since discovered near Lake Rudolph in Africa has now been accurately dated at 5.5 million years), man has been a hunter.

If this is so, if proto-man's leap from the trees was also a leap from vegetarianism to killing, the effects of a hunting heritage on our evolution must have been enormous. In *The Hunting Hypothesis* (1976), Robert Ardrey goes so far as to suggest that man developed the large, intricate brain which sets him apart from other species directly as a result of his need to survive in a world of faster, stronger, better-equipped hunters. "Man is man, and not a chimpanzee, because for millions upon millions of evolving years we killed for a living," writes Ardrey. Other anthropologists have suggested other less sweeping effects. In order to overcome prey larger and often more ferocious than himself, primitive man was forced to band together in cooperative hunting groups. These groups led, by necessity, to such things as food sharing and rudimentary language; in short, they constituted the first societies. Travel, too, probably stemmed from the dictates of a hunting existence; as prey was mobile, man also became mobile, his territorial boundaries expanding until they eventually encompassed most of the globe.

There are many other possible effects; indeed, just how far one can take these possibilities is currently the source of bitter dispute among anthropologists – is there, for example, a link between this hunting heritage and the wars, slaughters and Saturday night muggings within our own species? There is one legacy, though, which remains beyond doubt, and which most concerns us here. It is that sometime during the course of those three million plus years, mankind developed a taste for the violent hunting life, and not just for the end results it provided. Killing, in other words, became a pleasure.

It was perhaps inevitable that man should become attached to killing. All other behavior necessary to the survival of the species is accompanied by varying degrees of pleasure. Copulation and eating are just two examples; as naturalist Roger Caras observed in *Death as a Way of Life* (1970), "If sexual intercourse felt like shaving there would be no population explosion." So, too, with hunting which, for more than 99 percent of his time on earth, was as important to man as procreation. "Man takes pleasure in hunting other animals," concluded anthropologists S.L. Washburn and V. Avis. "Unless careful training has hidden the natural drives, men enjoy the chase and the kill." It is a statement that until only very, very recently, no hunter would have ever dreamed of disputing.

Thus equipped with the means and the motivation, man rapidly outstripped all his predatory competitors. In fact, he became a super hunter. Just how superior his skills made him can be judged by his early conquest of the North American continent. Twelve thousand years ago, bands of primitive hunters crossed from Asia into North America via the land bridge which once spanned what is now the Bering Strait. Within a few thousand years, these hunters, the forefathers of the American Indian, had stripped the continent of all its large game, mammoth included. It was an achievement which put man in a hunting league above all other species.

Of course, there is no way of judging how much of the slaughter was killing for killing's sake. Man was still totally dependent on hunting for survival and presumably the vast majority of creatures killed were eaten. But at the same time as these first colonists were decimating the American game, humans in other parts of the world were experimenting with a new method of survival based on the domestication of plants and animals which would, in time, remove the necessity from hunting, thus paving the way for another Roger Caras observation: ". . . no animal besides man kills wantonly and uselessly on a grand scale regularly and normally."

Ten thousand years ago the world held ten million hunters – one hundred percent of mankind. By Christ's time, that percentage had dropped by half, and by the discovery of the New World, it had dropped again by another quarter. Today out of a total world population exceeding four billion, barely 250,000 humans regard hunting as a matter of survival. But despite this agricultural explosion, the desire to hunt has remained. After three million years as the focal point of his existence, man was not about to forsake the pleasures of the hunt in a mere thousand years or two.

The ways in which the desire to hunt has been rechanneled in modern society is a topic which fascinates social scientists. Among the many examples offered, sport has always loomed large, and not without reason. Many sports – archery and javelin, for instance – are obvious extensions of hunting. Others are perhaps more obscure hangovers of a hunting past – the football team (hunting band) overpowering an opposition (the prey) to score (kill). Desmond Morris has even suggested that *all* sport is merely ritualized, symbolic hunting. In *Manwatching* (1978) Morris writes:

> Of all the hundreds of forms of competition we indulge in, only sports have the special properties of chasing, running, jumping, throwing, aiming and prey-killing. This is why, ultimately, only the transformed-hunting explanation will do.

It is an interesting hypothesis, especially when viewed against the violence underlying so many of our most popular sports.

But despite the enormous swing toward these "ritualized hunts," hunting in its original form has survived – indeed flourished – in modern times, and the way it has survived is, of course, as a sport itself. The chase and the kill have proved so appealing that hunting now continues for the sake of pleasure. As sport, its potency has remained undiminished. The violent destruction of life is still the end result of the hunt; in fact, throughout the history of sport hunting, killing has so often become the sole reason for the entire exercise. Today hunting remains man's most violent recreation.

The Sport of Kings

Exactly when hunting became pure sport can only be guessed at. Certainly by the time the Egyptian pharaohs had begun recording history, it had become, for them at least, purely a matter of entertainment. When Thutmose III slaughtered 120 elephants beside a waterhole in 1464 BC, and Ramses III inscribed in stone the words "With my own hand, I, the Pharaoh, killed from the chariot 102 wild-eyed lions," we can be fairly sure neither was hunting to stock the royal larders. Nor, too, was Ashurbanipal, ruler of Assyria, who bagged 450 lions, 390 wild bulls, 200 ostriches and 30 elephants during the course of a single hunt in 850 BC, the first – and most impressive – in a long tradition of regal overkills. They were warrior kings, exhilarated by the chase and, more importantly, attracted by killing.

As the civilizations these monarchs ruled grew progressively more stable, killing gradually became the predominant feature of the hunt, eclipsing the chase. Although they were surrounded by endless acres of rich game lands which could have afforded them any amount of exhilarating exercise, the Egyptian aristocrats preferred battue hunting. Under this method, beaters were employed to drive the animals – leopards, lions, deer, ibex, ostriches – into clearings which were surrounded by nets. The nobles, standing outside the circle of nets, were required only to aim and shoot. Even the carcasses were collected by servants.

The Persians and the Assyrians went one step further with the creation of permanent game parks – walled enclosures stocked with a wide variety of species ranging from deer to tiger. The king and his courtiers would ride into these enclosures to shoot their quarry at close range.

Under the Greeks and the Romans, hunting became a far more democratic pastime, open to any citizen wishing to participate. It was especially popular with the military, who viewed it as sound training for the violence of the battlefield (a philosophy which endured until earlier this century). Young Greek warriors enthusiastically hunted the European lion into extinction, often in savage hand-to-claw combat. The commanders of the

❝I am Ashurbanipal, king of hosts, king of Assyria. In my abounding, princely strength I seized a lion of the desert by the tail, and at the command of Enurta and Nergal, the gods who are my helpers, I smashed his skull with the axe in my hand. ❞

Ashurbanipal, *c.* 850 BC

Roman legions stationed abroad became famous for their hunting prowess. Less energetic citizens, however, kept to the game parks.

The Romans also added another twist to the sport – the *venationes*, the notorious hunts of the amphitheater. The *venationes* originated in the parades of exotic animals held by emperors and generals on their return from foreign campaigns. Elephants, bears, rhinoceroses and a host of other fantastic creatures were shipped back to Rome to amaze and win over the citizens. However, as the Roman taste in entertainment degenerated into a taste for bloodshed, these parades were transformed into highly stylized hunts – armchair safaris in which trained hunters known as *bestiarii* slaughtered wildlife from the four corners of the empire for the amusement of an audience. For the first time, hunting became a spectator sport.

The *venationes* were initially used as a sort of curtain raiser to the more popular gladiatorial displays. However, under the direction of such skilled impressarios as Pompey, who in 79 BC imported an entire tribe of desert nomads to slay elephants in the arena, they grew in stature until, by the completion of the Colosseum in AD 80, they had become immense and lavish spectacles quite capable of filling the arenas on their own. On the opening day of the Colosseum, Titus put to death five thousand wild animals; over the next one hundred days a further nine thousand were killed. Two decades later Trajan dispatched eleven thousand. Under the emperor Probus, the hunts scaled wild heights of fantasy; fully-grown trees were uprooted and replanted on the floor of the arena to form a shady grove into which thousands of ostriches, fallow deer, stags and bears were loosed to face hunters brandishing burning torches and armed with spears and javelins.

In time, no entrepreneur could afford to stage the Games without including a *venatio*. Across the empire an army of hunters – including the legions themselves – was employed chasing giraffe, elephant, auroch, bison, crocodile and bear to feed the insatiable appetites of Rome and her provincial capitals. In due course stocks were decimated, with some species being hunted to extinction. Once the animals were captured and caged, they were shipped to the amphitheaters where they were butchered in considerable style. Lightly clad *bestiarii* used hunting spears to bring down charging beasts as others, more heavily protected, fought with swords at close quarters. Still others hunted with arrows and some even used their bare hands, choking the big cats to death by thrusting an arm down their throats while gripping their tongues. Claudius and Nero, both ardent lovers of the arena, had the Imperial Cavalry conduct "campaigns" against "armies" of bears, lions and panthers.

Rome's fascination with the *venationes* lasted until AD 681, more than two centuries after the gladiatorial bouts had been abandoned. The dis-

---

**&& The chase, the sport of kings;
Image of war without its guilt. ⁷⁷**

William Sommerville (1675-1742), "The Chase"

---

solution of the empire, however, brought a temporary halt to sport hunting. The less sophisticated northern tribes who inherited the empire regarded hunting strictly in terms of the pot and keeping predators at bay. In England it was not until the arrival of William the Conqueror in 1066 that the hunt once again became the sport it had been under Roman occupation.

William pursued game as passionately and ruthlessly as he pursued his enemies, leveling whole villages – churches included – to build exclusive royal game parks such as the New Forest between London and Southampton. All game became the property of the king, to be hunted only by himself and his courtiers. Poachers were savagely punished by imprisonment, mutilation and sometimes death, a legacy which was to last for centuries.

Gradually William and his successors broadened the sport to include selected nobles, knights, clergy and the members of other elite social groups. They, too, took to hunting with a royal abandon. Their quarry was principally stag and deer, followed by wild boar, hare and several species of wildcat. These were pursued by packs of hounds which either pulled them down or ran them to exhaustion, thereby allowing one of the huntsmen to have the pleasure of the kill. Boars were also fought on foot by men with long spears which were used to keep the animals at bay until the hounds could disable them.

Sportsmen on the Continent hunted a wider variety of animals, from reindeer to dangerous big game in the form of black bear which was chased through the German forests by hunters dressed in full armor. But such savage delights, in England at least, were becoming increasingly rare. Even by Tudor times the wild and vigorous *par force* hunting of William and his cronies had been almost wholly abandoned in favor of less strenuous, highly stylized hunts conducted within the confines of a game park. Although Henry VIII hunted enthusiastically enough to wear out eight horses in the course of a day's chase, Elizabeth and her courtiers were content to quietly follow the "music" of the hounds from a distance. When they learned that a deer had been cornered, they galloped up to see it be killed. Elizabeth, who at seventy-seven was still deer hunting every second day, greatly enjoyed cutting the creature's throat with her own hand. Sometimes, rising early, she would ride to the game park where a waiting "nymph" would hand her a crossbow. There she would shoot the deer paraded before her to the strains of a small orchestra hidden among the trees. At Cowdrey in Sussex she did not even bother to shoot, but simply watched from a turret as sixteen bucks were pulled down by greyhounds for her after-dinner amusement. Once again, killing had become a spectator sport.

As the kill came increasingly to dominate the hunt, the rituals surrounding it became more and more elaborate. Each different species was dispatched and dissected in accordance with its own set of rules. Some were formulated to please the spectators and add to the performance; others to satisfy the hounds. Harts, for example, were ceremonially run through with swords by the hunters who would then dip bread in the gore to be fed to the hounds. Then various parts of the carcass were removed and awarded to selected hunters and onlookers. Blood in particular held an almost mystical fascination and was liberally smeared over all present, a ritual still observed today by the foxhunters who "blood" a newcomer. The early Stuarts went so far as to remove their riding boots to paddle barefoot in the blood and gore, believing that it somehow gave them strength.

But it was in France during the reign of Louis XIV, a monarch whose taste in hunting leaned heavily toward the bizarre, that the death spectacle reached its peak. It was Louis himself who invented *La Curée* (The Kill), a strange and sordid pageant which was performed whenever an animal was cornered. While the hunting horns trumpeted a special fanfare, the lead dog was encouraged to sink its teeth into the animal's skull. Then the rest of the pack was loosed to tear out its entrails.

At the beginning of the seventeenth century, James I, disgusted at the decadence of the English game park hunts, attempted to reintroduce the violent hunting tactics of William and the Normans which he had learned as a boy in the Scottish Highlands. These Highland gatherings, such as that hosted by the Earl of Mar at Braemar in 1618, were usually impressive affairs:

> all the valley on each side being waylaid with a hundred couple of strong
> Irish greyhounds, they are let loose as occasion serves upon the herd of
> deer, that with dogs, guns, arrows, dirks and dagger, in the space of
> two hours four score fat deer are slain.

The English, however, remained unimpressed, preferring to ride down their quarry one at a time, genteelly slaughtering it with ceremony. *Par force* hunting did not catch on.

James also made two other ill-conceived efforts to influence the course of hunting in England. The first was a futile attempt at restocking the royal forests with wild boar which had been totally hunted out during Elizabeth's reign; unfortunately they all died. Secondly, and more significantly, he legislated against a weapon which was just beginning to enjoy a measure of popularity among sportsmen – the "handgonne."

James was by no means the first English monarch to cast a cold eye toward guns. Fifty years before him, Edward VI had introduced "An Acte Against the Shooting of Hayle Shot" (small chunks of crudely rounded lead) which was, in turn, meant to reinforce a law drawn up by Henry VIII banning "handgonnes, hales and hacquebuttes." Indeed, the first firearms – simply a metal tube fastened to a wooden stock – had begun appearing as early as the mid-1300s. They were, however, unwieldy and dangerous, liable to explode in the face of the hunter. It was not until two centuries later with the invention of the wheellock and the flintlock that, in Edward's words:

> an infynite sorte of fowle ys killed and much Game thereby destroyed to the benefit of no man.

Sport into Slaughter

The introduction of the gun was the greatest single event in the evolution of hunting since primeval man cracked open his first skull with the jawbone of an antelope. In the expert hands of European gunsmiths, it fast became the perfect hunting weapon: quick, easy to use, accurate and devastatingly lethal. For the first time, hunters had at their fingertips the firepower to keep pace with their desire to kill.

As the gun underwent the continuing process of refinement and modification, the hunter's domination of the animal kingdom became even more complete. Together, the hunter and his gun formed a partnership which was to violently and drastically alter the pattern of wildlife around the globe. From this moment on, the history of sport hunting is, in large part, the record of mass slaughter on an extraordinary and ever-increasing scale.

Shooting in England was for many decades limited initially to "pot hunters" rather than sportsmen, who, like their monarchs, regarded guns

ᏎᏎ Something in the *power* of the double-barrel – the overwhelming odds it offers the sportsman over the bird and animal – pleases. A man feels master of the copse with a double-barrel; and such a sense of power, though only over feeble creatures, is fascinating. ᏅᏅ

Richard Jeffries in *The Open Air*, published in 1885, shortly after the appearance of the double-barrel shotgun with considerable disdain. Shooting was simply not considered sport, a prejudice which led to the sharp distinction made by English sportsmen today between "hunting" and "shooting." Continental sportsmen, however, quickly realized the sporting potential of the firearm. The game, enclosed in parks since the fifteenth century, presented an easy target for noble sportsmen experimenting with the new invention. Herded together and driven into nets, it was gunned down to universal delight.

As the seventeenth century progressed, such noble massacres grew increasingly more fanciful. The nets were replaced by painted canvas backdrops which routed the game over a series of jumps and artificial ponds toward a single narrow exit. There it was shot by the royal courtiers dressed in fancy costume (often, fittingly enough, Roman togas). Occasionally the animals themselves were dressed in clothing. Another sordid delight was the water hunt in which the game was driven toward a hedge cleverly disguising a sharp drop into a lake or river. The hunters shot from anchored barges or raised platforms built along the shore.

Such diversions were a favorite of the Spanish aristocracy, the French court of Louis XIV and George III of Saxony. They lasted for more than a century; as late as 1764 the Elector of the Palatinate was still busily entertaining his guests by driving vast herds of deer through triumphal arches into the rivers on his estate. On one occasion, during the first hour of the hunt, his party bagged 104 head.

But these spectacles were overshadowed by the sheer magnitude of the killings claimed by the crowned heads of Europe when they took to the open fields. In 1753 the German emperor Francis bagged 978 head of game in a single day. Two years later Louis XV led a twenty-three-man hunt through Bohemia which, in the space of eighteen days, slaughtered a staggering 47,950 animals, including 18,243 hares, 19,545 partridges, 9,499 pheasants, 19 stags, 17 roebucks and 10 foxes. The king of Naples had, by the age of forty, managed to kill 52,670 creatures by his own hand. The extravagancies of Saxony's George III may perhaps have merely been his attempt to live up to a formidable family tradition set by his father and grandfather. "This pair of ducal sportsmen," noted one early historian, "can claim to have been the greatest game slaughterers of whom we have any record, for between them in less than seventy years they killed 110,530 deer, 54,200 wild boars, 6,067 wolves, 477 bears, and of small game proportionate hecatombs."

But the most spectacular bags were achieved on the twenty-one square miles of parkland and the forty-eight square miles of forest belonging to the Condé family at Chantilly in northern France. From 1748 to 1799 more than a million head of game was killed: 587,470 rabbits, 117,574 partridges, 86,193 quail, 77,750 hare and an endless amount of duck, fox, hind, roebuck and wild boar. According to the estate records, "the pieces of game killed by Le Prince de Condé were, in number, 65,524." Included in the total bag were several hundred poachers hanged during the period.

By now England's sportsmen had seen the error of their ways and were embracing the gun with as much enthusiasm as their European counter-parts. During the eighteenth century "shooting flying" – the art of blasting birds on the wing – became fashionable, and by the mid-1700s shooters were killing twenty to thirty brace of partridge per gun a day. So popular was the sport that the grouse population, in particular, suffered a severe decline. By the century's end, according to the Reverend E.B. Daniel, game records in certain areas of the country revealed "such wanton registry of slaughter as no sportsman can read without regret." To offset this depletion and to ensure the continuance of the massive individual bags by which a sportsman's ability was now measured, game birds such as pheasant and partridge were hand reared and set loose on the day of the shoot. Rough shooting gave way to battues in which the near-tame birds were made to fly directly over the waiting guns. The desire for enormous bags began a spiral in which more birds were reared, more keepers and beaters were employed and stiffer game laws introduced. Poachers were sentenced to the navy, imprisonment or a whipping; if they resisted arrest they were hanged.

Game was also conserved in some measure by the evolution of a sporting code among the more gentlemanly shooters. This unwritten code, more a vague sense of duty than anything else, was summed up by Sir Ralph Payne-Gallwey in his book *Letters to Young Shooters*, which appeared in 1890:

> A man who is endowed with a true feeling of sport will always endeavour to give his game a chance – I can think of no better word to express what I mean – as much from the good old English feeling of fair play to all and everything as for any other reason.

Throughout the century, the shooting lodges began introducing fines for "poor sportsmanship," such as for killing a hen pheasant (£1.1.0), shooting at a pheasant in a tree (the same), shooting two or more partridges at one shot (5/-) and shooting a hare in her form (the same).

Such scruples, however, did not apply to the gentlemen who competed in the "Tournament of Doves," which flourished from the late 1700s. This sport was reputed to have begun in the "Old Hats" public house on London's Uxbridge Road, so called because the birds were placed in a hole and covered by a hat. When the hat was jerked away by a cord, the contestants aimed and fired. Pigeons were the main victims, but later, when the sport had become the height of fashion in refined circles, species such as the blue rock were specially bred to fill the demand. The gentry quickly warmed to pigeon shooting and the lawns at Hurlingham, the refined sports center, were often a swirling sea of white and crimson feathers. Dying birds dropped into the laps of the female spectators who found the whole effect utterly charming.

As the century progressed, however, some sections of society began to view the spectacle with increasing unease. Perhaps the most outspoken critic was *The Times*, whose editorial pages thundered:

> To walk out of the luxurious club rooms into an enclosed lawn with awnings and covered sheds, to enjoy the strains of operatic music till one's name is called from a printed list, to receive one's gun ready loaded from a servant, to choose one's own time for giving the signal to "let go" and at last to kill or maim a bird half dazed by its sudden release is assuredly the stupidest, tamest, lowest form assumed by the venatorial art since the age of Nimrod.

But despite the editorials, Parliament remained firmly behind the "Tournament of Doves." It was, after all, only a small step from killing pigeons to shooting hand-reared pheasants, and only an extremely rash member would have attempted anything so quixotic as to breathe a word against pheasants in a Victorian Parliament. In 1871 a tournament was even arranged between the Lords and the Commons. (The Lords lost, 71 birds to 60.) The sport only began to decline when the Prince of Wales in a fit of conscience withdrew from his gun clubs, and it was not until World War I, when live birds were replaced by clay pigeons, that the killing subsided. (Live pigeon shoots – albeit clandestine – can still, however, be found in certain areas of the United States and Australia.)

Despite its overwhelming popularity among bird "fanciers," the gun did not supplant the more traditional forms of English hunting. Deer hunting retained its preeminence as the royal pursuit, but as deer stocks dwindled during the eighteenth century, the sport became little more than a formalized ritual. Half-tame animals bred in paddocks were pursued and "carted" bucks and stags were loosed before a chase, sometimes deliberately maimed or lamed to ensure a successful hunt. More often than not they were saved from the hounds, crated up and returned to the game park for later sport. The extent of the deer's domesticity was reflected by hunts of the Earl of Derby, who twice a year made the two-hundred-mile journey from his summer home in Lancashire to his hunting lodge in Surrey. Not only did he take his huntsmen, horses and hounds, but he also brought with him his own supply of deer. The whole procession averaged twenty-five miles a day. Eventually the only deer hunted in the wild, apart from Highland stalking, was the red stag which survived in a small pocket of the West Country.

As deer hunting became increasingly an elitist sport, followers of the hounds turned their attention to other quarry. Otters were pursued along river banks and impaled on tridents. As Thomas Fairfax noted in his *The Compleat Sportsman* of 1758, the badger was also an enjoyable adversary:

> Her manner is to fight on her back, using thereby both her Teeth and Nails. . . . If the hounds either encounter him, or undertake the Chase before he can get into his Earth, he will stand at Bay like a Boar, and make most incomparable sport.

It was best, he added, to fit the dogs with broad leather neck straps to keep damage at a minimum.

The favorite animal entertainer of the eighteenth century, however, was the fox. Initially fox hunting had been treated as a minor amusement, a rather unseemly pastime something along the lines of badger digging. But with the shortage of deer the animal's sporting potential was given a re-appraisal. Fast, cunning and plentiful, the fox was soon providing endless amusement for members of the burgeoning hunt clubs, who killed it with an almost religious ardor.

As railways began to spread across the country in the early decades of the nineteenth century, the membership rolls of the more fashionable clubs swelled with the names of city dwellers. Although not cheap – a season's subscription to, say, the Quorn or the Pytchley could cost £100 or more – the clubs were a requisite stepping stone in higher society; a well-connected gentleman could be expected to belong to three or even more. Fox hunting had become one of the pinnacles of refined social living.

The railways also precipitated a boom in shooting, which, with an influx of cheap Belgian firearms, had become far more democratic than the mounted hunts. Each weekend trainloads of "sporting artisans" were ferried from town to coast to shoot seabirds, the "Cockney's Passion." Within a few decades, coastal wildlife had been decimated (albeit as much by the millinery industry with its appetite for feathers as by the sportsmen). Gulls, for example, declined so drastically that sailors accustomed to judging their distance from the shore by their cries began to run aground. Eventually the government was forced to introduce the Sea Birds Protection Act of 1869 to check the slaughter.

The last three decades of the nineteenth century were English hunting's golden age. With Queen Victoria's move to Balmoral Castle in 1848, the lush game fields of the Scottish Highlands had opened up before an onslaught of English sportsmen after red deer. The arduous task of tramping through the rugged landscape was by now a thing of the past; "gillies" – manservants – set out the night before, spotted the quarry and signaled the English laird, who was then taken up by pony and presented with a loaded gun. (By the end of the century telephone wires had been laid from lodge to hilltop, which made the process even easier.) The gillies also butchered the carcass and brought down the head and antlers. Even more popular was the battue hunt, as the author Robert Scott Fittis ruefully acknowledged in *Sports and Pastimes of Scotland* (1891):

> Now-a-days, much of the slaughter in our forests is effected by the system of *driving*, the deer being forced to run the gauntlet of a narrow pass, where the sportsmen, well and securely posted, fire away as fast as their gillies can supply them with loaded rifles.

In the south the fashion for big bags had reached grotesque proportions. Titled shooters advanced across the fields like an approaching army, snuffing out worlds of pheasant, partridge and grouse. On the Elveden estate in Norfolk in 1876, the Maharajah of Lahore bagged 789 partridge with a thousand shots in one day; over a nine-day period he killed 2,350. Twelve years later Lord Walsingham did marginally better – 1,070 in a day. In 1889 at Wemmergill, eight guns shot 2,079 birds and in 1896 another party of eight managed 2,234. A year later the Earl of Wilton's party scored 6,820 partridges in just over a week's shooting. Many of the finest bags were put together by the Prince of Wales (later King Edward VII), a sportsman with an almost pathological desire to kill game. On one of his expeditions to the home of Baron Rendlesham in Suffolk, the prince and his party accounted for 2,250 birds in a particularly frenzied afternoon's shooting. The most monumental lifetime's bag was the work of the Marquess of Ripon (1867–1923), who claimed the lives of some 556,000 game birds.

The mania for record bags continued well into the 1900s, although by the turn of the century there were indications that some hunters at least were beginning to have doubts about such massive campaigns in their war against the birds. In 1913 Lord Burnham invited George V to a battue in which four thousand pheasants were consigned to oblivion. On the return journey, George, who himself had accounted for a round thousand, was heard to remark to one of his aides: "Perhaps we went a little too far." In that line was the story of his generation.

❝ Very earnestly I ask you, have English gentleman, as a class, any other real object in their whole existence than killing birds? ❞

John Ruskin

33

Plundering the New World

The continent of North America was a huntsman's El Dorado. Forests swollen with exotic wildlife, the landscape a moving mass of grazing herds, skies dark with migrating wildfowl, the entire country rolled away from Plymouth Rock as one vast, unpatrolled game park. "How prodigal hath nature been," exclaimed John Fenwick, an early settler, as he cast his eye over what would one day become the industrial wastelands of New Jersey:

> to furnish this country with all sorts of wild beast and fowl, which every one hath an interest in and may hunt at his pleasure, where, besides the pleasure of hunting, he may furnish his house with excellent fat venison, turkies, geese, heath-hens, cranes, swans, ducks, pigeons . . .

The list went on and on, and the game seemed endless. When a group of aristocratic expatriates pining for some traditional English entertainment attempted to ride down a fox, as John Bernard recorded in his *Retrospections of America* (1887), "ten to one that at every hundred yards up sprang so many rivals that horses and hunters were puzzled which to select." The passenger pigeon, just one species in a plethora of winged wildlife, gathered in flocks forty miles long and several miles wide which literally turned daytime into night. They presented such a nuisance that one early bishop of Montreal felt compelled to excommunicate the entire species.

For the first settlers, hunting was largely a matter of survival. It was the shooter's task to stock the larder and keep, literally, the wolf from the door. But as Fenwick indicated, hunting for survival could also be a matter for sport. Even the Founding Fathers, those grimly starched Puritans intent on carving out their austere footholds in the wilderness, were not above sneaking a little pleasure out of killing. Cooperative hunts such as the wolf drives held on mid-winter Sundays after church became the closest thing to a public holiday the Puritans allowed themselves. Rounding up the wolves and driving them into a deep pit, the hunters took turns cutting them down from the rim. Later "circular hunts" became a regular feature of early farm life. Neighbors within a half day's ride of each other gathered at the home of the Grand Master of the Hunt before moving to a roped-off area where they stationed themselves fifty to seventy-five feet apart. As the *Pageant of America* recorded:

> No game of consequence was allowed to escape. Foxes and wolves were started from their lairs, while the hounds dragged down deer or treed bears. Occasionally a wild cat brought to bay wrought havoc amongst the dogs before he was despatched. As the hunters converged

toward the centre of the circle all firing ceased. The game had now been driven in a confused mass into a predetermined clearing where the best marksmen systematically completed the work of destruction.

It was, noted the *Pageant*, a "co-operative enterprise which combined the pleasure of pursuit with the satisfaction of exterminating prowling maurauders."

Other colonists threw themselves wholly into the business of hunting. These were the frontiersmen, forerunners of Daniel Boone, Davey Crockett and those other heroes of the American wilderness who lived by the Kentucky long rifle. They were professional hunters whose attachment to the gun became legendary. When they weren't killing for fur or food, they killed for fun, organizing contests among themselves such as "barking tournaments" in which they killed squirrels by firing directly below the creatures' feet and splintering the tree bark. They might, as the *Pageant* commented, "even be thought of as America's first professional sportsmen."

Both the settlers and the frontiersmen hunted with ruthless enthusiasm. Unfettered by the class-structured forestry laws of the Old World, they instituted a pattern of violent destruction which would eventually swallow up the fauna of the continent. Unlike George V, no American ever thought about "going too far"; excess was not a word to be heard from colonial lips.

Within eighteen years of the Plymouth landing, deer were scarce around the settlement, and as early as 1646 Rhode Island was forced to introduce a closed season. Passenger pigeons were slaughtered in enormous quantities. Clubbing them off their roosts at night with long poles, the hunters carted off as many as they could and then drove in hogs to finish off the rest. One hunter is on record as having netted five hundred *dozen* in a day. Sometimes the birds were taken live and sold to trap shooters; a dove tournament just wasn't a dove tournament in the colonies unless twenty thousand birds or more were released. Raccoons, hunted at night by torchlight, were also deemed unworthy of a bullet; the hunters simply chopped down the trees and collected the crushed bodies where they fell. The heath hen, rising slowly and clumsily from open spaces, was such a popular target that the servants of the Boston establishment stipulated the birds be served "only a few times a week." In 1708 the heath hen had received such a battering on its native Long Island that a closed season was introduced. Unfortunately, as with all game laws in the new home of democracy, it was universally ignored, and by 1840 the heath hen had entirely disappeared from Long Island. Half a century later it had also vanished from New York State and was a rarity in all its former strongholds – Virginia, Pennsylvania and the Alleghenies.

During the 1800s, town dwellers, secure in established offices and industry, took up hunting as their principal sporting recreation. Along the Eastern Seaboard wildfowl became the fashion among wealthy social circles, just as they had done back in England. In spring enormous numbers of curlews, plovers, godwits, sandpipers and tattlers migrated to the salt marshes where they were greeted by milling hunters who ambushed them from reed-covered boats or decoyed them within range of hidden gun batteries. Upland plover, a mindlessly easy target, was picked off from specially fitted-out horse-drawn gigs. Throughout the duck season the marshlands of Chesapeake Bay crawled with hunters. Other shooters cruised the bay in punts at night, blasting the flocks with scatter guns as they slept. Woodcock and bobwhite, both of which had the distinct misfortune of presenting unpredictable targets to marksmen, who relished the prospect of a "sporting flight," were shot to the point of extinction. In the Adirondacks city sportsmen chasing deer rubbed shoulders with professional hunters. The deer were either driven into lakes by dogs and fired on from boats, or were shot by torchlight at night as they clustered along the shoreline. Wild turkey, the staple of the first settlers, had by this time become figures of pure sport. Marksmen shot from a given range at birds tethered by their feet; for the more ambitious sportsman, the birds were enclosed in wooden boxes with only their heads showing. In the wilds the turkey was hunted relentlessly until in Massachusetts in 1851 some anonymous hunter gained the dubious distinction of killing the last of the original American stock.

There were several early attempts at establishing the English-style fox hunt on the American east coast. The landed Virginians, forever bent on emulating the sporting pursuits of the English aristocracy, took to the sport with enthusiasm, as they still do today. But despite the patronage of such luminaries as George Washington himself, the tradition of riding to hounds did not transport well to the New World. Shooting was the sport, and rough shooting at that; "gentlemen" shooting quail over a brace of pointers were generally more sneered at than admired. The idea was to roll up one's sleeves and slaughter as much as possible any way you could.

Throughout the nineteenth century America unfolded before the pioneers at a breathtaking rate. Jefferson's belief that the Louisiana Purchase would halt all further expansion for several generations was indeed short-lived; within three decades the frontier line had been pushed far beyond Louisiana. At each advance the pioneers discovered more and more game. On the western plains there were antelope and grouse, and in the Taos Mountains black bear and black-tail deer. Down the Rio Grande the newcomers wreaked havoc on the flocks of wild geese, and along the tributaries of the Arkansas "flocks of wild ducks kept the hunter's fowling piece warm from morning to night." To the pioneers the game still appeared inexhaustible, but behind them the pace of the slaughter was already beginning to tell.

In 1799 Daniel Boone claimed that the eastern woods had been all but hunted out which, although undoubtedly an exaggeration, was a clear indication of the precarious position of many species. Together with the heath hen the ubiquitous passenger pigeon was declining rapidly, and wildcats – lynx and cougar – were barely surviving the intensive hunting which was being carried out from the Carolinas to the Mississippi. The moose had disappeared from the eastern states, and by 1850 deer, bears, wolves and foxes had all been driven into inaccessible regions. Deer in particular were suffering relentless persecution. From 1755 to 1773, 600,000 deer skins had been shipped out of the port of Savannah alone, and by 1832 John James Audubon, the famous naturalist, was writing:

> The different modes of destroying deer are probably too well understood and too successfully practiced in the United States; for notwithstanding the almost incredible abundance of these beautiful animals in our forests and prairies, such havoc is carried on amongst them, that in a few centuries they will probably be as scarce in America as the great bustard now is in Britain.

The great American tragedy, though, was of course the buffalo – or bison, to give the unfortunate creature its correct name. In the early nineteenth century the buffalo ranged across nearly the entire North American continent – from the Canadian plains to the Gulf of Mexico, from the Mississippi to the Western Rockies. Some estimates put their numbers at fifty million; others said seventy. For centuries these great beasts, weighing two tons and more apiece, had thundered over the plains of the American heartland virtually unopposed. The Indians survived on them, eating their meat and using their hides for clothing and shelter. The braves hunted them with spears and lethal short-range bows; but often they merely stampeded the vast herds over a cliff, killing them in such numbers that much of the meat could not be reached under the crush of carcasses. For all their efforts, though, the Indians made not the slightest impression on the buffalo population. Yet within a century of the pioneers' first glimpse of those massive herds, the buffalo had vanished.

From the outset the white men found the buffalo an irresistible target. Apart from the animal's food value, buffalo robes soon came to be highly prized by the city folk back east. By the beginning of the century the hide industry had become a major economic consideration, and by 1843 Audubon was describing barges on the Big Sioux River which overflowed with skins:

One from St. Pierre had ten thousand buffalo robes on board. . . . The men reported that the country above was filled with buffaloes, and the shores of the river were covered with the dead bodies of old and young ones.

Amateurs also found the buffalo good hunting. John Palliser, an English sportsman, followed a herd in Yellowstone Park in 1847, an experience which he recorded in his book *The Solitary Hunter:*

Away went the huge mass raising a whirl of dust over the plain, followed by us in hot pursuit. We soon overhauled them, and continued loading and firing away into the herd. . . . Buffalo is a noble sport, the animal being swift enough to give a good horse enough to do to close with him; wheeling round with such quickness as to baffle both horse and rider for several turns before there is any certainty of bringing him down.

But these early buffalo hunters, like their Indian counterparts, made little dent in the herds. Although possessing the will, they lacked the firepower to do any lasting damage. The turning point came a year after Palliser's adventures in Yellowstone Park when Christian Sharps invented the breech-loading rifle. The Sharps rifle, together with other breech loaders from Colt, North & Savage, Warner and Remington, was a quick and efficient means of mass destruction. It fired soft-leaded bullets which flattened on impact. In the hunter's hands it effected, as Theodore Roosevelt remarked, a "merciless and terrible process of natural selection." A buffalo hunter who made his own bullets might leave base camp carrying half a ton of lead, expecting to return with not a single ball left.

Hunters flocked to the buffalo fields and were soon cutting a wide swathe through the herds. Men like Colonel William F. Cody ("Buffalo Bill") and Wild Bill Hickok delighted in riding close to the beasts and crippling them with a shot through the spine. Behind them they left a wake of paralyzed and dying animals. While providing food for the construction crews working on the Transcontinental Union Pacific Railroad, Cody boasted that in eighteen months he had killed 4,280 bison. Buffalo running became a competitive sport among the hide hunters who wagered large sums of money on individual totals.

"Pure" sportsmen poured in from the East and abroad – England and Scotland in particular. In a two-year expedition up the Missouri River around 1855, Sir St. George Gore of Ireland and his party bagged 2,000 bison, 1,600 elk and deer and over 100 bears. Sir George was accompanied by 40 servants, 112 horses, milk cows, oxen, over 40 hounds and a green-and-white-striped linen tent. The Grand Duke Alexis, son of the Czar of

Russia, was escorted to the herds by Cody and General George Custer – who was considerably more adept at killing animals than Indians – and came away with a respectable 25 heads to his own gun.

The massacre escalated in 1869 with the completion of the Union Pacific, three thousand miles of it. Splitting the animals into two distinct herds, the railroad brought hunters to the very center of the buffalo stamping grounds and provided a cheap and speedy means of transporting hides and trophies back east. Special trains were run packed with sportsmen who blasted away at the herds from the compartment windows, leaving beside the tracks a trail of rotting corpses and bleached bones. The German tanners added a further incentive in 1870 by perfecting a process for turning buffalo skin into acceptable leather.

By 1873 Kansas, the richest of the buffalo states, was played out, forcing the hunters to move on to Texas, then north to Montana, Wyoming and the Dakotas. By the winter of 1883–4 hide hunting had all but ceased. Even the teams of bone pickers which scoured the prairies were proving more successful than the hunters. In 1897 Roosevelt sadly recorded:

> A very few head are left in the Yellowstone National Park, but are being killed out by poachers. There are several small tame herds here and there; and there are one or two spots in the Rocky Mountains and possibly one or two on the Mexican Border where two or three individuals still linger in a wild state. These are all.

The slaughter of the buffalo was a monumental achievement by hunting man, unrivaled in scale and single-mindedness by any other hunting episode before or since, with the possible exception of the primitive men who pursued mammoths across the very same plains twelve thousand years before.

The buffalo's rapid decline was paralleled by an equally rapid increase in the ranks of the American sport hunter. In the last half of the century, reported the *Pageant*, these sportsmen grew into a spectacular army, "its ranks swelled to unbelievable proportions, invading every accessible portion of the nation." Fired by the Victorian enthusiasm to count, measure and mount their kill, this army fanned out across the country on sporting holidays and weekends, blasting away at anything with horns or feathers. They ranged from market hunters who sold game by the wagonload to finance their expeditions to wealthy sportsmen traveling in their own private railroad cars to the gamelands of the West. Both measured their trophies by the ton. The shotgun appeared and geese, duck and upland birds were destroyed in enormous quantities; the repeating rifle worked the same wonders with the larger game.

Hunting reached its zenith in the final three decades of the century with

---

❝ When man wantonly destroys one of the works of man, we call him a vandal. When he wantonly destroys one of the works of God, we call him a sportsman. ❞

Joseph Krutch, author, 1957

---

the opening up of the Rockies, the last remaining stronghold of American game. Trophy hunters from across the country and beyond flocked to the area, for by now the sportsmen of the entire Western world were gripped by a mania for big game. Some were content to shoot wapiti in the valleys – an easy target when ambushed on their undeviating paths to the feeding grounds – or to bring down antelope around the foothills. Others preferred trapping bear with huge steel gins attached to heavy clogs by chains. The more adventurous were met by guides at the rail heads and taken up to the crags to kill rare sheep, goats and grizzly bears.

The doyen of American hunters was an unlikely character, a pigeon-chested, short-sighted asthmatic named Theodore "Teddy" Roosevelt, the man destined to become twenty-sixth president of the United States. Roosevelt had taken up ranching in Dakota as a young man to forget early political disappointments and improve his health. Life in the wilderness of the Bad Lands entranced him and he became a passionate hunter – especially of big game, the rarer the better. Besides the continuous shoots around his own property he traveled the country collecting heads. As he wrote in *Ranch Life and the Hunting Trail*, it was nothing for him to mount an expensive expedition to the Rockies and "devote all my entire energies to the chase of but one animal, the white antelope-goat, then the least known and rarest of all American game." (He bagged several, including a female with a shot through the lungs – ". . . the light red frothy blood covered her muzzle . . . as she slowly walked along the log" – and her kid – "I fired, breaking the neck of the goat, and it rolled down some fifty or sixty yards almost to where I stood.") Although keenly aware of the general slaughter taking place around him – the mass destruction of the prong-horned antelope and the wapiti, the disappearance of the grizzly bear, wolf and buffalo – Roosevelt could not resist participating. In 1888 he sadly confessed that he had not shot a grizzly for four years: ". . . they are very shy, and live in such inaccessible places, that, though I have twice devoted several days solely to hunting them, I was unsuccessful each time." His finest sporting coup was bagging a buffalo when, by his own admission, the entire buffalo population could be counted on the fingers of two hands:

Mixed with the eager excitement of the hunter was a certain half-melancholy feeling as I gazed on these bison, themselves part of the last remnant of a doomed and nearly vanished race. . . . I aimed low, behind his shoulder, and pulled the trigger. . . . Fifty yards beyond the border of the forest we found the stark black body stretched motionless. He was a splendid old bull, still in full vigor, with large, sharp horns and heavy mane and glossy coat; and I felt the most exulting pride as I handled and examined him; for I had procured a trophy such as can fall henceforth to few hunters indeed.

According to his hunting companion, the elated Roosevelt performed an Indian war dance over the carcass.

Roosevelt was neither the best nor the bravest hunter of his generation. His friend General Wade Hampton, for instance, hunted bear with hounds and killed his quarry with a knife. The general was in at the death of five hundred bears during his sporting career, killing two-thirds by his own hand, including sixty-eight in four months and four in one day. It was Roosevelt, however, who captured the American public's imagination. Despite his vaguely ridiculous tailored fringed buckskins and sombrero hats, he came to epitomize all that was romantic about frontier life. To the city sportsman trapped in his office back east, he symbolized the free-roaming hunter wise in the ways of wilderness survival, who stalked ferocious animals across the range, bringing them down with a single thrilling shot and reliving the adventure in the nighttime glow of a prairie campfire. No matter that by this stage the popular image of frontier life had all but passed into myth, or that survival in the Bad Lands had more to do with ledger books and balance sheets than with a repeating rifle (Roosevelt's own experiments with ranching collapsed under debts totaling $20,000). To his Eastern readers Roosevelt was a link between the era of Boone and Crockett and the guilty comforts of the urban sprawl. His books, illustrated by Frederick Remington's stirring portraits of hard and heroic men, helped kindle a national fascination with "West-iana." To many eyes the hunter was seen as the true inheritor of the American ethos; hunting became almost an act of patriotism. Although the hunter would never again walk as tall and unquestioned through American society as he did during these few decades, Roosevelt and his dreams of wilderness left an indelible imprint on hunting in the twentieth century which still persists today.

Roosevelt's second hunting legacy was his concern to preserve enough game to aim at. By 1900 America's enthusiasm for killing had driven its wildlife to the brink. In that year the deer population reached its lowest point ever, and few other species were in any better shape to survive. Some, indeed, had already disappeared forever. The great auk had been the first extinction due primarily to overhunting, the last bird being sighted in 1844. It was followed by the Labrador duck (1875), the Eastern elk (1880), the Eastern cougar (1899)* and the Merriam elk of Arizona in 1900. Ten years later the Bad Lands bighorn was to vanish, followed by the Louisiana parakeet in 1912 and the Carolina parakeet (1920). In 1914 Martha, the last passenger pigeon, died in a Cincinnati zoo. The heath hen and the Eskimo curlew, a bird which had once migrated in untold millions across Texas, had not been sighted for decades by the time they were both officially declared extinct in the 1930s. It had been a wild party while it lasted, but looking ahead from 1900, the future for the American hunter looked bleak in the extreme.

In 1887 Roosevelt, together with twenty-three other sportsmen from the Eastern establishment, founded the Boone and Crockett Club. Although the primary aim of the club was ostensibly "to promote manly sport with the rifle," it was as an organization devoted to conserving game that it left its mark. Under pressure from it and other like-minded hunters' clubs, the twentieth century was to see a massive governmental and private restocking of the nation's dwindling game reserves. By its completion, America would once again become a hunting paradise, although this time the hunting would be meticulously regulated.

In time there would even be buffalo to kill.

Hunting the Antipodes

If the fauna of Australia fared marginally better than the American game at the hands of the early settlers, it was only because there were fewer immigrants. Certainly the Old World fervor for killing game did not diminish on the six-month voyage out to Botany Bay. Many of the newcomers were convicts transported for poaching; given free reign with a gun, they turned the areas around the settlements into a free-fire zone. Although, as on the American frontier, much of the early killing was carried out for purely utilitarian reasons, again the line dividing survival from sport was at best indistinct. Certainly some creatures such as the emu, Australia's huge flightless bird, were hunted purely for entertainment. The emu's misfortune was that it ran in a straight line; as such it was stalked and shot from horseback, or coursed with hounds which dragged it down by the neck.

---

* Small numbers of Eastern cougar have recently been sighted in the United States, and the species has now been dropped from the Department of the Interior's "Extinct and Presumed Extinct" list.

Less sophisticated hunters simply rode alongside it and smacked it over the head with a stirrup iron. By 1860 the emu had become scarce in settled areas.

After a brief flirtation with the native population, prompted by Rousseau's cloudy vision of the "noble savage," the colonists also came to view the aborigines as fair sporting game. In Lorna Lippmann's book *Words or Blows*, Dame Mary Gilmore recalled an incident she witnessed as a child on her grandfather's property. A neighbor returning from an unsuccessful hunt suddenly raised his gun and shot a black woman bathing in the river. When her husband rushed to her assistance, he too was shot. According to George Morrison, famous for his explorations in China, blacks were still being shot for sport in Queensland as late as 1882. Morrison was once a guest at a station "whose owner is said to have shot more blacks than any two men in Queensland." During the evening an aborigine was sighted near the stockyard and the station owner grabbed his rifle and headed off into the gloom. He returned an hour later "quite disappointed" that it was too dark to follow the black's trail. "The wretched blacks," wrote Morrison, "are shot without mercy." Eventually they were to suffer the fate of many other "game species," becoming "extinct" in Tasmania and "endangered" throughout the rest of the continent.

Australia's "buffalo" was the kangaroo. From the outset, the vast herds of this unique mammal, virtually untouched by centuries of native hunting, were the favorite target for colonial sportsmen. One early method of killing favored hunters working in pairs; one hunter stunned the animal with a lead-filled club, while his partner crept behind it and hamstrung it with a sharp knife. In later years kangaroos were coursed with greyhounds and ridden down by hunt clubs decked out in full English hunting regalia. Mostly, however, the creatures were simply shot. "Nothing stops a kangaroo so surely as a charge of No. 2 thrown well into the neck, at about twenty yards," advised naturalist Horace Wheelwright in 1861. Wheelwright was a leading expert on killing kangaroos. In the 1850s, when kangaroo battues became fashionable among wealthy sportsmen, he once led a party which in two seasons alone accounted for two thousand animals. Another party of the same period shot two hundred in a day with time enough for a possum shoot afterwards. By 1861 Wheelwright was noting that kangaroos were scarce even in the wilds. "I never could reconcile to my mind the wholesale and wanton destruction of this animal which is now being carried on all over the bush," he wrote in *Bush Wanderings of a Naturalist*. "It certainly used to go against the grain when I saw a kangaroo pulled down by dogs and left to rot in the bush."

Despite his great success at the sport, Wheelwright never really fancied shooting kangaroos. "There is a sameness in it," he complained, "which when carried on month after month is very wearying, even if followed as an amusement." He preferred to hunt possum with a dog; his record stood at ninety-three in one night. In 1867 the Prince of Wales on a hunting trip to America performed only half as well, bagging fifty-two (of which he brought home forty-three and left the rest in the trees).

But for all this abundance of native game, the expatriate sportsmen remained unsatisfied. There was no deer, no pheasant, no partridge . . . indeed, no creatures whatsoever "which afforded so much enjoyment to gentlemen elsewhere," as the *Bell's Life* of June 1865 complained. "We need to create in the southern hemisphere," continued *Bell's*, "an exact counterpart of that country which is so dear to most of us." Otherwise, it warned, why should any gentleman remain in the place?

There was, however, one landowner who had long been aware of the problem. Since 1859 Thomas Austin of Barwon Park in Victoria had been experimenting with a wide variety of birds and animals including partridge, deer, pheasant, blackbirds, foxes and thrushes. Although most of his efforts were failures, he did manage to produce one resounding success – rabbits. By 1865 Austin was killing twenty thousand rabbits a year on his property. So great was the achievement that during the royal visit of 1867, Prince Albert was taken to Barwon Park to see the famous rabbits, which at that time were still being bred in cages. The prince killed 86 and was so impressed by the sport offered that he broke his schedule to return the next day for a second outing. His party bagged a thousand, the prince claiming 416 to his own gun. At one point when the rabbits became bunched in a corner he killed 68 in ten minutes, his guns growing so hot they blistered his fingers. Albert's efforts notwithstanding, Mr. Austin's rabbits rapidly multiplied into the greatest and longest-running animal plague in history.

The hare was another English favorite to be introduced onto the Australian landscape. In the second half of the nineteenth century coursing became something of an obsession among the elite, with hares being shipped from England by the hundreds. Meets often lasted for three days, and with fifty courses a day the turnover in hares was staggering. Coursing reached its peak in 1882 when a record stake of £10,000 was offered as prize money. Thereafter its popularity declined sharply and by the turn of the century it had all but died out.

Hunting, however, continued to flourish – often with dire consequences as a *Bells Life* of 1861 recorded:

> Every Sunday thousands of fowlers leave not only the gold fields and great centres of population but every township and village throughout the country for the destruction of the animal kingdom. . . . In many

districts kangaroos are all but extinct . . . the turkey is unknown in many districts where it was abundant. . . .

Despite game laws introduced as early as the 1860s, this unrestrained killing continued until well into the present century.

On Safari

In his bestselling book *The Naked Ape* (1967), Desmond Morris writes of hunting man's inordinate enthusiasm for killing off species which he sees as competitors:

> Virtually any animal that is either inedible or symbiotically useless is attacked and exterminated. In the case of minor competitors, the persecution is haphazard, but serious rivals stand little chance. In the past our closest primate relatives have been our most threatening rivals, and it is no accident that today we are the only species surviving in our entire family. Large carnivores have been our other serious competitors and these too have been eliminated wherever the population density of our species has risen above a certain level.

From the sportsman's point of view, big game has long been the blue ribbon of hunting, unmatched in thrill, excitement or satisfaction. Although record bags of pheasant and partridge hold their own undeniable sporting attractions, from the mid-nineteenth century until only very recently a gentleman could not be considered a serious sportsman unless he had faced a "large carnivore" and brought back its head to prove it. As one early tiger hunter explained: "There is a stirring of the blood in attacking an animal before whom every other beast of the jungle quails, and an unarmed man is helpless as the mouse under the paw of the cat."

The finest big game fields were the safari countries of India and Africa. There the game ranged even more richly than on the plains of colonial America, "as thick as sheep standing in a fold," as one early explorer reported. India was the first to come under the sportsmen's guns, unfolding in the 1700s before the hunters of the British Raj. Sport hunting had, long before then, been a pastime of the rajahs who delighted in mounting massive battues of fifty thousand beaters and two and three thousand elephants to hunt tiger, leopard, rhinoceros and buffalo. Although the hunters of the Raj were considerably less flamboyant, they pursued the sport with equal enthusiasm.

The military, as it always had done, regarded hunting in much the same way as a hand might regard a glove. For the officers of the Imperial Forces,

---

❝ The thud of a bullet striking a sambhur stag is as welcome to a man's ear as the voice of her he loves. ❞

An old Indian hand, early 1800s

---

shikar was all but a duty. In the eyes of the high command, good hunters made good officers. Leave was invariably a carefully planned two-month expedition to the teak forests of the interior after elephant, tiger, panther, cheetah, bear, boar and bison . . . or to the Ganges Delta for rhinoceros, buffalo and big cats . . . or up into the Himalayas after bear, stag, wild sheep and ibex. Even as late as World War I, British officers were being recruited into the Indian forces by the promise from HQ of a "sportsman's paradise."

Shikar was also as much a way of life for the civilian population as for the military. Sport hunting was a social obligation, considered as a major thread binding together the white community, and even for those who could not stomach the thought of killing a tiger or an elephant, it was still nevertheless unthinkable not to at least own a rifle and a shotgun. For the planters, civil servants and "box wallahs" of the business community isolated in the interior, *shikar* was the only respite from unremitting loneliness, and many of them built their lives around it. One local magistrate became famous for moving his court out into the jungle before dawn so as to fit in a full day's hunting. In the towns more ritualized forms of hunting became popular, such as riding down jackals with hounds specially imported from England.

The most celebrated of these minor diversions was "pig sticking," a curiously English sport which was begun around 1800 by planters who speared sloth bear on the grasslands. When sloths grew scarce, the sportsmen turned their attentions to the wild boar which roamed over large areas of the subcontinent. It was an inspired substitution, from the sportsman's viewpoint at least; with the pig as the enemy, the sport became thrilling, difficult and dangerous. Beaters flushed the boar from the thickets and it was then ridden down, usually by two horsemen but sometimes by a dozen or more. After a mile or so the tiring boar would turn and charge the nearest horse, and at that moment the rider was required to run it through the shoulders with a bamboo spear. If he missed his shot, he could be in difficulties; boars weighed up to four hundred pounds each and used their nine-inch tusks like knives. One rider, slashed to ribbons as he lay stunned on the ground after a fall, required a hundred stitches in his back. Surprisingly, only two deaths were ever recorded.

Pig sticking rapidly became as formalized as the English fox hunt. Enthusiasts formed themselves into "tent clubs" and competed for trophies such as the Kadir and Muttra cups. Meetings sometimes lasted for two weeks and claimed over a hundred pigs.

According to Sir Robert Baden-Powell, the founder of the Boy Scouts who wrote a treatise on the subject, pig sticking offered:

> a taste of the brutal and most primitive hunts – namely the pursuit, with a good weapon in your hand, of an enemy whom you wanted to kill . . . you rush for blood with all the ecstasy of a fight to the death.

"It was a cruel sport," recalled another veteran pig sticker in Charles Allen's *Plain Tales from the Raj* (1975), "but the boar is a very valiant animal and he very often got away. When he died, he died gamely, charging you." What more could any sportsman have asked?

But for all its plucky fighting spirit, it was bigger game than boar that established India's sporting reputation. Up until the 1880s when game reserves began to run dry, the large predators of India were pursued the length and breadth of the subcontinent by a heroic band of quite remarkable killers. Few of them, as Major-General J. G. Elliot recorded, "knew or cared much about jungle lore." They were, simply, "fearless, hard hitting, straightforward Nimrods, ready to ride down with spear and rifle anything they came across." These were men such as Samuel White Baker, who killed 31 elephants in five days with a muzzle loader; Captain Thomas Williamson, who bagged 104 tigers in seven years; and H. A. Levesson, whose volumes of hair-raising sporting adventures enthralled generations of armchair hunters back home in Surrey. As he recounted in *The Hunting Grounds of the Old World* (1860), Levesson's specialty was elephant, which he exterminated with unbridled joy:

> I had hardly made sure of his being dead when . . . I saw the female . . . helping a young one over some rough ground about a couple of hundred yards distant. I took steady aim at the young one, hitting it severely and rolling it over; the smoke had scarcely cleared . . . when down she came on me with a hoarse roar of vengeance. I let her charge to within twenty paces from me, when I gave her a *right and left* full in the forehead, which stopped her career, and brought her to her knees. I reloaded the guns, and despatched the young one which could hardly drag itself along.

Not all such mid-Victorian encounters were as simple. Most Indian big game was potentially lethal, especially when wounded, and many hunting trips became a nightmare struggle for survival – on the part of the hunter, rather than the hunted. Levesson once found himself pirouetting in the arms of a bear, drenched in the blood and gore from the animal's mutilated face as his servant hacked away frantically with a bill hook. Lieutenant John Pester watched mesmerized as a blinded leopard crawled toward him up the bloody flank of his elephant. Stuart Baker, mauled by a panther, was left with one arm hanging by a shred of flesh which his wife trimmed off with a carving knife.

Arguably the most dangerous of all species was the tiger, which in 1860 had killed two thousand natives in Bengal alone. It was also the most coveted sporting scalp, presenting as it did an irresistibly violent challenge together with a perfect pelt. Here is Lieutenant Pester after discharging eight barrels into a tigress:

> [She] closed with the elephant nearest her, which she tore almost to pieces about the face, trunk and breasts. . . . After a furious fight (which drove us almost *mad* with the pleasure it afforded us) the elephant shook the monster off and struck it a violent blow with the trunk. . . . Our elephants were bellowing, and shewed every inclination to join in the combat; they seemed almost as furious as the parties engaged; in short we were *all mad together* . . . it was the *thing impossible* for a small party to be more happy and comfortable than we were.

The tiger was hunted mercilessly throughout the two-hundred-odd years of British rule. At their best its persecutors were men such as Jim Corbett who risked their lives many times protecting native villages from man-eaters. Less honorable sportsmen – by far the more frequent – were more easily satisfied sitting in a tree shooting tigers over a carcass staked out for bait. When the fashion for tigers was at its peak, an average sportsman could reasonably expect to collect thirty or forty heads by the end of his short span of Indian service. Soon it was considered crass to display a tiger skin in one's bungalow.

In the 1880s *shikar* underwent a marked change. By this time the freewheeling Nimrods of the early Raj had shot out much of their adopted homeland, and the government was forced to draw up a set of game laws to protect the surviving game. Only the maharajahs carried on in the traditional manner; from 1871 to 1907 the Maharajah of Cooch Behar bagged 365 tigers and almost equal numbers of leopard, rhino, buffalo, bear, sambhur and barasingh. By 1921 the Maharajah Scindia of Gwalior had 700 tigers to his credit and was still hunting. But for the average colonialist, unless he was lucky enough to receive an invitation to a royal or vice-regal battue, weekend forays against big game were now a thing of the past. Only the wildfowl offered an opportunity for unfettered sport, as Kenneth Mason recalled in Charles Allen's *Plain Tales from the Raj*:

More than once we got bags of more than a thousand duck in a day with eight guns. One's gun got so hot that you had to have a second gun because you could no longer hold the first.

At the Maharajah of Bikanir's annual Christmas sand grouse shoot, it was not exceptional for the thirty-five guns to dispatch fifteen thousand birds in a morning. So massive was the overkill that the servants stationed behind the butts had to use mechanical "clickers" to count the birds as they fell.

Man's boundless enthusiasm for wiping out large species was even more pronounced during the colonization of Africa. Although southern Africa was settled by the Dutch as early as 1650, it was not until 1836 when the Boer farmers broke from British rule and crossed the Orange River that the shooting began in earnest. Sportsmen were in at the very beginning of this "Great Trek." In May of that year William Cornwallis Harris, an engineer in the Indian Army, joined forces with a Bombay civil servant, William Richardson, and set off after the masses of game that had astounded the early explorers. They carried with them provisions for six months, eighteen thousand lead bullets, additional supplies of pig lead and a barrel of gunpowder. They were after sport and they were not disappointed. Entering Zulu country, they breached a rise and looked down on a plain which at first glance appeared to be in upheaval. On closer inspection they realized they had discovered an endless sea of game – gnu, hartebeest, buffalo, quagga, zebra, ostrich. . . . Slightly north of what is now Johannesburg they came across a herd of three hundred elephant. That night Harris could not sleep for excitement. "I felt my most sanguine expectations had been realized," he wrote, "that we had been amply repaid for the difficulties, privations and dangers we had encountered in our toilsome journey towards this fairyland of sport." In a land which "now presented the appearance of a vast menagerie," they counted no less than twenty-two white rhino a few hundred yards from their wagon. They brought back two heads of each species of quadruped in southern Africa, plus skins, antlers, tusks and horns.

Within forty years of the start of the Great Trek, most of southern Africa had been denuded of its big game. By 1850 eyewitnesses were recording the daily slaughter of elephants, lions, rhinoceroses, zebras, giraffes, leopards and hippopotamuses. The seemingly endless herds of springbok, wildebeest, hartebeest, quagga, eland and blesbuck were decimated by an ever-improving arsenal of weapons, notably the double-barrel breech loader. By 1870 the elephant had disappeared south of the Zambesi, fleeing to areas plagued by the tse-tse fly to escape the white hunters. In 1883 the last quagga died in an Amsterdam zoo, and the white rhino was on the brink of extinction.

❝ A sportsman is a man who, every now and then, simply has to get out and kill something. ❞

Stephen Leacock, British humorist

The blame for the bulk of this slaughter rested at the feet of the Boer settlers, whose sporting activities can most kindly be described as "indiscriminate." However, the sporting farmers were ably supported by a voracious collection of ivory hunters who lived by their guns – a profession brought to its peak by the famous Scot "Karamojo" Bell, who shot more than a thousand elephants before retiring in the 1920s – and a steady trickle of visiting sportsmen from Europe and Britain.

By the 1880s this trickle had become a flood. Fired by the best-selling books of the big game pioneers and driven by a desire for the record bags and trophies which had now become fashionable, an army of late-Victorian sportsmen – often titled and all wealthy – kitted themselves out with pith helmets and elephant guns and sailed off to the foreign game fields in search of amusement. Going "on safari" overtook the European shooting tour of a previous generation as the ultimate in sporting fashion. With a bit of careful planning, a man could travel to Somaliland, enjoy a two-week safari and be back in the London Shikar Club with a lion's head within the month. Africa became the first stop on a big game circuit that spanned the globe, stretching from India to the Rockies, Russia to Algeria, China to Australasia.

Heading the list of elite sportsmen who stalked this circuit was the British royal family, led by the Prince of Wales whose 1875–6 safari to India could be said to have started the titled bullets flying. There the prince bagged elephant, tiger, pig, jackal, cheetah and black buck with such royal abandon that one courtier was moved to report to Queen Victoria: "It was like winning a battle and proved he [Albert] possessed Royal qualities of courage, energy and physical power." From India the prince traveled to Africa (where he killed crocodile, hyena and a wide selection of exotic birdlife), America, Albania, Hungary (11,300 head in five days), Norway (60 elk in three days), Palestine and the Middle East (gazelle, vultures and even lizards), and Styria (30 chamois in three hours – "the prettiest sport I have seen for a long time"). In 1911 George v followed his father's intrepid footsteps to Nepal and killed 39 tigers in ten days. A decade later, *his* son toured India, killing 30 tigers, 10 rhinoceroses, 6 leopards, 3 elephants and 8,217 head of sundry smaller game.

Lesser royalty performed with equal enthusiasm. In 1910 the Duke of Connaught bagged the heads of thirty-two different *species* during a ten-week hunt through British East Africa, although encumbered by the presence of the Duchess and Princess Patricia. Lord Delmare shot fifty-two of the one thousand lions taken out of Somaliland during the brief decade before the country was deemed to have been shot out.

It should be noted that not all the stalwarts of the Shikar Club were male (although hunting has been an overwhelmingly masculine pastime since its inception, and remains so today). A Mrs. W. W. Baillie, the rather daunting wife of an Indian chaplain, killed considerable quantities of leopard, bear, bison, gazelle, ibex and tiger during her years abroad. Her finest moment came in 1913 when, confined to hospital after being badly mauled by a bear, she discharged herself against the doctor's pleadings, limped out into the jungle, climbed a tree and shot another pair of tigers with a "perfect right and left." In Somaliland a Miss Agnes Herbert and her cousin Cecily "walked up" a pride of lions with their double-barrel .500 Express rifles. Agnes bagged her first victim as it was clawing at Cecily's thigh.

Nor was membership of this exclusive fraternity confined solely to the British and Europeans. By the turn of the century there were a number of rich and prominent American sportsmen hunting in Africa and India; men such as Paul Rainey who in two years killed one hundred African lions with a pack of bear dogs specially imported from the U.S. They were, however, few and far between until in 1909, fifty years old and fresh from the White House, the indefatigable Theodore Roosevelt decided to mount a safari through the game lands of Kenya and East Africa. Roosevelt's inordinate love of killing was not without its detractors; the American press in particular had a field day, running cartoons of the former president striding purposefully over the African horizon as game fled in all directions. "I am not in the least a game butcher," railed Teddy. "My interest is that of a faunal naturalist." He then proceeded to kill a grand total of 296 animals – 9 lions, 8 elephants, 13 rhino, 7 hippo, 6 buffalo, 15 zebra. His son Kermit – who, together with another son Theodore, was later to cover himself in glory by being the first man to shoot a Tibetan giant panda, the rarest creature in existence – bagged a further 216. The safari took a year and at the end the party returned home with 14,000 "zoogeographic" specimens, many of them the bodies and bones of dead animals.

Roosevelt's safari captured the imagination of American sportsmen; after him, safari hunting quickly became recognized as the ultimate sporting experience for the well-heeled adventurer. Each successive wave of visitors added to the continent's mystique, and with the arrival of the author/ hunters – Ernest Hemingway first, Robert Ruark later – the safari became a status symbol even for those who had never touched a gun before in their lives. For Hemingway, Africa was the perfect theater in which to explore the mysteries of courage and death; a crucible of manliness alive with challenge and danger. His *Green Hills of Africa*, published in 1936, was vintage Hemingway, and like Roosevelt's safari, it brought many more guns to bear on Africa's and India's big game.

Unhappily the realities fell rather short of the image. Even before Roosevelt had set out, the dangers inherent in killing big game had been greatly reduced. By the turn of the century weapons had improved enormously both in range and, with the invention of high velocity ammunition, in "stopping power." Bullets were now designed to mushroom on impact, carving out lethal gaping wounds in the thickest of hides, "the head with its tremendous velocity dragging and catching with its edges the flesh and viscera," as Edouard Fou observed in *After Big Game in Central Africa* (1901). "It often happens in the case of delicate animals," added Fou, "that upon leaving the body it makes a hole as big as the crown of a hat." Gone were the days when one blindly blasted away, praying for a bullet to hit a vital organ.

The dangers were further decreased with the appearance of the first "white hunters" around 1910. Tough, experienced professionals, they watched over their clients like hawks, steering them away from trouble and coolly correcting their mistakes with an unhurried shot from behind. Some of the more timorous – or idle – clients such as the Duke of Orleans even had their white hunters do all the shooting themselves, claiming the credit on their return to civilization.

Access to the game also became progressively less hazardous. Initially it was the railways which opened up the country to the safari sportsmen – with devastating effect. A single page from a game control officer's notebook of 1908 recorded 996 rhinoceroses shot in one hunting area alongside the Mombasa railroad. Then came the gasoline engine and with it the motorized safari – or "champagne safari," as it was more aptly known. Convoys of sportsmen fanned out from Nairobi into the game lands, some of them not even bothering to leave their seats to take their shots. It was little wonder that motorized hunting parties in such places as the Serengeti regularly "hit a century" (one hundred lions) in the course of a single expedition. In six weeks a modern sportsman could bag what would have taken his father seven months to kill, a situation which shocked many old hands. In a letter to *The Times* during the 1920s a veteran hunter complained:

> All this really makes a farce of the whole thing and it only means that the so-called "big-game hunter" comes back at the end of six weeks with a fine bag obtained with practically no work, absolutely no hardships and very little danger.

> **I fired, plowing more than three tons of missile energy into his brain. Instantly decerebrated, he remained frozen in death, still on his feet. Then, under impact of an insurance shot into his heart, he plunged to the ground. The exhilaration, triumph and emotional fever of an elephant confrontation cannot be adequately described except, perhaps, to another hunter.**
>
> **Dr. Edward S. Bundy, American big game hunter**

Although the excitement of brushing with death may have been eroded, the thrill of killing large creatures remained. Violent death was what India, Africa and the other safari countries offered and it was an invitation accepted with very few reservations. But reservations there were. Some hunters such as H. L. Lempriere, stalking in South Africa, strove to avoid killing certain animals for various personal reasons. Lempriere's object of mercy was baboons; they were simply "too human":

> On one occasion I saw one which had been hit in the breast. It cried like a child, and tried to plug the hole with some twisted grass until a merciful shot put it out of its misery.

Others found that killing did not agree with them, vomiting with shame beside the carcass of their first tusker or in old age hanging up their guns in disgust. "I am sorry for all the fine old beasts I have killed," wrote William Cotten Oswell, one of the earliest and most voracious of the hunting titans, "but I was young then, and there was excitement in the work. . . ." Scores more lamented the visible year-to-year decline in the amount of game, and a few even curbed their hunting appetites voluntarily because of it.

But such sportsmen were rare. For most, the opportunity of killing big game was simply too good to pass up. The experience was, as E. M. Sinauer, another notable turn-of-the-century sportsman, breathlessly put it after a successful elephant battue, "really great fun."

Half a century later the American author Robert Ruark was still obsessively blazing away along the same safari trails, although by now the target was something rather less grand than an elephant:

> I shot him nine times with the .220 Swift. I hit him every time, and every time the bullet splattered on his outside. One time I hit him in the face and took away his lower jaw and still he didn't die. He just bled and began to snap fruitlessly at his own dragging guts. I spoke

my first command in Swahili. . . . "The big one. Gimme the .470."
I held it on the gory hyena and took his head off.

Mopping Up

Since those heady days of limitless bags and unalloyed enjoyment, sport hunting has undergone a series of radical and profound changes, not the least being the absence of game throughout many of the most popular hunting grounds. Soon after the beginning of this century, a fateful combination of encroaching civilization, the greed of market hunting and the excesses of sportsmen had cut swathes through animal populations around the globe. Some countries managed to step back from the brink, forcing a jarring reorganization upon the sport. Others, such as the safari countries, were not so fortunate.

Although the masters of the British Raj had long recognized the dangers inherent in leaving India as a sporting free-fire zone, even before the end of the empire the future of hunting on the subcontinent was already apparent. By the 1930s and '40s poaching had become widespread, feeding a well-established market for hunting trophies. Heads and hides from Kashmir and the Central Provinces were finding their way to the large stores of Bombay and Calcutta where they were sold, as one contemporary author remarked, "at the most amazingly high rates" to the growing number of tourists who desired a trophy without the effort. The poachers were, in the main, the native *shikaris*, the descendants of those faithful servants who had learned their trade from the Pesters and Levessons, and learned it well. It was a fateful legacy.

The British withdrawal from the subcontinent in 1947 was the signature on the death warrant of India's wildlife. As one Indian prince later recalled: "War broke out against the animals." With the lifting of restrictions, the Indians blazed away with total abandon: the villagers, in their desire for meat and to protect their crops; the hide and trophy hunters, spurred on by eager foreign markets; and the sportsmen, mimicking the obsessions of their former masters. Dr. Salim Ali, now one of India's most renowned ornithologists, remembered the period in an article in *National Geographic* (September 1976):

> At that time we all shot. In a morning you could easily bag three or four blackbucks. And every hunter with any ambition wanted a tiger. Some shot five, then, thirty. I remember once, about 1953, when I was doing some fieldwork in Madhya Pradesh, I met the Maharaja of Surguja. He was an old man with palsy and braced himself with a stick. "I am

very happy today," he told me. "Why?" I asked. "Because today I have shot my 1,100th tiger!" He ended with 1,157.

Shooting in large parties by day and from Jeeps equipped with spotlights at night, their ranks swelled by British, European and – especially – American sportsmen following the tracks of Hemingway and Ruark in increasing numbers, the hunters decimated their prey. In 1948, less than a year after independence, the last surviving Indian cheetah was shot, and, until the beginning of this decade when most states belatedly adopted the Wildlife Protection Act, it seemed certain that other game would follow suit.

Today the situation is far from rescued. Whereas at the turn of the century there were 40,000 tigers in India alone, there are now probably less than 1,800, with maybe another 200 in the Himalayas and 20 or so in Bangladesh. (Elsewhere in the world there are perhaps another 2,800, but that is possibly an overoptimistic figure; certainly more tigers now exist in captivity than in the wilds.) According to the latest count, there are now only 7,000 Indian elephants, 2,000 buffalo and 900 rhinoceroses. The snow leopard has almost disappeared along with the brown antlered deer (25 at last count), the Kashmir stag (250) and the Markhor goat (250). Even the blackbuck is only a shadow of its former self. For those birds and animals not confined to the small number of reservations set aside by the government, the odds against survival are not encouraging. The Indian Summer has now reached its dismal end. "India," said Colin Platt of the International Society for the Prevention of Cruelty to Animals (ISPCA), "is a classic example of animals being hunted to virtual extinction."

In Africa the devastation has been even more complete. Such was the pressure of the motorized safaris that by the end of World War 1 game laws had been instituted across the most popular hunting stretches of the continent. Not that they did much good; a license to hunt in Kenya and Uganda, for instance, cost only £100, peanuts considering the expense of mounting a safari, and entitled the license holder to a full ninety-six head of game. An elephant cost £15 extra (or two for £45), a giraffe another £15, a rhinoceros £50.

The safari continued as the rich man's status symbol, passing from the aristocracy of England and Europe into the hands of the rich American, who pursued his sport with a single-mindedness which even included light aircraft. Safari hunting was a race to kill the biggest and the rarest. Having your own white hunter was akin to having your own personal attorney. Throughout the century they "filled their cards" with fierce enthusiasm, either unconcerned by or oblivious to the background of steadily vanishing game.

THE FLUSH TOILET SAFARI

Even denuded of game, the Indian subcontinent still holds a powerful fascination for royal hunters; or at least it did until the shift in popular opinion of the last decade or so moved big game hunting closer to murder than to sport. The most famous royal safari of modern times was Queen Elizabeth of England's short excursion into the foothills of the Himalayas in 1961. As an exercise in convenience hunting it surpassed even the tiger battues of the old maharajahs. To ensure that his guests enjoyed their afternoon's outing, the host, King Mahendra of Nepal, ordered a large area of jungle cropped and sprayed with DDT. Royal tents were then erected for the visitors, complete with zinc bathtubs and flush toilets (the queen's was equipped with a red velvet seat cover). After a picnic banquet of boar shashlik and venison curry prepared by "the famed Yak and Yeti Bar in Katmandu," as *Sports Illustrated* reverently reported, the safari set off on the backs of 305 elephants specially imported from India (two of which were walking bars).

Despite all the preparation, the queen was content only to shoot pictures, while the Duke of Edinburgh pleaded a sore finger and also declined a gun. The rest of the party, however, banged away enthusiastically. The first trophy to fall was a female rhinoceros, who was duly measured and photographed once her baby had been driven off. In fact, a mother rhino, despite its bulk, was something rather less than a perfect target, as *Sports Illustrated* pointed out: "Rhinos are not considered sporting trophies in Nepal since only 80 are left in the country and poachers threaten them with extinction."

The safari soon took a turn for the better, however, with the sighting of a tigress – not an entirely unexpected event considering that the night before she had been ringed by Nepalese beaters and fed a buffalo calf to slow her down. Even so, she still proved an elusive target; Britain's foreign secretary Lord Home missed her four times, leaving the kill to another gun (nobody was sure exactly whose). When the smoke had cleared what remained, in *Sports Illustrated*'s estimation, was one "runty" tigress, measuring "a disappointing 8 feet 8 inches."

Today Africa's wildlife is in an appalling state, the destruction compounded over the past decade by the marauding gangs of native poachers. Hardest hit has been the elephant. In Kenya there are now only sixty thousand, with that number perhaps decreasing by as many as twenty thousand a year. In Uganda there are now probably little more than three thousand elephants in the entire country. Likewise the spectacular Grevys zebra: in Kenya whittled down from fifteen thousand a decade ago to apparently less than two thousand, according to one estimate; wiped out in Somalia; and all but gone in Ethiopia. The white rhino is virtually extinct and the leopard is not expected to last in its wild state to the end of the century. The rest of the game has been massively depleted.

It would be wrong to lay the blame for these tragedies solely at the feet of sport hunters. The inevitable expansions of the human population have contributed far more to the decline of big game than the safari hunter, high velocity ammunition notwithstanding. But the sportsman's contribution has been real enough – not only through his own voracious efforts at extermination, but also indirectly, by the fashions he set and the markets he established. It was the sportsman who made trophies – the head over the mantlepiece, the zebra skin on the wall, the stuffed polar bear in the hall – desirable, and when the fashion extended to those unable to obtain the trophies by their own hand, there were any number of willing middlemen to meet the demand by supplying secondhand souvenirs of frozen violence. As Colin Platt of the ISPCA told me:

> It is a European syndrome, this. We started the evil and other people
> have cashed in on it for different reasons. The gazelles, the ikudu, the
> African antelopes – all were originally slaughtered for trophies.
> We're suffering from the backlash of the hunting of many species.
> Between them, the trophy hunters and the fur industry have been
> responsible for the decimation of all the spotted cats . . . tiger, jaguar,
> panther, ocelot, cheetah, leopard – one is now talking of only a few
> thousand. The root of this decimation can be traced back to sportsmen
> without any doubt.

Perhaps the most disturbing fact in the long-running tragedy of the sportsman's relationship with big game is that the safari is still very much with us. Despite the nightmare slide of big game toward extinction, it is still possible for the well-heeled hunter to follow Papa Hemingway's footsteps across the Dark Continent – or bits of it, at least – and elsewhere in search of prey. "Every hunter would love to go on safari," said George Martin, publisher of *Petersen's Hunting* magazine. "The worldwide super-trophies – the African Big Five [elephant, leopard, lion, rhino and buffalo], *shikar* in India and Asia for tigers, Himalayas for sheep, polar bear out of Norway on the sealing boats – sure, every hunter would love to do it." And many of them do.

In the 1975 edition of *Petersen's Hunting Annual* there appeared a lengthy article by hunter John Wootters entitled "Hunting Africa Today," which urged all those who "have dreamed of an African hunt since boyhood" to embark on a safari without delay. From between $6,500 and $9,000 – a price which allows "somewhere around twenty trophy animals per hunter, plus the odd shot at a baboon, bustard or spurwing goose" – Africa "is still worth it." "Yes," Wootters concluded:

> Africa and everything surrounding a safari is changing. No longer do you take a steamer through Suez to Mombasa and trek overland at the head of three hundred head-burdened porters. No longer does your license include hundreds of head of game. No more are lions listed as vermin, with no bag limit. But no longer is African hunting an exclusive pastime of the super-rich, nor does a safari require six months or a year away from home. Now you can be stalking Cape buffalo on one day and on the day after tomorrow step off a jetliner in your home city. Modern, motorized safaris permit you to look over more game heads in three weeks than you could have in three months in the old days. . . . Perhaps Sir Samuel Baker, Selous, Speke, Teddy Roosevelt and even Akeley, Martin Johnson, and Taylor would be horrified by today's Africa. But to the American on his long-dreamt-of first safari, Africa is still everything you thought it was. The important thing is to go while that's still true.

In other words, hurry while stocks last!

Safari hunting may not be the exclusive preserve of the super-rich, but it does help to be a little more wealthy than merely well off. Wayne Preston is a Dallas agent who specializes in packaging expensive hunts for expensive clients. Preston can arrange trips anywhere in the world where they allow hunting; he schedules flights, arranges visas, obtains permits, organizes food and accommodation and so on. Customizing is his specialty; if you have a burning desire to kill a kangaroo in Australia or bag a mountain sheep in Mongolia, Preston is your man. "I've been to Iran, Afghanistan, New Zealand, South America, Mexico . . . all over, organizing trips," he told me. "We're now sending people to Russia in the Eastern Section. The last American to go there was President Teddy Roosevelt!"

In Africa, Preston has links with a number of game ranches in Rhodesia and South Africa. Although Kenya is the most popular safari country, he said, he still prefers to send his clients to Botswana given "this on-again, off-again thing with the elephants." (At the time we spoke, Kenya had just declared one of its frequent moratoriums on elephant scalps.) There were also more trophies to be had in Botswana, he added, including leopards. "I'd say that on a twenty-one-day hunt in Botswana you'd probably take twenty trophies."

Preston's comprehensive services do not come cheaply. A twenty-one-day African safari costs around $12,000, for example. But, he said, "it's surprising the number of folks that'll lay out that kind of money. It's a goodly number." Each year Preston alone handles some four hundred international safari hunters from around his area who each pay on average $6,000. That figure is increasing, he said, what with the advantages of jet travel and the lowering of the minimum number of days required of each hunter by most safari countries. Once they demanded at least a month's trekking, said Preston; now a hunter could be there and back with his heads in ten days.

The sportsmen who use Preston's services and the services of the others like him are the elite of the hunting world. They are invariably rich, powerful and successful men who are viewed by less fortunate fellow hunters with awe and envy, and by unkind psychiatrists as inadequates forced to beat their chests with the butts of elephant guns and measure the length of their penises with rifle barrels in order to affirm their manhood. The most dedicated of them return again and again to the safari grounds, filling their homes with fantastic collections of bird and animal trophies: heads and antlers, hooves and hides, bears stuffed and frozen at the moment of assault, giraffes which seem to step out of walls. They are men such as California's C. J. McElroy, whose trophy room was appraised by *Sports Illustrated*'s J. D. Reed in 1974:

> The room is overpowering. Tier upon tier of heads go up the dark, shadow-lighted walls; full-body mounts make the room an obstacle course of teeth, claws, snouts and legs. Trying to get a better look at a rampant polar bear guarding a freshly killed young seal, I get poked in the chest by a leopard tail. And many trophies haven't even been put up. They lie face down on the leather couches, tilted into corners, and wooden crates marked NAIROBI promise further overcrowding. There are more than three hundred animals in the room.

For Europeans the advent of the African package tour has meant that the safari has become increasingly democratized. "Giraffe, kudu, lion, black rhinoceros," wrote one journalist of Kenya in early 1977, "they can all be shot down quite legally by any German factory worker who can afford the $300 package tour." However, there are still some heads of state carrying on the sanguinary traditions of the European aristocracy, most notably President Giscard of France.

Like that other statesman-sportsman Teddy Roosevelt, President Giscard's assaults on wildlife have become the stuff of legends. His African safaris, which have taken him through Zaire, Gabon, Central Africa, Mozambique and Kenya, have given rise to a hit pop song which has a mother elephant patiently explaining to her infant why the president of France is trying to kill him. His favorite prey would appear to be bear, and he has shot bears in Poland and Romania, although it was later revealed that his Romanian trophy had been released from a zoo prior to the shoot. Which might not have perhaps worried Giscard unduly. According to reports in the French and British press, his gamekeepers in France say that the president shoots hand-reared boars and on one memorable day's outing, he dispatched 1,200 hand-raised pheasants. Most countries try to indulge the president's tastes, which often include shooting protected or out-of-season animals. So far only India and Malaysia have balked at a Giscard request; what he asked for was, predictably, a tiger hunt. Giscard has on several occasions been accused of bending the rules to allow the importation of his trophies, and public criticism has been widespread and vocal. Nevertheless Giscard remains unfazed. That old adage of the redneck gun lover – "I will give up my gun when they pry my cold, dead fingers from around it!" – would appear to apply to localities other than just those situated south of America's Mason-Dixon line.

According to the ISPCA's Colin Platt, the fate of the world's big game with respect to sport hunting is improving. India's protection is still in force, however shakily; the polar bear has recently been added to the protected species list; and with growing pressure for conservation from such international bodies as the United Nations, more and more safari countries are realizing that their big game is worth considerably more on the hoof than hung above a mantlepiece in New Jersey or Düsseldorf or Surrey. Take Kenya, for example. During 1974, the last year in which figures were published, the government issued nearly five thousand hunting licenses which netted more than $9 million. There were even elephants available for anybody who could manage the $1,500 license fee. The streets of Nairobi were lined with dozens of "game trophy" shops offering a full range of heads, hides and so on. Then in May 1977, following strong international pressure, Kenya banned all hunting. Soon after the government outlawed the trophy trade. The East African Professional Hunters Association disbanded, its 106 professional hunters (all but 16 of them white) and the 1,000 Africans employed as safari hands finding themselves out of jobs.

How long Kenya's hunting ban will remain is difficult to judge, but given the Third World's willingness in the past to trade its game to wealthy sportsmen for a quick return, it is likely to be considerably short of forever. "Wave enough money," said Colin Platt gloomily, "and anything is possible." And even if Kenya does hold firm, there are plenty of other safari countries still on offer to the hunting elite. South America is now only just becoming popular, and although the continent's big cats are already sorely pressed, it would seem likely that, as a hunting ground, the area has a rosy future.

Certainly the threat of extinction will not deter sportsmen. In his article of 1974, J. D. Reed talked with another doyen of the big game circuit – Harry Jersig, owner of Texas's Lone Star brewery. It is Jersig's pleasure to possess probably the finest set of trophy rooms in the country – the African Hall, the Hall of Feathers, the North American Hall, the Boar's Nest – crammed with hundreds of deer heads, thousands of antlers, moose, rhinos, lions, etc. "I could be mad for clothes," he told Reed, explaining his passion, "go all over the world looking for a certain suit style or a ring or something. But I like to find things typical of a country, of a time and place. Things that are vanishing, just like that grass gazelle on the wall there. . . ."

Sport for All

"Our humanity evolved as a portion of our hunting way," wrote Robert Ardrey in *The Hunting Hypothesis*, "and the hunting way, regrettably, is gone." Well, yes and no. While it is true that less than a quarter of a million humans around the world hunt for survival, there are today far more hunters on the face of the earth than at any other time in history. Sport it may be, but it is sport on the grand scale.

Europe, despite its many physical limitations, is still a major hunting center. Italy alone houses well over two million hunters, all of them possessed by the sport. Each year they fire on average eight hundred cartridges per gun, killing a staggering two hundred million birds and fifty million animals. Cynics have estimated that if every Italian entitled to shoot were to take up his position on the land available for the sport, there would be seven hundred guns blasting away on each square kilometer. The annual turnover in guns and ammunition in Italy is almost $400 million, which for a country in such dire economic straits reflects an unparalleled dedication. Every August 28 – "Black Sunday," the opening day of the songbird season – more than a million shooters take to the valleys and hills, some to purpose-built concrete bunkers giving a clear view down the valleys. Between them they massacre something on the order of six to twelve million songbirds (a conservative estimate). On August 28 only the foolish stroll through the Italian woods.

The French are only slightly less avid. In late 1978 a light aircraft was shot down by a party of a dozen hunters. Police later dug 120 bullets out of its fuselage. When confronted, the hunters readily confessed to the attack. The plane, they said, had been scaring the birds.

Belgian hunters pay out almost $4 million each year on licenses; the French, whose licenses are ridiculously cheap, $32 million. In the USSR some three million hunters stalk the landscape. In Germany would-be hunters line up for the privilege of sitting long and arduous examinations in order to become eligible for a license. The privilege is not cheap.

Elsewhere in the world the enthusiasm for killing is equally as strong. In Australia, where the strong passion to hunt has only in the last few years been tempered by truly protective legislation, hunting remains one of the great national pastimes. During the 1950s and '60s hunters – mainly professionals, but also a large sprinkling of amateur sportsmen – came close to endangering the survival of several species of kangaroo, notably the red kangaroo. By the late '60s, 'roo shooting was accounting for two million red and gray kangaroos each year, a slaughter rivaled only by the massacre of red deer in neighboring New Zealand. "Spotlighting" – shooting at night by transfixing the animals in the glare of a spotlight – although hardly sporting was the favored method of hunting (as it still is today, despite its being outlawed). Safaris and the handbag trade also threatened the native crocodiles of the tropical north. From 1945 to 1960, 284,724 giant emus – a unique creature of absolutely no value to anyone save as a target – were slaughtered in Western Australia alone. Duck hunting is now the Australian hunter's delight, and in the season the bays and marshes become a battleground. "One could devote much . . . space to the Australian sport of killing," concluded author Keith Dunstan wryly.

In Britain the turn-of-the-century status quo has been preserved and expanded despite some often spectacular opposition. Today some two million sportsmen shoot and hunt, decimating worlds of pheasant, partridge, duck, snipe and quail, riding down an estimated forty thousand foxes, shooting deer, setting the hounds on stags and coursing innumerable hares.

Fox hunting in particular has never been more popular. The 180 fox-hound packs which mustered after the war have now grown to 206, despite the encroachment of civilization with its motorways and barbed wire. More than that, hunting to hounds has become a sizable spectator sport, with around a quarter of a million devotees careering cross-country every Saturday on bicycle, car and foot following the hunt proper. So, too, with the tradition-steeped stag hunts of Exmoor, an exercise which ends with the stag either being dispatched with a "humane killer" or having its throat slit with a knife. The challenge is to be present at the kill. According to one hunter I spoke to, a stag hunt is to the locals what football is to a Londoner: "It's their Saturday afternoon sport and there'll be probably a thousand of them in Land Rovers flying about the countryside."

Beagling – the art of walking up a hare with a slow-moving pack of beagles and maneuvering it toward a kill – has also increased; there are now eighty-one packs fielded in England. So, too, has the number of harrier packs increased. There are eighty coursing meets a year, the main one – the Waterloo Cup – drawing upwards of one thousand spectators to muddy fields to watch a pair of greyhounds snap the back of a hare. In Scotland, Highland deer stalking and bird shoots reap some £3 million each season. At one of the more famous estates – the Duke of Athol's – four thousand stalkers and shooters pay £700–800 each a week.

Against this vivid background of chasing and killing, only the otter packs have succumbed. In 1977 there were seventeen active otter packs, but with the otter population disastrously reduced, first by relentless hunting and, more recently, by stream pollution, they could manage to kill only three. In 1978 otters were belatedly listed as an endangered species (there may be only thirty-two pairs left in the most popular haunts) – much to the chagrin of the otter hunters themselves, who argued in the tortuous logic common to many hunters regardless of their country of origin that only by hunting otters could the creatures be saved.

But it is bird shooting which is Britain's most popular hunting pastime. Today the exclusive grouse moors and preserves of the English landowners have been thrown open to the syndicate shooters – groups of businessmen and wealthy city dwellers who club together and hire a stretch of shooting territory, sometimes for as much as £250 per gun per week for a prime strip. Although looked down upon by the more traditionally minded sportsmen, the syndicate shooters have created a boom in bird shooting.

To meet the demand, British landowners have long been accustomed to artificially rearing stocks. Eggs are produced in game farms (some years ago it was estimated that a million pheasant eggs were being produced annually) and sold to the estates, both commercial and private. The birds are then hand-reared by the gamekeeper who feeds them, places them and protects them from predators until they are ready to be shot by sportsmen. It can be an enormous business; the Earl of Aylesford, for example, reportedly adds six thousand reared pheasants to his existing stocks of five thousand birds each year and rears some three thousand mallard. According to one article designed to attract American shooters to the earl's Packington Hall, the results of this human intervention are supremely satisfying:

> Each day, over one thousand pheasants will be flushed and shown over the guns . . . you can shoot as many teal, wigeon, pochard, tufted duck, golden-eye and pintail as come within range, and there are no bag limits on anything you can shoot . . . you will readily appreciate that the shooting can get fast and furious . . .

Indeed. In one recent season, according to the blurb, eleven thousand birds were dispatched.

In effect, game management has meant that the modern British sportsman has now solved the problem of supply and demand. Nature, until now unable to withstand the enthusiasm of hunters equipped with sophisticated weapons, has been improved upon. It is now no longer just birds that are artificially reared; even the fox population is reinforced by the purpose-built lairs which have been found on the estates of the very best people. (This makes rather a mockery of the fox hunting fraternity's expressed aim of ridding the countryside of "vermin." It does, however, make for better hunting.) Indeed, without the rearing of game specifically for destruction at the hands of sportsmen, the chances of the most popular forms of hunting continuing at their present levels in Britain would be slim in the extreme. And what is true for Britain is even more true for the United States.

Meat on the Hoof

The regeneration of hunting in America is one of modern man's most spectacular triumphs over nature. At the turn of the century, most authorities held little hope of the larger species of American game lasting much beyond the 1920s. Today the United States is the home of modern hunting.

Ironically it was the hunters themselves and their organizations – Theodore Roosevelt's Boone and Crockett Club, the Audubon Society – who were largely responsible for reversing the course of hunting. Even while Roosevelt was trying his hardest to kill what was, by his own estimation, one of the last half dozen buffaloes on the plains, he was exploring means of conservation – a contradiction which most hunters blithely accept without question. Roosevelt's conservation was, of course, conservation of a particular kind – the preservation of game to allow the continuance of sport hunting. Yet it had its desired effect; the game survived and Roosevelt became a hero of conservation.

Through the lobbying efforts of the various hunting clubs and the influence of Roosevelt as president, a number of important measures designed to control the killing were passed, much to the disgust of many free-reigning hunters. (In certain quarters of the National Rifle Association,

Roosevelt is still villified by hard-line hunters pressing for a return to un-restricted killing.) The U.S. Forestry Service was set up, followed by the Wildlife Refuge system which provided a sanctuary for game. (Unfor-tunately for the animals, the sanctuaries were again opened to hunters during the last decade.) In 1916 the Department of the Interior, which had long struggled in vain to introduce curbs on hunting, signed an agreement with Canada on the protection of migratory birds.

It was not until the 1930s and the introduction of game management programs, however, that the situation began to change radically. The combination of game management by the state and the occasional private concern (such as Ducks Unlimited which has, since 1937, established 1,200 "duck factories" on Canadian marshland) together with more stringent hunting legislation, license fees, gun and ammunition taxes, and the systematic destruction of predators such as wolves, pumas and coyotes, laid the foundations for an enormous regeneration of game. By the 1940s the New York businessman could leave his office Friday evening, fly out to the Rockies to meet his outfitter, and be back at his desk by Monday certain of a trophy. More significantly, the game regeneration meant that any of his blue-collared employees could venture out into the Pennsylvanian woods, confidently expecting to bag a deer and drive home with it strapped across his fender. As the car allowed more and more people to travel away from home, weekend hunting became almost a ritual. Supply, controlled by the game managers, followed demand, and game populations exploded.

Today the reversal is complete. A continent which less than half a century ago was facing wildlife problems equal to those of modern Africa, has once again become a hunting haven. Populations of whitetail deer – the most popular of large game targets – have soared from a total of half a million at the turn of the century to a current total of sixteen million. There are now twenty-four times the number of elks that there were in 1907, and seven times the number of antelopes. Wild turkey, which even as late as the 1950s numbered less than one hundred thousand, now total well over a million and a quarter. In 1915 the wood duck was on the verge of extinction; today it is the most common breeding waterfowl in the East, a region which is a duck hunting paradise. In addition to this rebirth of native game there have been several spectacular successes with imported wildlife, such as the Hungarian partridge and the Indian chukar. The ringneck pheasant, unknown on the continent a century ago, now numbers in the millions.

There are now even buffalo – some ten thousand of them scattered throughout the U.S. And, contrary to Roosevelt's projections, they are there to be hunted. Wayne Preston, for example, sells shots at Texan buffalo for $7,000 each, including air travel, wining and dining, accommodation and trophy mounting. He said he got the idea from Neiman Marcus, the Dallas department store which specializes in lavish Christmas gifts. One Christmas the store was offering a matched male and female buffalo for $11,550. "I thought," chuckled Preston, "if Neimans can help propagate the buffalo world, maybe we can help to cut it back a bit." So far the package has proved successful.

Game control in America has developed into a highly technological and sophisticated science. Populations are checked and monitored, licensing is strict, "harvests" are controlled. Limits for ducks and geese are determined by satellite photographs. Large game is fitted with radio-controlled collars to keep track of its movements. When anti-hunters point to drops in elk or deer populations caused by overhunting, they are merely indicating the surface ripples on a vast reservoir of game which is watched over by more than twenty-five thousand state and federal "wildlife conservation" workers and supported by a budget of more than half a billion dollars.

The aim of modern game management is as Roosevelt hoped – to perpetuate a "hunting surplus" which sport hunters can "harvest" for a minimal fee. Game is regarded by the wildlife departments as a "renewable resource" to be put at the disposal of hunters, or, in the official jargon, to be "oriented to mass recreation." As one former department official quoted in *The Saturday Evening Post* remarked: "You may be hired as a wildlife manager, biologist or whatever, but you soon find that you are paid to put out so much meat on the hoof."

The effect of this abundant "crop" has transformed sport hunting. Within the space of a lifetime, people who had grown up in the belief that hunting, inevitably, would one day come to an end, have witnessed the growth of a sport which could conceivably continue indefinitely. And over the years, as the game grew more and more abundant, more and more people took up the sport until hunting became a major participatory recreation.

It is difficult to convey the sheer enormity of hunting in the United States to anyone who has never been near Pennsylvania or Utah or Texas during the season. Before the start of 1978, it was estimated that twenty-two million Americans would hunt during the year – one-tenth of the entire population. In America today there are more sport hunters than Jews or Mormons or Southern Baptists or Episcopalians. In 1975, 16,597,807 hunters paid $154.9 million in state hunting license fees, bringing the total payment since 1923 to $2.3 billion. In 1975 duck hunters purchased more than a million federal duck stamps. The taxes on arms and ammunition has provided $600 million over the last thirty-five years and with each new season adds another $55 million to the government coffers. Hunting equipment, ranging from automatic duck pluckers to specially fitted-out four-wheel-drive vehicles, has grown into a \$2 billion-a-year industry – half a billion of which is spent on guns and ammunition alone. As one wildlife department official shrugged, indicating the nearby offices of a leading cartridge manufacturer, "DuPont owns the state of Delaware." Until 1977 it was estimated that two million waterfowl were dying every year, not from gunshot wounds, but from eating the lead shot which now carpets the bottom of many waterways. In some popular hunting areas it was discovered that there were as many as 120,000 misplaced pellets lying on every acre, part of 6,000 *tons* of lead shot spent each year.

The National Rifle Association (NRA), the hunters' most prominent pressure group, has a membership of more than one million, 75 to 85 percent of whom are hunters. The organization employs 250 full-time staff, owns an office block in the center of Washington, D.C., and is larger than all but three of the country's biggest labor unions. Its annual budget is \$10 million and its assets total in the region of \$24 million. It is the NRA's proud boast that it can deluge a politician with thousands of telegrams from hunters around the country within twenty-four hours of any speech against either guns or hunting. Its views are echoed by the National Wildlife Federation, another Washington-based pro-hunting organization, which claims a membership of 3.7 million.

Besides this love affair with the gun, many sportsmen have also reverted to more traditional forms of hunting. Between one and two million Americans now hunt with bows and lethal steel-tipped arrows. Another two million are trappers, accounting for an estimated seventeen thousand birds and animals *a day* – 6.5 million a year. Of these, only some twenty thousand are full-time professionals; the rest trap solely for the sport, as Georgia trapper Dorothy Gooch explained to *Sports Illustrated* in June 1976:

> There ain't no way I can tell you the thrill of trappin'. There ain't nothin' to compare it with. There's makin' love. And fishin'. And gettin' high on somethin'. And trappin' – well, trappin' kind of stands alone, I'd say.

Thousands more have been drawn to the recent vogue in antique weapons such as muskets and muzzle loaders. Not so long ago I watched a young Californian, Jim Porter, hunting with a hawk on a stretch of wasteland in the heart of Los Angeles. As the cars sped by on the adjacent highway, Porter's majestic creature hovered motionless in the warm air before swooping to snatch some small ground animal in its talons. By Porter's estimation there were at least a thousand falconers practicing the sport in California, and perhaps three or four times that number elsewhere in the States. "It's gotten real popular in the last few years," he said.

Although the backbone of the hunting fraternity still tends to be the blue-collar worker from a rural background, the social spectrum is all-embracing, ranging from the "good old boys" in the pick-up trucks with "Register Communists Not Firearms" taped to their bumpers to the corporate executives entertaining clients on their company-leased game ranches. "Hunting is not an elitist sport in America," an NRA spokesman told me pointedly. "In America *everybody* hunts."

The effects this hunting army has on American wildlife are, to say the least, impressive. During the 1975-6 hunting season, according to the NRA hunting annual, the modern American Daniel Boone killed:

2,600,000 deer	102,000 elks
21,000,000 waterfowl	84,000 antelope
94,000,000 upland game birds	67,669 moose
32,000,000 squirrels	55,000 caribou
27,000,000 rabbits	24,000 bears

All in all, well over 250,000,000 birds and animals, and these figures are far from complete. What this means is that every American hunter chalks up at least a dozen kills each year, and that figure could easily be double.

One final statistic should be added to this list of violent destruction and that is the number of hunters killed each year while pursuing their sport. According to the National Safety Council, at least 700 people die in hunting accidents every season. (State figures, generally acknowledged to be incomplete, put the figure for 1974-5 at 322 fatalities, while the NRA, obviously not wishing to add fuel to any fires, claims between 300 and 325.) In addition, the NSC lists 5,500 woundings (the states, 2,500).

The main point about these private tragedies is that they reflect not so much the fact that Americans are worse shots than anyone else (a distinct possibility, given the general lack of licensing tests), nor that they become impossibly frenzied at the touch of a gun (for many, a certainty), but the sheer log jam of humanity which now follows the sport. As one hunter education officer from Pennsylvania, a state which attracts a million deer hunters to its limited hunting grounds on opening day, recently remarked, "Even if they used baseball bats there would be some accidents." For the majority of sportsmen, hunting in America today is about woods crawling with Day-Glo orange jackets, country roads choked with traffic and gunfire echoing off the hills like fireworks. Teddy Roosevelt and his visions of wilderness seem part of a long time ago.

The Joy of Killing

The urges which drive men to become hunters in a modern society are more elusive and clouded than perhaps anything else in the relatively uncomplicated world of sport. At its best, hunting is an uncomfortable and dangerous pastime which offers few benefits, either physical or financial. It is both expensive and time consuming, and to the majority of nonhunters, a sordid and disgusting practice. So why hunt?

The reasons proffered by hunters themselves cover a wide territory. The most frequently heard explanation concerns urban man's return to nature – the attractions of Roosevelt's wilderness, if you like, said George Martin of *Petersen's Hunting* magazine:

> It's a way of life . . . and this gets trite; I've never seen it successfully put into words because it's too inner, too gut, too intimate . . . but hunters still thrill to the bugling elk, glistening wings in the morning sunlight, that sort of thing. It's neat and it sends a chill up your back.

The spokesman from the NRA quoted from José Ortega y Gasset's *Meditations on Hunting*, the thinking hunter's bible. To Ortega, hunting was "a vacation from the human condition":

> This is the reason men hunt. When you are fed up with the troublesome present, with being "very twentieth century," you take your gun, whistle for your dog, go out to the mountain, and, without further ado, give yourself the pleasure during a few hours or a few days of being "Paleolithic." . . . "Natural" man is always there, under the changeable historical man. We call him and he comes – a little sleepy, benumbed, without his lost form of instinctive hunter, but, after all, still alive. "Natural" man is first "prehistoric" man – the hunter.

Most hunters are generally less erudite. To them, hunting presents a deliciously seductive image comprised of many parts: the joys of all-male companionship, the thrill of facing nature at her most ferocious (it is no coincidence that most big game trophies are set in unnaturally threatening poses), the simple pleasures of the collector – "Some people collect stamps; I collect trophies." The American fascination with guns is also a powerful attraction. "That's the way our country was won," said Dallas hunting packager Wayne Preston, proudly eyeing a large wall map of Texas. "That's the way we opened up these areas. Now we use the gun as a sporting device. You're never going to stop the gun thing." As Roger Caras once wrote, if guns looked like sewing machines there would be far less hunting.

American sportsmen talk of tracking, stalking and the "satisfaction of squeezing off the perfect shot." English foxhunters recount the glories of "the chase." Other hunters cite the need to cull herds for conservation, or to help keep the foxes down – in other words, the urge to do one's duty. To renowned big game hunter Harry Jersig, hunting provides many school-children with their one chance to see animals they otherwise could only read about – an "educational program." Still others put forward different reasons – patriotism, the assertion of masculinity in an otherwise softening world. And most would probably just echo the hunter interviewed by CBS television who struggled to articulate his feelings with: "I dunno, it's just . . . just somethin' in the blood . . . I just . . . *enjoy* it."

There is, however, one reason which hunters never offer: that hunting is killing, and that killing – the violent destruction of life – is supremely enjoyable. In the past there was rarely any such equivocation; hunters hunted for the pleasure of killing. Indeed, for many the lust to kill was a source of pride. Put a civilized man before a fine head, wrote British MP and crack sportsman Sir Henry Seton-Karr in *My Sporting Holidays* (1904), and:

> he will straightway be seized with an inordinate desire to slay the animal in question. . . . Only those who have experienced it can realize the strength of the hunter's lust to kill the hunted, though they may find it difficult to explain. It is certain that no race of men possess this desire more strongly than the Anglo-Saxons of the British Isles. . . . Let us take it that in our case this passion is an inherited instinct – which civilization cannot eradicate – of a virile and dominant race and that it forms a healthy natural antidote to the enervating refinements of modern life . . . the pursuit and slaughter of wild game is a per-fectly natural, healthy and widespread trait of humanity, even necessary in some cases for health and happiness.

More recently, the University of Arizona published a pamphlet entitled *Values of Hunting and Fishing in Arizona in 1965* which contained a number of quotations from hunters:

> I like the excitement of killing. You get a feeling of accomplishment when you kill something.

> [It] satisfies a basic human need, in some people, to kill.

> Killing a deer is relief; it takes out inhibitions, and it's good to take it out on the animals.

But these are the words of another generation. Today, in an era which has seen the demything of killing and the sport of hunting laid under

---

ᴬᴬ It's a good thing there's laws or else I'd get myself a tank or a howitzer and I'd kill deer by the bus loads. **ᵖᵖ**

Herb Miller, American deer hunter, 1975

---

vigorous siege, such confessions have become decidedly unfashionable. It is simply no longer good form to mention hunting and killing in the same breath. Of all the hunters I interviewed – on both sides of the Atlantic – only one, *Petersens*'s George Martin, came even close to echoing the sentiments of his hunting predecessors. "There's no point in trying to put your head in the sand," he admitted. "Killing and blood are very definitely an important part of it. I don't feel bad if I go hunting and fail to kill anything, but I feel a helluva lot better if I *have* killed something. That's the climax." But in the next breath he quickly added with narrowed eyes, "I'm not prepared to say that there are not those who get their jollies out of watching blood run, but I've hunted forty years and I've never run into anyone who I ever thought was masking that attitude."

Today's hunter does not even use the word *kill* in his language; game is "culled," "harvested," "reduced," "cropped" or "controlled." State and federal fisheries and wildlife departments are specifically barred from using the word *kill* in their reports and literature. "There's an awful lot of guilt among hunters," explained Mr. McGarvey, press officer for the Washington bureau, himself hardly an anti-hunter. "It feels good to kill things, but they don't want to admit it."

There is very little room for killing in the modern hunter's own self-image. At most, killing is regarded as an incidental, almost embarrassing side effect. In a poll involving over a thousand hunters which was conducted by a University of Wisconsin student named Lowell L. Klessig in 1970, only 30 percent of those questioned gave bagging game as a primary motivation for their hunting. The majority considered either social or appreciative reasons to be more compelling. When CBS televised the controversial exposé of modern American hunting *The Guns of Autumn*, it was reviled by hunters – not for its facts, which were beyond dispute, but, in the words of one critic, for its "stressing the kill and not the hunt." "Violence?" said the spokesman for the British Field Sports Society with raised eyebrows when I approached him. "My first reaction is why come to me? I have nothing to do with violent sports."

The ideal firmly fixed in most hunters' minds would appear to be that demonstrated in a recent story in *Sports Illustrated*. After spending hours tramping through the woods alone, raising a sweat, watching the game, listening to the sounds of nature, the writer wound up not firing a shot. It was, he concluded, "the perfect hunt."

Yet it was one of the leading hunting figures of recent times, John Madson of the Olin munitions works, who bluntly punctured this near-universal vision of the bloodless hunter. During an address to the NRA, Mr. Madson was reported to have said:

> The hunter often deludes himself and buries his motives. Yet, his ultimate motive in hunting is to kill. All other reasons, however important, are secondary. Remove the conscious intention of shooting at something and a hunt is simply a walk in the country.

Today killing is still very much the mainspring of hunting, as it always has been.

There are, of course, exceptions. Apart from the handful of huntsmen at the core of a foxhunt – the Master of the Hunt and his cohorts – whose job it is to exterminate foxes, most supporters hunt solely for the excitement of the ride. "I can't tell you what it's like at the moment when you think you're going to have a run," bubbled one female foxhunter I spoke to. "Something just goes down your spine. It's rather like the Queen going past." Only occasionally catching a glimpse of the fox and rarely participating in the kill, it is probable that most English foxhunters would be just as at home riding with a hunt from upstate New York, one of whose members recently confided that if they ever *did* kill a fox, they would all most likely burst into tears. So, too, with the coursing fraternity, disgusting though the tearing apart of hares may seem to the uninitiated. The interest in comparing the skills of their dogs far outweighs the fascination of seeing a hare done to death, for most coursers at least.

In America there *are* hunters who lose themselves in the wilderness, living out Roosevelt's dreams to their fullest. Mr. McGarvey cited the example of a colleague who backpacked three weeks out of every year through the wilds of South Dakota after bighorn sheep. "He'll go for days and not fire a shot," he said. "He's done it for fifteen years straight, and he hasn't got one yet. If everyone hunted like him in this country, we'd have no problems."

Unfortunately for McGarvey's department, everyone doesn't hunt like that; in fact, most don't. The cherished self-image of the hunter is a far cry from the realities. Today the wilderness hunter is about as scarce as the much shot-at whooping crane. Game management, while ensuring an endless supply of targets, has also had the effect of reducing hunting in America, Britain and Europe to the level of supermarket shooting. The self-image of the tracker penetrating deep into the wilds is a modern myth, even by George Martin's reckoning. "Probably no more than 25 percent of American hunters will get more than a mile or so from the road," he told me. "We're a nation – certainly the last couple of generations – of people who want the regenerating that wilderness areas are able to give us. We want that, but we're not willing to give up our creature comforts for it. It's the soft life."

The spectacle of American hunting today is far more often that described by James Selk, a columnist for the Madison, Wisconsin, *State Journal*, after covering the opening of the deer season:

> I saw the traffic jam of cars and trucks and campers crowded onto shoulders and pull-offs. I saw hundreds of orange-clad hunters stalking their prey in large groups a few hundred yards off the highway. I saw a wounded deer limping across the road and several others, panicked, chased across the road by men and small boys blazing away with their guns. I saw huge blotches of blood and gore at close intervals on the highway. At one . . . spot, I saw a bloody carcass, split in two, half on one side of the road, half on the other. . . . I took a different route back and found much the same thing . . . crowds of hunters among cars and trucks, apparently discussing their next forays into the brush; panicked deer, blood, cars with gutted deer lashed to bloody bumpers. . . . Maybe all the slob hunters were on those small stretches of road last weekend, but I doubt it. I think they represented a pretty fair cross section of the entire breed.

This in a state whose hunters denied that killing game was a major motive to hunt.

The development toward making hunting easier and more certain has now reached a plateau. The only danger remaining is the danger of being mistaken for an elk by one's fellow hunter. Bear, America's great domestic "killer," is now totally outmatched, and has been since Roosevelt's time. "On the whole," wrote Roosevelt in *The Wilderness Hunter*:

> . . . the danger of hunting these great bears has been greatly exaggerated. At the beginning of the present century, when white hunters first encountered the grizzly, he was doubtless an exceedingly savage beast, prone to attack without provocation, and a redoubtable foe to persons armed with the clumsy, small-bore, muzzle-loading rifles of the day. But at present bitter experience has taught him caution. He has been hunted for sport and hunted for his pelt and hunted for the bounty and hunted as a dangerous enemy to stock, until, save in the very wildest districts, he has learned to be more wary than a deer and to avoid man's presence almost as carefully as the most timid kind of

---

❝ There's something special about bears. They're a very dignified animal. I guess that's why I love to hunt them. ❞

Fred Bear, veteran American bow hunter, 1976

---

game. Except in rare cases he will not attack of his own accord, and, as a rule, even when wounded, his object is escape rather than battle.

Today in the bear hunting regions of Montana, bears are pinpointed by light spotter aircraft, "hunted" down back country lanes by convoys of four-wheel-drive vehicles, shot out of trees and gunned down from car windows.

Even the big game safari has long since had its teeth pulled. In Africa and elsewhere, safaris are as harmless as any other package tour. To obtain the ultimate North American ferocious animal, according to Roger Caras, all one has to risk is money. "If you can afford ten thousand dollars to put a Kodiac bear in your lobby," he said, "you can put a Kodiac bear in your lobby." Caras himself has toured the Kodiac hunting grounds with hunting parties. "You don't have to know how to shoot or track. Your life's never in danger. Your white hunter is never more than three feet away."

When Fred Bear, doyen of American big game bow hunters and the man most responsible for the renaissance in bow hunting, faces bears, tigers or African elephants, he does so with a battery of rifles at his back. His first two Arctic polar bears were gunned down by this back-up crew when they refused to succumb to his arrows. It was not until his third attempt that he could rightly claim to have personally killed a representative of the species.

Along with the challenge of the wilderness has disappeared another Rooseveltian ideal, the joy of surviving by one's own hand. Of the thousand-plus Wisconsin hunters polled by Lowell Klessig, only 3 percent gave hunting for meat as their primary motivation. Even more significantly, a mere 14 percent considered that providing low-cost meat was *any motivation at all*. The most popular target in North America, the morning dove, is in many states not even considered a game bird but a songbird, as fit for eating as a squirrel, a groundhog or many other species of popular but unpalatable hunting prey. Like the Dallas couple from Indian Creek, many hunters do not even eat the ducks they kill, let alone the venison. Similarly, according to an article in *Sports Illustrated* some years ago, 10 to 20 percent of all the trophies taken to taxidermists are never picked up.

All of this points to the inevitable conclusion that killing, for the modern sportsman, is not just *a* major reason for hunting, but *the* major reason.

"These hunters – attorneys, welders, high school students, accountants – have no need for the game they kill, and little respect for its source," wrote journalist Craig Waters in *New Times*. "Hunting is a divertissement, a different way to spend one's weekend; it is a brutal game which people other than pro athletes can play." And the way the game is being increasingly played leaves less and less room for the illusions. According to Ortega y Gasset's *Meditations on Hunting*, as hunting grew more sophisticated:

> man imposed more and more limitations on himself as the animal's rival in order to leave it free to practice its wily defenses, in order to avoid making the prey and the hunter excessively unequal, as if passing beyond a certain limit in that relationship might annihilate the essential character of the hunt, transforming it into pure killing and destruction. Hence the confrontation between man and animal has a precise boundary beyond which hunting ceases to be hunting.

Throughout the hunting world – and especially the American hunting world – that boundary has now been breached to the point of disintegration.

It is purely the joy of killing which has made legitimate sporting events out of such pastimes as the "bunny bashings" of Boise, Idaho, and Harmony, North Carolina. Hundreds of hunters, young and old, are attracted to these events – held ostensibly to assist the farmers – often driving hundreds of miles to herd thousands of rabbits into pens and club them to death with branches, sticks, boots and baseball bats. In Tasmania, the Australian state which exterminated its aboriginal population in the mid-1800s, occasionally in the name of sport, wallaby drives take the place of the bunny bash. The Avoca Football Club has carved out its own niche in hunting lore by organizing afternoons whereby two hundred and more Tasmanians pay $2 a head for the privilege of gunning down herds of penned wallabies. Once again, culling is the traditional justification – and indeed there may well be a need for controlling the wallaby population – but that is hardly why people attend.

It is the joy of killing which prompts hunters to bag Montana's elks by firing point blank into the herds from their car windows, and which is responsible for the slaughter of South Dakota's foxes by hunters shooting from ski-equipped light aircraft. "Have you ever watched a plane run down a fox?" asked one farmer appalled by the killing which in the winter of 1971–2 accounted for twenty thousand creatures. "The animal doesn't have a chance."

It is the joy of killing which accounts for the piles of dead songbirds shot over the Italian Dolomites and left to rot, and the expensive Arctic safaris which, until very recently, guaranteed clients one polar bear apiece and as many seals as they could be bothered to fire at. The beauty of such Arctic hunts, as one wildlife expert informed me, is that the animals "are just sitting ducks." Clients were not even required to step down from the ship, merely firing from the deck as it passed through the ice flows. There were even helpers to load the guns. Until the polar bear was listed as an endangered species, one American travel agent was packaging eight such safaris a year on specially chartered ships.

In Arizona hunters wait a decade for their number to come up in a state-run lottery which will entitle them to a once-in-a-lifetime shot at a buffalo. Each lucky winner pays $500 for the privilege. The buffalo is chosen by a game warden and it is gunned down over a distance of only a few hundred yards as it grazes. There is no shortage of hopeful entrants and no complaints, even when a few years ago the animals earmarked for execution were first corralled and then run out of a chute to be shot at point blank range. "It is a true hunt, the way we're doing it now," commented one Arizona game warden proudly.

In the tiny township of Copper Harbor, Michigan, hunters – many of them from out of state – flock to the local dump on the opening day of the season to shoot bears which, after living on garbage and handouts for most of the year, are almost completely tame. "It's sort of like a small war out here," one resident told a CBS reporter. "Last year they came out here in lounge chairs drinking beer and just sitting back and waiting for the bears to come in the dump." In Lennox, Massachusetts, hunters could not even wait for the animals to arrive, tame or not; instead, they shot two fallow deer penned in a private zoo.

It is the urge to wreak violence which turns otherwise reasonable men into bands such as the group of New Jersey hunters described by a *Sports Illustrated* writer, himself a pro-hunter:

> The guys I knew there hunted in full camouflage outfits, with jump boots and flak vests, with more armament than the 101st Airborne and they didn't just shoot at anything that moved – they just shot. They shot at parked cars, telephone poles, turnpike toll stations, road signs, and one guy I knew even blew in the side of his own Dodge truck.

Such behavior is not merely confined to a small core of rogue "slob" hunters bent on excess, as the NRA and its kindred bodies would have the world believe. It is simply the pieces of a deep-seated hunting pattern which have bubbled to the surface naked and undisguised. In Britain, a nation whose hunting custodians throw up their hands in horror at the mere thought of America's ways of shooting for sport, the pinnacle of sporting refinement is still the grouse shoot. From the first day of the season – the

"Glorious Twelfth," as it is known – covey after covey of grouse is driven over the guns in their butts. On many of the most popular moors, the shooters, who pay heavily for their entertainment, do not even keep their kills; those remain the property of the estate. The attractions are purely "sporting."

But whatever the devilries of grouse shooting, they are considerably less than those of its sister sport, the pheasant battue. Shooting hand-reared pheasants on an English country estate is about as sporting a proposition as killing bears at Copper Harbor dump. The birds are hand-fed twice a day by the gamekeeper who invariably whistles them up from their carefully selected coveys so that they grow familiar with him. Then one day, instead of bringing corn, he arrives with a syndicate of shooters who advance on the pheasants in a line as the birds are chased over the guns by beaters. It is the gamekeeper's task to encourage the birds to present a "sporting" target, which, in the words of one gamekeeper, can mean "that you have a devil of a job getting [them] into the air so that they can be shot." One common method is to force the pheasants to fly from hilltop to hilltop, with the guns stationed in the valley below. "There is no valid reason why such immense trouble should be taken to rear and maintain a bird which can just as well be brought up on a farm like any other creature designed for the use of man," commented author and hunting historian L. G. Pine. "It is the desire to kill something which makes the pheasant into the figure of preservation that it is."

Such practices have steadily become fashionable elsewhere in the world, particularly in the United States. Not only do the various wildlife bureaus now release penned birds into the wilds to promote hunting in desired areas, but over the past three decades America's much-vaunted hunting democracy has suffered the growing intrusion of private shooting clubs providing hand-reared birds on tap for the enjoyment of members only.

As with the English shoots, the different clubs prefer different methods of exposing their game – pheasant, duck, partridge, among others – to the guns. At some clubs the birds are placed in the field the day before a shoot to be flushed out by dogs when the time is right; at others they are released immediately prior to the hunters' arrival. If the gamekeeper has difficulty in making them fly, he will often release them from platforms hidden in the trees, or drive them up a wooden ramp so that they are forced to fly over the waiting guns. One standard trick involves training the birds to fly from their pens to a pond some distance off each day for feeding. Generally overfed and used to a life under wire, the birds present easy targets, but just to make sure, some clubs go to the added extent of clipping their wings. There have even been reports of stunned birds being placed in front of the sportsmen's guns. According to one estimate of a few years ago, there are some three thousand such clubs offering hand-reared birds to paying customers. They would appear to be especially popular with the executive class of shooter – wealthy businessmen, corporation heads and so on.

From wildfowl preserves, it was only a small step to the no-game-no-pay guarantee hunts of exotic preserves such as Richard Grona's Indian Creek Ranch with which this chapter began. Since the 1940s when they were first introduced, exotic ranches have become a major feature in the overall pattern of American hunting. They can now be found in Vermont, Tennessee, Iowa, Nebraska, Pennsylvania, New York, Michigan, New Mexico and California, offering mouflon ram from Sardinia, Barbary sheep from North Africa, sika deer from China and Japan, axis from India. There are now more blackbuck antelope in Texas alone than on the entire Indian subcontinent, from whence they originated; in fact, Texas ranches are now involved in shipping the creatures back to India to replenish the native stocks. One Texas ranch which experimented with a pair of nilgai antelope from Africa wound up with a herd of more than four thousand animals. No one in Texas imports exotic animals now; the state is crawling with them.

At Oregon's Ponderosa Buffalo and Wildlife Ranch, hunters can shoot a yakalo (a cross between a buffalo and a yak) or a zonie (a cross between a zebra and a Welsh pony). Both are man-made species, purpose-built for hanging above a mantlepiece.

Although the figures are uncertain, there are thought to be well over two hundred such ranches scattered across the country. (In Texas alone I counted thirty.) Some cover areas of more than 125,000 acres; others are so small that you can see fences from wherever you are standing. According to the Fisheries and Wildlife Department in Washington, game ranches may already account for as much as 10 percent of the nation's hunting, and that is a percentage which is expanding rapidly. Barring any unforeseen changes of direction, it seems very likely that the game ranch is destined to become the future of American hunting, a prediction I heard expressed by hunters, anti-hunters and government officials alike.

The attractions of the game ranches are obvious; they are quick, clean and, for what you get, relatively inexpensive. "They can hop on a jet, come down here and be home in two or three days with their trophy," said the travel agent when recommending Indian Creek, "and nobody knows if it came from Africa or India or wherever. And unless you ask, they're not going to tell you." But there is one reason above all others which best explains the popularity of the game ranch, and that, according to Richard Grona, is the simple fact that game ranches don't merely offer hunters the promise of killing – they *guarantee* it.

It is Roger Caras's firm belief that game ranches spell the eventual end of hunting. "You see," he told me:

> they're very good in this way: they are an abomination so far as sportsmanship and humanity goes. The hunter survives with an incredible image of himself. It's a multibillion-dollar industry creating this image: the tattoo on the back of the hand, the incredible knife, the beautiful gun (which is always a female – *she's* great, *she's* lovely; never a man, nobody ever says isn't *he* great), and he's got his killing knife, and his killing gun, and his killing clothes on, and his killing words, his own language, got his own organization which tells him he's the only conservationist in the world, he's the only man in the world, everybody else is either a Communist or a homosexual (you've got your choice), there's the good old dog by the fire, and they put flies in their hatband, and no one else knows about it, and they drink beer, do the whole big thing . . . and then they come back to the city and they're an effete fart like everybody else, Park Avenue campfire boys. But out *there*, they've got their thing. Okay. The fact that he goes out there and does something disgusting depends on his self-image. Take the image away and he'll stop doing it, eventually. Which is what these shooting galleries do, they take it away. There's no self-image *possible*. These animals are fed from that truck until *you* get in it and they take *you* out and the animal comes up to get fed and you shoot it. You can't make your penis grow doing that.

Much of what Caras said is true; game preserves not only eliminate the hunt from hunting, they also destroy any possible illusions about "sport." However, if hunting is to suffer a future decline, it will be a decline forced upon it by external pressures – by the ever-shrinking amount of land available to the sport or by legislators and activists morally offended by the killing of animals for entertainment. It will certainly not be through voluntary surrender.

English field sports in particular are now under extremely heavy attack – and from both sides. On the one hand legislation seeking the abolition of various forms of blood sport is now regularly being introduced into Parliament, and despite furious opposition, some of it manages to get passed. (The recent act protecting the otter was largely the work of anti-hunting lobbyists.) Hare coursing would seem to be the next area of hunting to be legislated out of existence, possibly in the very near future.

At the other end of the scale from these Parliamentary lobbyists is a large and extremely active body of demonstrators who devote their Saturday afternoons during the season to physically disrupting hunts and hare courses.

The violence of hunting is now mirrored by the violent clashes of hunters and anti-hunters; fistfights, whippings, damaged cars, smoke bombs, fire-crackers and mass arrests are now a common feature of the English hunting scene. Most weekend fox hunts can now expect to meet some form of opposition, be it false scents, misleading hunting horns or physical obstruction. Hare coursing, because of its relatively stationary nature, is especially vulnerable to disruption. I have attended meets where almost every course has been ruined by anti-hunting activists who, on one occasion, even hired a helicopter to hover over the coursing field and frighten away the hares. I have also met anonymous representatives of a clandestine organization called the Animal Liberation Front who have boasted how they routinely destroy hunting equipment, smash horse trailers and hunters' vehicles, and wreck vivisection laboratories – damage which runs into tens of thousands of pounds – all at the personal risk of long prison sentences (three years for one offender). Already one person has been killed in the hunting war – an anti-hunter, shot dead by a pigeon shooter during an argument over blood sports – and it seems extremely unlikely that there will not be more people at least seriously injured before the thing is finally settled. Faced with the commitment of the anti-hunting brigade – both lobbyists and activists – I personally can see little future for hunting in England.

But England is an extreme; a small country where hunting is an obvious and unnecessary toy of a wealthy elite, whatever the British Field Sports Society might say to the contrary. Although English hunters may not all be unspeakable, the creatures they hunt are either patently uneatable or left uneaten. Hunting in England is hardly the preserve of the common man – fishing yes, but hunting no. In America, of course, hunting is the sport of the average man, and although anti-hunting organizations point gleefully to a slight fall in the percentage of hunters as against the total population, it would seem likely to remain so for a very long time to come. Commercialism, government game management and the sheer popular enthusiasm for killing conspire to make it extremely difficult to imagine that there will ever be a time when America will not hunt. There are simply too many American hunters willing to hold onto their guns with "cold, dead fingers," even if it means having to purchase their game at the gate of a fenced-in hunting preserve one acre square. Indeed, that is the way many prefer it.

A Boar Hunt on the House

Initially I had passed through the high wire gates of Richard Grona's Indian Creek Ranch with considerable misgivings, for I had been warned that the press and Indian Creek did not enjoy particularly amicable relations. Not so long before both the ranch and its manager had been featured in the controversial CBS program *The Guns of Autumn* and neither had been cast in anything that could be considered as a sympathetic light. The CBS reporter had asked Richard Grona if he had ever arranged "easy" hunts for clients, and Grona had laconically replied: "We kind of got what a guy wants. If he wants a hard hunt, we'll give him a hard hunt. If he wants an easy one, we can make it easy." Which meant, the reporter later added, that Grona released animals – boars included – from pens, allowing them to be gunned down by undiscerning clients from myopic distances.

Needless to say, I fully expected Grona to be less than friendly toward further press inquiries. To my surprise he was the epitome of candidness and hospitality, driving me around the spread, showing me how tame the animals were, even revealing that in winter some of the bolder game actually approached vehicles looking for handouts. He seemed totally unconcerned about what I might write. I soon discovered why.

"That CBS thing," he said, shaking his head at the memory, "what they did the time they came here was they twisted everything around." Then he looked across at me and grinned and added with a chuckle, "But *really* what they did was they give us lots of advertisin'. Just like these movie stars doin' somethin' bad for publicity. Hell, we couldn't have *paid* for that . . . we got *nationwide tee-vee!*"

You mean, I ventured, that people – hunters – actually phoned up and made reservations at Indian Creek after seeing the ranch pulled apart on national television?

Grona nodded happily. "Hell," he said, "you can write anythin' you like . . . just give me the publicity. You give me that publicity and I'll tell you what I'll do. Next time you're down here I'll give you a boar hunt – on the house!"

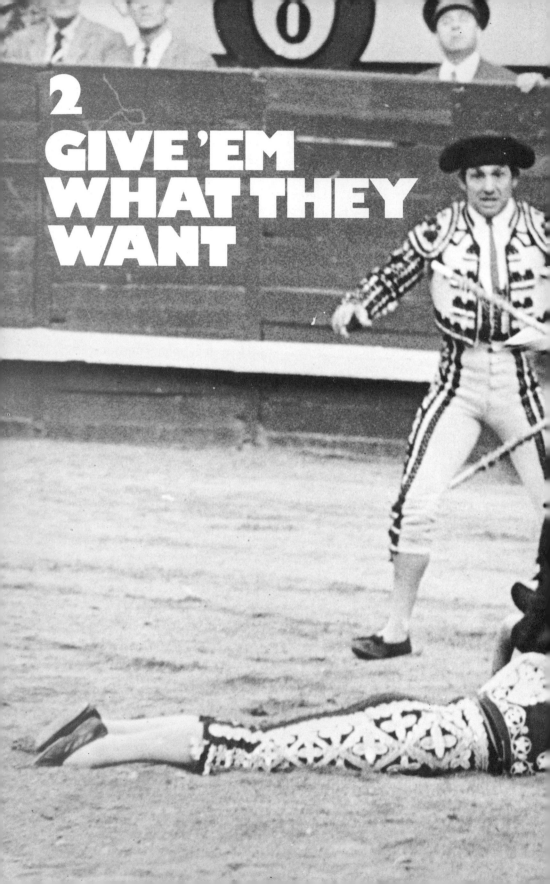

2
GIVE 'EM
WHAT THEY
WANT

2 Give 'Em What They Want
Death as a Spectator Sport

Aside from being shot, stabbed, ridden down by horses and torn apart by hounds, animals have long figured in a wide range of other bloody diversions perpetrated in the name of sport. Since antiquity man has been busily encouraging lesser species to tear themselves to shreds for his entertainment, carefully nurturing their territorial and hierarchical instincts into violent sporting spectacles. And given the average lifespan of most sports, the animal pit has proved remarkably durable. Although some once-popular events such as the bear bait have fallen by the wayside (due as much to a general dearth of bears as to any other reason), others – cockfighting, dog fighting, the bull fight – have survived virtually unchanged for almost three millennia. Today they are still very much in evidence. In many Eastern and Latin countries, fighting cocks is more popular than spending a night at the movies; throughout Spain and South America the matador is still the modern folk hero; and in the United States, a country whose sophistication has given it the potential to destroy whole nations at the touch of a button, Sunday afternoon for hundreds of thousands of people means dying chickens, mutilated dogs and pools of blood on packed-dirt floors.

From Sacrament to Sewer

Cockfighting, the most pervasive of all pit entertainments, holds valid claim to the title of the world's first spectator sport. It originated as part of the religious ceremonies practiced in southern and southeastern Asia more than three thousand years ago. In Sumatra, for instance, temple priests staged cockfights to ensure the fertility of both their congregations and the soil, and in some primitive societies the cock is still regarded as sacred. Eventually, though, much of its religious symbolism was abandoned in favor of the more secular god of sport, and cockfighting began a gradual spread northward, first into India and then across into Persia.

Europe was first introduced to the sport in 479 BC by the Greek general Themistocles. While campaigning against the superior armies of Persia, Themistocles used a pair of sparring cocks as a symbol of unquestioning bravery to inspire his men. His subsequent victory was the sort of happy accident that modern sports promoters would give their right arms for;

THE NATIONAL BACKBONE

Cock- and dogfighting are a nation's salvation, according to many of today's pit sportsmen. As Themistocles inspired his soldiers with a lesson from the pit, modern cock- and dogfighters believe that the fighting spirit of today's animals also rubs off on them and their spectators, infusing them with courage and dedication which, in times of crisis, can affect the performance of a nation.

In talking with cock- and dogfighters I have heard everything from the Korean stalemate to the decline of the British economy blamed on anti-pit legislation and sentiment. Women, rarely pit enthusiasts, are apparently particularly guilty. "The Ladies League came in, and when the women control you, that's it," remarked one Salt Lake City dog breeder bitterly while explaining the direct link between a recent piece of anti-pit legislation and the fall of Saigon. "We have the biggest defense force in the world, but it's like having a big tough dog with no guts to fight. And when you haven't got the guts to fight, you're in big trouble." Unfortunately he was at a loss to explain how Israel had managed to survive for so long with neither a dog- nor a cockpit in Tel Aviv.

overnight the grateful Greeks embraced cocking as a national sport, setting aside one day each year for matches financed by the state.

After initially scorning cocking as a "Greek diversion," Rome also adopted the sport and it spread throughout the empire. It took root particularly well in England where, with cocks cheap and plentiful, it became one of the few sports to fall within the grasp of the common man. From the twelfth century onward, it gained great popularity among all social classes; from the nobles seated around Henry VIII's cockpit in Westminster palace to the schoolboys who took cocks to classes on Shrove Tuesday and spent the morning pitting them under the approving eyes of their masters. By 1615 Gervase Markham, a prolific historian of rural sports, could write without fear of contradiction from any Englishman who considered himself a sportsman: "There is no pleasure more noble, delightsome, or void of cozenage and deceit than this pleasure of cocking."

By Markham's time, cocking had become a serious commercial proposition, both for participant and promoter alike. Prize birds were imported from India and Asia and carefully bred to emphasize their natural aggression. Their offspring were exercised, fed elaborate diets (which usually

86

included a liberal dose of the cocker's own urine to "scour and wonderfully cleanse both head and body") and sold for large sums. Permanent cockpits proliferated throughout London and the other big cities, attracting a varied and often violent crowd. As Pepys noted in his diary in 1663, a commercial London cockpit was no place for a man of refinement:

I did go to Shoe Lane to see a cocke-fighting at a new pit there, a sport I was never at in my life; but Lord! to see the strange variety of people, from Parliament man . . . to the poorest 'prentices, bakers, brewers, butchers, draymen and what not; and all these fellows one with another in swearing, cursing and betting. I soon had enough of it, and yet I would not but have seen it once, it being strange to observe the nature of these poor creatures, how they will fight till they drop dead upon the table and strike after they are ready to give up the ghost, not offering to run away when they are weary or wounded past doing further, whereas where a dunghill brood comes he will, after a sharp stroke that pricks him, run off the stage, and then they wring his neck without much ado, whereas the other they preserve, though their eyes be both out, for they breed only of a true cock of the game. Sometimes a cock that has had ten to one against him will by chance give an unlucky blow and will strike the other stark dead in a moment, that he never stirs more. . . . One thing more it is strange to see how people of this poor rank, that look as if they had not bread to put in their mouths, shall bet three or four pounds at one bet and lose it, and yet bet as much the next battle.

In this atmosphere of blood, poverty and heavy gambling, the violence on the pit floor inevitably spilled over into the spectators' stands. Angry mobs often stormed the pit when the betting went against them, and many cockfights ended up as riots. Eventually pit owners were forced to hire guards to protect their interests and ensure the continued patronage of their more profitable clients. "Gentlemen shall be accommodated with a glass of excellent wine and care taken to prevent disturbance by the mob" ran one reassuring advertisement of 1725.

Although undoubtedly the most popular, cockfighting was only one of several pit sports to surface in "Merrie England." From Tudor times baiting, which pitted specially trained dogs against various other species of animal, was a favorite of both city and country dwellers, rivaling on occasion even the popularity of cocking. Baiting came to England by way of the Romans who, during the heady days of the empire, delighted in matching every species of bird and beast they could lay their hands on: lions *vs.* bulls, bears *vs.* pythons, lions *vs.* crocodiles, seals *vs.* bears, rhinoceroses *vs.* anything and everything. Sometimes the animals were linked by a chain to heighten the excitement. By this method of trial and error, the Romans came to rank the British bear as one of the most satisfactory fighting species, and under their occupation vast numbers of bears were captured and shipped back to the Colosseum. When the empire collapsed, the Britons continued the sport on their own.

Baiting's Golden Age began under Henry VIII, who divided his leisure time between his Westminster cockpit and the Bankside Bear Garden, which he built in the early 1500s. A special herd of bears was kept outside London to meet the demands of the capital's sportsmen; in the provinces town councils promoted official bear baits to keep their electors happy. By this time bears had grown scarce in England, so baits were usually halted before the bear was actually killed. The careers of champion bears were followed as closely as the careers of modern boxers. Sackerson, Blind Robin, Tom of Lincoln and Ned of Canterbury all gained considerable reputations as champion fighters, and Old Nell, a famous Middlewich bear, was regularly taken to an alehouse after a bait and stood rounds of beer by her admirers. To the enthusiast, a glass of beer was a small price to pay for the delights of a bear bait, as Robert Laneham described in 1575:

> It is a sport very pleasant to see the bear, with his pink eyes leering after his enemies approach; the nimbleness and wait of the dog to take his advantage; and the force and experience of the bear again to avoid his assaults; if he were bitten in one place, how he would pinch in another to get free; that if he were taken once, then by what shift with biting, with clawing, with roaring, with tossing and tumbling, he would work and wind himself from them; and when he was loose, to shake his ears twice or thrice, with the blood and the slaver hanging from his physiognomy.

Another favorite baiting animal was the bull. A pack of dogs, often numbering as many as six at a time, would be set on a chained bull with the object of their "pinning" the animal by its nose or dewlap and forcing it to its knees. It was a formidable task, given that a good fighting bull could toss a dog thirty feet into the air with a shake of its horns and open its belly like a zipper. The tenacity of these dogs was legendary, however; one owner was recorded as having cut the legs off his dog one by one in order to demonstrate that it would not release its grip. (Gradually the muzzles of these dogs became flattened through selective breeding – to give them an even better grip – producing what is now known as the "bulldog.")

Other animals besides bears and bulls were also baited, but more in the nature of novelty acts than as serious sport. In 1667 the diarist Evelyn recorded with intense disgust a rural horse bait in which the unfortunate animal was eventually run through with swords. Elizabeth I, who enjoyed the sport so much that she banned the production of plays on baiting days, once saw an ape baited, and James I experimented, somewhat unsuccessfully, with lions in the Tower.

The most prevalent of these sundry diversions was badger baiting. A savage fighter that refused to give up its life easily, the badger was a perennial favorite with rural sportsmen – especially the young gentlemen of Eton – who chained it to stakes or nailed its tail to the ground before setting their dogs on it. During the breeding season dogs were placed into a badger hole to draw the female away from her young. Captured badgers were shipped by the dozen to Smithfield in London where they were secured in boxes. Bets were laid on the number of times a terrier could draw the creature from its sanctuary before it succumbed. When the terrier fastened on, it was the handler's task to bite it on the leg in order to loosen its grip. One unfortunate badger is on record as having being drawn seventy-four times in ten minutes.

The dogs bred for baiting, especially a ferocious breed known as the Staffordshire bull terrier, became celebrities in their own right during the eighteenth century with the rise to prominence of dogfighting. As with fighting cocks, pit dogs were bred for aggression and pampered like princes, often eating decidedly better than the families of the poverty-stricken men who invariably owned them. The fights lasted on average two or more hours and were protracted displays of naked savagery. The animals fought in an unnerving silence, broken only by the shouts of encouragement from their backers and their own heaving and wheezing. Bouts usually ended in death for one or both combatants. A water barrel was commonly provided to drown "curs" who fled the pit.

Smaller terriers were bred for "ratting," a particularly unsavory pastime which flourished throughout the nineteenth century. The object of the sport was simple enough; a terrier was placed in the pit with a given number of rats and set to work, the spectators betting on how many the dog could kill within a given period. Rules were strict: broken backs did not count as a kill unless the rat was unable to crawl outside a circle the size of a dinner plate; a dog was disqualified if it left more than a specified number of rats alive, or if it leaped from the pit.

In 1851 Henry Mayhew, a diligent explorer of London's underworld and author of *London Labour and the London Poor* (1851–2), attended a match in the upstairs room of a "sporting" pub. Although only a minor event, the spectacle attracted an eager crowd which included a fair sprinkling of army officers and gentlemen. After a few preliminary skirmishes, the pit was cleared for the main bout in which fifty rats were to be killed:

The floor was swept, and a big flat basket produced, like those in which chickens were brought to market, and under whose iron top could be seen small mounds of closely packed rats. This match seemed to be between the proprietor and his son, and the stake to be gained was only a bottle of lemonade. It was strange to observe the daring manner in which the lad introduced his hand into the rat cage as he fumbled about and stirred up with his fingers the living mass, picking up, as had been requested, "only the big 'uns." When the fifty animals had been flung into the pit, they gathered themselves into a mound which reached one-third up the sides, and which reminded one of the heap of hair-sweepings in a barber's shop after a heavy day's cutting. These were all sewer and water-ditch rats, and the smell that rose from them was like that from a hot drain. When all the arrangements had been made the second and the dog jumped into the pit. The moment the terrier was loose he became quiet in a most business-like manner and rushed at the rats, burying his nose in the mound till he brought out one in his mouth. In a short time a dozen rats with wetted necks were lying bleeding on the floor, and the white paint of the pit became grained with blood. In a little time the terrier had a rat hanging to his nose which, despite his tossing, still held on. He dashed up against the sides, leaving a patch of blood as if a strawberry had been smashed there. "Hi, Butcher! hi, Butcher!" shouted the second, "good dog, bur-r-r-h!" and he beat the sides of the pit like a drum, till the dog flew about with new life. "Dead 'un! Drop it!" he cried when the terrier nosed a rat kicking on its side, as it slowly expired of its broken neck. "Time!" said the proprietor, and the dog was caught up and held panting, his neck stretched out like a serpent's, staring intently at the rats that still kept crawling about.

Sometimes by way of variety a man would enter the pit with his hands tied behind his back to compete against a dog, biting the rats terrier-style with his teeth. On other occasions the pit was roofed over with chicken wire and cats were substituted for rats.

Despite the appalling odor thrown up by the sewer rats which turned the pits into reeking cesspools, ratting attracted a large and faithful following. By the mid-1800s there were more than seventy permanent rat pits in London alone, and the sporting journal *Bell's Life* was packed with advertisements such as: "Ratting! Ratting!! Ratting!!! There will be an extraordinary number of rats destroyed on Monday evening at J. Ferriman's Graham Arms, Graham Street, City Road" and "Ratting every Saturday. Best of wines and spirits. *Bell's Life* at the bar . . ." One rat-fancying publi-

CHAMPION RATTERS

Numerous ratting terriers won widespread fame for their lusty work in the pits, and although contests were often rigged in their favor – the rats being dosed with laudanum or some other soporific – the feats they performed were often remarkable. Three dogs in particular were hailed as true champions of their squalid sport. In 1848, a black-and-tan ratter named Tiny (who weighed a bare $5\frac{1}{2}$ pounds and wore a woman's bracelet as a collar) was given three hours in which to kill 300 rats; he finished the job in 54 minutes 50 seconds, to universal acclaim. Three years later Henry Mayhew was privileged to witness the corpse of Billy who had been stuffed to commemorate his feat of dispatching 100 rats in 5 minutes. The most sustained performance was given in 1862 by a dog named Jacko, who ate his way through 1,000 rats in less than 1 hour 40 minutes.

can, Jimmy Shaw, was buying from three hundred to seven hundred rats each week at anything up to a shilling apiece and boasted at least two thousand rats on his premises at any one time. It was said that he employed twenty families to meet his requirements.

Pit sports reached their zenith around the turn of the eighteenth century, perhaps as one would expect given the prevailing brutality of the age. By then the pit had become almost the exclusive preserve of the London poor, those condemned to a life of squalor amidst the East End slums with all their attendant miseries of disease, starvation, gin addiction and violent crime. It is hardly surprising that the sports they turned to during their scant periods of leisure also revolved around bloodshed and brutality. Indeed, the pit was by no means the most violent spectacle thrown up by the times. Until the Capital Punishment Amendment Act of 1868, tens of thousands – and sometimes as many as 100,000 – flocked regularly to Newgate and the other large prisons to watch what common parlance termed "a hanging match." There they jostled for positions nearest the gallows, joked or fought with each other and cheered the hangman's assistant as he tugged on the legs of the struggling condemned. The only real difference between a hanging and a sporting crowd, as Kellow Chesney noted in his history of covert Victorian life, *The Victorian Underworld*, was that no one was interested in betting on the outcome.

Despite this increased attention from the lower classes, pit sports continued to attract gentlemen from the higher reaches of English society – notably the flamboyant collection of rich young swells known as the "Fancy," whose love of the pit was only surpassed by their predilection for bareknuckle prizefighting. This smattering of gentry lent an air of legitimacy to the increasingly violent spectacle of the pit, and as such they were accepted by "every greasy hero or sooty chief," as Pierce Egan, the eccentric chronicler of the English sporting scene, reported. But no matter how well the swells blended with the throngs surrounding the cockpits, they remained outsiders, drawn as much by the thrill of mixing with the London lowlife as by the sports themselves. When, during the 1820s, they tired of the riffraff and withdrew their patronage, they left pit sports wide open to social reform.

Indeed, at no time during its history did the pit go entirely unopposed. Throughout the seven centuries during which it flourished, the pit was the subject of numerous attacks by a wide assortment of politicians, clergymen and humanitarians all anxious to stamp it out. The Puritans, who in the words of Macaulay's celebrated jibe undoubtedly deplored baiting "not because it gave pain to the bear but because it gave pleasure to the spectators," were the most successful. But even the efforts of Cromwell (who saved bears only to tie them to trees and have them shot) made little difference in the long run. It was not until 1800 when the upper classes, apart from the Fancy, had largely deserted the pit, that humanitarians felt confident enough to place before Parliament a bill designed to outlaw bull baiting. It was defeated, largely by the efforts of the secretary of war, William Windham, who argued that Parliament had no right interfering with the "robust and hardy" sports of the poor. Two years later a bait at Bury St. Edmunds in which a bull was forced to perform with its hooves cut off, prompted another bill, which was also defeated. It was another twenty years before the first piece of animal welfare legislation finally passed through both houses, and another thirteen years after that, in 1835, before baiting, cockfighting and dogfighting were all declared illegal.

Pit enthusiasts, however, did not succumb without a struggle. In 1836 the village of Stamford held its annual bull run in which a bull was chased through the streets and beaten to death in the adjoining fields. Of the eight people arrested, five were acquitted – a verdict that was seen as giving tacit approval to the bull runners. It was only after a pitched battle between troops of the Fifth Dragoon Guards and four thousand sympathizers on the day of the bull run in 1839 that the town finally capitulated. Elsewhere in England bull baits persisted at county fairs well into the second half of the century.

The more concealable sports of dog- and cockfighting carried on behind

---

❝ Wild animals never kill for sport. Man is the only one to whom the torture and death of his fellow creatures is amusing in itself. ❞

James Anthony Froude, British essayist, 1886

---

closed cellar doors or inside the forecourts of sympathetic inns. Dog-fighting also survived under the guise of ratting, which was not banned until 1912; nineteenth-century animal lovers found it an impossible task to drum up sympathy for rodents. The sport was given added impetus in 1860 when James Hinks crossed a bull terrier with a white English terrier and a dalmation to produce "the perfect pit dog." In London it became fashionable to own a "white 'un" even if one had no intention of fighting it – although many, of course, did.

Six years later, however, all Hinks's good works were undone when a London journalist, James Greenwood, caused an uproar with his account of a fight between a pit dog and a dwarf in the mining town of Hanley. Green-wood had been taken to a basement by dogfighters promising him "a bit of sport it would do any man's heart good to see." One one side of a makeshift pit was tethered a dirty-white bulldog named Physic, already quivering in furious anticipation; on the other was the dwarf, Brummy, also tethered and showing the scars of two recent bouts. Greenwood's description of what followed remains the most chilling picture of pit sport on record:

> The man was on all fours when the words "Let go" were uttered, and, making accurate allowance for the length of the dog's chain, he arched his back, cat wise, so as just to escape its fangs, and fetched it a blow on the crown of its head that brought it almost to its knees. The dog's recovery, however, was instantaneous; and before the dwarf could draw back, Physic made a second dart forward, and this time its teeth grazed the biped's arm, causing a slight red trickling. He grinned scornfully, and sucked the place; but there was tremendous excitement among the bull-dog's backers, who clapped their hands with delight, re-joicing in the honour of first blood. The hairy dwarf was still smiling, however, and while Dan'l held his dog, preparatory to letting it go for Round 2, he was actually provoking it as much as he could, "hissing" at it, and presenting towards it the bleeding arm. The animal, flushed possibly with his first success, made for its opponent in a sudden leap, but the dwarf leapt forward too, and smote the bull-dog such a tremendous blow under the ear as to roll it completely over,

evidently bewildering it for a moment, and causing it to bleed freely, to the frantic joy of the friends of the man-beast. . . . By the time Round 10 was concluded the bull-dog's head was swelled much beyond its accustomed size; it had lost two teeth, and one of its eyes was entirely shut up; while as for the dwarf, his fists, as well as his arms, were reeking, and his hideous face was ghastly pale with rage and despair of victory. Fate was kind to him, however. In Round 11 the bull-dog came on fresh and foaming, with awful persistence of fury, but, with desperate strength, the dwarf dealt him a tremendous blow under the chin, and with such effect that the dog was dashed against the wall, where, despite all its master could do to revive it, it continued to lie.

When Greenwood's report appeared in the *Daily Telegraph* in 1866 it provoked a storm of outrage in Parliament. Any hopes dogfighters may have held of re-establishing their sport on the open market were dashed along with the unfortunate Physic. Thirty years later the miners of Hanley were still threatening Greenwood with physical injury if he ever set foot in their town again.

In 1921 L. Fitz-Barnard published his famous book *Fighting Sports* in which he relived a lifetime's devotion to the English pit and offered advice – including tips on how to avoid the law – to all those sportsmen whom he hoped would follow his example. Fitz-Barnard was the last of his kind, however. In a country which had come to pride itself on an almost obsessional concern for the welfare of its domestic animals, the pit found it impossible to survive the twentieth century on any scale. Today, although matches do undoubtedly take place in the East End of London, the Midlands and the mining towns of the North, cock- and dogfighting as viable sporting propositions are as dead as the British bear.

Pit Sports, USA

The spectacles of the pit received a somewhat mixed reception in the New World. For a time baiting, together with a variety of sundry rural brutalities such as "cat-in-a-barrel" and "pulling-the-goose," gained some sporting currency in the early northern settlements. In 1763, for instance, a large crowd witnessed a bear baited to death outside an inn called the De Lancey Arms in New York. But on the whole the colonists preferred shooting their animals to tormenting them, and baiting soon died out.

Cock- and dogfighting, on the other hand, fared considerably better than baiting when transplanted in the New World. From the first days of settlement, cocking was a favorite of all classes, who practiced it from

Annapolis to Charleston. Although generally held in low esteem by the more respectable Northerners (as early as 1705 Cotton Mather was denouncing it as one of Boston's iniquities), cocking flourished above the Mason-Dixon line for almost two centuries. In New York cockers gathered twice a week near Broome Street in the Bowery, and George Washington, Andrew Jackson and Abraham Lincoln were all sometime enthusiasts. (According to cocking lore, Lincoln earned his nickname "Honest Abe" during his days as a cockfight referee.)

It wasn't until Pennsylvania passed an anti-cocking statute in 1830 that Northern sportsmen turned to other amusements. In the South, however, cocking had become as firmly entrenched as the mint julep. The wealthy landowners of Virginia and the other plantation states, imitating the sporting habits of the English aristocracy which, ironically, were already fast disappearing in the Mother Country, devoted themselves to the cockpit, often at the expense of their farms and business.

In 1787 a New England merchant, Elkanah Watson, came across a main while traveling through Virginia:

> The roads as we approached the scene were alive with carriages, horses and pedestrians, black and white, hastening to the point of attraction. Several houses formed a spacious square, in the centre of which was arranged a large cock-pit; surrounded by many genteel people, promiscuously mingled with the vulgar and debased. The moment the little birds were dropped, bets ran high.
>
> (*Men and Times of the Revolution*, 1856)

Watson "soon sickened at this barbarous sport, and retired under the shade of a wide-spread willow," but for most Southern gentry cocking, horse racing and the prize ring were all-consuming passions. Animal welfare legislation was winked at by judges and sheriffs, who were often cockfight enthusiasts themselves; in some Southern states the cockpit has still yet to be declared illegal. Well into this century advertisements for big-money mains were appearing openly in local newspapers, and in 1937 the Acme News Agency reported that the State of Carolina had staged a twelve-day party for one hundred visitors which included an exhibition of cockfighting.

Today the genteel cockers of the South are still very much a force to be reckoned with. On May 7, 1976, a young deputy sheriff leading a posse of twenty state troopers raided a cockpit at Inglecress Farm, near Charlottesville, Virginia, and caused a wave of outrage which rippled the entire length of the Blue Ridge Mountains. Eighty Virginian gentlefolk, including some of the most established names on the state's social register, had assembled

SOUTHERN COMFORTS—COON BAITIN'

Although most American wildlife has long been protected against baiting, there is one notable exception – the racoon. Since pioneer days coons have provided America's rural communities, especially those of the Deep South, with endless hours of sporting entertainment.

Like the English badger, coons have sharp teeth and powerful jaws and put up a spectacularly bloody fight when set upon. As with badger baits, the basics of coon baiting are simple enough: a dog attempts to draw out the tethered racoon; fastest dog of the day wins the money. However, over the years cooners have devised a range of variations with which to enliven proceedings. First there is a coon-in-a-hole, which has the coon chained to the bottom of a pit. Then there is coon-in-a-barrel, the barrel swinging from a rope to make it more difficult for the hounds; coon-on-a-pole, with the coon tethered by a long rope to the top of a six-foot pole and the dogs trying to drag it down; and coon-in-a-box. The most novel is the Texan favorite, coon-on-a-log. The coon is chained to a log in the middle of a river and the dog has to swim to the log and pull the coon into the water.

Most coons die during an afternoon's cooning; those that don't are recaged and kept for the next date. Such spectacles are found most commonly in Alabama, Texas and the other Southern states, but cooning also occurs further north in places like Ohio. For big meets, cooners will travel from all over the state with their dogs to compete for prize money which can run as high as $12,000. Although cooners disguise their activities with such euphemistic titles as State Championship Field Trials and Water Races, it is the battle between dogs and coons which draws the crowds. When ordinary time trials are inserted into the program, people tend to drift away.

for cocktails and cockfighting when the troopers burst in and arrested eleven of the ringleaders. To Northerners, unfamiliar with the sporting diversions of Southern aristocrats, the episode was seen as another amusing example of Southern gothic behavior. But in Albermarle County the case of the Inglecress Eleven became a *cause célèbre* in which the very foundations of a whole lifestyle came under scrutiny.

I spoke with Mrs. "Mama" Jones, matriarch of the rich, rolling fields of Inglecress Farm, some nine months after the raid. She had seen her first chicken fight at the age of seven, she remembered, and now she was eighty-eight. "I've grown up with cockfighting," she said in a voice that still cracked with emotion when she recalled the deputy's raid. "My father did it and my grandfather before him. My son fought chickens. My husband fought chickens. We've been fighting chickens since the Civil War! And we *never* got in trouble in our lives before! This is an animal farm; always has been!" The interior of Mrs. Jones's rambling weatherboard mansion verified what she said. Every inch of wall space was covered from floor to ceiling with framed photographs of herself and her relatives leaping rail fences on horseback, posing in hunting pink with their fox hounds and ruffling the feathers of their prize fighting cocks. Miniature silver cocks cluttered the mantlepieces and above the hearth hung an antique steel engraving of two Regency swells – one suffering from gout – fighting a pair of cocks on a marble floor. The title underneath read "The Ruling Passion."

Outside the crowing of three dozen fighting cocks undergoing surgery on their combs drifted up to the house. In a few weeks Mrs. Jones and her two hired hands would begin toughening them up by throwing them into the air so they landed on a spring mattress. "Ten or fifteen times you throw them up," she said. "Some of the fat ones you have to throw up forty times." Raising even three dozen cocks was a long and expensive business, she declared; ten dollars a week for feed plus the wages of her handler and his assistant. But to a devoted cocker, it was surely worth it. "It's just a great sport . . . a great entertainment."

Despite her failing health, Mrs. Jones still planned on entering at least five fights during the coming season. Her best birds she would save for her own invitation-only tournament in the round "chicken mill" she converted from a dairy barn, the one that was raided by the state troopers. Her tournament wasn't the biggest affair of the season, she hastened to add. That honor belonged to the Claymore, which was held each year on a neighboring property by a gentleman who, Mrs. Jones candidly estimated, had more money than anyone in the United States. Upwards of four hundred people attend the Claymore, she said. "People come from all over . . . Maryland . . . New Orleans . . . Pittsburgh . . . Georgia. The *nicest* people . . . Mrs. Thouron – a DuPont! Mrs. Scott – a DuPont! Mrs. Scott, she's got a *lot* of chickens!"

At that point Mrs. Jones's two nurses decided that the old lady needed her rest. As I was leaving, she leaned over and confided something which had been troubling her for the past nine months. "You know," she said in a shocked whisper, "if I hadn't come home early that night, *they would have got me, too!*" Not that it would really have mattered in the long run; according to the judge who presided over the subsequent trial, cockfighting is only illegal in Virginia when it is accompanied by gambling. As the police could produce no evidence that money had changed hands in Mrs. Jones's chicken mill, the case was dismissed. The only person to come out of it badly was the young deputy sheriff, who was placed on six months' probation by his superiors.

For all their wealth and influence, Virginia's chicken-milling aristocrats are merely the tip of a cocking pyramid which has grown to encompass every strata of American society. Over the past three decades, cockfighting has enjoyed a considerable renaissance. Although accurate figures are naturally hard to come by, it would not seem unreasonable to suppose that there are now roughly half a million practicing cockfighters operating in hundreds, if not thousands, of pits across the country, ranging from makeshift arenas in converted barns to air-conditioned, purpose-built stadiums complete with bleachers, snack bars and permanent coops for visiting chickens. "I suppose there's thirty-five or forty public pits within a radius of fifty miles from where you're sitting right now," one cocker arrested at Inglecress told me. In New York, where the influx of Puerto Rican immigrants has caused the sport to boom, enthusiasts claim there are between two hundred and a thousand mains scheduled on any given weekend.

Like other fast-growing sports, cockfighting has become a multimillion-dollar business. The sport literally consumes hundreds of thousands of birds each season which average around $100 apiece and can cost up to $1,000. In 1971 there were an estimated seventy thousand full- and part-time professional breeders supplying the domestic market as well as the flourishing export markets of Mexico, the Philippines and much of Latin America. The back pages of the three nationally distributed cockfighting monthlies offer an enormous range of expensive cocking paraphernalia: hand-forged gaffs at $60 a pair, carrying boxes at $270 a gross, $75 scales, personalized belts and billfolds, and a host of patent medicines such as "Blitz Drops," "No Bleed" and "Sure Sharp" to keep a bird in trim.

"Cockfighting has reached a new level of respectability in this country," said Frantz Dantzler, chief investigator of the Humane Society of the United States. "It's reached the point where they have actually hired their own Washington lobbyists." According to a 1971 study by sociologist William C. Capel and psychologist Bernard Caffrey, respectability would appear to be a hallmark of the average modern American cockfighter. Those cockers polled by Capel and Caffrey proved to be staunch law-and-order supporters who were concerned with their health, believed in firm discipline for children and planned ahead for the future. Forty-four percent earned more than $175 a week which, in 1971, put them firmly into the "comfortable" bracket. The study concluded that cockfighters had more in common with people rated "good credit risks" than with people rated "poor credit risks." In other words, far from being a "deviant outsider," the modern cocker is apparently a law-abiding, god-fearing, solid son or daughter of middle America.

A visit to Arizona's Ehrenberg Game Club confirmed the suspicion. Ehrenberg is little more than a flyspeck in the Colorado Desert. A ramshackle outpost of tin huts and dirt roads, the sole advantage it holds over its larger and more prosperous neighbor of Blythe, a half-step away over the Californian border, is that it happens to be in Arizona, a state whose legislators have as yet not seen fit to rule against organized cockfighting. As such, on this particular Sunday – listed as Derby Day in the cockers' calendar – the parking lot out front of the Ehrenberg Game Club was a sea of late-model sedans, campers, caravans and pick-up trucks, many of them bearing out-of-state license plates.

Outside the cavernous corrugated-iron building, groups of men crouched around portable television sets watching the afternoon's football game as some women prepared meals on camp stoves. Inside, an audience of some seven hundred or so spectators studied the action from tiers of solid, purpose-built bleachers. Together they encompassed the entire spectrum of age groups, from teenagers in pressed denim jeans and cowboy hats silently holding hands with their girlfriends to wrinkled old men dressed in buttoned Sunday suits croaking out their bets. Squatting on the dirt floor at the front, dozens of small children pressed their faces against the chicken-wire cages. Almost a third of those present were women. In a small kitchen at the rear of the building, three cheerful stalwarts of the cockers' women's auxiliary grilled hamburgers and dispensed Cokes for a nominal charge. Above them a large notice warned sternly NO DRINKING! With only a small stretch of the imagination, the entire scene could have been that of a union picnic or a PTA fund raiser.

The contrast between this happy family-outing atmosphere and the spectacle which it surrounded, however, could not have been more stark. Even as performed in the affluent circles of middle America, cockfighting remains at heart as violent and grisly a display as anything thrown up by the East Enders of Regency London.

Each battle began in the large cage in the center of the pit. The birds were first taken to one corner by their handlers where they were weighed. They were then held beak-to-beak for several seconds before being placed on their respective scratch marks. At the referee's command, the two birds flew toward each other in a whirl of feathers, slashing the air with their three-inch, needle-sharp steel spurs. Sometimes the fight ended in this first furious rush, one bird dropping like a stone with a gaff through its eye or skull. More often, though, both cocks would continue to hack and peck each other to the vast encouragement of the crowd. If a spur became embedded in an opponent's body, the two birds were separated and the fight restarted from scratch. As a bird grew weak from loss of blood, its handler might try to revive it by placing its head in his mouth. At other times the handler would blow on an open wound to prevent its stiffening, or, in the case of an internal injury, breathe down his bird's throat to force air into its blood-clogged lungs. If, after a set period of time, there was still no winner, the fight was adjourned to one of the two smaller "drag pits" adjoining the main cage. Often there would be three fights in progress at the same moment, all within a few feet of each other.

Most fights were continued on to the death in hopes of witnessing one of those rare occasions so dear to cocking lore whereby a mortally wounded bird struggles back from death's door to win the day. This meant that birds who were unable to stand, or whose eyes had been pecked out, or whose neck muscles could no longer support their heads, were repeatedly brought back to scratch. Fights in the drag pits generally wound up as totally one-sided affairs, with one contestant casually pecking at the head of its opponent lying helpless on the ground. "If neither of them can't cut," one cocker informed me, "then, hell, it'll go on for an hour or more!" The longest fight I saw lasted forty-five minutes.

Fighting continued from around midday until well into the evening without interruption. As each bout lasted no more than five minutes in the center cage, there must have been over a hundred separate fights during the day. A steady stream of birds ferried back and forth between the pits and the row of coops running along one side of the auditorium. Winners were carried back to be rested and revived before fighting again; losers made their exit upside down, hanging by their feet. After the first few hours, large patches on the dirt floor had soaked a deep purple and the handlers were spattered with blood.

The audience accepted all this with a singular lack of passion. For most, so it seemed, these brief rituals of blood and glory stirred about as much visible reaction as an afternoon spent glued to a television. Only the serious gamblers, waving fistfuls of banknotes and shouting out their odds across the pit, displayed much enthusiasm, and then only for as long as it took a bird to gain ascendency over its opponent in the main cage. The grim dramas in the drag pits went largely ignored, save for the children pressed against the wire who watched on in wide-eyed fascination.

The fortunes of cockfighting in the United States have been closely shadowed by those of the dogpit. Dogfighting was first introduced to the States during the 1860s by English breeders who, battling a rising tide of public disapproval and parliamentary legislation at home, had begun to explore other markets for their animals. First adopted by South Carolina, the sport rapidly spread throughout the South; indeed, the locals were so impressed by the tenacity of the imported Staffordshire terriers that they renamed them "Yankee terriers." For the next forty years English and Irish imports monopolized the American dog rings. Then, around the turn of the century, local breeders came up with their own champion dog which they called the "American pit bull terrier." Larger and stronger than the Staffordshire, with a wide, shovel-shaped skull and slanted eyes protected by a massive ridge of frontal bone, the American pit bull was the ultimate canine assassin, a brute capable of delivering a bite of two thousand pounds per square inch.

Within dogfighting circles the pit bull caused a revolution; but the increase in the sport's popularity anticipated by breeders failed to materialize. The dogpit was essentially a poor man's pleasure (although willing to embrace cockfighting, wealthy Southerners found it hard to stomach the more obvious gore of a dogfight) and as the cost of buying and keeping a serious fighting animal was high, the sport remained beyond the reach of those most eager to participate. It was not until the affluent years of the post World War II economic boom that the situation changed. In the 1950s and '60s a dogfighting network stretching from Texas and Florida across to California and eventually to the big Northern cities such as Boston, Chicago and New York was quietly established. For the first time fights were organized on a national scale, with some dog owners traveling thousands of miles to conventions which lasted three days and longer. Dogs were registered along with their stud history to give backers an idea of their fighting form, and three pit dog magazines – one claiming sales of three thousand an issue – began to circulate.

According to Duncan Wright of the American Society for the Prevention of Cruelty to Animals, who has been studying the sport since the early 1970s, over the last decade the number of dogfighters in the United States has doubled and then doubled again. In 1974 the *New York Times* estimated that a thousand dogfights took place every year. Today, says Wright, that figure may be closer to three or four thousand, with perhaps five thousand active dogfighters involved. "These are big-money matches we're talking about," said Wright, "not what goes on in some neighborhood basement a couple of times a month in front of six or eight people. That stuff is countless. What we're talking about are fights which attract three and four hundred people."

As it now stands, the dogfighting fraternity is split into two camps: the professionals, who use the sport as a means of making money; and the purists, for whom pitting dogs is a matter of sport. It is this first group, says Wright, that has been largely responsible for dogfighting's recent boom in popularity. Highly organized dog rings now travel throughout Texas and the South, stopping in a place for two or three days before moving on to another site. Besides the spectacle of a dogfight and the opportunity for heavy gambling – up to $100,000 changing hands on good nights – they offer alcohol, prostitution and drugs. They are also apparently closely linked to organized crime. In this atmosphere, spectator violence is common; fights are frequent and shootings have occurred. In December 1973 the bodies of two men, both connected with dogfighting, were discovered on a riverbank outside Dallas with their hands tied behind their backs. Both had been shot through the head, allegedly in a dispute over a dog. In May the next year a humane society officer testified that he had been fired at while driving in Texas after investigating the dog rings. "I'll tell you one thing that I always see at these fights," said a Dallas dogowner at the time, "and that's pistols."

The purists of the dogfighting world operate far less volatile events. They are breeders who arrange their own fights amongst themselves, usually with formal written contracts. Fights are generally attended by no more than a few dozen carefully screened spectators and individual bets rarely exceed two or three hundred dollars. Spectator violence is far less evident than on the professional circuit, although guns still figure prominently as symbols in the ritual. A winning dogfighter in Salt Lake City, for example, wears a .38 revolver on his belt as a mark of his success; the owner of a champion progresses to a pearl-handled derringer.

Like its sister sport of cocking, the mechanics of the modern dogfight have changed little over the centuries. High-priced puppies are still feted and trained, fed stray cats or housedogs from the pound for practice, and run for miles on treadmills or on a lead behind a slow-moving pick-up truck. At sixteen months the ring candidate is pitted against a veteran; if after twenty minutes it still shows fight, it is considered eligible for the real thing.

Fights are conducted under a strict set of rules, on a regulation canvas floor 16-foot-square which is surrounded by a 2-foot-high knock-down plywood wall. Each dog is washed by its opponent's handler to ensure that coats have not been laced with drugs or poison. At the referee's command "Face your dogs!" the animals are turned toward each other, brought up to their respective scratch marks and set to work. What follows is described by an extract taken from the Texas magazine *Pit Dog Report*:

Dogs meet hard in the center of the pit with Lou going for the shoulders and Missy holding her out with ear holds. Both dogs fighting fast with Lou throwing Missy with cheek holds and ear holds. At five minutes Lou gets into the shoulder deep and throws Missy and bites hard, making Missy cry out, but Missy gets on the nose and starts biting hard. Lou stays in hold as Missy is biting the nose very hard and busts an artery on the side of cheek of Lou. Missy brings Lou off the shoulder and dogs go mouth to mouth. It is plain to see that both of these dogs are very hard biters as Missy has been dog bit in the shoulder. Lou is getting weak from the loss of blood, having a hard time breathing. She is swallowing a lot of blood from the mouth.

An average fight lasts between one and two hours. Often a dog will maintain a hold for ten minutes or more. When a dog turns its head and shoulders away from its opponent, the referee pries the animals apart with a "breaking stick" and they are taken back to their corners. If, after thirty seconds, a dog fails to come up to scratch, it is declared the loser. Dogs often simply drop dead in the ring, and many die later from exhaustion or internal injuries. One concession to progress made by modern dogfighters is that the water barrel of eighteenth-century England has been done away with; the accepted way of dealing with a cur is now a bullet through the head or an ice pick driven through the heart.

"They're a wonderful dog," said Ralph Greenwood, who runs the American Pit Bull Register in Salt Lake City. "Them dogs'll hit the center of the pit like two cannons. They're fighters! That's what they were bred for and that's what they're for, like the fightin' chicken. Now, if I was a chicken and I had my pick of being an eatin' chicken or a fightin' chicken. I know which one I'd pick."

There are many reasons put forward by cock- and dogfighters as to why the pit in all its bloody glory still survives – and thrives – in twentieth-century America. On face value, the pit offers the opportunity to gamble and the bond of comradeship which comes with belonging to an illicit organization. But while big money and the secret-society mentality are undeniably important factors in the pit's continuing popularity, they are not the only explanations. According to several recent psychological surveys, the reasons why men fight cocks and dogs run deep. To some sportsmen, the pit provides, like other more legitimate contact sports (although the theory is now much under attack), a catharsis for bottled-up violence. As one unusually perceptive cocker put it:

We exploit animals for our psychic existence – to provide the emotional outlet through which daily tensions can be relieved, thereby enabling man to exist in the world without those shocking outbreaks of violence such as occurred not so long ago in Dallas and Chicago. Man has a real need for activities which can channel those impulses left over from more primitive days into socially harmless modes and then dissipate them.

Others see the pit, in the best Hemingway tradition, as providing one of the few opportunities left in modern society to take a long, hard stare at death. "It is the aspect of death that holds a particular fascination," wrote sociologist Clifton D. Bryant, citing one cocker who told the *Saturday Evening Post*: "Sure it's death. You put those padded muffs on cocks, the way they do for sparring them, and see how many people come to your cockfight. Death and money – that's the attraction – death and money and honor."

But for the majority of its adherents, the grisly struggles of birds and dogs extend beyond animal instinct into a personal trial of the men and women who rear them. "The cocks become an extension of, and symbolic

---

PEACHES

It is every cock- or dogfighter's desire to breed an unfalteringly game contestant. When such creatures do appear and seize the opportunity to show their worth, their exploits, like those of the old ratting champions of Victorian London, continue to be passed around long after they are gone.

One of the best examples of gameness in recent times was that concerning a dog named Peaches. After a particularly grueling bout, Peaches was left in a seemingly impossible position. Her owner, Chicago construction worker Pat Podzianowski, recounted the event in *The New York Times* in August 1974:

Her front leg was broken and sticking through the skin at two places. It would jab holes in the canvas when she walked. The guy said, hell, she couldn't make it over the line again, so I let her go. That dog didn't know what was wrong, she tried to run at the other dog and that stub of a leg would hit the floor and she'd tumble. She finally turned almost a flip into the boards and landed under that dog and dug in. You tell me that dog didn't have heart?

Peaches' opponent, incidentally, was already dead.

---

of [the cocker's] own ego," wrote Bryant, and the issues at stake in the pit are courage, integrity, virility and, as the *Saturday Evening Post*'s cocker noted, honor. "Gameness," the willingness to keep snapping or slashing right to death's door, is the quality most prized by dog- and cockfighters as a reflection of themselves. Sentiments such as "There isn't a man here who is not just as game as his damn rooster" are almost clichés of cocking literature, and if a man's rooster fails to come up to scratch, it is more than just a matter of losing the money. As *Esquire*'s columnist Harry Crews put it:

> I don't expect many people to sympathize with it or even understand it, but when a man's Kelso or Blueface or Gray or Whitehackle or Allen Roundhead quits – when a man's cock quits in the pit, he suffers profound humiliation. *When a man's cock quits.* Yes, that's part of the ritual, too. Perhaps the biggest part.

How long these archaic epics of death, money and honor will continue in American society is currently a matter of considerable speculation. In August 1974 Wayne King, a latter-day James Greenwood, infiltrated a Chicago dogfight, and his series of articles in the *New York Times* sparked a long-overdue flurry of police activity and a congressional hearing into the sport. Since then, dogfighters have cut a considerably lower profile. In April 1976 President Ford signed into law the Animal Welfare Act Amendment which made the transporting of animals and birds across state lines for the purposes of fighting a federal offense, punishable by a heavy fine and a prison sentence. The amendment was hailed as a major victory for humanitarians, who felt that pit sportsmen would no longer be able to enjoy a cozy relationship with law enforcement officials. "The thing that really frightens them is going to the slammer," said Duncan Wright. "If we can nail a few, it will change a lot of things."

According to Ralph Greenwood, dogfighters have already thrown in the towel:

> They might mess with a misdemeanor law – things like gambling and prostitution – but when they come into those heavy laws, a man would be a damn fool to fight a dog, now wouldn't he? The dog men are all paranoid. I have an old dog here that's fourteen years old that I bought from a man in Texas and he has got a broken front leg and scars all over him . . . he's an old man. And I'm paranoid to let anybody see him, because they'll point the finger and say "You fight dogs!" Now isn't that disgusting? It's like an old punch-drunk fighter with cauliflower ears being paranoid about being seen in public. Now I'm

afraid to tell them that was a game dog and a fighter. In America I'm afraid to say that was a fighter! The sport dies when it starts that kind of stuff. They break the back of it.

But for all Mr. Greenwood's understandable assurances to the contrary, pit sports – even the dog pit – have yet to succumb. In Mrs. Jones's chicken mill, the Ehrenberg Game Club and a thousand other basements and corrugated iron sheds across America, it is still business as usual. In Salt Lake City as I left, humane investigator Lonnie Johnson was awaiting the arrival of a champion pit bull terrier from Denver which had been scheduled to meet the champion of Salt Lake in what aficionados were hailing as "The Dogfight of the Century." The plate glass windows in Johnson's office were a mass of white insulation tape. A few days earlier they had been riddled with bullets by the local pit sportsmen.

The Fiesta Brava

The supreme spectacle of violent death remains today – as it has done since the demise of bear baiting – in the bullrings of Spain and South America. The bullfight is death on the grand scale; a "ritual tragedy," as the aficionados claim, in which the man always (or nearly always) triumphs and the bull always dies. It is a spectacle lifted intact from the floor of the Colloseum which has enthralled Spaniards for nine centuries and Latin Americans since the conquistadors, as it now enthralls the tens of thousands of tourists who flock to it from countries where even greyhound racing is often considered a cruelty. They attend for many reasons: the tradition, the beauty, the spectacle. But above all else they attend because bullfighting offers the fascination of violence and death.

"The only place where you could see life and death, i.e., violent death now that the wars were over, was in the bullring," wrote Hemingway in 1932, "and I wanted very much to go to Spain where I could study it." He was not shortchanged; after watching bullfights for five years, Hemingway became an authority on violent death and produced what remains still the best book on bullfighting in the English language, *Death in the Afternoon*. If Hemingway were to repeat his experiences today, it is unlikely that he would be any the less satisfied. In Spain alone each season there is a *corrida* – six bullfights one after the other – every Sunday afternoon in the Madrid Plaza, a hundred towns stage their annual Fiesta Brava (some lasting for as long as two weeks), and between six and seven thousand carefully bred fighting bulls end their lives as half-ton corpses dragging behind a team of mules.

The bull, like the fighting cock, has been revered since antiquity as a symbol of strength and virility. Throughout ancient Egypt, Phoenicia and the Levant, bull gods were worshiped as a source of fertility. In 3,000 BC the Minoans of Crete fostered a bull cult which included the first, albeit bloodless, bullfight; Minoan acrobats, after inciting the bull to charge, grasped the creature's horns and were tossed over its back in a ritual display which combined both religion and sport. The Greeks regarded killing a bull as the ultimate test of manhood, both for mortals and the gods of mythology. In Rome, disciples of the Sun-Bull cult of Mithra worshiped the bull and bathed in its blood.

The Romans also keenly pursued a less religious relationship with the bulls. As was previously mentioned, bulls were one of the star attractions of the *venationes*. So well regarded as a source of amusement was the bull that special gladiators known as *taurarii* or *taurocentae* were commissioned to face it. The *taurarii* used pikes or swords and fought in a style directly related to the methods used to dispatch modern fighting bulls. Today's matadors still wear small pigtails – usually artificial – into the bullring, the caste mark of a Roman gladiator.

Bullfighting died in Rome with the collapse of the arena during the reign of the Christian emperors, but on the Iberian peninsula, home of the most prized bulls and the source of much of the Roman stock, the Visigoth invaders preserved the sport, chasing the animals across the plains on horseback and fighting them in the arenas left by the Romans. By the time the Visigoth empire fell to the Moors, bullfighting was widely practiced throughout Spain as a test of courage and leadership, an ideal enthusiastically endorsed by the Christian nobles who replaced the Moors. Even the popes failed to make any lasting impression on what many of them felt to be a decidedly un-Christian pastime. In 1567 Pope Pius V, concerned at the rising mortality rate of Spain's nobility, banned bullfighting on pain of excommunication; less than a decade later popular opinion forced Pope Gregory XIII to recant.

The nobles of the seventeenth century fought on horseback in the style of their Moorish predecessors, aided by foot peasants who maneuvered the bull with capes. Although many peasants gained considerable followings for their bravery and capework, the sport remained firmly in the hands of the aristocracy until 1702 when Philip V, displaying a refinement which came with a French education at Versailles, barred his courtiers from the bullring. Only after losing and then regaining his throne did he relax his ban in a bid to cultivate popular support, but by then the peasants had taken control of the sport and foot fighting had become the fashion. Mounted bullfighting never recovered its preeminence, although it is still practiced in Portugal and by the *rejoneadors* of Spain.

These early foot fights were crude, brutal battles between man and beast, designed solely to kill the bull as quickly and unceremoniously as possible. It was not until the latter half of the eighteenth century that the sport took on any semblance of the art form its proponents now claim it to be. The first of the great "modern" bullfighters was Pedro Romero (born 1754), whose grandfather is credited with having introduced the matador's red cloth, the *muleta*. From 1771 to 1799 Romero killed a staggering 5,600 bulls without suffering a single injury. He died in bed at the age of eighty-four. Besides this extraordinary carnage, Romero is best remembered for his remark "The coward is not a man, and to fight bulls men are necessary," which comes as close as anything to explaining why so many Spaniards have risked life and limb in the bullring over the centuries. He is also remembered for the bullfighting school he founded in Seville. Together with Joaquín Rodriguez Costillares, another great bullfighter of the same period who learned the trade in his father's slaughterhouse, Romero and his pupils refined and formalized the spectacle, paving the way for the first set of official regulations which were drawn up in 1852. Since then the rituals of the bullfight have altered little; only the names of the matadors change to mark the end of one era and the beginning of another.

The two key attractions for the serious bullfighting aficionado are death and danger – death for the bull, and danger for the man. The whole process of the bullfight is geared to producing these two elements and anything else that eventuates, even the spectacular cape and *muleta* passes, are by way of a bonus.

The first two acts of the bullfight, although spectacular enough in their own right, are basically preliminaries, designed primarily to reduce the bull both in body and in spirit, transforming it from the wild animal which charges madly about, snorting and slamming its horns into the boards the moment it sets foot in the ring to the weakened and wary creature which will stand feet together and head lowered as a matador runs it through with a sword. The first of these acts involves the use of the *pic*, a long, wicked steel-tipped lance. Picadors mounted on heavily padded horses enter the ring, and as the bull charges the horse, the picador leans down and buries $4\frac{1}{2}$ inches of lance tip into its neck several times. This tears the muscle, making it difficult for the bull to toss its horns.

Next, three pairs of *banderillas* – wooden sticks tipped with barbed iron points – are driven into the bull's neck slightly behind the *pic* wound. These also serve to tire the tossing muscle. Throughout both these acts, the matador goads the bull to charge the cape, bemusing it and forcing it to expend its energy. When the matador is satisfied, he exchanges the cape for the smaller *muleta* and continues his passes. Eventually he will so dominate

BLOOD AND SAWDUST

Originally the picadors' horses – invariably scrawny, ill-nourished creatures – entered the ring unprotected and were disemboweled at the first charge. Most, but not all, died – survivors were led out and sewn up, the cavity in their abdomens packed with sawdust. The turnover in horses was, of course, enormous: in 1846, for instance, 7,473 horses were killed in 427 bullfights, slightly more than half the country's cavalry force at the time. In 1927 the Spanish government, in deference to the burgeoning tourist trade, introduced compulsory quilted padding, a move that was strongly opposed by aficionados (Hemingway included) who objected that it would lessen the bull's opportunity for proving its killing power and detract from the overall spectacle.

Today, although anti-bullfighters claim that two hundred horses still die in the ring each year, the most one is likely to see would be the horse and rider brought crashing to the ground by a bull's charge.

the bull that he can do as he wishes, even to the point of touching the point of its horns with his own forehead. When this stage is reached, the matador steps away from the bull, draws himself to his fullest height, sights along his sword at a small gap between the animal's shoulder blades and runs toward it.

There is no sight more overwhelmingly violent in all of sport – and precious few elsewhere – than the sight of a man driving a three-foot sword into a half-ton bull. To Hemingway it was a moment of supreme emotion and beauty: ". . . that flash when man and bull form one figure as the sword goes all the way in, the man leaning after it, death uniting the two figures in the emotional, aesthetic, and artistic climax of the fight." To Alfred Weirs, secretary of the International Council against Bullfighting, it is "a bloodbath . . . the bloody torture of a living creature."

However it is viewed, the bloodshed is inescapable. Even if the matador hits his narrow target and the sword cuts the aorta as it slides in, the bull does not necessarily drop immediately. Usually it staggers around for several seconds, sometimes managing one or even two complete laps of the arena before collapsing. Often a matador will move the bull's head with the *muleta* so the rigid sword cuts up its insides, or he will remove the sword to allow air into the wound. If the bull continues to stand, the *coup de grace* will be inflicted by a smaller sword, a *descabello*; if it falls and still lives, a short dagger called a *puntilla* will be driven into the back of its head.

Bad kills are far bloodier, and far more frequent. Sometimes the sword will hit bone and fly up into the air, or the matador will puncture a lung, in which case the bull will vomit blood and take longer to die. If the bull is still standing fifteen minutes after the first *muleta* pass, it is sent back to the corrals where it is given the *puntilla*.

The moment of killing is also the most lethal point in the fight for the matador. To kill correctly, he must drive in over the bull's lowered horn, leaving himself exposed from chin to groin. If he is unlucky – for at this point it is all a matter of luck – and the bull chooses to toss its head, a goring is almost inevitable. At worst, he will die like Manuel Granero, nailed to the *barrera* of the Madrid ring in 1922 by a horn through his eye, or like Gitanillo de Triana, hurled three times against the same *barrera* in 1931, the last time by a horn which drove clean through his pelvis and tore out the sciatic nerve by the root – "as a worm may be pulled out of the damp lawn by a robin," wrote Hemingway. He died weighing sixty-three pounds after two and a half months of agony. "The people who say they would pay to see a bullfighter killed would have had their money's worth when Gitanillo became delirious in the hot weather with the nerve pain," Hemingway concluded. "You could hear him in the street."

Since 1850 more than 520 deaths have been recorded in Spanish bull-rings. Hemingway in 1932 estimated that a full matador stood a one in a hundred chance of dying in the bullring. A later estimate held that 10 percent of bullfighters were killed in the arena, 13 percent were crippled, and 40 percent wounded at least twenty times in their careers. Luis Freg, a matador of the 1930s, received ninety horn wounds during his career, seventy-two of which were classified "severe." Freg was given extreme unction five times but still managed somehow to survive, although in Barcelona once he came close enough to death to see it. "I see it clearly," he screamed. "*Ayee. Ayee.* It is an ugly thing." Carnicerito de México received over fifty wounds which were diagnosed as "fatal." The last one killed him.

Since the introduction of penicillin, the odds of a matador's dying from a horn wound have lengthened considerably, a fact fully appreciated by the bullfighters of Spain who have erected a statue to the drug's inventor, Dr. Alexander Fleming, at the entrance to the Madrid Plaza. In the last decade only three full matadors have reportedly been killed in Spain (though many more obscure bullfighters and novices have undoubtedly died in the provinces). It is difficult, however, to sit through more than three *corridas* in a row without witnessing at least one tossing or goring. During his career, even the celebrated El Cordobes suffered more than a dozen horn wounds.

"Before every season I know very well I shall be gored," said matador Antonio Ordóñez in 1960. "I know this, you must understand. It is therefore foolish to pray to the Virgin that I shall not be hurt. Yet I do pray in the bullring chapel before every fight. I pray to God that when I am hurt the wound will not be too big." As *banderillero* Ricardo Aguilar once remarked: "Nobody gets out of this business without knowing they were here."

Critics of the modern bullfight point to this low mortality rate as indication that the popular image of the matador as a man dueling with death is a myth, fabricated to entice the gullible. "It's not a dangerous sport," Alfred Weirs told me. "There are far more severe injuries sustained on British rugger fields than in Spanish bullrings." Which may indeed be so. But illusion or not, the aura of danger and imminent death hangs over the bullring like a shroud. "Whether you like it or not," wrote former bullfighter Antonio Diaz-Cañabate, "the whole essence of the bullfight stems from the danger of man mastering the bull." Or, in the words of author and sometime bullfighter Barnaby Conrad: "The aficionados go for one reason: to see the almost-death of the matadors."

When audiences feel that a cowardly matador has cheated them of the danger, they are merciless. In 1976 I witnessed a *corrida* in the Spanish city of Albacete featuring one Curro Romero, a matador who not so long before had been vigorously promoted as the greatest event in bullfighting since penicillin. The bulls on that particular afternoon were an unpredictable and difficult bunch, and from the beginning it was clear to everyone that Romero had made up his mind that a provincial town like Albacete was not worth the risk of a horn in the chest. With his first bull he ran so wide of the horns at the kill it took him six attempts to finish off the unfortunate beast. The crowd whistled and jeered in disgust. With his second he ran even wider, scrambling past the lowered head and eventually stabbing it sideways through the lungs. By now the audience was beside itself and showered Romero with a hail of cushions as he stood tight-lipped, watching the animal stagger about on the sand blowing a thick mist of blood from its nostrils with each dying breath.

Unhappily for Romero, one of the other matadors had been gored earlier, and as the senior fighter it was his duty to kill his colleague's second bull, a task which he performed quickly and grimly without any attempt at style, striding off across the sand as soon as the animal had fallen. Knowing full well they had been swindled, the spectators rose as one, howling and whistling, and pelted him with everything they could lay their hands on – shoes, cushions, wineskins and beer cans. At the exit gate Romero halted, turned to them and spat contemptuously in the sand. At that precise moment a beer can hurtled out of the stands and struck him flush on the

THE BULL RUN

The thrills of the arena sometime goad spectators into more positive participation. Occasionally a would-be matador – an *espontaneo* – will smuggle a *muleta* into the stands and leap with it into the ring at an opportune moment (a practice strongly discouraged with stiff fines and jail sentences). A more legitimate way for amateurs to experience the dangers of the ring is Pamplona's annual running of the bulls. On the morning of the *corrida,* six bulls are driven through barricaded streets to the bullring, led by a mass of runners. The sport is in staying one step ahead of the horns for as long as possible.

Deaths and injuries are common, particularly if the runners fall at the bottleneck entrance to the arena. The American matador John Fulton in his book *Bullfighting* described just such a pile-up in 1970 which trapped both himself and fellow American Ron Vavra:

> We made the sprint down the ramp and to our horror heard the shouts of *"El Montón—El Tapón."* Some runners had fallen and others stumbled over them, and in no times there was a mountain of mon blocking the entrance to the ring. It was too late to do anything, and the bulls and oxen smashed us against the walls of the tunnel and into the human blockade. I had one bull's head on my chest and could smell its sour breath as I tried to keep its horns from hitting me in the head. Over its shoulder was another bull whose horns framed Vavra's bleeding face, and behind him was still another animal. We were at the mercy of the bashing horns, flailing hooves, and immense bodies of the animals as they tried desperately to climb this bizarre obstacle.

The run lasted six minutes and forty-one seconds and claimed one dead and thirty-eight injured.

In 1977 one person was killed and thirty-six injured running the bulls at Pamplona. (In 1978 the running was postponed because of riots between Basque separatists and police.) Yet despite the annual casualty toll, the bull run has become a remarkably popular participant sport, so much so that runners now have to be sent off from the start in relays.

head. As his legs buckled and his assistants rushed forward to support him, the mob gave a resounding howl of delight.

The demands of the crowd have literally driven bullfighters to their deaths, forcing them to choose between the jeers and catcalls, and a move which crosses either the limits of sound judgment or their own abilities. Hemingway cited the example of the Spaniard Manuel Vare ("Varelito"), a fighter whom the novelist considered "probably the best killer of my generation." In 1922, after returning to the ring too soon following a horn wound suffered the previous season, he was unable to kill with his old flair and the crowds turned against him. During the April fair in Sevilla he turned his back on a bull after he had put the sword in to please the crowd, and was shockingly gored near the rectum, a wound which perforated his intestines. Hemingway described what followed:

> As they were carrying him down the passageway around the ring to the infirmary, the crowd, which had been hooting him a minute before, now murmuring with the rush of talk that always follows a serious cogida, Varelito kept saying, looking up at them, "Now you've given it to me. Now I've got it. Now you've given it to me. Now you've got what you wanted. Now I've got it. Now you've given it to me. Now I've got it. Now I've got it. I've got it." He had it although it took nearly four weeks for it to kill him.

The list of crowd victims also includes several of bullfighting's most famous names; accomplished and spectacular matadors, their only fault – as the spectators saw it – was that their superior skills made them appear as invincible. Such a victim was the great Manolete who, from 1939 to 1947, ruled as the undisputed monarch of the Spanish bullrings. Manolete fought with an iron nerve, allowing the bulls to pass so close to his chest that their horns caught the brocade of his jacket. For seven years he was the idol of Spain, feted by an adoring public which showered him with a fortune of more than four million dollars. Then, in 1946, his public turned against him.

"He was fighting as well as he ever had," recalled Manolete's friend and fellow matador Carlos Arruza, "but after a while audiences became infuriated by his perfection. They kept demanding more and more of him with every

---

ᏻ My knees start to quake when I first see my name on the posters and they don't stop until the end of the season. ᏻᏻ

Manolete, 1947

---

fight." "I know very well what they want," Manolete told Arruza on one occasion as the jeers of the crowd echoed around the arena, "and one of these afternoons I might just give it to them to keep the bastards happy."

In August 1947 Manolete was gored in the groin by the bull Islero and died within hours. Overnight the public's hostility toward him evaporated, and his memory was embellished to the point of deification. Barnaby Conrad, Manolete's biographer, explained the transformation with these telling words:

> When he was killed, he died such a beautiful dramatic Spanish death that I swear, in spite of the great funeral, the week of national mourning, the odes, the dirges, the posthumous decorations by the government, that in his heart of hearts, every Spaniard was glad that Manolete had died. They, the Spaniards themselves, had murdered him.

What leads men to fight bulls is a complex combination of the tangible and the intangible. The business side of bullfighting cannot, of course, be overlooked. Top matadors earn enormous fortunes – ten thousand dollars a *corrida* and more; a million dollars a season – and in countries where, as the old bullfighting adage goes, "Hunger wounds worse than the bulls," fortunes are a powerful spur to ambition. But money does not explain it all. The stark realities are as daunting as they are widely known: of the ten thousand aspirants who attempt the art each year, only two dozen will ever become full matadors, and of these, only a handful will ever earn a decent living at the business. Also, millionaires do not continue in an occupation which causes their knees to shake, leaves their mouths as "dry as the Sahara" and turns their faces gray with fear solely for more money.

Rather, the main attraction of the ring is perhaps best described by that well-whipped word *machismo* (or, if you like, another word frequently bandied about in bullfighting circles – *cojones*, or balls). The arena is the greatest masculine showcase left in the world (that and, arguably, the motor-racing circuit). The matador is the epitome of *machismo,* from the moment he strides on to the sand to the moment he draws himself proudly erect and dedicates his efforts to the crowd with a theatrically arrogant sweep of his hand. A successful matador is the very image – deserved or not – of bravery, courage and man's triumph over death, and for many aspirants that alone is more than enough.

For the crowd the bullfight presents something more; there is the vicarious pleasure to be drawn from the matador's triumph and the grace with which it is performed, but there is also the spectacle of blood and death at first hand, and the delicious attractions of fatal danger. (This last point is perhaps best illustrated by the Spanish artist J. Jíminez Aranda's work of the late 1800s *An Accident in the Bull Ring*. The picture shows the eager spectators climbing on to their seats and scrambling over themselves in the frenzy to catch a glimpse of the goring which is taking place outside the frame.) In the Hollywood bullfight epic *Blood and Sand*, Tyrone Power as the matador about to step into the arena and meet his audience remarked: "Out there is a beast, a beast with ten thousand heads." It was one of Hollywood's more profound lines.

Dodge City Revisited

The sport which comes closest to mirroring the spectacle of the bullring is rodeo. Although usually stopping well short of the deaths so avidly retailed by bullfighting (and thus is considered to be a very poor relation indeed by all true aficionados), the rodeo remains at bottom line the violent struggles of man against wild beast.

Rodeo grew out of the great American cattle drives which traversed the Southern states immediately after the Civil War. In these drives vast herds of Texan Longhorns were rounded up and driven north along the Chisholm Trail to the railheads of Kansas, where they were shipped off to the markets back East. The cowboys who rode the Chisholm Trail were genuinely tough characters. Southern Civil War veterans and hardened drifters from the Eastern states, they were one of the few groups of men to live up to the brawling, whisky sodden reputation which Hollywood was later to bestow on the "wild" West. (It was the Chisholm cowboys who were largely responsible for shooting up such towns as Dodge City and Abilene.) To relieve the monotony of months on the trail, they staged impromptu roping and horse riding contests amongst themselves. Not surprisingly, these sporting events were as much a test of strength and courage as of skill, in keeping with the cowboys' manners.

The cattle drives lasted twenty years. When they ended, rodeo continued as the cowboys' sport. Gradually other events such as bareback and bull riding were added to the card. Many of these new events had little connection with ranch work; they were purely entertainment. In 1903, for example, a cowboy named Bill Pickett, infuriated by a steer which refused to be corralled, leaped onto the animal's back, sank his teeth into its lower lip like a bulldog baiting its opponent, and wrestled it to the ground by its horns. His colleagues were so impressed that they adopted steer wrestling – or "bulldogging" – as a rodeo event, although the business with the teeth was soon dropped.

Rodeo reached a far wider audience as part of the Wild West shows which toured the nation and abroad around the turn of the century. However, as a sport in its own right, rodeo remained very much a fledgling, ill paid and poorly organized. It was not until 1936 when contestants scheduled to perform in the Boston Gardens struck for higher prize money, forming what was to become the Professional Rodeo Cowboys Association (PRCA), that rodeo could claim any sort of professional sporting legitimacy.

Since then rodeo has boomed. Today ten thousand contestants compete annually in the six hundred professional rodeos endorsed by the PRCA, watched by fourteen million paying spectators. Together with attendance figures for amateur, intercollegiate, high school and "Little Britches" rodeos, the total number of Americans actively following the sport is estimated to be forty million, not including television audiences. Rodeo has now spread across the entire country (there are now more rodeos staged in New Jersey than in Arizona) and further afield to Canada, Australia, and elsewhere (the biggest rodeo of all is Canada's Calgary Stampede). Although television coverage in the past has been sporadic, plans have now been drawn up for a National Rodeo League which would play off teams from major American cities for the benefit of television audiences. "We have an exciting, colorful, dangerous sport," said NRL organizer Wayne McLaren. "It has to succeed."

The dangers inherent in tackling one-ton brahma bulls and wild horses hand picked for their "meanness" are obvious. Mason Smith, writing for *Sports Illustrated*, attended a rodeo with veteran rider Darrell Winfield, the original "Marlboro Man." The first contestant they saw was a female:

> [The horse] veers at the fence, jerks her loose, and while she is in the air beside him, whacks her with his head and smashes her into the calf-chute. The cowboys on the rail nearby turn their heads with mild interest. A bronc bucks his rider off balance and goes for a gallop closer to the rail with the cowboy hanging out sideways and finally wipes him off against the main gate. The noise is awful. Winfield and his cronies guffaw at a photographer who turns away with a hand over his eyes, appalled. Suddenly Tom Lozier is down in the dirt at the far end, a bone sticking out of his leg. He sits up and calls for an ambulance . . .

Such injuries are commonplace in rodeo. The pages of the *Rodeo Sports News* often read like casualty reports from the front. One recent issue featured such mishaps as Chris Le Doux's broken collarbone ("I could feel the bone just pull in two while I was riding . . ."), Denny Flynn's goring by a bull ("the horn barely missed his heart, and Denny was back in action again two months later!") and a host of other contestants' broken legs, smashed wrists and cracked ribs. *Show* magazine once asked veteran rodeo star Bill Linderman which bones he had broken. He nonchalantly replied:

Headbone for one, fractured skull that is. Broke my neck and back in the same accident in Deadwood, South Dakota, when a bull fell on me . . . Broke my right arm four times. Broke a leg twice. Ribs? Lost count. Hands and feet more or less broken. Collarbone. Oh, hell, if you're going to count collarbones. Yeah, I broke my collarbone, quite a bit, but I can't remember the exact count.

Others are not so fortunate, as this poignant letter from another recent issue of *Rodeo Sports News* illustrates:

Dear Editor:
I have a friend who was paralyzed from a bull riding injury last September, and I thought if some of the PRCA bull riders would write to him he might get into a little better spirits and maybe recover faster. The doctors in Houston thought this was a good idea. He's James Henson, and he was paralyzed from the neck down. . . .

"It's a rough contact sport," Randy Witte, editor of *Rodeo Sports News* told me. "Accidents can happen and a guy can get hurt. Take bull riding now, there's probably more injuries in that than any of the others – guys getting stepped on by bulls . . . they can move amazingly fast for their size." He added, however, that there were surprisingly few critical injuries; mostly rodeo was about broken arms, legs, ribs, shoulders and a lot of bruises. "We have a few what you would call bad injuries every year, and occasionally there is a death. But you get that in any sport. We might go two, three years and not have anyone killed, then in one year we might have a few guys . . . a bull might step on a guy's head or something and kill him."

There is a studied air of casualness that most rodeo contestants adopt when discussing their injuries. It is a nonchalance bred from the cowboys' own self image of the Chisholm Trail veteran still firmly fixed in the Wild West. As with bullfighting, rodeo is a solid bastion of overt masculinity, and although the executive jet is now the hallmark of the successful rodeo star, like bullfighting, the heavy flavor of *machismo* is a strong motivation behind the rodeo. To most cowboys the sport offers one of the last chances for independence, challenge and the satisfaction of doing a man's job in a man's world. Fred Schnell, author of *Rodeo! The Suicide Circuit* (1971):

The modern competing cowboy is the direct, lonely descendant of the individuals of a century ago who braved the formidable prairie with little equipment and little companionship. Today's rodeo cowboy also stands alone in the arena – a two-legged animal battling a four-legged animal. A rodeo athlete rides bulls or horses and wrestles steers for the same irresistible reasons that a man climbs mountains, pushes racing cars to the edges of adhesion, or dives from airplanes: for exhilaration, pride in himself, and the feeling he's conquered nature – at least this time. . . . No one forces these cowboys into rodeo. They have chosen their own battleground – the last frontier of rugged individualism.

No matter that the modern up-and-coming contestant is more likely to be a college graduate who calls his elders "Sir" than a whisky-swigging cowhand. The image remains. As Bill Linderman once snorted when he heard a contestant's college credentials being read out over the loudspeaker: "People aren't going to come to a rodeo to see a bunch of college kids compete. They want to see real cowboys!" Against this background, injuries are regarded almost as a badge of courage.

Rodeo can be equally punishing on its animals, a fact which has earned it the enmity of several humane organizations including the Humane Society of the United States (HSUS). A recent two-year HSUS investigation into rodeos in Montana, Wyoming and Colorado found "visible injuries to a significant number" of animals. "The injuries," continued the report, "were indicated by broken limbs, dazed or unconscious animals, flank sores, open wounds, abrasions, spur marks in the neck and shoulder areas, and broken horns." A 225-pound calf roped while traveling at its normal speed of 27 miles per hour was subject to enough force to injure it, often severely, claimed HSUS. The report concluded that some 12 percent of calves suffered irreparable injury. As a result of such pressure, several of the more violent events – wild horse racing and bull busting in particular – have now all but disappeared from the rodeo circuit. Rodeo has also often been charged with using cattle prods and bucking straps to enliven animal performances, an allegation which the PRCA strenuously denies.

But cattle prods or not, it is violence and danger – or "excitement and action," as rodeo prefers to call them – which provide the sport's biggest drawing card. In 1972 a Rodeo Information Spectator Survey found that of the twelve events regularly featured in rodeo, bull riding – by far the most violent and dangerous – was the overwhelming fan favorite. It was followed by the three next most grueling events – bareback, saddleback and steer wrestling.

"People buy rodeo for two reasons," said author Roger Caras, "first because it's pseudo Americana, and secondly because it's deliciously violent. You might see someone get killed or broken up; you certainly see a lot of animals get thrown up in the air and smashed. Violent physical activity is what our good people crave." Bluntly put, but perhaps not all that far from the truth. Certainly the promoters of Los Angeles' 1977 indoor rodeo held a clearly defined idea of what they thought the public wanted. Every hour on the hour Los Angeles radio broadcast this message: "The roughest, toughest, fiercest, finest, most exciting damn sport in the whole wide world . . . *Rodeo!*"

From the Colosseum to Shea Stadium . . . and Back Again

The list of animals which have been baited, pitted and destroyed over the centuries for man's entertainment is astonishingly wide-ranging. The redoubtable Captain L. Fitz-Barnard alone recorded seeing such divers sporting spectacles as rams against rams, buffaloes against buffaloes and elephants against elephants in India, a boar pitted against a tiger, another boar pitted against a buffalo, stallions fighting stallions, stallions fighting tigers, and, in a Spanish bullring, a bull fighting a bear:

> The bear was game and tried to fight, and, rising on his hind limbs, struck savagely at the charging bull; but he had no chance against those horns and was soon a somewhat mangled corpse.

The fascination still lingers. In India tourists now pay one dollar each for the chance of photographing a mongoose chewing the head off a cobra. Fighting crickets have been a favorite of the Chinese since the thirteenth century who, up to the Revolution, pitted them in glass jars before huge audiences packed around the town squares. (In Canton during the 1920s it was not uncommon for sums of $100,000 to change hands over a single match.) Today the sport survives in Thailand and several other Asian countries, together with the better known Siamese fish fighting. Turkish entrepreneurs are currently busily reviving the traditional Turkish sport of camel wrestling for the predilection of the tourists. "Our hope," said Mr. Halit Cayirli, chairman of the Association for the Protection and Development of Camel Wrestling in the Aegean Region, "is to turn them, like the bullfighters in Spain, into an attraction sought for by all the people of the world."

The bloodless bullfighters of Portugal have also recently cast envious eyes at their neighbor's Fiesta Brava. In 1977 Portuguese matadors defied a two-hundred-year-old law prohibiting them from killing bulls in the arena by slaughtering six animals at Vila Franca de Xira, north of Lisbon, to chants of "Kill! Kill!" from the crowd. For years, Portuguese aficionados have slipped across the border to watch Spain's "death bulls" in preference to their own bloodless spectacle. Now Portugal's National Union of Bullfighters is lobbying to have the ban on killing lifted. The Union promises that "real" bullfights will attract as much tourist revenue to Portugal as Spain now receives. It is probably right.

In more affluent countries the lure of closed-circuit television has fostered a rash of ambitious plans. A Tampa promoter battled to have cockfighting legalized in Florida, claiming that regular matches could draw a live audience of twenty-five thousand and a national audience of millions. In 1977 a New York entrepreneur planned a bullfight on three acres of inter-connected barges anchored off Coney Island beyond the three-mile limit, and a Mr. Co managed to persuade the Haitian government to let him stage a "fight to the death" between a karate champion and a "wild Bengal tiger" for the benefit of American closed-circuit viewers. Both spectacles were thwarted only at the eleventh hour by pressure from the humane societies. The "wild Bengal tiger," it later transpired, was in fact nothing more than a broken-down circus reject.

With the release of the movie *Jaws*, sharks suddenly shot into vogue. Evel Knievel filled a tank full of small sharks (*very* small sharks, by all accounts) and attempted to vault his motor bike over them. Unfortunately he crashed during practice, leaving an embarrassing gap in the TV special scheduled for later that evening. Even more ambitious was the contracting of Australian shark hunter Ben Cropp to fight a shark to the death in a sixty-foot under-water arena off Samoa for a million dollars. "It's a sick idea," one of the promoters candidly confessed. "Listen, you've got a society and social system that's obviously sick enough to make rich men out of all of us." "If the guy gets eaten," crowed his partner, "the film rights will be very valuable." After several false starts, the Great White Shark Duel eventually sank under its own financial shortcomings.

How long such delights will be with us is, of course, impossible to predict. But judging by current trends and the weight of history, the future for many animals would still appear to be rather bleak. Certainly bull fighting will remain for many years to come, and may even spread further afield under its comparatively recent guise of "art." What presumably began as an affirmation of man's mastery over beast has long since become a spectacle of violence for violence's sake, and that has always been able to command an audience.

There are other attractions to the pit; the matador's capework, the bull-fighter's bravery, the historical trappings of the rodeo, the promise of illicit gambling. But at base root the pit offers violence, blood and death in varying degrees, the same attractions which filled the Colloseum two thou-sand years ago and which even the sophistications of twentieth-century civilization find difficult to dull. It is, after all, the affluent Western tourist who feeds the cobra to the mongoose, the same tourist who is responsible for keeping alive many of Spain's bullfights. The largest club of bullfighting aficionados outside the bullfighting countries is in England, a country whose passionate defense of animals often extends beyond its concern for mankind itself. And in many parts of America the neighborhood sporting hero is just as likely to be a cockfighter or a dog fancier as a baseball star. Civilization, as most people would recognize it, often seems a very thin veneer.

"We *are* becoming more civilized," said Roger Caras, when I spoke with him in New York. "Everything's better than it was. We do a lot less of this stuff than the Romans did, for instance. But if you were to announce tomorrow that you were going to kill a thousand lions in Shea Stadium, the goddamn line would stretch from here to Alberquerque, New Mexico, and back." With the Ehrenberg Game Club playing to a full house every Sunday, who can argue against that?

3
BLOOD AND CANVAS

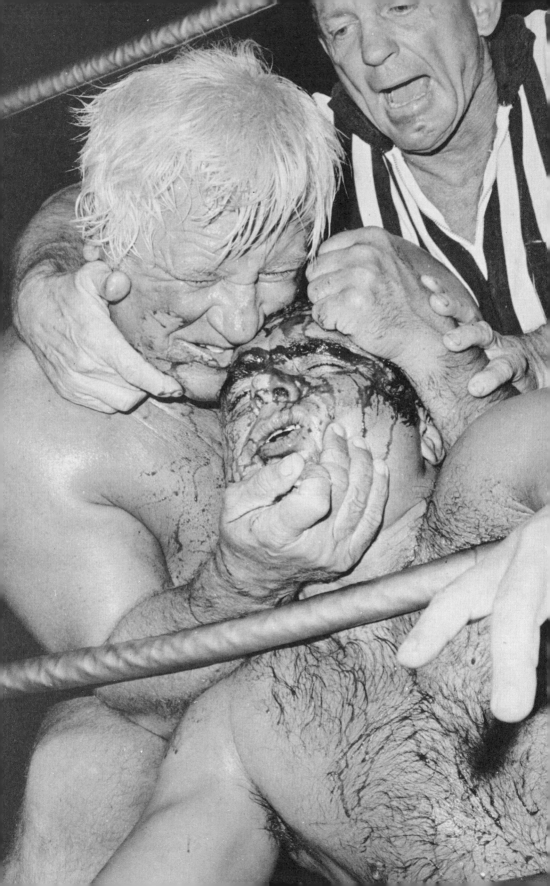

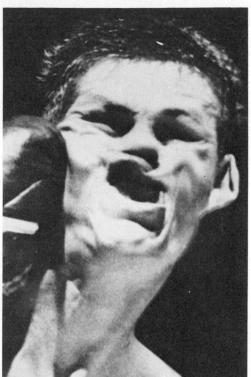

3 Blood and Canvas
Combat Sports

The first time that I was made aware of the realities of boxing was in 1974 when Muhammad Ali fought George Foreman for the world heavyweight crown in the ramshackle city of Kinshasa, Zaire. Until then I had always thought boxing a game, in which the contestants – even the heavyweights – were more or less normal human beings whose punches were tactical weapons and therefore somehow less painful than punches thrown in anger during, say, a bar-room brawl. Then again the closest I had ever been to a major heavyweight bout was six feet from a television set, which, as I soon discovered, was about as useful for understanding boxing as trying to study the surface of the moon through the wrong end of a telescope.

The first blow to my preconceptions came when George Foreman entered the gymnasium for his first training session. The thing about Foreman was that he was unlike any other person in the room, sparring partners included. He was a monster, the heavyweight champion of the world, a man-machine who exuded doom and destruction like the sweat which trickled down his enormous shoulders. The punches that he landed as he attacked the big punching bag were equally inhuman. I had tested the bag earlier, punching it as hard as I could. I had not been able to leave more than the slightest dent in its leather surface; in fact, the thing had barely moved on its heavy chain. Before Foreman began his assault he had his manager, Dick Saddler, grasp the bottom of the bag and lean into it with his shoulder. The first punch he threw jacknifed the bag like a snapped breadstick and sent Saddler reeling back a dozen paces. It was an awesome display of power, and I was not the only one awed. "Prizefighters do not, of course, train to kill people at large," Norman Mailer later wrote in his book on the coming struggle *The Fight* (1974). "To the contrary, prizefighting offers a profession to men who might otherwise commit murder in the street. Nonetheless, the violence capable of being generated in a champion like Foreman is staggering to contemplate...." Quite. But at the time Foreman's homicidal capabilities did not really register. I saw the champion cripple the punching bag and shook my head in sorrow for Ali's probable fate, but the thought that Foreman might actually snap Ali like a breadstick never really entered my mind. Boxing was, after all, only a game.

The first punch which caught Ali's rib cage disabused me of that simple-minded belief. It landed with a sickening crunch which cut through the shouts of the crowd like a laser beam through butter. Seated at ringside a yard away from the two fighters, I could see Ali's face contort with agony and hear the rush of air as he tried to suck in his next breath. He lay back on the ropes directly above my head and Foreman went to work using the same staggering blows which he had used to destroy the big bag. For the first time I realized why people pay so dearly for ringside seats at heavyweight title fights. When you are close enough to be showered by sweat after each blow it becomes stunningly obvious that boxing is not sport but mortal combat, a primitive blood battle in which two giants smash at each other with their fists with all their might. It is savage, bloody and cruel, and also entirely mesmerizing.

Foreman kept up his lethal barrage for seven rounds. In the end he was beaten by the uncontrollable rush of his own brute power which slowly drained away as he hammered Ali, a fighter whose own iron physique had been carefully disguised by the graceful proportions of his body. Foreman was a man trained to bludgeon to pulp anything that stood in his path; Ali was a fighter who had trained solely to absorb punishment. On that night in Zaire Ali's training proved the more effective. It was as simple as that. Early in the eighth round, with Foreman's misguided bombs still whistling around his head, Ali stepped forward and landed two lightening punches flush in Foreman's puffed and bloody face. They connected with the pistol crack of leather against bone and they sent the champion spinning helplessly to the canvas. He tried to get up but he couldn't. I could see his body quivering with the effort.

I returned to London a few days later and caught a cab at the airport. I began chatting with the cabbie and inevitably the conversation turned to Zaire and the fight. I gave him a few impressions of the fight and at the end he half-turned in his seat and said with a knowing grin, "But it was a fix though, wasn't it." "Come on," he continued as I looked at him in astonishment, "you can't tell me they were *hurtin'* each other in there. Big George Foreman bangin' away? Jeez, I coulda done better myself! And that last bit where Ali put 'im down, those punches wouldn't 've hurt my bleeding grandmother." He had seen it all with his own eyes, he said. He had paid ten pounds and taken his seat in a cinema showing a live relay of the fight on one of those larger-than-life closed-circuit screens. "You see everything on them," he declared. "See right up their bleeding noses if you want."

How can you argue against ten-foot video? I turned away and stared out the window, remembering poor George mumbling inanities in his dressing room after the fight, and how the morning after Ali had kept getting up from his seat in the sun on the banks of the Zaire to check whether he was still pissing blood.

Combat à la Grèque

The first form of man-to-man combat to become a game was wrestling. Several archaeological discoveries have determined that the Egyptians and the Assyrians were applying headlocks and half-nelsons for sport as long as five thousand years ago. In the temple tomb of Beni Hasan on the Nile there survives a remarkable series of sophisticated wrestling poses – 250 in all – which can only be taken as some kind of early wrestling manual, and the holds it details are as valid today as they were when they were first drawn.

Wrestling was an early favorite with other ancient civilizations as well. A statue known as the Olmec wrestler, which depicts a warrior with shaven head squatting in a fighting stance, dates wrestling in ancient Mexico to at least 200 BC, and if the fighter's deformed head is any indication, the Mexican variety was a more violent sport than that practiced by the Egyptians. In Afghanistan early folk legend boasted of a giant wrestler named Rustum Zoal, who stood nine feet tall and weighed 650 pounds. During his formidable career, Zoal snapped the necks of hundreds of opponents, retiring only when he unwittingly killed his estranged son. In Japan, Sumo giants, inbred over centuries in the hope of increasing their strength, fought each other in protracted life-or-death struggles as early as 23 BC.

But the most enthusiastic wrestlers of antiquity were the Greeks. Hellenic legend is studded with the epic bouts of heroic wrestlers, among the most famous being Ajax *vs.* Ulysses and Hercules *vs.* Antaeus. Such early encounters were desperate and bloody affairs, a far cry from the Egyptian style of fighting. One hero, Theogenes, who lived around 900 BC, was credited with an unblemished record of 1,425 victories – all of them clean kills. A Greek kylix of the same period shows a pair of wrestlers attempting to gouge each other's eyes with their thumbs while an onlooker, presumably a referee, stands poised with a pronged stick ready to intervene. Gradually, though, the sport was toned down and the *palaestra*, or wrestling school, became a common feature of urban social life. Two centuries after Theogenes the sport had become respectable enough to be included in the Olympic Games, victory being won not through an opponent's death but with the more conventional three falls.

The Greeks were also among the first to devise a form of boxing. On the isle of Santorni there is a fresco dating back to 1520 BC which appears to depict two athletes boxing with rudimentary gloves, and Greek literature contains several descriptions of bouts which sound remarkably similar to the brutal bare-knuckle prizefights of Regency London.

The Greeks credited the Athenian hero Theseus with the invention of boxing. Theseus, a man who so loved mortal combat that his pulse was said to quicken at the sight of blood, was apparently also responsible for attempting to replace the soft leather straps which early pugilists used to protect their knuckles with spiked gloves, thus predating the vicious Roman *caestus* by several centuries. Theseus's gloves did not, however, gain great acceptance, and the soft ox-hide thongs survived as a feature of Greek boxing until the end of the fifth century BC. A Greek fist still left its mark, though. Perhaps the most famous of all Greek statues of athletes is of a battered veteran boxer whose features display what was to become the trademark of his profession – a cauliflower ear.

Boxing was introduced into the Olympics of 688 BC, and it quickly became a favorite event. Nor did the battering stop with boxing and wrestling, however. So much did the two sports appeal to athletes and fans alike that in an uncharacteristic fit of brutality, the Greeks devised a third form of sporting combat which wedded, and if anything intensified, the violence of both sports. This was the *pankration*, which first appeared in the Olympics of 648 BC. Unlike wrestling where contestants strove to win by unbalancing each other, combatants in the *pankration* tried either to force a submission (as in the all-in wrestling of modern pro bouts, which owes much to the *pankration*), immobilize their opponent by breaking his limbs, or kill him, usually with a strangle hold. Although certain tactics such as biting and gouging were specifically banned, the *pankration* was essentially a brutal free-for-all.

For decades the sport was dominated by a legendary character named Milo of Crotona. It was said that he could hurl a three-hundred-pound man twenty feet with one hand, tear up trees by the roots, and carry a full-grown ox around the arena before killing it with his bare hands and devouring it raw within the day. He could also slay an opponent with a single blow of his fist. But despite Milo and other endemic perils, the *pankration* remained a popular amateur sport until the fourth century BC. However, as the stadium grew increasingly more favored as a venue for mass spectacles, the amateurs gave way to professionals who did not hesitate to encourage the crowds' taste for violence. Records of prize money indicate that soon the *pankration* had become the most popular event on the Greek athletic program.

Enter the Gladiators

The Romans, always eager to try any sport which might satisfy and reinforce their appetite for battle, readily adopted both wrestling and boxing. Somewhat surprisingly, they toned down the crueler aspects of wrestling, devising a modified "Greco-Roman" style which confined attack to the upper part of the body. (This style is still widely practiced today, most notably in Olympic competition.) With boxing, however, they leaned heavily in the other direction. The soft thongs of the Greek pugilists were replaced first by a glove incorporating a hard leather ring over the knuckles, and then, during the empire, by the *caestus* – a leather glove loaded with lead. (In a later and still more vicious form the *caestus* was studded with brass or iron spikes.) Blows which were initially directed against the body were eventually confined solely to the head. With the spiked gloves, the fighter landing the first solid blow was usually the winner.

But it is not for this dubious contribution to the evolution of boxing for which the Romans are best remembered in the field of combat sports. Rather it is for their success at promoting death as a spectator sport with the Games of the gladiatorial arena. Gladiatorial combat originated as an Etruscan funeral rite sometime around the sixth century BC. The Etruscans believed that the spirits of the deceased were propitiated by human blood and so it was their custom to have small numbers of slaves fight to the death before a corpse. This ritual was inherited by the Romans who, in keeping with their pronounced taste for blood and battle, soon dispensed with the religious aspects and savored the spectacle purely as sport.

The first Roman Games were held in 264 BC and involved a mere three pairs of slaves. From this modest beginning the spectacle mushroomed, rapidly increasing in both size and frequency under the demands of a populace whose appetite for such entertainment soon grew to be boundless. Two centuries later Julius Caesar was exhibiting 320 pairs of gladiators and an army of wild animals in an arena paved with silver plates. Fifty years after that, Augustus had produced eight games which included a total of ten thousand gladiators. By the end of his reign a full ninety days had been set aside on the Roman calendar for gladiatorial games. Trajan went even further by setting ten thousand gladiators against one another to celebrate one single victory, and at the end of *his* nine-year rule, no less than twenty-three thousand gladiators had entered the arena in his name.

Gladiating was by no means a glamorous calling; as a profession it ranked near the bottom of the Roman social order along with prostitution. For the most part its recruits were the dregs of society – slaves, prisoners of war, condemned criminals – who had been conscripted very much against their will into the harsh gladiatorial schools where they were taught how to kill skillfully and die honorably. It was only very occasionally that a freed man or Roman citizen, perhaps laboring under the faint hope of amassing enough money to pay off a debt or regain a squandered fortune, sold himself voluntarily into service.

The public's attitude toward this domestic cannon fodder was decidedly schizophrenic. Gladiators as a class were regarded with disgust and loathing, yet those who managed to survive while showing a degree of flair and courage were rewarded by an adulation bordering on the hysteria which greets today's pop stars. Befriended by emperors and showered with favors by females of the highest social standing, they were able to command huge sums of money for rare performances. In this, the gladiators of Rome were in roughly the same position as today's boxers – ridiculed as a class, idolized as champions.

But successful gladiators were few and far between. Generally the life of a gladiator was as unrewarding as it was short, a fact poignantly illustrated by the handful of epitaphs which have survived the centuries. "Here lies a 22-year-old gladiator who died after five fights in the sixth year of his marriage . . ." is typical. Although Romans often justified the gladiatorial games by arguing that gladiators enjoyed the battle – in much the same way as modern hunters sometimes claim that the fox enjoys the chase as much as those who are chasing it – it is highly improbable that any gladiator ever chose his profession out of pleasure. Trainers, who stood at the shoulders of the fighters as they performed, were often required literally to whip up enthusiasm with leather straps and red hot irons, and the history of the Games is studded with instances of men pressed into service who preferred suicide to combat. According to Symmachus, twenty-nine Saxon prisoners of war once strangled each other in their cell rather than face the arena.

The Games reached their dizziest heights at the hands of the young Titus, whose inauguration of the Colosseum in AD 80 remains an unsurpassed monument to man's enduring struggle to save his fellow creatures from boredom. The festivities were preceded by a build-up worthy of a modern heavyweight title fight; weeks in advance the city was plastered with posters. On opening day Rome seethed with foreigners from as far afield as Abyssinia, Arabia and the upper reaches of the Nile. Titus, blessed with a fortune left to him by his penny-pinching father Vespasian, did not disappoint his guests. The vast animal slaughters with which he opened the program would alone have ensured his place in showbiz history. But it was with the gladiators that Titus excelled himself.

The first duels involved the cream of the Roman gladiatorial schools – hard, tough professionals who could be relied upon for skill and courage. These individual bouts were punctuated by spectacular massacres pitting mounted warriors clad in chain mail and vizorless helmets against charioteers, much to the delight of the crowd (chariot fighting was at that time still a novelty). Then large numbers of gladiators formed ranks and divided themselves into two armies – "lights" *vs.* "heavies" – and set upon each other in a lethal game of human chess in which the pieces were replaced the instant they fell. Slaves dressed as the Etruscan deity Charon moved through the surging masses cracking the skulls of the fallen to ensure they were dead. Other slaves dressed as Mercury, the guider of departed souls, hauled the corpses from the arena with grappling hooks. A pitched battle on such a scale would have been the crowning glory of any other Games, but Titus was determined not simply to satisfy his subjects but to stun them. As the Colosseum was cleared, it was flooded and small ships appeared to act out an historic sea battle between Corinth and Corfu.

So ended the first day of an extravaganza which was to last a hundred. During its course every gladiatorial twist in the Roman repertoire was displayed. Never was so much blood shed by so many for the entertainment of so few. Titus, of course, became the hero of his age and on his death two years later was immediately deified. When Suetonius pronounced him the "darling of the human race," he was undoubtedly expressing the sentiments of every loyal and noble Roman.

After Titus's Hundred Days, gladiatorial games became a Roman obsession. Half the capital's population could pack the Colosseum at any one time, which they did with grim regularity. Throughout the empire every provincial outpost of any consequence was able to boast its own amphitheater, some of which still survive. The mania for games even touched the scholarly Greeks, who passed laws allowing men to kill each other for the pleasure of spectators.

On the few occasions that the Romans bothered to analyze this addiction – and it is some indication of the Games' pervasive popularity that even the most humane of Roman scholars rarely questioned them – they arrived at conclusions which have much in common with those put forward by apologists of our own pit and combat sports. The Romans' primary belief was that the spectacle of violence somehow engendered courage in the spectator. Courage – "gameness" to a cockfighter, "bottom" to a Regency prizefighter, "guts" to the followers of our own contact sports – was the quality the Romans demanded of their gladiators above all others. If a gladiator fell after putting up a brave showing, he stood a good chance of escaping death at the hands of the crowd. "*Mitte!*" the spectators would cry, "Let him go!" and the director of the games, who ignored the judgment of the audience at his own peril, would grant a reprieve. If, on the other hand, the crowd decided a fighter lacked courage, he would die with the shout "*Jugla!*" – "Throat!" – ringing in his ears.

A gladiator was required to show courage even at the point of death. The

---

❝ We hate those weak and suppliant gladiators who, hands outstretched, beseech us to live. ❞

Cicero

---

schools taught students how to die honorably; after falling to his knees the beaten gladiator gripped the leg of his vanquisher and thrust out his neck to meet the sword. If a cowardly fighter managed a courageous death, the disgrace of a poor showing was expunged. The sight of a gladiator performing well and dying courageously was held by spectators to be an enobling and uplifting experience, and well worth the price of a life. Most dog- and cockfighters pursue the same line of reasoning.

The Romans also prized the Games as an exhibition of skill, and not without some cause. Although facets of the Games later degenerated into artless massacre, the backbone of the spectacle remained the professional gladiators, men who were highly trained and extremely competent sword fighters. Training was as meticulous as it was rigorous, and when the Games were at their most popular it could take years before a student was deemed sufficiently skilled to try his hand in the arena. Moreover, the gladiators' armor was specially designed to emphasize skill rather than haphazard slashing. Fighters' limbs were heavily protected and the only vulnerable target was a narrow opening in the breastplate, which veteran fighters always kept covered with their shields. It was an unlucky veteran who died from a wild blow landed by a novice.

For at least a certain percentage of the audience, then, gladiatorial combat was an exercise in "science," a term still often applied to today's boxing matches. For many Romans the fact that gladiators died in the arena was as incidental as the split faces and broken noses are to modern fans seated at the ringside. But the overwhelming appeal of the Games was in their bloodshed. It was the *munera sine missione* – no mercy shown – which the impressarios advertised in order to attract the crowds. "In the morning they throw men to the lions and bears; at noon they throw them to the spectators," wrote Seneca after witnessing a procession of condemned criminals forced to kill each other one by one before a wildly applauding audience.

Many Romans were no doubt fully aware of this appeal. The fate of the young Alypius as recounted by his friend Augustine displays a complete understanding of the dreadful fascination of gladiatorial combat. Dragged to the games by his friends against his wishes, Alypius steeled himself to remain with closed eyes and blocked ears for the performance, but at one point he weakened, glanced up and succumbed totally to the spectacle:

He saw the blood and he gulped down savagery. Far from turning away, he fixed his eyes on it. Without knowing what was happening, he drank in madness, he was delighted with the guilty contest, drunk with the lust of blood. He was no longer the man who had come there but was one of the crowd to which he had come, a true companion of those who had brought him. There is no more to be said. He looked, he shouted, he raved with excitement. He took away with him a madness which could only goad him to come back again, and he would not only come with those who first got him there; he would go ahead of them and he would drag others with him.

It is easy to dismiss this lust for blood as some monstrous defect in the Roman character. But the Romans were not a race of perverse monsters, savage accidents of human evolution. The Games they so passionately cultivated were not the result of a vicious twist in their character; rather they were derived from a series of interlocking circumstances which first allowed and then accentuated to an appalling degree the fascination with blood and battle common to most societies – our own included.

To begin with, Roman society was grounded in slavery, which enabled and encouraged citizens to regard a large percentage of the population as virtual subhumans totally without rights – even the right to life. This unthinking callousness, developed over centuries, was also extended to the large numbers of prisoners of war who were captured as the empire expanded. Of course, many other civilizations have been based on equal callousness, yet have not enthused over gladiatorial bouts. What led the Romans down such a bloody path was the exploitation of this insensitivity by successive governments who discovered in the Games a means of retaining power.

In the hands of the Roman rulers, gladiatorial combat was used deliberately and skillfully as an instrument of domination. By pandering to base tastes in order to gain popularity with the masses, the leading political figures of Rome succeeded in institutionalizing those tastes, making cruelty and bloodshed respectable. Not only that, they actively encouraged excess, often by their own example. The emperor Commodus regularly entered the arena and, as Dio Cassius records, "sliced off the noses of some, the ears of others, and sundry features of still others." Drusus, whose love of gore embarrassed even the members of his own entourage, was so meticulous in ensuring the sharpness of the gladiators' swords that he lent his name to one particularly lethal weapon. Caligula dreamed up bouts between aged fighters and unskilled criminals, and Domitian set women, dwarfs and cripples against each other.

By the beginning of the empire, the citizens had come to regard the Games as a birthright. As the historian Fronto observed:

> the people are, all in all, less avid for money than for spectacles; and that though distributions of corn and foodstuffs are enough to satisfy men as individuals, spectacles are needed to satisfy the people as a whole.

Panem et circenses – bread and circuses, as Juvenal wryly remarked, with circuses taking precedence over bread. For an emperor to deny the plebs their circuses was to flirt with revolution, as Trajan, Marcus Aurelius and Hadrian, all of whom attempted at various stages of their careers to replace the Games with bloodless mock battles, discovered. Indeed, Trajan learned the lesson so well that his Dacian Games were one of the more brutal milestones in the sport's brutal history.

In the final analysis the Games were a monument to excess – excess brought about largely through the unrestrained and single-minded pursuit of the philosophy of "Give 'em what they want." Perhaps it is worth noting that the same philosophy is often heard in today's sporting boardrooms as justification for the increasing violence of several modern contact sports.

Royal Pleasures, Rude Pursuits

The collapse of Rome left a considerable gap in the evolution of combat sports. Although trials of strength in various forms did undoubtedly continue, it was not until the more romantic age of knighthood and chivalry with its jousting and tournaments that a direct heir to the Roman arena was discovered.

Despite its beguilingly innocent ribbon-and-lace trimmings, a tournament was a full-blooded war game in which heavily armored knights on horseback supported by squads of foot soldiers fought each other with battle axes, massive two-handed swords, maces and lances. For the royal and noble spectators looking on from their reserved seats – like the camp followers who crowded the Crimean hilltops to watch the Light Brigade's ride to extinction – tournaments offered a thrilling face-to-face glimpse of warfare, without risk of personal injury. Participants, however, were rarely so fortunate. The earlier tournaments in particular often proved extremely bloody, with knights trampled underfoot and armor split by the heavy swords. In 1249 sixty knights lost their lives in a single tournament at Neuss, near Cologne (although it is believed some may merely have choked to death in the dust). The sport was banned in England until 1135 when Stephen allowed his nobles to adopt the French fashion as a means of proving honor and valor during peacetime. (The church, however, forbade tournaments for their entire existence.)

Jousts differed to tournaments in that only two knights participated, each riding at the other with an iron-tipped lance. Although weapons were usually blunted, in the popular *joute à l'outrance* pointed lances were used, often with fatal results; Henry II of France, for one, ended his life on the end of a jousting lance. In 1443 the risk of a serious injury was reduced by the introduction of a wooden barrier separating the riders which allowed the blows to glance off more easily. These tamer jousts, which eventually displaced tournaments, soon ended up as mild social occasions offering more of an excuse for drinking and wenching than for violence. Eventually they, too, were replaced by an even less dangerous practice – riding at the quintain (a wooden figure balanced by a heavy sandbag which swung on a pivot and clouted inexperienced riders).

Jousts and tournaments were exclusively aristocratic affairs, limited strictly to knights and nobility. Those of lower birth contented themselves with more humble forms of sword play, notably contests with the sword and buckler (a small round shield). These duels were usually extremely wild and unrefined, involving much kicking, grappling and the clubbing of opponents' heads with the sword pommel. The buckler was often fitted with a sharp pike up to three feet in length which could either be used to break an opponent's sword or be thrust into his face. By 1286 sword-and-buckler matches were causing so many injuries that all public displays – generally little more than all-out street brawls – were banned and all schools closed on pain of forty days' imprisonment. Sword play continued to flourish, however, and by 1540 it had once more earned royal patronage in the form of Henry VIII, whose "Maisters of the Noble Science of Defence" gallantly pursued the "playing with the two hande sworde, the Pike, the bastard sworde, the dagger, the Backe sworde, the sworde and Buckeler, and the staffe and all other maner of weapons apperteyninge to the same science." The heyday of this noble company came during Elizabeth's reign when young courtiers flocked to receive tuition and a degree from the Maisters. Thereafter the company gradually declined. It was one of the few sporting institutions not revived during the Restoration.

Public sword fights remained popular, although in the growing professional climate they rapidly became prizefights for money rather than for honor or a degree. Bands of rural gladiators – known as "swash bucklers" (after the sound of a sword striking a buckler) or "ruffians" (after Ruffian Hall, a famous venue) – roamed the countryside performing in theaters and inn yards, causing mayhem and murder wherever they went. These professionals normally used blunted swords, but as one contemporary writer noted in an illuminating aside on public taste: ". . . as they were obliged to fight till some blood was shed, without which nobody would give a farthing for the show, they were sometimes forc'd to play a little ruffly." Another contemporary was even more direct, stating that the spectacle was "becoming a blood bath."

Prizefights were a regular attraction at London's Bear Garden, with swordsmen arranging bouts through open challenges in print, a practice which later became popular with the bare-knuckle pugilists. On May 27, 1667, Samuel Pepys visited Bear Garden Stairs "to see a prize fought" between a butcher and a waterman. The crush of spectators was so great that he was forced to slip into the hall through an adjoining alehouse and view the contest from the floor of the bear pit. Unfortunately for Pepys, the contest erupted into a riot when the butcher delivered a foul blow:

> Lord! to see in a minute the whole stage was full of watermen to revenge the foul play, and the butchers to defend their fellow, though most blamed him; and there they fell to it, knocking down and cutting many on each side. It was pleasant to see, but that I stood in the pit, and feared that in the tumult I might get hurt.

Such rather base exhibitions were by no means the only representations of sword play during Pepys's time. Refined society had by now discovered the fencing foil, and fencing was sweeping the more fashionable drawing rooms. The first light weapon, the rapier, had appeared in England a century before during Elizabeth's reign, brought over from Italy and, to a lesser extent, from Spain. The Continentals had mastered the art as early as the sixteenth century and regarded it as the only method of gentlemanly self-defense. Fencing schools flourished, with masters jealously guarding their secrets like precious jewels. Duels were even recognized by law as a means of settling personal disputes.

In England the rapier encountered considerable opposition from brawny advocates of the battle axe and the broad sword who despised such effete foreign fashions. One such stalwart, Henry Porter, was still lamenting the death of manliness as late as 1599: "this poking fight of rapier and dagger will come up; then a tall man, that is, a courageous man, and a good sword and buckler man, will be spitted like a cat or a rabbit." However, with the armor-piercing two-handed sword rendered obsolete by the introduction of gunpowder, it was inevitable that gentlemen would turn to lighter weapons for their sport. By the middle of Elizabeth's reign, the rapier had become an essential article of every gentleman's apparel.

The foil replaced the court sword at the beginning of the seventeenth century, but it was not for almost another hundred years that safety measures such as a button on the foil tip and mesh face guards were introduced and fencing became the virtual bloodless exercise that it is today.

Another combat sport to survive the collapse of Rome was wrestling. Besides the countries which had developed their own wrestling traditions without Roman influence – China, Turkey, Japan – the sport survived and flourished throughout Europe, particularly in medieval England. There, annual "trials of strength" were traditionally held on the curiously violent religious holiday Lammas Day, usually amid scenes of intense rivalry. In 1222 at Clerkenwell, for instance, a wrestling match between the men of London and the men of Westminster turned from simmering resentment into a full-scale riot which ran unchecked for several days. Three centuries later the sport had penetrated the royal court, again through the patronage of Henry VIII. In 1520 Henry challenged the French king Francis I following a drinking bout and the two grappled angrily until their courtiers managed to separate them. Later they fought again; according to the English version of the bout, Henry had the upper hand until Francis unsportingly pinned him by his bad knee.

Wrestling was further popularized among the aristocracy by the well-known Cambridge mathematician Sir Thomas Parkyns, who in 1660 authored England's first wrestling manual. A keen wrestler himself – he fought regularly until the age of 78 – Sir Thomas established an annual tournament at his property Bunny Park, near Nottingham. The prize was a gold-laced hat. Sir Thomas viewed the sport as a "regimen of education" and tried to modify what was still essentially a brutal and dangerous activity, as can be seen by his list of "prohibitions" – strangle holds, head blocks, eye gouging and leg, toe and finger twisting.

The attentions of various amateur gentlemen such as Sir Thomas Parkyns apart, however, wrestling was a predominantly rural pastime practiced chiefly by the peasants of Devon, Cornwall, Cumberland and Westmoreland. It was a standard fixture at rural fairs with the local heroes battling each other for such traditional prizes as a ring and a ram.

Each region developed its own style, the toughest being that of Lancashire, where veterans delighted in boasting how often they had "stopped the smoke of a chimney" (i.e., choked an opponent to death). During the Restoration, when wrestling became a professional spectator sport, the various county champions capitalized on their skills and reputations by competing in much publicized bouts. In 1667 the diarist Evelyn together with the king and several of his courtiers watched a wrestling match in St. James's Park "'twixt the Western and Northern man" for what was then an enormous purse of £1,000.

The sport enjoyed its greatest prominence after the turn of the eighteenth century – the era of the prize ring – when large numbers of sportsmen and gamblers would travel miles to watch a championship bout. Such matches usually opened with several rounds of furious shin kicking, which caused the "claret" (blood) to flow freely. Opponents were then finished off by staggering body slams which often rendered a man unconscious for long periods. John Jordan, "The Devonshire Giant," was the most formidable shin kicker of his time, apparently capable of raising "violent contusions" below the knees of his opponents.

County fairs were also the home of several other rough rural sports. Quarter-staffing, which involved the use of a six- or eight-foot wooden pole gripped in the middle and at one end, was one such country favorite. The object of the contest was to "break the head" of an opponent by drawing blood anywhere above the eyebrow. Robin Hood was reputedly an early champion; his bout against Arthur-a-Bland was said to have lasted more than two hours, the blows falling so heavily that "all the wood rang with every bang."

In back-swording, fighters rained blows on each other with an ash stick fitted with a large basket handle. To protect the exposed side of their head, they looped a leather strap around their finger which they then fastened to their left leg. Standing three feet apart, they struck and feinted until one yielded or blood flowed. According to Thomas Hughes, author of *Tom Brown's Schooldays*: "If good men are playing, the quickness of the returns is marvellous; you hear the rattle like that a boy makes drawing his stick along palings, only heavier." Hughes had the young Brown attend a match between a gypsy and Joe, the village favorite:

> The gypsy is a tough active fellow, but not very skillful with his weapon, so that Joe's weight and strength tell in a minute; he is too heavy metal for him: whack, whack, whack, come his blows, breaking down the gypsy's guard, and threatening to reach his head every moment. There it is at last – "Blood, blood!" shout the spectators as a thin stream oozes out slowly from the roots of his hair.

Cudgeling was a kindred stick sport which remained popular until the early nineteenth century. In 1719 Delforce – "The Finished Cudgeller" – was challenging "any man in the kingdom to enter the lists for a *broken head* or a *belly-full!*" A century later an advertiser in the *Reading Mercury* was having to entice contestants with cash – 18 pence to every man who broke a head and a shilling to those whose heads were broken. Even then there were easier ways to make a living.

Crosses and Claret

The fairs and wakes of England were rough and riotous affairs, conceived solely to alleviate the tedium of a year's unremitting toil with a few days of boisterous mayhem. It is therefore hardly surprising that the sports thrown up by these violent gatherings were chiefly violent pleasures – wrestling, back-swording and so on. It is also hardly surprising that it was the English fairgrounds which fostered the resurgence of an archaic and brutal sport forgotten since the fall of the Roman Empire – boxing.

It is an interesting point, that. We tend now to think of modern boxing as the end result of a long and glorious history, dating back thousands of years; in fact the reverse is true. The sport began as a disreputably brutal practice, flourished under the Romans as a supremely lethal blood sport, and then, for well over a thousand years, vanished entirely from the history books. From the decline of Rome until the early 1700s there is not one clear historical reference to sportsmen fighting with their fists. The reason, although never stated, seems fairly obvious: it was simply considered beyond the pale of sporting sanity. Whereas even a timid sportsman might willingly take up his buckler or flail about at a companion with a stick happily risking a cut scalp, only a madman would ever contemplate entering a contest in which *inevitably* one side retired with at best a swollen head or a battered face and the other with bruised or broken hands.

The resurrection of boxing is credited to a professional showman by the name of James Figg. Although Figg was more concerned with demonstrating the "Manly Arts of Foil-play, Back-sword and cudgelling," it was as the first English champion of pugilism (1719–1730) that he is now remembered. Pugilism, as practiced by Figg and his contemporaries in their fairground booths at Southwark, Moorfield and Smithfield, was a decidedly primitive ancestor of modern boxing, owing nothing to skill and everything to brute strength and the ability to soak up punishment while remaining on two feet. Like the Greek *pankration*, it was a cruel combination of boxing and wrestling, fought with bare knuckles toe to toe at a chalkmark. To retreat or attempt to avoid a blow was unthinkable. Fighters who threw their opponents crashed down on top of them with their full weight. Eye gouging was both common and popular with the spectators, and "purring" – the art of sinking a hobnail boot into one's fallen opponent – was considered only right and proper. With weight divisions still a thing of the far distant future, only the heaviest of the heavyweights survived for long.

Figg's prowess as an exponent of the "manly art" (it could hardly yet be said to have earned the euphemism "sweet science") won him widespread acclaim, not only from the members of his own class but also from the higher echelons of London society. After a visit to London during the 1820s, the Frenchman de Saussure reported with considerable distaste that dueling had been abandoned by a gentry which demeaned itself by brawling in the street with the lower classes. It was to be an attitude which disgusted foreigners would hold for the rest of the century, much to the delight of "manly" Englishmen of every social persuasion.

Figg was succeeded as champion by several minor celebrities – Pipes, Gretting, Taylor – until in 1740, the year of Figg's death, there appeared another giant of the prize ring, Jack Broughton. According to a treatise on boxing published by a John Godfrey in 1747, Broughton was the "Captain of the Boxers," a giant of a man who soaked up punishment like a sponge before pole-axing his opponent:

> Broughton steps boldly and firmly in, bids a welcome to the coming blow; receives it with his guardian Arm; then with a general Summons of his swelling Muscles, and his firm body, seconding his arm, supplying it with all its weight, pours the pile-driving Force upon his man.

But for all this relentless iron-fisted put and take, one of Broughton's main contributions to the embryonic sport was his introduction of movement. Under his influence it was soon no longer necessary for a fighter to stand in the direct line of a blow (although to retreat was still unthinkable). For the first time, skill began to raise its feeble head in the ring.

Another Broughton invention was the "muffler," the first boxing glove. Broughton made his living by teaching young gentlemen the art of prize-fighting at his Haymarket Amphitheatre, an awkward profession given the inherent savagery of the sport and the delicate constitutions of the majority of his pupils. In 1747 in the hopes of attracting more delicate customers he advertised the use of mufflers for sparring, promising that they would "effectually secure [pupils] from the inconveniency of black eyes, broken jaws and bloody noses." Prizefighters themselves, however, shunned Broughton's mufflers; they were, after all, the manly sons of John Bull. It was to be another century before gloves appeared outside boxing academies and exhibition halls.

But the innovation for which Broughton is best remembered is his set of rules (see p. 143). There is a persistent story that Broughton formulated his rules in a fit of remorse following a fatal bout. (George Stevenson, the "Fighting Coachman," is often cited as the unfortunate victim, although the essayist William Hazlitt wrote of his meeting Stevenson when he was an old man and Broughton long dead.) It is far more likely, however, that he drew them up to win the confidence of the gamblers who were fast becoming the backbone of the prize ring. After all, Broughton's rules,

BROUGHTON'S RULES

To Be Observed In All Battles On The Stage. As agreed by several Gentlemen at Broughton's Amphitheatre, Tottenham Court Road, August 16, 1743.

1 That a square of a Yard be chalked in the middle of the Stage; and on every fresh set-to after a fall, or being parted from the rails, each second is to bring his Man to the side of the square, and place him opposite to the other, and till they are fairly set-to at the Lines, it shall not be lawful for one to strike at the other.

2 That, in order to prevent any Disputes, the time a Man lies after a fall, if the Second does not bring his Man to the side of the square, within the space of half a minute, he shall be deemed a beaten Man.

3 That in every main Battle, no person whatever shall be upon the Stage, except the Principals and their Seconds; the same rule to be observed in bye-battles, except that in the latter, Mr. Broughton is allowed to be upon the Stage to keep decorum, and to assist Gentlemen in getting to their places, provided always he does not interfere in the Battle; and whoever pretends to infringe these Rules to be turned immediately out of the house. Every body is to quit the Stage as soon as the Champions are stripped, before the set-to.

4 That no Champion be deemed beaten, unless he fails coming up to the line in the limited time, or that his own Second declares him beaten. No Second is to be allowed to ask his man's Adversary any question, or advise him to give out.

5 That in bye-battles, the winning man to have two-thirds of the Money given, which shall be publicly divided upon the Stage, notwithstanding any private agreements to the contrary.

6 That to prevent Disputes, in every main Battle the Principals shall, on coming on the Stage, choose from among the gentlemen present two Umpires, who shall absolutely decide all Disputes that may arise about the Battle; and if the two Umpires cannot agree, the said Umpires to choose a third, who is to determine it.

7 That no person is to hit his Adversary when he is down, or seize him by the ham, the breeches, or any part below the waist: a man on his knees to be reckoned down.

whatever else they were, could hardly be considered protective legislation. Whatever their origins, Broughton's rules were introduced in 1743 and remained the bible of the prize ring until 1838 when they were superseded by a more humane code. As much as any single thing they were responsible for the ring's rise to prominence.

Broughton lost his title in 1750 to the Norwich butcher Jack Slack. It was a memorable bout, displaying all the blood and suicidal courage that even the most critical ring adherent could have wished for. In the first two minutes the "Knight of the Cleaver," as Slack was known, landed a devastating blow on Broughton's forehead, closing both his eyes. "I am blind, not beat," cried Broughton to his patron, the Duke of Cumberland. "Only let me be placed before my antagonist, and he shall not gain the day yet." Slack, however, coasted to victory in fourteen minutes. The duke, who had bet Lord Chesterfield £10,000 to £400 on a Broughton triumph, was so incensed that he hurried a bill through Parliament making prizefighting illegal. All boxing amphitheaters were closed, Broughton's becoming, much to the disgust of one early ring historian, a Methodist meeting hall.

All of which did not, of course, end prizefighting. But with Slack as champion, the ring fell rapidly into disrepute. Even for those unpolished times Slack was a remarkably dirty fighter. His specialties were the "chopper" – a backhand blow which involved more fist than elbow – and the "rabbit punch" – a karate-type blow to the back of the neck. Even more damaging to the ring's prestige than these "unmanly" tactics were the rumors of fight fixing, "crosses," which flourished during Slack's reign and which kept the gambling fraternity away in droves.

It was not until 1786 that the ring regained its squandered respectability. In that year a glittering collection of French and English nobles reputedly led by the Prince of Wales (later to become George IV) turned out to witness Richard Humphries batter Martin the Bath Butcher at Newmarket. Blessed with such influential patrons, prizefighting was catapulted back into vogue, a position it maintained for the next forty years thanks largely to a succession of honest and popular champions – Tom Johnson, Humphries, Daniel Mendoza and so on. So began the age of Regency Boximania, an extraordinary chapter in sporting history which saw pugilism sweep the country and the bare-knuckle ring become an inspiration for patriotism and fierce national pride.

Despite its illegality and all that that entailed – harrassment from zealous county magistrates, lack of permanent venues, long journeys to obscure rural destinations – by the turn of the century the prize ring had grown into a social phenomenon of enormous magnitude. Although the pugilists themselves were drawn exclusively from the lower classes (butchers, coal heavers and carriagemen predominated) and, more than that, usually from an un-fashionable ethnic minority (Irish, Jewish or Negro), their supporters en-compassed the entire English social order.

At the head of the "Fancy" (as ring enthusiasts dubbed themselves) was a solid knot of royalty – the Prince of Wales and his brothers, Prince Frederick, Duke of York, and the Duke of Clarence (later William IV). Indeed, it was Clarence's property Moulsey Heath which was to be the scene of many of the prize ring's epic moments. Next came a wide selection of lesser nobility – lords, barons and earls, including the poet Lord Byron whose famous bedroom screen pasted with contemporary newspaper clippings survives as a unique record of the prizefighting era. They were followed in descending order by the "Corinthians," the rich and idle young swells of the Regency period; the butchers, costermongers and other assorted East End traders who constituted the bulk of the Fancy; and, at bottom, the large and shadowy collection of thieves, cutthroats and pickpockets, in-cluding John Thurtell, the most celebrated murderer of his age. Even scholars were not immune to the prizefighting frenzy; support for the ring ran as high as in the East End. In the 1820s an Eton schoolboy complained that his colleagues' conversation revolved solely around prizefighting, a charge which could, in fact, have been leveled against almost any Corinthian. Only the emergent middle classes remained unmoved, their affected gentility requiring them to sniff disdainfully at such a common spectacle.

This extraordinarily varied support could best be seen when the Fancy made its way to Moulsey Heath, dressed in its greatcoats, pearl buttons and knotted handkerchiefs, and strung out for miles on horseback, carriage, cart and foot. As Pierce Egan, author of the prize-ring classic *Boxiana* and self-appointed mouthpiece of the Fancy, described it:

> From the *brilliant* of the highest class in the circle of Corinthians *down to* the Dusty Bob graduation in society; and even a *shade* or two below that. Lots of the Upper House; the Lower House, and the *flash* house. Proprietors of splendid parks and demesnes; inmates from proud and lofty mansions; groups from the most respectable dwellings; thou-sands from the peaceable cot – and myriads of *coves* from no houses at all.

For a "Grand Mill" this sporting subculture turned out in remarkable numbers – to wit, when Jack Scroggins met Ned Turner in a field near Hayes in 1817, thirty thousand people out of a total British population of less than nine million made the long overnight journey through driving rain to attend.

What the Fancy expected to see once it had taken up position beside the ring was a bloody lesson in protracted brutality, often lasting for six or seven hours and eighty or ninety rounds. Although Mendoza, and later Jem Belcher, revolutionized the sport with their footwork and "scientific" bobbing and weaving, milling remained basically a matter of brute blows delivered by iron fists. After the opening rounds any science displayed by the fighters invariably disappeared. Although grappling still played an important part, it was the bare-knuckle blows which caused the most damage, cutting and ripping the face and throat. Mendoza's prime targets were the eyebrows, the bridge of the nose, the temple arteries and a spot below the left ear. He also recommended the kidney punch, which "deprives the person struck of his breath, occasions an instant discharge of urine, puts him in the greatest torture and renders him for some time a cripple." Another favorite was the "suit in Chancery" in which an opponent's face was smashed repeatedly while being held in a headlock.

Such blows also caused considerable damage to the fists, and fighters were instructed to use only the larger knuckles on the top of the hand as the smaller knuckles in the middle of the finger "frequently give way." To toughen their fists they pickled them in a variety of heady brews such as a mixture of turpentine, whisky vinegar, horseradish and saltpeter. However, before a fight had gone too many rounds, each man's knuckles had usually puffed out and softened to the consistency of a modern boxing glove.

Much of the prize ring reporting of the time was an entertaining blend of Fancy slang and euphemism, especially as penned by the prolific Pierce Egan in *Boxiana* and the sixpenny sporting journals he contributed to. "Ogles" were blackened, "peepers" plunged into darkness, "tripe-shops" received "staggerers," "ivories" were cracked, "domino boxes" shattered, and "claret" flowed in a steady stream. But for all this picturesque turn of phrase, the early ringside scribes still managed to convey the naked brutality upon which the prize ring was founded. In 1821 Egan described a bout between Jack Randall and Martin the Baker on Crawley Downs:

> Catching Martin in his right arm he fibbed him with his left hand with such rapidity that the eye could do no more than follow the motion of his fist; he then changed arms and repeated five or six blows on the face and neck with his right hand, operating so decisively, that the eyes of Martin turned up, and he foamed at the mouth as he struggled to extricate himself. A few drops of claret fell from his listener, Randall punishing him almost to the ground, when his head and neck come roughly against a post and both men come down *wop*. . . . Martin was picked up in a state of stupor, and was certainly not in fighting trim until long after "time" had been called!

146

❝ We live in a freakish world, a vicious world. People like to see blood. ❞

Muhammad Ali, after destroying his mismatched Belgian opponent Jean-Pierre Coopman in 1975

Egan's report of the tenth round between Jem Belcher and Jem Bourke on August 20, 1802, was equally as explicit:

Belcher, losing no time, cut Bourke under the left eye; under the right; and another blow so dreadful in its effect between the throat and chin as to hoist Bourke off his feet, and he came down head foremost. Belcher also fell from the force which he gave it. Both on the floor, when Bourke squirted some blood out of his mouth over Belcher: Jem threatened that in the next round he should have it for such conduct – but Bourke declared it was accidental.

Bourke eventually surrendered, "his face so disfigured that scarcely any traces of a human being were left. . . ."

In a later bout Belcher "materially altered" his opponent Dougherty's face: "His mouth and lips were so lacerated, that it resembled what is termed 'a *hare's lip*.' Three of his teeth were completely knocked out from a tremendous blow of Belcher's. His appearance was truly piteous." Both Big Ben Brain and Tom Johnson were bleeding so badly after twenty-five minutes of a bout at Wrotham in Kent that "it was almost a difficulty to distinguish the face from the hind part of the head." After forty-three rounds with Henry "Game Chicken" Pearce in 1805, John Gully's head was "truly terrific, and had a giant-like appearance, from being so terribly swelled, and the effect was most singular, from scarcely any of his eyes to be seen." Likewise, to distinguish Cribb from the Negro Molyneaux by their features after forty rounds of action on Copthorne Common in 1810 "would have been utterly impossible, so dreadfully were both their faces beaten – but their difference in colour supplied this sort of defect."

But the most graphic description of the effects of bare-knuckling came not from the ring's self-appointed spokesman, but from the pen of the essayist Hazlitt, who was among the thirty thousand who traveled to Hungerford in Berkshire on December 11, 1821, to witness the underdog Neat from Bristol administer a terrible beating to Tom Hickman, the "Gas Light Man." The turning point of the bout, as described by Hazlitt in his essay "The Fight," came in the eighth round:

Neat just then made a tremendous lunge at him and hit him full in the

---

❝ Games is just for a little while. Your face and teeth is all your life. ❞

Muhammad Ali

---

face. It was doubtful whether he would fall backwards or forwards – he hung suspended for a second or two – and then fell back throwing his hands in the air and with his face lifted up to the sky. I never saw anything more terrific than his aspect just before he fell. All traces of life, of natural expression, were gone from him. His face was like a human skull, a death's head, spouting blood. The eyes were filled with blood, the nose streamed with blood, the mouth gaped blood. He was not like an actual man but like a preternatural, spectral appearance, or like one of the figures in Dante's *Inferno*. Yet he fought on after this for several rounds.

Many fighters suffered permanent injury or died early as a result of the beatings they received. Big Ben Brain, for example, was punished so severely during his victorious bout against Johnson that he died a few months later. Few pugilists managed to fight more than a dozen times in a career, mainly because recovery from injuries was such a long and painful process. Surprisingly, there were few deaths in the ring during major bouts, although they did sometimes occur; the Prince of Wales was said to have retired from the ringside after witnessing a fatal bout between Earl and Tyne at Brighton in 1788. During provincial and minor bouts, however, deaths were considerably more frequent.

Much of the blame for serious injury can be attributed to the fighters' seconds who alone judged when a man had received enough punishment. More often than not the second had a vested interest in his man's returning to scratch after a knockdown, and the history of the prize ring is littered with sad examples of befuddled fighters being propelled back to the mark by mercenary cornermen. In the fatal bout between Deaf Burke and Simon Byrne, Byrne was literally carried to scratch.

But if a fighter's friends were bad, his enemies at ringside could be infinitely worse. With thousands of sovereigns riding on each major bout, the temptation to alter the course of events proved irresistible to many gamblers. It was an easy enough task to achieve, considering that the ring, as such, was merely the unfenced eye of a seething whirlpool of people. If the fight began to go against the betting, an angry army of gamblers would often surge forward and attempt to break up the event. In later years consortiums of gamblers hired East End bullies to watch over their favorites and ensure that the results were as they had predicted. At one famous mill, Spring fought Langan in a packed ring crowded with thugs and officials "kicking, pushing and striking with whips and sticks." When Jem Smith faced Frank Slavin, Smith was surrounded by armed ruffians who attacked Slavin whenever he approached. Slavin's ear was torn off by a knuckle-duster. Eventually the situation became so bad that a group of honest pugilists joined forces to keep order in the inner circle of the ring. Unfortunately these vigilantes had little effect and rioting became a standard feature of large bouts, contributing heavily to the ring's eventual demise.

Bare-knuckle prizefighting remains as the most calculatedly brutal sport ever evolved by the English sporting fraternity. Just as the cock and dog pits of the same period demanded a total lack of sensitivity toward the sufferings of animals, so too did the prize ring require an equal callousness toward the sufferings of men. (Indeed, many of the ring's supporters were the same people as those who crowded round the pits, and it was no accident that bull baits were often held alongside major prizefights.) As such, the ring was completely in tune with its times, and in order to explain pugilism's spectacular leap from fairground sideshow to national obsession it is necessary to first weigh the ring against the social background of those times.

The common denominator of eighteenth and early nineteenth century life in England was violence. Although most contemporary histories, concentrating as they did on the lives of the aristocratic and wealthy, tended to present a gilded picture of luxurious well being, this was a distortion, wholly unrepresentative of the great mass of the population. For the majority, violent death was a casually suffered fact of life. In the mid-1700s – the height of the gin era – burials in London were double the number of baptisms. By the end of the century there were more than two hundred types of crime listed on the statutes as capital offenses, most of them concerned with violence against property rather than person, which was treated with a marked leniency. Women were still being burned to death as late as 1790 (although by then the executioner would usually first strangle his unfortunate victim as an act of mercy), and criminals, homosexuals and other social outcasts were dying in the pillories. Thieves, cutthroats and murderers thrived amid the hopeless poverty and dreadful squalor of London's festering slumland, ill-controlled by a makeshift force of Bow Street Runners. (Not until 1829 did the capital finally receive a proper police force.) By the 1830s Sir Edwin Chadwick was reckoning that eleven thousand Britons died each year from acts of violence. It was perhaps not insignificant that flagellation became known on the Continent during this time as *le vice Anglais*.

With violence so permeating every corner of lower-class life, it is unfair to expect the popular leisure tastes of the period to reflect any more compassion or humanity than the surroundings which fostered them. For decades public hangings vied with the prize ring as the country's most popular spectator sport. "Hanging matches" at Newgate, the most famous venue, regularly attracted thirty thousand people to its narrow surrounding streets, and at the better-positioned jails – Liverpool's Kirkdale Jail, for example – upwards of one hundred thousand might turn out to see a famous murderer swing.

Executions usually took place on the Monday, and by early Sunday evening the first spectators had invariably arrived to secure the best positions close to the gallows. Soon the ledges and parapets of the surrounding buildings would be crawling with paying customers; a room with a view at Newgate could cost as much as £25 for the evening. Refreshment peddlers, pie men, fruit sellers and pamphleteers hawked their wares through the festive and boisterous throng which would regularly burst into a chant – "Oh, my! – Think I've got to die!" – or a collective song just like the English soccer crowds of today. "The conduct of the people was so indescribably frightful, that I felt for some time afterwards almost as if I were living in a city of devils," wrote Charles Dickens after witnessing the hanging of a husband and wife at the entry to Horsemonger Lane Prison. Few of his fellow countrymen would have agreed; a hanging match was grand sport.

It was against such a background that the prize ring grew and prospered, drawing on the vast pool of ill-paid and unemployed men for whom smashing a man with their bare fists was far more lucrative than sweating for poverty wages, and providing savage entertainment for an audience inured to violence. If there is any excuse to be made for the rise of so brutal a national sport it is that pugilism was simply a product of its environment. The ring was a cracked mirror which reflected a disastrously flawed age, a fact indelibly underlined by a bout on Wimbledon Common in 1800 in which Jem Belcher fought Andrew Gamble under the shadow of the hanged highwayman Jerry Abbershaw, who creaked overhead chained to his gibbet.

The reason for the aristocracy's involving itself in such a base pleasure is rather more complex, a curious mixture of hypocrisy and heart-felt sentiment. At the root of the obsession was the fact that pugilism came to be widely regarded as the only way for an Englishman to display his manhood. Although testing masculinity had been one of the mainsprings of violent sports ever since the first Greek youth faced his first wild bull, to the upper crust of the Fancy the love of "manly" self-defense was prized as a peculiarly English trait – which indeed, at that particular time, it was.

&& The gladiatorial displays of the Romans we admire not, nor any public exhibitions tending to degrade mankind; but the manly art of boxing has infused that true, heroic courage, blended with humanity, into the hearts of Britons, which have made them so renowned, terrific and triumphant in all parts of the world. 🥾🥾

Pierce Egan

"Foreigners can scarcely understand how we can squeeze pleasure out of this pastime," wrote Hazlitt; "the luxury of hard blows given or received; the joy of the ring; nor the perseverance of the combatants." While visitors might regard prize fighting with the same disgust they reserved for dog fighting and bull baiting, the English soon came to view their love of fisticuffs as a national asset, something which set them a cut above other races. Whereas the Frenchman would shoot you in the back with a lead ball and the Italian stab you with a concealed dagger, an Englishman settled his differences the honorable way, face to face with his fists. The prize ring, of course, provided the perfect expression of such sentiments, and although the fighting may have been undertaken exclusively by the lower ranks, it was easy enough for a Corinthian to apply to himself the manliness and "bottom" he saw in a Bristol butcher or an East End coal heaver. They were, after all, all sons of Mother England.

Such jingoism reached full fruition during later matches when English champions and foreign fighters met; Cribb's two successful title defenses against the former Virginian slave Tom Molyneaux, for instance, earned him the status of national hero. But it was during the twenty years of intermittent warfare against the French spanning the turn of the century which laid the groundwork. With England under constant threat of invasion, pugilism was raised on a pedestal and hailed as exemplifying all that was courageous about the British race. "The English are led to the attack or sustain it equally well, because they fight as they box, not out of malice, but to show *pluck* and manhood," wrote Hazlitt in 1825 in his essay "Merry England." *"Fair play and old England for ever!"* When the czar of Russia, the king of Prussia and various other Allied leaders visited London in 1814, it surprised no one that they were taken to Lord Lowther's house in Pall Mall and urged to witness what was still technically an illegal activity – "the national sport of boxing . . . a peculiar trait of the brave natives of England." It was the prize ring's finest hour.

There was, however, another, far less comfortable, reason why England's gentry occupied much of their time journeying to and from prize rings. It was that, despite all Pierce Egan's pious protestations to the contrary, the Fancy were passionately in love with the gladiatorial blood and gore of bare-knuckle prize fighting. Egan's own ringside reports betray him, gleefully retailing as they do every sanguinary detail. So, too, does the behavior of the spectators at ringside that he recorded. Fighters fought until they dropped and were urged on to do so by near-hysterical crowds even when the outcome was already clearly beyond doubt. It was not only the gamblers who goaded on the lost cause; it was everybody who had arrived expecting a good show, and that included gentlemen.

But it was the prize ring's sister sport – the hanging match – which effectively gave much of the game away. Public executions were nothing more than artless exhibitions of violent death. They had precious little to do with skill and even less to do with courage or bottom, and even the most fervent jingoist could not have read any source of national pride into the disgraceful scenes which occurred outside Newgate's grim gates. Yet it was to hangings that the stalwarts of the prize ring Fancy flocked, willingly handing over their £25 for a window giving a clear view of the condemned man's death struggles. The familiar faces around the foot of the gallows were those of sportsmen, Corinthians such as the Marquis of Waterford – "the young and rakish head of the great sporting clan of Beresford," as Kellow Chesney described him – whose absence at a famous execution was enough to excite "surprised comment."

Members of the Fancy, both humble and grand, attended public executions for one reason – the sensation of witnessing a spectacle of violence. And although they were loath to confess it even in those unabashed times, they attended prize fights for very much the same reason. With Figg, Broughton, Cribb and the rest, the gladiators had returned to the sporting scene. They have remained with us ever since.

The lingering death of the prize ring began a mere decade after Lord Lowther's patriotic exhibition, even as Hazlitt was brimming with fair play and old England. In 1824 Tom Spring, the last true titan of milling, retired after two memorable defenses against John Langan, leaving behind him a sport riddled with fraud, corruption and crowd violence. Fixed fights had become the rule rather than the exception, and pugilists who refused to bend to the wishes of the gamblers were intimidated with threats and assault. Even at championship level foul fighting was rife. At ringside the casual violence of the spectators matched that of the pugilists; any honest spectator foolish enough to show support for an unpopular fighter was swiftly dealt with. Thus it was that when Spring threw in the towel in 1824, Tom Jackson, whose presence at the ring had always guaranteed an honest bout, followed suit and closed his Rooms in Bond Street, abandoning the sport in disgust.

The Corinthians, in turn, followed Jackson's lead, appalled by the fixing which deprived them of their gambling pleasures and embittered by a crowd which would just as soon pick their pocket as take their wagers. With them went the ring's last vestiges of respectability, and the sport was left wide open to the concerted harassment of the magistracy. In 1824 Ned Neale and Jem Burns were prosecuted after a bout at Moulsey, and the celebrated venue was closed down. Pronouncing judgment at Kingston Assizes, Mr. Justice Burroughs ruled that prizefights only served to indulge the vicious and to encourage gambling. He regretted that there had been gentlemen of rank present at the event, although by that time there could not have been many. By then even Pierce Egan had turned his back on the ring, writing mournfully in that year:

> All things, it is said, must have an end, and *Prize Milling* has already, if not quite, arrived at this Climax . . . the thing altogether has degenerated, and the highest patrons of the P.R. have retired in disgust.

But it wasn't just the ring that was changing, it was the times themselves. A new moral climate which was to achieve full bloom under Queen Victoria was already evolving in reaction to the flashy habits and loose living of the Regency swells. William Windham, champion of pit and prize ring, was gradually being overshadowed by Humanity Martin, friend to the animal kingdom. Sports which would once have been accepted with casual insensitivity were now being openly questioned. This new wave of humanity came sharply into focus in 1830 when the Irish champion Simon Byrne beat Sandy McKay in a brutal forty-seven rounds. McKay died as a result of the beating and Byrne was arrested and tried for manslaughter. Although the fighter was acquitted, the case caused a flood of revulsion toward the ring. Three years later Byrne himself died after going $3\frac{1}{4}$ hours and ninety-eight rounds against Deaf Burke.

Despite the efforts of a hastily convened "Fair Play Club," the prize ring continued on its downhill slide from grace. Following another fatal bout between Owen Smith and Brighton Bill in 1838, the Pugilistic Benevolent Association was forced to replace Broughton's Rules with a milder ring code. Just how violent the sport was even at that late date can be seen from the tactics the association felt compelled to outlaw by name – among them, butting, kicking, gouging, biting, tearing the flesh and falling on an opponent with elbows and knees. Under this new code the ring lingered on, occasionally throwing up popular heroes such as Deaf Burke and the much-acclaimed Bendigo, who achieved enough fame for the Irish miners of Australia to name a not inconsiderable gold-mining town after him. But as a national pastime prizefighting was patently moribund. In 1840 *Tom Spring's Life in London* sorrowfully noted the trend toward "a system of cowardly assault and treacherous revenge displayed in the murderous use of the knife – a weapon which is now becoming almost as common in England as in Spain and Italy." Lord Lowther would have turned in his grave.

The last bare-knuckle bout of any consequence fought on English soil was in 1860 between Tom Sayers and the American champion John Camel Heenan. It was a mill which came close to matching the brutality and the jingoistic fervor of a bygone era. *The Times* reported that the blows on Heenan's ribs "sounded all over the meadow as if a box had been smashed in." With Heenan all but blinded, the crowd, closely followed by the police, broke the ring and stopped the fight, much to the chagrin of sportsmen from across the Atlantic. In the wake of the publicity, police, clergy and humanitarians redoubled their efforts and the ring was driven further into the shadows. Seven years later a Cambridge undergraduate named Chambers drew up a far stricter set of rules under the patronage of the eighth Marquis of Queensberry. These rules introduced fixed rounds, rest periods and a ten-count to end a contest, replacing the old Broughton philosophy of fight-till-you-fall. Skin-tight gloves became fashionable and were in turn replaced by a modified version of the Broughton muffler.

Bare-knuckle bouts continued in the fairground boxing booths which traveled up and down the country under the watchful eye of the police.* As late as 1886 the Constabulary was still breaking up prize mills on Glasgow Green, one of which ended in tragedy when a fighter dived into the Clyde to escape arrest and was drowned a few feet from the bank. But bare-knuckling had run its course. When boxing was finally declared legal in 1891, the pubs, clubs and halls had all long since bowed to the Marquis of Queensberry whose rules, in the eyes of the law, were leniently interpreted as promoting self-defense rather than cold-blooded murder.

The ghost of the prize ring still hovers over London's East End, however, in the shape of the unlicensed "pirate" or "charity" matches which surface every few months. These matches, although outlawed by the British Boxing

---

* The fairground booths which gave birth to the prize ring remained the first home of many boxing champions and contenders in England and, later, in Australia, where Jimmy Sharman's tent with its troupe of pugilists lined up outside on the catwalk was for decades the primary entertainment for many bush towns. In Britain, the booths have now declined almost to the point of extinction; whereas only a few decades ago there were one hundred, now there are two. "You just can't get the boys today," explained Ron Taylor, one of the surviving owners. Much to his displeasure he has been forced to include wrestling on the bill: "When the women come, they want the wrestlers; it's what they're used to on television."

Board of Control, regularly draw upwards of three and four thousand hard-core fight fans at £10 per head. What the fans come to see is a steady stream of "pugs" batter each other until the canvas turns red – retired boxers, disbarred boxers, ex-convicts and pub bouncers who have earned their reputations street brawling and in the "garage fights" which can be found in the East End if one knows where to look. They are rarely disappointed. With winnings reportedly running as high as £15,000 and age no barrier (many of the pugs are well over fifty), there is never a shortage of contenders.

The long-standing champion of this largely unpublicized circuit was until mid-1978 a granite-fisted bruiser who fought under the misnomer of Roy "Pretty Boy" Shaw. One of Shaw's last matches was against an American heavyweight, Ron "The Butcher" Stander, whose main claim to fame was that he had once appeared in the same ring as Joe Frazier. It was a bout which produced all the flag-waving jingoism – and all the blood and gore – of a Cribb-Molyneaux mill, coming as close to the philosophy of the Regency prize ring as any fight could where the pugilists used gloves. After a bludgeoning, bloody, no-holds-barred first round, it ended with The Butcher doubled up underneath the ropes by a blow which had landed somewhere between his knee and his navel. This was too much for Stander, who up until then had found Pretty Boy's ring tactics bewildering, to say the least. When he had recovered his breath he hurled himself at Shaw, scattering supporters in all directions, and wrestled him to the canvas. Unfortunately for the American the fall was disallowed.

The last bout on the card involved two aging bouncers, one a gray-haired old pug rumored to be well in his sixties. It ended with the victor having to be hauled bodily off his insensible opponent who lay prone on the canvas, the victim of a roundhouse punch which had lifted him clean off the floor. The audience was delighted.

A few months prior to this, Shaw and his seconds had thrown the Marquis of Queensberry to the winds and had agreed to a full-blooded bare-knuckle grudge match against one Don Adams. However, word of the affair was somehow leaked to the police, who were granted a restraining order by the courts. The match was eventually held in a circus tent at Windsor, outside London, on the understanding that gloves would be used – but only for the opening round. As it happened, the bare-knuckle question was rendered academic when Shaw flattened Adams in the first thirty seconds. However, the rest of the evening more than did justice to the spirit of the prize ring. The trouble began when a challenger leaped into the ring from his seat and smashed his opponent's face to a pulp before the referee could finish reciting the pre-bout rules. The audience, as film director Peter Clifton recalled, erupted:

They just went crazy . . . berserk . . . smashing into each other with fists and chairs. It sounded like an earthquake, the most incredible sound you've ever heard. They were telling the blind kids (who had been collected at ringside in deference to the evening's charitable overtones) to crawl toward the ring, but my God! the sound that must have been ringing in their ears!

But what shocked Clifton, a man of some sensitivity, more than the riot itself was the crowd's reaction to the bloodbath in the ring. "I had my cameras on the audience's faces during the most violent bits, and they were *smiling*! All of them! It was a consistent expression!" Such a revelation would have come as no surprise to John Ford, historian of the Regency ring. "Gentlemen fanciers might on occasion turn away from a bloody battle," he wrote in his book *Prizefighting*, "but a true fancier never."

The Ring in America and Abroad

The prize ring was the foundation of boxing not just in Britain but throughout the empire and beyond. In Australia fist fighting had arrived with the First Fleet, but it was not until the first match under Broughton's Rules was held at Sydney Racecourse on January 7, 1814, that the sport took root. It lasted sixty years, its finest moments coming during the gold rush when the miners would pour out of the diggings in their wagons and bullock carts on the day of the fight in their thousands, presenting a similar if shabbier version of the procession to Moulsey Heath. The bouts were as equally hard fought as at Moulsey; in December 1854 Irish Jim Kelly fought Jonathan Smith from Norwich for a full six hours, the first round alone lasting for two.

But as with the Motherland, the forces of moderation soon began to gain the upper hand. Attendance at a mill became a cat-and-mouse game with the police, involving boats chartered for unspecified destinations and private trains which stopped along deserted stretches of track to let the whole crew – fighters, seconds, referee and spectators – disembark to continue the entertainment. Such necessary tactics caused a severe setback to the ring's fortunes in the winter of 1867 when six of the Fancy were drowned while negotiating the surf on a barren strip of Australian coastline. Four years later the sport was revived by a series of brutal and hysterical "religious" bouts between Larry Foley, a staunch Catholic, and Sandy Ross, an Orangeman.

When the religious fervor had burned itself out, gradually but inexorably the ring declined. The end came in 1884 when James Lawson laid out a 27-year-old novice, Alex Agar, with a terrific blow over the left eye. Agar died in a hansom cab on the way to the hospital and Lawson served six months for manslaughter.

Prizefighting also enjoyed a brief period of popularity in Canada, but it received its warmest welcome south of the border in the United States. The first bouts were organized by the cotton aristocrats of Carolina, Georgia and Virginia, who had quickly discovered that their strongest slaves could be put to more profitable use as stand-up pugilists rather than as plantation workers. The most famous of these slave fighters was Tom Molyneaux, who made his name fighting Tom Cribb one frozen winter's day on England's Copthorne Common. After a bruising thirty-three rounds Molyneaux collapsed, raising his hand and uttering the immortal line as he sank to the ground, "Me can fight no more." A second bout was held a year later before twenty-five thousand spectators. The American had Cribb in trouble from the outset until John Gulley, Cribb's second, lanced his fighter's closed eye. The Englishman went on to win in the eleventh round.

Molyneaux's "bottom" endeared him to the Fancy (although perhaps it was merely gratitude for his loss), and his fame was carried back to his homeland, thereby laying the foundations for a future boom in bare-knuckling. The first major prizefight on American soil was held in New York in 1816 between Jacob Hyer and Tom Beasley. Police pressure kept the sport to a low profile, however, and for the next thirty years bouts were largely confined to the back rooms of waterfront taverns. The pugilists were mostly sailors who had caught the prize-ring fever on voyages to England.

The turning point came in 1841 with the arrival of James Sullivan in San Francisco. Sullivan, a twenty-year veteran of the Australian penal colonies, immediately staked his claim to the American championship, a title which he held for a dozen years. Sullivan's popularity lent the sport an air of semilegitimacy, a legacy which was inherited by his successor, John Morrissey. After Morrissey had retired to a business fortune and, later, a successful career in New York politics, the title was assumed by John Camel Heenan.

Although the outcome of John Camel Heenan's abortive 1860 bout with Tom Sayers was bitterly disputed by the American Fancy, the match itself proved something of a blessing in disguise for them. The increased police activity in England which followed the bout served to drive many of Britain's best pugilists across the Atlantic to the more relaxed atmosphere of the United States, specifically to a small town on the Pennsylvania–West Virginia border called Collier's Station. Over the next two decades, what had once been an exclusive preserve of the British now became a wholly American pastime. This transition was sealed in 1882 with the emergence of another Sullivan, the magnificent John L., a ten-year champion with an invaluable flair for self-advertisement.

On winning the title from Paddy Ryan, Sullivan became the first of the idolized American heavyweights, much to the regret of *Leslie's* newspaper which wailed: "The worship of brute force has filled the boxing schools of New York. Let prize-fighters be once more regarded as outlaws, and not as public 'entertainers.' " Sullivan's appeal, however, was magnetic, and when he visited England in 1887, he, Buffalo Bill and the Prince of Wales all competed on equal terms for newspaper column inches. Sullivan even engineered an introduction to the prince (which mortified Queen Victoria, in the middle of celebrating her Jubilee), and ended up training at Windsor. After this coup, even the New York press were forced to grudgingly admit that Sullivan had something. "There is hardly a more disreputable ruffian now breathing than this same Sullivan," reported the *Tribune*, "but with all his brutality, his coarseness, and his vices, he certainly is not afraid of meeting any living man with his bare fists."

In fact Sullivan actually preferred fighting with gloves. But the American sporting public, fascinated by the bloody machismo of the London prize ring, was slow to accept Queensberry Rules, and it was on his bare fists, carefully coddled in a potent brew of turpentine and walnut juice, that Sullivan's fame was founded.* His greatest bout was in 1889 against Jake Kilrain, the last match to be fought under the rules of the London prize ring.

Sullivan lost the title in 1892 to James J. Corbett, who ushered in the era of glove fighting. But even in defeat, Sullivan remained the people's champion. When Teddy Roosevelt set out to slaughter African big game in 1909, it was Sullivan's gold-mounted rabbit's foot that he carried in his fob pocket for luck. "The boxing public generally are a bloodthirsty lot," wrote former British heavyweight champion Henry Cooper in his autobiography. "They like to see a good hard fight, and if there's plenty of gore and snot flying about they love it." Sullivan certainly gave them plenty of that, and they loved him for it. So, too, did the prize ring, and for close on two centuries they loved that, too.

---

* The former world heavyweight champion Joe Frazier, a boxer whose bludgeoning skills very definitely reflected their historic origins, was also fond of pickling his flesh. When training for a fight he soaked his head every day in a bucket of rock salt and water. "It makes me mean and toughens my skin," he explained.

Blood and Ketchup

Wrestling also made the crossing from England to the Americas, one of the few sports to be brought to the New World aboard the First Fleet. One early record of the first settlement mentions that at Plymouth in 1621 the founding fathers wrestled braves from the friendly Massasoit tribe as an exercise in strong-arm diplomacy. Under the influence of rugged, frontier living, wrestling in America grew progressively more ferocious, eventually outstripping even the wildmen of Lancashire. In his book *Five Years' Residence in the Canadas*, published in 1824, Edward Allen Talbot wrote that wrestling "in the modern style of *rough* and *tumble*" was sweeping the country, unchecked by either good sense or feeling:

> Instead of fighting, like men whose passions have gained momentary ascendancy over their reason – which would to all intents be bad enough – they attack each other with the ferociousness of bull-dogs, and seem in earnest only to disfigure each other's faces, and to glut their eyes with the sight of blood. . . . The principal object of the combatants appears to be the *calculation* of *eclipses*; or, in other words, their whole aim is bent on tearing out each other's eyes, in doing which they make the fore-finger of the right hand fast in their antagonist's hair, and with the thumb, as they term it, *gouge out the day-lights*. If they fail in this attempt, they depend entirely on their teeth for conquest; and a fraction of a nose, half an ear, or a piece of lip, is generally the trophy of the victor.

Gouging was even more popular further south. The Irish adventurer Thomas Ashe gave an account of a gouging match on the banks of the Ohio in his book *Travels in America, Performed in 1806*:

> The Virginian never lost his hold; fixing his claws in his hair and his thumbs on his eyes, gave them an instantaneous start from their sockets. The sufferer roared aloud, but offered no complaint. The Kentuckian not being able to disentangle his adversary from his face, adopted a new mode of warfare. He extended his arms around the Virginian, and hugged him into closer contact with his huge body. The latter, disliking this, made one further effort and fastening on the under lip of his mutilator tore it over the chin. The Kentuckian at length gave out, on which the people carried off the victor, and he preferring a triumph to a doctor . . . suffered himself to be chaired round the grounds as the first rough and tumbler.

Gouging was not the only style of wrestling to become popular in

America, merely the most vicious. (Although even in this it had its rivals, notably the shin-kicking and head-butting contests of Pennsylvania and North Carolina and the free-for-alls of Virginia which allowed fighters to grab each other's testicles.) As early as the mid-1700s the more refined had adopted several milder styles, and although true champions still based their reputations on the number of fatal bouts they had survived, soon large numbers of quite respectable people were learning to grapple. George Washington, at 18 a local champion of a style known as "collar and cuff," was the first of a whole series of wrestling presidents, among them Lincoln, Teddy Roosevelt, Taft and Coolidge.

The sport achieved added popularity during the Civil War when it became a favorite recreation of the Union troops. A decade later its position was further enhanced by a craze for Greco-Roman wrestling which was enjoying a renaissance on the Continent. The greatest home-grown exponent of Greco-Roman was William Muldoon, the "Father of American Wrestling," who fought dressed as a Roman gladiator half a century before professional wrestling had become synonymous with show business. Muldoon had learned his trade during the Civil War, afterwards perfecting it in tavern back rooms before audiences waiting to cheer on bare-knuckle prizefighters. He first reached national prominence in 1880 when, still a New York policeman, he wrestled Professor William Miller to a 9 hour 35 minute draw. This was followed by three classically brutal bouts, all ending in draws, against Clarence "Kansas Demon" Whistler, each bout split half and half between Greco-Roman and the more popular – and violent – catch-as-catch-can.

Professional wrestling of the period was rugged and bloody, a contest for iron men who could accept broken ribs and limbs, torn ears and open wounds as standard hazards of their chosen calling. Just how tough it was can be judged by Muldoon's laconic description of Whistler after their first bout: "In getting out of a neck lock I had fastened on him, Whistler partially tore off his left ear and the left side of his face was swollen to the size of a boxing glove. One of his fingers was also broken." Muldoon himself was in no great shape after the match; Whistler had used his head as a battering ram against the Roman Gladiator's chest until it was raw.

But for all his fighting prowess and ability to draw blood, Muldoon could not lift wrestling's popularity any higher than a very poor second to the prize ring. While occasional wrestlers could achieve a measure of fame and fortune through grappling, it was the prizefighters – and later the boxers – who dominated combat sports, a point brought home bitterly to Muldoon when he tackled John L. Sullivan in 1887 before a crowd of two thousand. As Muldoon slammed Sullivan to the canvas and gathered himself for the *coup de grace*, the audience surged forward and stopped the fight.

By the turn of the century wrestling had split into two distinct camps – amateur and professional. The amateurs were the young men who flocked to the college gymnasiums and sporting clubs of the big Eastern cities as part of the craze for physical fitness which had gripped the nation since the 1880s. Wrestling to them was wholly a recreation, a means of keeping fit and, to a lesser extent, of testing skill and strength. It was designed solely for participants, not for spectators. On the amateur mats the overt brutality and bloodshed which had long been the hallmark of the sport gradually withered away, paving the way for the bloodless bouts of college, amateur club and Olympic wrestling. Today's amateur bouts are hardly what the television commentators would describe as "crowd-pleasing"; slow and protracted, violent injury is almost nonexistent. Indeed, violent is not really a word which applies to amateur wrestling; a better word might perhaps be gymnastic – at least certainly in comparison to the professional sport. For professional wrestling, as any late night television addict is only too well aware, has followed a strikingly different path to that of its less well-known sibling.

According to social scientists Alan G. Ingham and Michael D. Smith in their report "The Social Implications of the Interaction between Spectators and Athletes" (1973), all spectator sports are faced with a fundamental dilemma: how to remain legitimate sports satisfying the needs of their participants, and yet, at the same time, be entertaining enough to entice the fans back week after week. Most of the more popular sports manage this more or less successfully, balancing the game against the spectacle – with the spectacle, if anything, taking second place. Professional wrestling, however, constantly overshadowed by the more popular prize ring, struggling for an audience and faced with the grim prospect of life forever on the box office breadline, resolved the dilemma and gambled its future by throwing the "game" out the window and plumping solidly for "entertainment." It was a simple enough transition; pro wrestling had always inclined heavily toward showmanship – to wit, Muldoon's gladiator outfits. When in 1912 Frank Gotch, the Iowa farmer who was the last of the great "legitimate" wrestlers, retired, the sport had already moved far into the realm of theater. Thereafter, whatever the wrestling scribes might say to the contrary, only very occasionally did individual wrestlers rise above the showbiz.

It was as a particular kind of theater – a theater of violence – that pro wrestling secured its future. Some denied it; ring historian Nat Fleischer, for instance, wrote in his 1936 study of wrestling *From Milo to Londos*:

We are a red-blooded race, a people who like thrills, but we are not blood thirsty. There is a limit, beyond which line we call a halt and that's why science, rather than brute strength, is the keynote to modern wrestling.

But by then wrestling had long since realized that what the crowds were flocking to see was not science but raw violence. The most popular style was

---

TRICKS OF THE TRADE

It is extraordinarily difficult for nonparticipants to gain admittance backstage at professional wrestling bouts. If one does manage to get backstage, the reasons immediately become obvious. For a start the relaxed, fraternal atmosphere of the dressing rooms is in direct contrast to the murderous atmosphere which surrounds the ring. In private, wrestlers happily share rooms, talk and joke with the same opponents who a few minutes before they were threatening with death and damnation. Pain also seems less of a feature than it does outside in the stadium. Injuries which cripple men in the ring necessitating their removal by stretcher are invariably far less severe back in the dressing room.

Even more exposed are the professional tricks which help fulfill the publicity, especially those which sustain the steady flow of blood in the American rings. According to one former wrestler I spoke to, bleeding on demand used to be achieved by breaking a small capsule of stage blood at an opportune moment. Later, when the audiences demanded more realism, real blood was actually drawn from the opponent – with his prior consent, of course – by nicking him with a sliver of razor blade palmed in the hand. Today the razorblade slivers have gone, the blood being produced by a nip with the teeth on the vulnerable anatomy – usually the forehead – of a "bleeder."

On a visit backstage in Los Angeles I came across one such fellow, a comparatively slight and not very impressive performer who had earlier stumbled from the ring, his face a mask of blood. Standing next to him, I saw that his forehead was scarred and mottled and looked like nothing but an old-fashioned corrugated washboard. Although he denied being a willing accomplice to having his blood spilt, he did say that his career was progressing splendidly.

"all-in" wrestling (known as "bear-cat" wrestling in Britain), a style with as few restrictions as the Greek *pankration*. What rules there were seemed made to be broken by a foul blow on the referee's blind side or a knuckle-duster concealed in the trunks. Soon even the referee himself became part of the act, a willing accomplice to the rule breaking, and what little of the game remained was further diminished.

Of course, wrestlers could not actually *kill* each other week after week; this was, after all, the twentieth century. However they did provide the next best thing for their gullible and uncritical audiences – the semblance of enraged, uncontrolled, no-holds-barred brutality. Whereas the manly ethics of boxing discouraged its contestants from displaying their pain and injury to the crowd, agonized grimaces, screams of suffering and howls of anguish became the stock in trade of the pro wrestling circuit. Prematch publicity was ripe with promises of impending bloodshed, all of which was dutifully engineered one way or the other.

Professional wrestling grew increasingly outrageous. The spectacle became a "passion play," as Stone and Oldenburg put it, in which carefully selected "good guys" battled evil in the shape of an endless stream of "bad guys." "Red Indians" fought "cowboys," "Nazis" fought "Jews," and "Koreans" attacked archetypal blue-eyed all-American heroes. Next came Tag Team matches which allowed four wrestlers to slug it out in the ring to the "despair" of the referee, followed by Battle Royals which filled the ring with a dozen contestants, the winner being the last man standing. Today the Stretcher Match is the big attraction: "No fouls, no time out for injuries, counts, stops or anything – the only way there will be a winner is when one man goes out on a stretcher!"

Just how much of the "game" remains in professional wrestling is a question as indeterminable as it is irritating for the wrestlers to whom it is monotonously directed. For their part, wrestlers are unanimous in their claim that, although the action may fall short of the grimaces and groans which resound from the ring, the sport is still a hard, painful and serious contest. In their defense they cite long lists of injuries.

George Kidd, Britain's former world lightweight champion:

> I have two cauliflower ears and I'm deaf in one of them. I've had broken ribs, a broken nose and have a torn tendon which made one calf permanently smaller than the other. Wrestling can kill a man. And has on two or three occasions. It's the constant pounding rather than the one bad fall that does the damage. Two wrestlers, well-known ones I remember, both died from kidney trouble brought on by the punishment they had taken over the years in the wrestling ring.

Les Kellett, an English wrestler for forty years:

What really hurts is when people say it doesn't hurt. I had one [injury] where the bone was split lengthwise from the knee to the elbow. I've had my ankle broken, and I was in hospital for four months with two operations to remove abcesses on my back caused by body slams and falls. [*He points to a cauliflower ear*] That was done with the elbow . . . I could cut the ear open now and it would be like a piece of black pudding. All congealed blood! When you go into the ring, you've just got to reconcile yourself to the fact that it's hurt or be hurt.

Brian Glover, a twenty-two-year veteran of the British ring, now better known for his acting and playwriting:

Injuries? Terrible! I can tell wrestlers a mile off. They can never bend their elbows high enough to comb their hair. I've had both cartilages done, but I've never had a broken bone yet. I've been fortunate. I saw a bloke in Newcastle with a compound fracture of his shin . . . the bone sticking out. Martinson died at Bellvue. Another fellow died in Sheffield . . . banging him on his head. A fellow throws you around the ring, a punter jumps up and throws a chair in the ring. Bang your bloody head and you're dead. A lot of bad backs. There's always "sugarbagging" going on to jerk the vertebrae. They always say the wrestlers' injuries are bad backs and piles. It's the banging.

Mike Moreno, another popular British veteran:

Take a good look at my face . . . I wasn't born in this condition. I've had fourteen or fifteen cuts across my eye and to show you how weak it is . . . [*He pinches his eyebrow together and it stays pinched, like a ball of putty.*] I've two very well-bent cauliflower ears as you can see . . . dislocations . . . wrenches. Everything hurts. There's nothing in this business that doesn't hurt. Let me give you a little for instance . . . [*He leans across and applies a small amount of pressure to a point at my elbow which numbs the forearm to the fingertips.*] We are pros – past masters at submission wrestling. Everything hurts.

British promoter Mike Judd said:

I wouldn't let my son go into it. I've seen some of the old wrestlers and the condition they're in, and I can't equate that with money. There *can't* be enough money. Bert Asserati was probably one of the greatest wrestlers ever, a fearsome man. Now he is a cripple – lives in Brighton, walks on two sticks, can only see out of one eye, joints all locked together. He's got everything wrong with him you could possibly imagine. Can't be worth it, can it?

"Professor" Tanaka, a Japanese star on the American pro wrestling circuit:

> When people say wrestling fake, I tell 'em, "My friend, I tell you what. You go into ring and make eighty thousand dollars a year fake! Go! I see how long you stay inside ring. If wrestling fake," I say, "what all these scars I get? What all these hospital bills?" My hospital bill big, believe me!

Given this litany of verbal and visual ills, it is difficult to dispute that the blood on the canvas is not all just ketchup. According to Brian Glover pro bouts are rigged but only in the sense that the top wrestlers only face the men they know they are certain to beat: "So the stars never lose, they never fight the men who can beat them." According to others close to the sport, however, rigging extends further than that. As Dr. J. G. P. Williams of the Farnham Park Rehabilitation Center near London, an institution which specializes in sports injury, told me:

> Injuries are very rare. These chaps don't hurt each other except by accident. They couldn't do the things they do if they were wrestling seriously. In fact, I've had patients who have been wrestlers and I've helped them plan for their next fight to keep the strain off the particular injured part: "Now it's your turn to throw me . . ." It's all done by that.

It is difficult to determine how seriously fans take their sport. Most spectators I spoke to believed in the genuineness of the assaults. Others said that they knew all along that it was a fraud. And for some at least, it is a bit of both. Stone and Oldenburg reported hearing a lone beer drinker once scream, "I don't give a damn if it is fake! Kill the son-of-a-bitch!" But however the fans choose to view the spectacle, it does not stop them from coming. Today, as it has been for decades, wrestling violence is big sporting business.

Although spectator statistics are hard to come by, pro wrestling is clearly one of the few major international sporting attractions. A 1972 survey by Triangle Publications estimated that in the United States alone, $5\frac{1}{2}$ million viewers tuned in to pro wrestling. Top stars like André the Giant are today reputed to make around a quarter of a million dollars at the sport each year, with lesser figures such as Butcher Vachon earning close on $80,000 in a good year. Wrestlers regularly perform six and seven times a week all year round and are still forced to turn engagements down. In Britain Mike Judd's Dale Martin organization stages a thousand promotions a year before crowds averaging around two thousand people. In Japan Antonio Inoki – a "Samurai warrior" (as his press agent would have the world believe), who plunges his fist down the throats of live pigs and rips out their hearts – is a national idol confident enough of his drawing power to pay Muhammad Ali several million dollars for a match. From Australia to Spain the wrestling fans are there.

What these fans pay to see is violence – either real or imagined – and the more violence, the better the show. In the candid words of Miz. Lillian, mother of President Jimmy Carter and a staunch pro wrestling fan, "The more brutal it is, the better I like it." "We as promoters prefer to put on nice clean wrestling matches," Mike Judd told me, "and sometimes we kid ourselves they come to see those nice clean wrestling matches. But I doubt it. It's like going to watch the man who jumps over the buses on a motorbike. They don't really come to watch him jump over the buses, they go to see him hit the last two buses and land in a terrible mess."

Like many other violent sports, pro wrestling suffers an increasing amount of crowd trouble. More often than not it is the women to blame.

Mike Judd:

It's getting worse, no question about it. People are becoming more violent. It's harder to control people now than it was ten years ago. I evicted a woman last night for attacking one of the wrestlers as he was leaving, completely without any purpose Raining blows on him she was, not that she hurt him. It's rare, but it is becoming more frequent.

In a brief career lasting, so far, less than a year, Magnificent Maurice, a British successor to America's late lamé-clad sensation Gorgeous George, has already been stabbed in the ring. "If I go in with a nice lad," he said, "the women want to kill me, want to hurt me." Other British wrestlers complained of chairs being hurled at them, being hit with everything from bottles to umbrellas, and having cigarettes stubbed out on their flesh. Crowd violence has become so bad on the Continent – especially in Spain – that several wrestlers have taken to wearing leather helmets in the ring.

The fans are even more demonstrative on the American circuit, where wrestlers have to break through a gesticulating mob whenever they leave the ring.

Professor Tanaka:

I been hit with whisky bottle, beer bottle, beer can, chair, stool, food, big bricks, knife . . . you name it, I been hit hard. People are very violent. Home town team lose, hometown people chase referee out of ring.

LADIES' NIGHT

Miz. Lillian is not the only mother harboring a deep-seated love of pro wrestling. Apparently the popular image of the wrestling audience as being packed with little old ladies knitting furiously while the heads roll is more than just an image. In his book *The Hidden Persuaders*, Vance Packard cited a Neilsen rating which determined that female wrestling fans outnumbered their male counterparts two to one. While Queen Elizabeth is reportedly an ardent viewer of televised pro bouts, studies have confirmed that the greatest concentration of fans is comprised of older, lower status women. Why women have adopted pro wrestling as *their* contact sport – to the virtual exclusion of all others – is difficult to say. Most of the wrestlers I interviewed attributed the female presence to straight sex appeal, and certainly the sexual aspects of the sport, heightened as they are by the blatant posturings of many of the participants, cannot be ignored. (One psychologist has gone so far as to postulate that female fans experience "vicarious gratification from the pain inflicted by one [male] wrestler upon another in the sexually suggestive position.")

Sex, however, does not explain the popularity of female wrestlers among female fans. Pro wrestling is one of the few heavy contact sports in which women can become stars – albeit less brilliant stars than men. Although they were undoubtedly introduced to whet the lascivious lips of the male spectators, it was not long before they became considerably more than just sex objects for the men. As one British promoter explained after being censured for televising an all-female bout: "It was the women who asked. They said, 'When are we going to have women wrestlers like in America?'"

Perhaps the real reason for pro wrestling's popularity with women is rather more simple. Dismissed as harmless theater by males, until only recently it afforded females the only acceptable opportunity for viewing violence. Whereas a husband could laughingly shrug off his wife's obsession with two grown men growling and mincing around a ring, he would have been sorely perplexed had she enthused over gridiron or hunting or even boxing (the first female spectators were not admitted to a boxing match until 1919). That was man's stuff.

The violence includes even the women wrestlers. The heroine of American wrestling, Fabulous Moolah, recalled being knifed after a bout in Oklahoma City:

> I was wrestling a full-blooded Indian girl named Celia Blevins, and after I beat her and I was walkin' toward the dressing room, this big Indian guy – he was the biggest man I'd ever seen – come at me with a knife. I started backin' up, and then he took a swipe at me, cut me right here on the shoulder before the crowd closed around him and I got away. Sumthin' like that kinda scares you. You wonder.

"Wrestling feeds on the hatreds of the spectators to fuel the fighting in the ring," wrote American journalist Mike Roberts in his 1976 book *Fans! How We Go Crazy over Sports.* "It took decades of synthesizing hatred before pro wrestling finally got what it bargained for." What Roberts was referring to was an incident which occurred in January 1975. A ringside fan, believing his hero was about to be unjustly beaten by the villain, whipped out a pistol and fired off two shots, wounding five spectators. Police subsequently discovered that all those injured were seated on trajectories between the gunman and the referee. Wrote Roberts: "Witnesses told a reporter they had talked wrestling all evening with the man; he was a real aficionado." That night at least no one was in any doubt about the genuineness of the blood being splashed about at ringside.

The Sweet Science

The beginning of the twentieth century marked a renaissance in pugilism. With the advent of gloves, the ring soon found itself blessed by an unaccustomed air of acceptability. The sporting public, caught up by the mania for muscular development, suddenly decided that a sport which had been base and ignoble when practiced with bare fists, was somehow transformed by gloves into an instrument of virtue. "Boxing is not degrading," declared the Belgian poet Maeterlinck. "It is the discipline of violence. Combative instincts are an integral part of our nature. They who lack them, lack mental energy." Across the Atlantic, Teddy Roosevelt assailed boxing's dwindling number of detractors with similar theories of fitness and manhood. "The boy that won't fight is not worth his salt," thundered Teddy, declaring that he was of two minds whom to beat the hardest, the son who was cruel or the son who backed away from a fight. Roosevelt's fellow legislators were in total agreement, and state after state legalized the ten-round bout.

In fact, the ring's transition from bare-knuckling to boxing was, in practical effect, only a slight move forward. True, boxers now padded their fists with cowhide, but in many instances it would perhaps have been safer if they hadn't. Gloves weighed only four ounces – half the weight of those used today – and they were "loaded" with heavy insulation tape which was bound around each fighters' fists before every bout. Gunboat Smith, the first of boxing's White Hopes, once recalled tearing an opponent's ear clean off with a loaded four-ouncer. Less law-abiding pugilists doctored their gloves with studs or pins, and gouging with the thumb at the eyes remained a hazard of the profession.

There was still no time limit set on fights, and bouts continued to run for hours. Indeed, the longest fight ever recorded took place between Andy Bowen and Jack Burke at the beginning of the gloved era, on April 6, 1893, in New Orleans. It ran 7 hours and 19 minutes and 110 rounds, and when it ended, eyewitnesses reported that the faces of both fighters looked "like hamburger." Referees were loath to halt matches; the only winner was the man who actually knocked out his opponent, and as a result injuries were frequent and severe. Jack Dempsey, for example, won the world heavy-weight title and earned himself the nickname "Man Killer" by flooring Jess Willard seven times in three rounds. Willard was helped from the ring, his face almost shapeless, his jaw broken and several of his ribs cracked, the victim, so it was later rumored, of gloves filled with plaster of Paris. Damon Runyon was at ringside to report the slaughter:

> The right side of Willard's face was a pulp. The right eye of the fallen champion was completely hidden behind that bloody smear. His left eye peered over a lump of flesh in grotesque fashion. The great body of the giant was splotched with red patches. They were the aftermath of Dempsey's gloves thumping there and giving back a hollow sound as they thumped. At the feet of the gargantuan pugilist was a dark spot which was slowly widening on the brown canvas as it was replenished by the drip, drip, drip of blood from the man's wounds. He was flecked with blood from head to foot.

Other fighters lost eyes, their hearing and their minds. Some, inevitably, lost their lives: Walter Croot died the day after a bruising fight with Jimmy Barry in 1897; Luther McCarty, another White Hope, died a few minutes into a bout with Arthur Pelky (he had entered the ring with a broken collar-bone); Frankie Jerome was battered for twelve rounds by Bud Taylor in 1924 and died later in a hospital. And these were well-known boxers; how many minor fighters' deaths went unrecorded is impossible even to guess at. "Every fight in there was a fight," recalled Charley Phil Rosenberg, world bantamweight champion of 1925. "It wasn't one of them dances or waltzes or anything."

Throughout the early 1900s boxing's stocks continued to soar. The enthusiasm of the amateurs in their gymnasiums and sporting clubs spilled over to include the professional circuit as well. Increased newspaper coverage brought the sport to an ever-widening audience; at important bouts the crowd would be studded with wealthy bankers, leading businessmen and movie stars – "lots of the Upper House; the Lower House, and the *flash house*," as Pierce Egan would have put it. There was even talk of allowing women to attend, although not without considerable opposition from the sporting press. "I know from observation that a fight arouses certain cruel instincts which we prefer to regard as nonexistent in the fairer sex," growled one writer in a statement which revealed as much about fight crowds in general as about early twentieth-century chauvinism. "It is not nice to see a woman's eagerness for the destruction of a fighter or to find her reveling in a fierce exchange of blows and indifferent to the sight of blood." As it happened, women were not destined to make much impact on boxing's gate receipts. Not that that would have concerned many early promoters; by the 1920s there were more than enough men fighting to fill the arenas.

On July 2, 1921, the mercurial George L. Rickard staged a bout between the young Jack Dempsey and France's handsome heartthrob, Georges Carpentier, the Orchid Kid. On that night a sell-out audience of eighty thousand, including the cream of East Coast society, watched as Dempsey took the Frenchman apart in a field outside Jersey City known as Boyle's Thirty Acres. It was the first "Battle of the Century" and, more importantly for boxing's future, the first million-dollar gate. It also marked the beginning of what is now regarded as boxing's Golden Age.

For the next three decades boxing enthralled America. For those who could fight their way out of the tough urban ghettos – a struggle made even tougher by the depression of the '30s – there was a chance for fame and, if a man managed to avoid the thieves and ring sharks, fortune as well. In addition to Dempsey, a flock of fighters became household names across the nation – Gene Tunney, Jack Sharkey, James J. Braddock and, greatest of all, Joe Louis. With such attractive and celebrated personalities sharing the limelight, America – and the world – grew comfortable about boxing.

But success only came after a long and painful education in blood and bruises. Behind the title Golden Age and its million-dollar gates, prewar boxing remained as squalid and brutal as ever. For every Jack Dempsey there were thousands of Jack Powells who could recall finishing one bout and then being called back into the ring to fight another bout later that same night. Boxers fought four and five times in a week, starting out at age 12 or 13 as dollar-a-head sluggers in blindfolded Battle Royals. At the end of their career, many could boast upwards of five hundred fights.

The bouts remained vicious and brutal, acknowledging little to either science or progress. Heads and thumbs were still considered tools of the trade, and the referee remained very much the third man. Champions returned home after a match, passed blood and rested up in a hospital until the next match. The rest selected an alias, crossed the state line and fought again a day or so later. Reports from the era would have done justice to the pen of Pierce Egan.

Nat Fleischer:

Battered and bruised, lips badly cut, a severed artery bringing forth the claret in spurts, face cut into crimson ribbons, one eye closed and the other puffed, but game to the very last, Braddock lay unconscious on the rosin-covered canvas. . . .

The memories of boxers who fought through the period, as recorded by Peter Heller in his excellent 1973 collection *In This Corner!*, are equally as graphic.

Tommy Loughran, light heavyweight champion from 1927 to 1929:

I couldn't see anything, my eyes were filled with blood, and he threw a right hand at me and I put my head to the side and as I did my eyes began to roll. The blood in there acted like a lubricant and I couldn't raise my eyes, if I put my head this way they'd roll that way. I couldn't control my eyes. The only thing to do is move in close . . . it was a championship fight and they wouldn't stop it.

Fritzie Zivic, welterweight champion of 1940:

After about five rounds I got mad and started to hit him low, choke him, foul him, and everything else. The referee in the sixth round stopped the fight, looked at Armstrong, looked at me, and said, "If you guys want to fight like this it's OK with me." That's all I wanted to hear. I pulled my trunks up and went to work on him. I busted him up, cut him here and cut him there. I'd get him in a clinch. He'd have his head down trying to give you that head, I'd come up on the other side. When the eye was cut, I'd rub it with the laces to open it up a little more. Then he's watching this cut and I'd cut [his other] eye. His mouth was cut real bad. He was too proud to spit the blood out. He swallowed it. Swallowing the blood made him sick. . . . [The public] put a label on me as a dirty fighter, but I never lost a fight on a foul in my life. I'd give 'em the head, choke 'em, hit 'em in the balls, but never in my life used my thumb because I wanted no one to use it on me. But they accused me of that. I used to bang 'em pretty good. You're fighting, you're not playing the piano, you know.

**❝ To listen to the noise and to watch the faces of the specta-
tors at a heavyweight championship bout is to observe
human beings at their worst – uncontrolled, and indulging
in an orgy of cruelty. Of course the spectator always claims
that he is only interested in technique, and this may be true
of a few. . . . The fact is that a pleasurable feeling is induced
by the sight of one man beating another into insensibility,
and this primitive emotion, which in civilized people should
be disciplined, is fostered by those responsible for staging
these bouts.** ❞

**Baroness Summerskill, English MP, in *The Ignoble Art* (1956), published at
the height of her crusade against boxing**

Billy Conn, light heavyweight champion, 1939–40:

I hit him in the balls and knocked his ass through the ropes in the
thirteenth round. You're supposed to do anything you can to win,
see? You're not an altar boy in there. Hit 'em on the break, backhand,
do all the rotten stuff to 'em. What are they going to shoot you for it?

"I fought for twenty years," welterweight champion Jimmy McLarnin
told Heller, ". . . boxing's a very hazardous business and anybody that
goes into that for fun has got to be out of their entire cotton pickin' minds,
because it's a rough, rough business."

By the 1950s a large section of the general public had come to agree with
McLarnin. After the boxing boom which immediately followed the war
had run its course, it became apparent that what had been blithely accepted
during the '30s and '40s was no longer permissible. Critics of the sport,
who still saw the shadow of the Colosseum hanging over the ring, grew
increasingly vocal, demanding reforms and in some cases abolition. In
1948 boxing writer Jimmy Cannon rounded on the sport in an article published in *Esquire* magazine. "It is a filthy enterprise," Cannon wrote, "and
if you stay in it long enough your mind will become a concert hall where
Chinese music never stops playing. Old fighters who do not go insane are
considered fortunate and those who leave the ring with breakfast money are
exceptional. . . ." In Britain, Baroness Summerskill, a Member of Parliament, drew widespread support for her attacks on a pastime whose primary
object was "to render a man unconscious as fast as possible" and that could
leave men such as welterweight contender Art Doyle dead on the canvas.
In 1954 Belgium banned boxing because of the injuries it caused and the

"degrading spectacle" it presented. A year later Paul Gallico, the sports-writer responsible for the famous Golden Gloves amateur tournament, also disowned the sport:

> The object of the game is to destroy the opponent by beating him and rendering him helpless. It would be less cruel if a knife or a gun were employed because one shot or one cunning slash or stab would do the trick. Beating a man into insensibility with a padded fist takes time. The first rule of the sport is to weaken the opponent by belaboring him in painful and vulnerable spots such as the kidneys, the stomach, the solar plexus and the heart, as well as the head. If a cut or abrasion appears upon the face this must be enlarged. A broken nose is to be hammered, a torn ear further lacerated.

Opposition to boxing reached a crescendo following the death of Benny "Kid" Paret at the hands of Emile Griffiths on March 24, 1962. Griffiths, incensed by a prematch jibe, had smashed more than twenty consecutive blows into Paret's head as he slumped senseless against the ropes before the referee stopped the match. The only thing Griffiths could remember about the fight was his instructions to "keep punching" if he hurt his man. After the Paret tragedy there followed a series of ring deaths which had several states seriously considering the abolition of boxing. In September of that year, Alejandro Lavorante was battered into a coma; six months later he was still unconscious. A year after Paret's death almost to the day, featherweight champion Davey Moore was relentlessly beaten by Sugar Ramos and died in a hospital bed seventy-five hours later. One week later three more boxers were killed in the ring – two in Australia and one in Pennsylvania – and six months after that, Ernie Knox died following a fight near Baltimore. Even the Pope was moved to call for boxing's abolition. However, the custodians of the sport managed to duck the attacks and boxing, after some hasty rule revisions, remained legal.

Today, as the sport's officials would have it, boxing has long outgrown the horrors of the '30s and '40s. They claim that stringent medical examina-

❝ The moment has come that boxing should no longer be officially encouraged, but generally prohibited. A way of acting that in everyday life is punished by prison, hard labor, and even death, is rewarded in boxing with publicity, gold medals and money. ❞

Dr. E. Jokl, German neurologist, 1962

tions, stricter control of bouts by referees and longer breaks between fights have combined to produce a marked decline in ring deaths. According to *Boxing Illustrated*, worldwide ring fatalities – around five hundred since 1900 – have dropped from a 1953 high of twenty-one to a 1973 low of three. The British Boxing Board of Control, universally recognized as the sport's strictest controlling body, admits to only eight ring deaths in Britain in the past thirty years. Although accurate overall casualty figures are as impossible to obtain for boxing as for most other contact sports, it would appear that there is now considerably more chance of witnessing a death or a serious injury on a football field than in a boxing ring. Lacerations have become less apparent and the cauliflower ear, once the stigmata of the profession, is now all but unknown among younger boxers. "We aim to see boys leave the sport in exactly the same condition as when they entered it," said Dr. Adrian Whiteson, the British Board's medical advisor.

Other countries are considerably less safe for boxers than Britain. In America it is still possible for a boxer to fight one night, move across a state line and fight again the next night; it is still possible to produce a bout that will leave a Chuck Wepner with 120 stitches in his face after facing a Sonny Liston. In Australia, now notorious among British boxers, the game is still firmly in the hands of the promoters who control the match, the venue and the referee. Premature stoppages are a rarity in Australian rings. Injuries, however, are not. In one sixteen-month period dating from late 1970, two top Australian boxers died after hard bouts (for one it was his fourth professional fight in as many weeks), and two others were reduced to mental cripples. More recently a 22-year-old American, Chuck Wilburn, suffered a brain hemorrhage following a barrage of punches during a bout in Australia and later died. "The Australian sport," wrote journalist Fred Dartnell in the 1920s, "likes his boxing to be highly flavored with plenty of good red blood and pepper in it, so to speak." That would still appear to hold true.

Among the most recent ring tragedies was the death of Italian middleweight Angelo Jacopucci in late July 1978, which occurred just as I was putting the finishing touches on the typescript of the final chapter. Jacopucci suffered a cerebral hemorrhage following a prolonged battering received at the hands of England's Alan Minter. He underwent a three-hour emergency operation and was put on life support machines, but two days later he was declared clinically dead. There had been strenuous criticism of Jacopucci's being pitted against Minter prior to the bout, especially after the Italian had developed physical problems following several earlier fights. However, the Italian boxing board let the match go ahead as planned. What was even more disturbing was that this was one of boxing's prestige bouts – a European title fight – and supposedly subject to infallible controls. In that same week a Spanish boxer, Salvador Pons, was beaten into a coma during a fight in Spain. He lasted six days before hospital officials pronounced him dead.

Lax and corrupt management is one thing; however, it is extremely doubtful whether boxing can live up to Dr. Whiteson's admirable intention and leave its participants in the same condition at the end of their careers as at the beginning, even given perfect supervision. Neurologists especially have reservations. It took many decades for the boxing world to accept that smashing a fist into another man's head could cause permanent brain damage, although evidence of such damage has abounded since the earliest days of the London prize ring. Ring historian John Ford considers that many bare-knucklers suffered brain damage to some degree: ". . . one thinks of such men as Jack Scroggins and Caleb Baldwin as likely subjects for this diagnosis." In *Claret and Cross-Buttock* (1976) Joe Robinson gave a description of his great great uncle Johnny Robinson, British lightweight champion of 1884, which would be immediately familiar to any medical investigator concerned with the effects of boxing:

> He looked dazed and he was always whisperin' silly things to himself. Havin' daft dreams that scared him. God made him to be champion of the world, but by the time he was thirty-five, he was nowt but a dirty, drunken tramp.

It was not until 1928 that the possibility of a link between boxing and the mental wrecks who shuffled around boxing gymnasiums was first postulated. In that year H. S. Martland examined five former boxers and coined the phrase "punch-drunk" to describe what he had seen. Since then a steady flow of medical evidence has pointed to the existence of an identifiable neurological syndrome – variously labeled dementia pugilistica, traumatic encephalopathy and psychopathic deterioration – developed by boxers.

Some fighters had long recognized many of their colleagues as being "punchy," "slap happy" or "goofy." Some even noticed disturbing changes in their own behavior – prolonged periods of grogginess, double vision and amnesia. The most famous case was that of Gene Tunney. Hit on the temple during training, he continued to spar, knocking out one opponent and boxing three rounds with another, and next morning awoke with a totally blank memory. Tunney later wrote in his autobiography:

> As I lay in this state of returning consciousness, I became greatly frightened. Gradually my name came to me. That I was a pugilist soon followed, then the thought of being a champion – impossible, un-

believable. I must have had a long dream. Gradually the realization came that I had not been dreaming. I rose and asked guarded questions. I wanted to know all about the events of the day before. For three days I could not remember the names of my most intimate acquaintances. I had to stop training. I did not leave my cabin except to eat or take a short walk. On these occasions all seemed queer. I was unable to orientate myself. The sensation I had was as though hot water had been poured through a hole in my skull and flowed slowly over my brain to my eyes, leaving a hot film. . . . The first seed of retirement was sown then. The possibility of becoming punch-drunk haunted me for weeks.

Despite such evidence, many of those connected with the sport remained unconvinced. "The so-called punch-drunk syndrome has become symbolic of brain injury," wrote a contributor to the 1959 *American Journal of Surgery*. "It has never been proved to be a neurological syndrome peculiar to boxers and produced by boxing. It has, unfortunately, become a slick medical cliché with which to label any boxer whose performance and behavior in or out of the ring is unsatisfactory or abnormal." As recently as 1974, one former heavyweight champion felt compelled to tell me in all sincerity that punch-drunkenness was nothing more than myth, and doubtless there are others who still share this view. However, within the last decade or so the realities of punch-drunkenness have been placed beyond dispute.

In 1969 Dr. A. H. Roberts, senior registrar at the London Hospital's Department of Neurology, set out to examine the prevalence of punch-drunkenness in former boxers. Selecting at random the names of 250 former boxers from the 1929–1955 records of the British Boxing Board of Control, he managed to trace and test 224. Of these, thirty-seven showed signs of traumatic encephalopathy – 17 percent of the group. Of this 17 percent, a third were either moderately or severely affected. "The study has shown the relationship to occupational exposure of an easily recognizable and relatively stereotyped syndrome of disturbed neurological function," Roberts concluded. He added that there were possibly six or seven hundred former British boxers currently suffering the same affliction. Two years later J. Jedlinski of Poland found that of the sixty *amateur* boxers he examined, half displayed neurological abnormalities, five of whom eventually required hospitalization.

In 1973 a leading London neurologist, Professor J. A. N. Corsellis, examined the brains of fifteen deceased former boxers – twelve professionals (including two world champions) and three amateurs – who had displayed signs of punch-drunkenness during their lifetimes. What Corsellis was seeking to determine was whether or not brain damage was actually visible. In the majority of cases he discovered unique and sometimes widespread structural damage which he concluded could only have been caused by boxing. Some of this damage, he decided, was the result of scarring from direct blows. However, much more was caused by an unidentifiable degenerative process which attacked the nerve cells and which he could only attribute to the constant battering undergone by the boxers. In light of this it would appear that it is not the isolated knock-out punch with its danger of brain hemorrhage which is the boxer's worst enemy, but the steady dosage of violent punishment that is not only inherent in the sport but acceptable to its custodians.

Boxing's defenders argue that, as with ring deaths, punch-drunkenness has been all but eliminated through the introduction of stricter safety measures. And indeed, as Roberts reported, there would appear to have been a marked decrease in its incidence since the days when boxers suffered enormous amounts of weekly punishment during the course of hundreds of fights – sometimes as many as seven and eight hundred in a career. "I don't think in twenty years' time we are going to get the same neurological problems that we are getting today from the prewar period," said Dr. Whiteson, and that may well be the case. However, according to Prof. Corsellis, by the time a fighter has had even as few as 150 bouts, "he is really, I think, very likely to have suffered brain damage." He would, he told me, strongly discourage any son of his from taking up the sport. "There is an appreciable risk even today, although it's almost certainly less than it used to be. If you see the human brain it is soft tissue . . . imagine it as a sort of jelly inside the skull. It is a bit of a nonsense, actually, to bash it around. Just on common-sense ground I would strongly advise any relative, or anybody actually, not to box."

There is support for Professor Corsellis's reservations about boxing. In 1974 he asked 169 British neurologists if they had ever encountered sportsmen suffering from suspected brain damage. The replies showed 290 suspected cases attributed to boxing; the next highest incidence was in horse riding – 12. All of the suspected boxing cases may have been hangovers from the seven-hundred-fights-a-career era, but maybe not. In that same year P. Harvey and J. Davis described the punch-drunk syndrome in a 25-year-old fighter whose ring career had begun in 1962. He had had seventy-two amateur bouts and sixteen professional bouts when symptoms developed – slurred speech, shuffling gait, aggression, acute depression and paranoia. Eventually he was admitted to a psychiatric unit. In 1977 British heavyweight champion Joe Bugner announced his retirement from the ring. He was, then, at the peak of his career, receiving offers to fight the world's leading heavyweights for purses ranging from £150,000 to £300,000. He was retiring, he said, simply because he feared for his future health:

> After ten years in a tough business, I still have my marbles. I believe I'm going to make it as an actor, and to tell you the truth, I want no bloody part of boxing. If you go for fifteen or twenty years you're not going to be sane, and if you're not sane you can't spend the money. Other people will spend it for you.

The Last of the Gladiators, Baby

Whatever the efficacy of the ring's new and improved safety nets, boxing is still, in the words of former light-heavyweight champion Willie Pastrano, "the last of the gladiator sports, baby." The game is as it has always been, a contest in which two men climb into a restricted area and try to ensure that only one climbs out. The object of the game is still to purposely knock an opponent senseless. Its side products are the cut eye, the broken nose, the cracked rib, the blood in the urine, the detached retina. Its *pièce de résistance* is the punch which accelerates at sixty times the force of gravity to land at a speed of 30 mph with full body weight behind it. It is, in effect, still man-to-man warfare.

Joe Frazier, former heavyweight champion of the world, a fighter who studied the Book of Judges before each bout because it put him in mind of war:

> In the ring it's me and you, baby, and I'm gonna be sure it's you. There's a man out there trying to take what you got. You're supposed to destroy him. He's trying to do the same thing to you.

John Conteh, former light-heavyweight champion of the world:

> By the time I reach the last couple of weeks, when I'm coming to my peak, I start to get really mean and edgy, and I build up this burning hatred for my opponent. Because he's trying to destroy me, isn't he?

❝ I could throw a nice little left hook to the liver. I've had guys literally scream out at that. They used to go down paralyzed. I've won a good many fights that way. ❞

Henry Cooper, former British and European
heavyweight champion, 1972

> **I don't want to knock him out. I want to hit him, step away and watch him hurt. I want his heart.** **"**
>
> **Joe Frazier, former world heavyweight champion, 1975**

He's going into that ring for one reason only, to hurt me, smash me, stop me from breathing. You can't expect me to send him hugs and kisses. Maybe I sound hard, but this is what the fight game's like – kill or be killed.

"Science," for all Ali's fancy shuffling, still runs a poor second to brute violence.

Which is how the fans prefer it. With the exception of Muhammad Ali, it is still the slugger who draws the crowds, fighters like lightweight champion Roberto Duran who can put his opponents out for eighty minutes and into a hospital bed for five days with concussion, as he did against Ray Lampkin in 1975. And if the slugger happens to be a heavyweight, he is worth his weight in ticket stubs. "There's usually a bit more blood about," explained British promoter Beryl Gibbons, "a bit heavier punching." Blood – "gore and snot," as former British heavyweight Henry Cooper put it – is what the fans want to see, either side of the Atlantic. "The people that come to Steelworkers don't want no gimmicks," said Eli Hanover, Baltimore boxing promoter. "They don't want no free T shirts. They don't want no free boxing gloves. They want to see blood, that's what they want to see – blood. As long as it isn't theirs." "Which is why so many people are irate in this country," said Dr. Whiteson. "When people go to boxing it does, to a certain extent, bring out the animal instincts and they, I suppose, want to see far more of a show than we are prepared to give them." Like the gentlemen of the Regency, and the solid citizens of Rome before them, we too have grown comfortable with the ring's bloodshed.

In his 1948 boxing classic *The Harder They Fall*, author Budd Schulberg had his protagonist sum up fight crowds with these words:

Every heavyweight fight is a simulated death struggle. Those fans who rise up in primeval blood lust and beg their favorite to "Killim! Killim!" may be more in earnest than they know. Death in the ring is not an everyday occurrence, not every month or even every year. But it always adds a titillating sense of danger and drama to all the matches that follow. For the sadism and cruelty of the Roman circus audience still peers out through eyes of the modern fight crowd. There is not only the conscious wish to see one man smash another into insensibility, but the subconscious, retrogressive urge to witness violent tragedy, even while the rational mind of the spectator turns away from excessive brutality.

Coming from such a confirmed fight fan as Schulberg, this judgment seems surprisingly harsh. Yet it is the viewpoint that Mando Muniz repeated to me early in 1977 a few days after losing his welterweight title bid in a hard, brawling bout against Carlos Palomino:

Back in Roman times, the gladiators – it wasn't so much a sport perhaps, but an exhibition of violence – they filled the arena and made the people go wild. I *think* it's the same urge with boxing. It's something innate in us. We can't change it. Now, I don't think anyone will tell you, "Sure I go to a fight because I just *love* to see somebody get knocked out!" And yet, in a fight, in a big fight, somebody goes down and the whole arena goes wild. Same thing with car racing – car turns over and we all stand up. Perhaps it's bad for people to be that way, but unfortunately we are just that way. There's an accident on the street – somebody gets splattered on the corner somehow or other. Everybody from this block and around are going to come over here. They hate it. But they're looking at it, they're looking at the blood and the guts and everything. You can't explain that. You ask them, "You like that?" "Oh my God, I *hate* that! Jeez!" "Why are you looking at it?" "Oh, curiosity . . ." I think there's just a deep down thing in us that we have to see this stuff. It's fantastic for me because I make my living out of boxing.

Fight fans, however, are often not content with merely watching. Since the days of the Regency, boxing has been plagued by riots at the ringside. Much of the trouble stems from the sport's unavoidably personal method of picking its winners. Even more has come from the blatant racial overtones which have long been a feature of prizefighting. The most memorable crowd battle was fought in Reno, Nevada, on July 4, 1910 after White Hope Jim Jeffries had gone down to the notorious Jack Johnson, the first black heavyweight champion. Although all spectators were searched for guns, the authorities were not prepared for the riots that erupted elsewhere in the US when Jeffries slumped to the canvas in the fifteenth round. In West Virginia a crowd of blacks held the town of Keystone for twenty-four hours. In Uvaldia, Georgia, three blacks were killed in a gun battle, and in Muskagee, Oklahoma, another two were attacked by a knife-wielding white claiming to be John L. Sullivan's second cousin. A detachment of marines was called out to restore order in Norfolk, Virginia, and there were reports of rioting from Arkansas, Colorado, Maryland, Mississippi, Missouri, Ohio and Pennsylvania. When the trouble finally petered out, the total stood at 19 dead, 251 injured and 5,000 arrested.

Throughout the '20s New York bouts regularly developed into riots, with chairs broken up and used as missiles and referees forced into hiding. "It is a violent primitive bias," wrote a happily shocked Fred Dartnell, "and your English spectator accustomed to the comparatively decorous progress of a match at home, would be amazed at the extraordinary manifestations which are common at boxing bouts." When Joe Louis fought Mussolini's hope, Primo Carnera, in 1935, 1,300 police ringed Yankee Stadium while 300 plainclothesmen mingled with the crowd. Wrote black sociologist E. Franklin Frazier: "Joe Louis enables many lower class youths to inflict vicariously the aggression which they would like to carry out against whites for the discrimination and insults they have suffered." Ten years later a brick-throwing mob in Mexico City took back American Ike Williams's newly won title belt at gunpoint.

Little has changed today. The ethnic crowds who wrecked the old Madison Square Garden with such monotonous regularity that the weekly boxing card was canceled – on one occasion things got so out of hand that the stadium organ was pushed through a retaining wall – now smash up seats and tear toilets from the walls in the Felt Forum. "I've got a great fight," matchmaker Teddy Brenner was once reported as saying, "Frankie Benitez of Puerto Rico against Villomar Fernandez of the Dominican Republic. But I don't care to put it on. It's too explosive." In Los Angeles, the current commercial "home" of US boxing, it is the Mexican-American fans who hurl the bottles in the ring and brawl in the aisles. On the black/white front, Muhammad Ali, the Jack Johnson of the 1960s, can – or at least *could* – work his followers into a frenzy with talk of jihads and holy wars; men have been killed defending or reviling his name. In Kuala Lumpur when Ali fought Joe Bugner, local newspapers refused to publish many of his remarks for fear they would lead to a resurgence of the bloody rioting between Malaysia's Moslem and Chinese populations.

Most of boxing's crowd troubles are, of course, a direct outgrowth of the social tensions – racial, religious, nationalistic – which underlie most societies. It is significant, however, that these tensions erupt so frequently around boxing rings. It is difficult to imagine, for instance, black America igniting following the defeat of Arthur Ashe at Forest Hills. Like its bare-knuckle predecessor, boxing is both a mirror to the eruptions of a violent society and a party to those eruptions.

Boxing today is in generally poor shape. Whereas in prewar Britain there were between three and four thousand registered professional boxers, there

---

❝ I don't think normal everyday living should consist of getting whacked around. I never thought people were born for this: to destroy one another. ❞

Paul Pender, middleweight boxer, 1961

---

are now scarcely four hundred. In the United States numbers have been declining steadily since the war, and in Australia, once a boom country for boxing, the sport is dying on its feet. It is now only the top fighters who can earn a decent living at the game, and only the best of the heavyweights who can make their fortune.

The reason for this decline most frequently voiced both from inside the sport and out, is that boxing only thrives when times are hard. Given a choice, men usually prefer to make their living in a less violent fashion. "Any man with a good trade isn't about to get knocked on his butt to make a dollar," remarked Miami promoter Chris Dundee. It is a strong theory.

Money – or social advancement, if you like – has long been the primary motivation behind boxing, more, perhaps, than for any other sport save perhaps bull fighting. It has traditionally been the sport of the poor man or the deprived. Indeed, the broad history of boxing can be read in terms of the continual upward shift of ethnic minorities: initially it was Jewish boys who were forced to turn to the ring in order to make money and gain respect; next it was the turn of the Irish; next it was the blacks. But today's comparative affluence has sapped boxing in the West of much of its motivation. Not only are there more "good trades" about, but for the deprived youngsters there is a whole new range of sporting outlets – pro football, basketball, soccer, baseball – offering better opportunities for fame and fortune than the ring, without the ring's incessant pain and violence. And so Western boxing is on the wane, waiting, as one English manager told me with a wistful look in his eye, for a "good depression." (And indeed, in London's East End, growing steadily more depressed each day, there is now the beginnings of a boxing revival; amateur clubs are filled with youngsters, their eyes all firmly fixed on a professional career.)

Today it is the "hungry" countries of Latin America and South East Asia that are boxing's most enthusiastic supporters. In Bangkok there are three cavernous boxing stadiums which offer among them a bout every night of the week. In Mexico alone there are currently some seven thousand professional fighters, including five world champions. "They all have the same look," remarked the proprietor of one of Mexico City's nine flourishing boxing gymnasiums, "flat bellies and hungry eyes."

One area of combat sports which is booming despite Western affluence is that devoted to the Oriental martial arts. Although designed initially solely as a means of unarmed self-defense, as sports, karate and judo are proving immensely popular with Western youth. In Britain alone there are at least one hundred thousand people involved in some form of martial arts. Many of these are working class youths who up until a few years ago would have been spending their evenings in boxing rings. In America the boom is even more pronounced.

How long Oriental martial arts will continue to gain what boxing loses is debatable. Martial arts promoters are optimistic, however, particularly for the success of their own brainchild, "full contact karate." In 1971 karate bridged the gap between participant and spectator sport with the introduction of full contact. Whereas participants had previously pulled their punches during competition, under full contact they were now allowed to land their blows, cushioned by a set of styrofoam gloves. To date there have been several deaths during full contact bouts in both Britain and the US, prompting a spate of angry articles condemning what one writer labeled the "gladiatorial syndrome." So far, however, the promoters have remained unfazed. "Full contact is coming. Definitely!" said Ed Parker, doyen of Los Angeles's martial arts fraternity. "The people who come and see it, they love it." Which, if true, seems certain to ensure the sport a long and lucrative life, the "gladiatorial syndrome" notwithstanding.

How far we have taken our combat sports away from the Roman arena is of course a matter of opinion; however, it is perhaps considerably less than what we would like to think. We don't kill people for sport (not intentionally anyway; maim, disfigure and drive insane, yes, but not kill). Nor do we entertain ourselves by watching other people intentionally kill themselves in combat (although to borrow Roger Caras's point, if someone was to advertise a fight to the death in Shea Stadium tomorrow, it is extremely unlikely that everybody would survive the rush to the box office). However, I find it difficult to believe that it will not be considered a reflection on our society by future generations that our single most prestigious, most lucrative and most enthralling sporting event is the spectacle of two heavyweight fist fighters slugging each other into insensibility.

THE BRAWL GAME

4

4 The Brawl Game
Ball Sports

As veteran LA Rams lineman Merlin Olsen once said, "They don't call the middle of the line The Pit for nothing. We really do get like animals, trying to claw one another apart in there. It is very hard in The Pit. No matter how it seems, no matter what the score, it's always hard. We get so bruised and battered and tired we sometimes wind up playing in a sort of coma. By the end of the first half your instincts have taken over. By the end of the game you're an animal."

When Olsen retired from pro football at the end of the 1976–7 season, he was ushered from the field to universal applause (as universal as any applause could be, that is, given the rabidly partisan world of football support). The television cameras picked him out for special attention during his last game, the sportswriters wrote columns about his achievements, and fans around the country looked on with a respect which bordered on awe. Olsen, they agreed, was something special.

It wasn't that Olsen had been one of football's overexposed superstars; compared to the Joe Namaths and Jim Browns of the NFL galaxy he hadn't been. What he had done, however, was to survive an extraordinary length of time – fourteen full seasons – in a game which habitually destroys the majority of its players within three to four years, and which counts fourteen-season veterans on the fingers of one bandaged hand. For fourteen years Olsen had survived and flourished in the eye of the holocaust. That was why the announcers spoke so glowingly of him, and rightly so.

Olsen's game, American pro football, together with our other heavy contact ball sports (rugby, ice hockey, Australian Rules and so on), are the end products of centuries of sporting violence. Games which began as the delight of kicking about a ball have now grown into preposterously over-blown spectacles of all-out assault, as hard and as punishing as any could be without the conscious inclusion of death as an attraction. Today there is no group of sports more relentlessly violent. There is also none more popular.

From Rome to Rugby

The history of ball sports is as ancient almost as sport itself. The ball has delighted the sportsmen of countless civilizations since the time of Thutmose, Ashurbanipal and the other great royal hunters of antiquity. The pharoahs, the ancient Greeks and the Chinese ruling classes of 2,500 years ago all amused themselves with various long-forgotten types of ball games. Later references range from the Eskimo tribes of North America to the Maoris of the South Pacific. And these are only several of many.

How violent these early games were has gone largely unrecorded. However, in some instances at least, it appears that ball games were little more than a broad invitation to disorder and riot. As early as 600 BC, teams of Persian warriors, often numbering a thousand a side, battled over a carved willow root in a frenzied game which, as polo, would later come to be regarded by the pukka sahibs of the British Raj as the height of sporting gentility. In neighboring Afghanistan mounted hill tribesmen played – as they still do today – *buzkashi*, which substituted a dead calf for a willow root (a choice of "ball" which would tend to support the theory of ball sport's being merely an extension of hunting). "*Buzkashi* can probably best be described as a combination of polo, mounted football and unorganized mayhem," recorded one eyewitness. "Cracked skulls are common and quirt-like riding whips draw blood freely from both horse and men. The general tendency seems to be to hit an opponent or an opponent's horse if one gets in a tight squeeze" – a tactic which soccer fans will recognize as the "professional foul."

Even more bloodthirsty was *peloya*, a game popular with Mexican tribes from around 800 BC. Players were equipped with wide leather belts, leather aprons, chest protectors and thick leather gauntlets to protect themselves from the solid rubber ball which hurtled around the court like a bullet. Even this was often not enough, as the Spanish priest Diego Duran recorded: "Many players were carried off the field dead when the ball had hit them in the stomach or over the heart, knocking the breath out of them so that they fell down dead." To win at *peloya* was for a time just as lethal; archaeologists believe that the colossal stone heads which are scattered around the coastal regions of the Mexican Gulf may be monuments to Olmec *peloya* champions beheaded by their adoring publics in order to speed their entry into heaven. Later the Olmecs adopted a more modern attitude toward sporting victories and executed the losers.

The roots of modern ball sports probably sprang from a rather less demanding game, the Roman sport of *harpastum*. From the few passing references that have survived, it would seem that *harpastum* was a primitive version of American gridiron or rugby. Goals were placed at either end of a confined area and two teams attacked them with a ball roughly the size of a

---

66 Sport is an expression of the barbarian temperament. **99**

Thorsten Veblen, *The Theory of the Leisure Class* (1899)

---

modern soccer ball. As witnessed by the second-century Roman physician Galen, it was an intensely physical game which relied heavily on tackling. As such it was, not surprisingly, widely used to toughen up the Legions.

Although there is evidence that several forms of ball games were being played in Britain and Europe before the Roman conquest, it is probable that the intervillage brawls which came to be graced by the name "fote-ball" owed much to this legionnaires' war game. The annual Derby game, for instance, one of the most famous of England's annual football matches, did not begin until well after the initial invasion – ironically in celebration of a Roman military defeat. When the empire collapsed, *harpastum* was almost certainly one of the legacies the Romans left behind.

By 1175 "the ball game" had become an established annual event in London, played noisily through the streets by mobs of students and apprentices. Indeed, from its earliest, football – if it can be called such – was simply a running free-for-all, part of the amicable territorial rivalries which set street against street, parish against parish and town against town. In addition to the London game, days were annually set aside up and down England for the local youths to flex their muscles and display their courage. At Derby on Shrove Tuesday the parishes of All Saints and St. Peter's chased a ball to a gatepost a mile out of town. At Ashbourne the town divided and surged through rivers and streams out across the open fields. At Haxey, in Lincolnshire, the villagers fought over pieces of rolled-up canvas and leather, and in Leicestershire on Easter Monday, Hallaton and Medbourne battled to propel a small barrel of beer down a hill and across a river. In East Anglia the game was known as "camp ball," and when it was played with boots on, "savage camp." "When the exercise becomes exceedingly violent," wrote Joseph Strett, "the players kick each other's shins without the least ceremony, and some of them are over-thrown at the hazard of their limbs."

All of these battles, together with their counterparts in Scotland and Ireland, were bruising affairs waged with few rules and even less restraint. Teams often numbered in the hundreds and usually fought all day, mowing down fences and hedges, trampling spectators and settling the score with an all-in brawl. Injury and shortened life were inevitable at such events, and indeed much of football's early history can be gleaned from the death certificates and injury reports of its victims. The first known football fatality occurred in 1280 when Henry, son of William de Ellington, accidentally impaled himself on a knife belonging to David le Ken during a game at Ulkham on Trinity Sunday. Henry succumbed the following Friday. Forty years later Pope John XXII granted a Norfolk canon, William de Spalding, a dispensation for his part in a similar fatality: "During the game at ball as he kicked the ball, a lay friend of his, also called William, ran against him and wounded himself on a sheath knife carried by the canon, so severely that he died within six days." In 1567 Henry Ingolde of Essex died after a particularly nasty tackle and at Ashbourne a villager drowned in the River Dove. A coroner's inquest during Elizabeth's reign found that Roger Ludford had died after being sandwiched between two players, one of whom had delivered a short-arm blow under his breast; and in 1796 at Derby John Snape was "an unfortunate victim to this custom of playing at Football at Shrove Tide." Hurling fatalities in Cornwall had become so numerous by the late 1700s that Cornishmen became wary of the game and it all but disappeared.

Lesser injury was even more rife. "Broken shins, broken heads, torn coats and lost hats are among the minor accidents of this fearful contest," wrote Glover in his *History of Derbyshire* of the early Derby game, "and it frequently happens that persons fall, owing to the intensity of the pressure, fainting and bleeding beneath the feet of the surrounding mob." It would be difficult, he added, to give an adequate account of such a "ruthless sport." An early eyewitness to the Chester game – which apparently started as a kick-about with the head of a Danish prisoner – reported that "much harme was done, some in the great thronge fallinge into a trance, some having their bodies bruised and crushed; some their arms, heades or legges broken, and some otherwise maimed or in peril of their lives."

Many such injuries were by no means accidental. A village football match crashing through the countryside provided perfect cover for settling old scores, or beginning new ones. In 1583 three weavers, a fuller and a tailor were heard to shout as they set about an opposing player, "We are making work for the surgeon!" Their victim died soon after. Fifteen years later John and Richard Gregorie of North Moreton were killed by a player called Ould Gunter. According to the parish register, "Gunter's sonnes and ye Gregories fell together by ye years at footeball. Ould Gunter drewe his dagger and broke booth their heades, and they died booth within a fortnight after."

Football matches could, on occasion, stir up enmity between entire towns. The Sheffield/Norton game of 1793 gained particular notoriety, with Sheffield enlisting the help of outsiders and Norton sending out press gangs to scour the countryside for recruits. The match lasted three days with "many slightly injured, but none killed." For the next few years, however, the people of Norton dreaded visiting Sheffield "even about their necessary business." As late as 1815 Sir Walter Scott was writing that it was unsafe to hold intervillage football matches in Scotland "as the old clannish spirit is too apt to break out."

In London it was not long before the city fathers were up in arms. It was not so much the injuries and the fist fights which led to a growing disenchantment, but rather the damage to the city's windowpanes and shop fronts wreaked by the mobs of apprentices surging through the narrow cobbled streets. In 1314 the merchants of London petitioned Edward II to speak out against the game, which he duly did. "For as much as there is great noise in the city caused by hustling over large balls from which many evils might arise, which God forbade," proclaimed Edward's minister, "we command and forbid on behalf of the King, on pain of imprisonment, such games to be used in the city in future."

For the next five hundred years with a few rare exceptions, football was an outlawed sport. Although Cromwell attended a hurling match between 150 Cornishmen and Charles II was entertained by his servants kicking a football, the majority of monarchs and rulers viewed the game solely as an illegal and ignoble riot for apprentices and peasants. Football was specifically banned by acts and proclamations in 1349, 1388 and 1410. Henry VIII, besotted as he was with outdoor sports, legislated against it, as did his equally sporting daughter Elizabeth, who again made it a prisonable offense.

The Puritans, of course, were piously mortified by the spectacle, the most withering attack coming from the pen of that grim prophesier of hellfire and damnation, Phillip Stubbes:

> For as concerning football playing I protest unto you that it may rather be called a friendlie kinde of fyght than a play or recreation – a bloody and murthering practice than a felowly sport or pastime. For dooth not everyone lye in waight for his adversarie, seeking to overthrow him and picke him on his nose, though it be hard stones . . . so that this means sometimes their necks are broken, sometimes their backs, sometimes their legs, sometimes their armes, sometimes their noses gush out with blood, sometimes their eyes start out, and sometimes hurte in one place, sometimes in another . . . for they have the sleights to meet one betwixt two, to dash him against the hart with their elbowes, to butt him under the short ribs with their griped fists, and with their knees to catch him on the hip and pick him on his neck, with a hundred such murthering devices.

Even allowing for his righteous wrath, there was more than a grain of truth in Stubbes's words. James I, a decidedly un-Puritan monarch, also considered football "meeter for laming than for making able the users thereof," and banned his son from playing. During his reign the Manchester city council canceled the annual match because of mobs "breakinge many men's windowes and glasses at their pleasures and other great enormyties."

The practical effect of all these various decrees with their threats of fines, floggings and imprisonment was, however, marginal. Certainly matches were broken up and, as the court records of the fifteenth, sixteenth and seventeenth centuries show, a steady trickle of culprits did find themselves before the magistrates charged with disturbing the peace. But despite this, the sport continued. By the seventeenth century more than forty separate communities throughout England were gathering every Shrove Tuesday to play football. There were even teams of women.

By the mid-1700s "mob" football had reached a peak. Over the decades it had slowly developed from a rowdy expression of boisterous high spirits into an instrument which threatened open social revolt, a recurring nightmare for the English judiciary who had on more than one occasion banned the sport on the grounds of possible insurrection. In the cities the apprentices, a traditionally underpaid, overworked and generally disaffected lot, were using football as an excuse to congregate and flex their political muscles, often forcing the authorities to send in the dragoons. In the provinces peasants objecting to some new feature of the landscape – a fence or a dam – would "throw up a ball" and steam-roller the offending article en masse. In 1740, for example, it was recorded that "a Mach of Futtball was Cried at Kettering of five Hundred Men of a side, but the design was to Pull Down Lady Bety Jesmaine's Mills."

It was the grimy hand of the Industrial Revolution that managed what legislation and the dragoons had failed for so long to achieve – the defusing of mob football. As the country moved rapidly from agriculture to the harsher realities of coal, pig iron and steel, football was simply squeezed out of the working man's life along with the rest of his leisure-time diversions. A worker in industrial England was nothing more than a tool to be used day in and day out. He was to remain as such until the factory acts of the mid-nineteenth century grudgingly granted him a limited reprieve. By 1801 Strutt was forced to concede that football was played only rarely.

Some traditional matches did survive, however. As late as 1903, the Workington game – a pitched and bloody battle between the town's colliers and sailors – was reportedly attracting fifty thousand spectators from all over England. Today the men of Hallaton and Medbourne still spend Easter "bottle kicking," and at Ashbourne on Shrove Tuesday the locals still lumber through the river in a massive scrum. However, mob football is now no more than an historical curiosity, kept up for the sake of tradition.

But if the working man was forced to abandon football in favor of the factory floor, elsewhere on the English social scale there was another group willing to adopt and develop it. Ironically, the instrument of this development was the English public school system, the preserve of the rich and titled, the very people who had traditionally aligned themselves against the game. In fact, football had been an intermittent part of public school life since at least 1466, the year Christopher Robson kicked a ball into the Minster at York and received "six yerkes with a birchen rod on the buttocks." A game which was rooted in disorder and mayhem was indeed admirably suited to the public school system as it then stood.

Until well into the nineteenth century, the realities of life at an English public school were light years away from the now-popular image of a world of boater hats, impeccable manners, and tea and crumpets beside the fire in one's study. What a late eighteenth-century father was consigning his son to – wittingly or unwittingly – was, in the words of a former Charterhouse pupil, "a sort of hell on earth. " Masters were expected to be savage, and men such as Eton's Dr. Keate and his predecessor, Dr. Heath, surpassed all expectation, flogging boys – sometimes a hundred at a time – until they raised scars which lasted a lifetime. After being birched a boy could spend all night with his friends peeling off his shirt and removing slivers of wood from his back. Some even died of their wounds. When a boy ran away he was returned, fettered like a criminal. And if the masters were bad, the pupils themselves were appalling. Boys were roasted in front of open fires, scalped in blanket tossings, locked choking in trunks filled with sawdust and, occasionally, even murdered by their peers.

What organized recreation there was leaned heavily toward blood sports. One Eton favorite, for instance, was the annual ram hunt in which a ram was driven through the streets by a howling mob of students wielding wooden clubs. Later, the strenuous exercise involved in chasing a ram during the summer months was deemed unhealthy for the boys, so the unfortunate ram was hamstrung and clubbed to death within the confines of a school courtyard. Against this background, football was merely another piece in a jigsaw of brutality.

Until the 1820s the football played at the public schools was exactly that of the common folk. Violent, unorganized and dominated by the big and beefy, it was an agent as well as a symptom of the general chaos which surrounded it. As such it was feared and discouraged by the schools' authorities, who saw in it the possibilities of violent insurrection. By the beginning of the nineteenth century, the public schools had already been rocked by a succession of student riots and rebellions, with masters stoned, windows smashed and buildings set alight. In this tense climate a school football match involving hundreds of young men fighting and brawling without restraint must have terrified the authorities.

"It's no joke playing-up in a match, I can tell you," Scud East informed the Rugby new-boy Tom Brown. "Quite another thing from your private school games. Why, there's been two collar-bones broken this half, and a dozen fellows lamed." East was not exaggerating. Rugby's "bigside" matches of the early 1800s were truly awesome affairs, furious battles of blood and mud which pitted sixty boys of one house against the rest of the school, all in all more than three hundred players. There were few rules and players showed no hesitation in trampling or maiming their opponents. For long periods the ball simply disappeared, trapped under the massive heaving scrum.*

The other public schools devised games which were equally as forbidding as Rugby's. At Charterhouse football was played with complete abandon along the lethal brick cloisters of an old Carthusian monastery. Fifty or sixty boys would be crammed in on top of each other, all lashing out with their boots and shoving and pushing to extricate the ball, sending the smaller players skittering head first over the stones. The only rule was against breaking the windows. Eton's famous Wall Game – a sort of trench war played alongside a school wall – had become so brutal by 1827 that it was banned for a decade. After its reinstatement, the players adopted padded caps complete with ear flaps and "wall sacks," coarse sacking jackets which predated American football armor by more than half a century.

It was the "educational revolution" begun by Rugby's Thomas Arnold – "The Doctor" of *Tom Brown's Schooldays* – which lifted football from the sordid corner of public school life and bestowed on it the respectability needed to ensure its development. Arnold was the first headmaster to regard it the duty of the public schools to instill in their pupils such lofty tangibles as Character and Morality and Manliness, and in so doing he transformed school life.

Actually it was not Arnold but his disciples who translated such sentiments into sport. Although the writings of such Arnold admirers as Thomas Hughes credited the Doctor with the introduction of organized sport to the public school syllabus, it is doubtful that Arnold ever saw games such as football as anything more than minor evils. It would appear that sport bored him, and if football flourished during his period at Rugby as much as

---

* The popular belief as to the origins of modern rugby is that during one of these bigside brawls in 1823, a student named William Webb Ellis – a chap "with a fine disregard for the rules of football as played in his time," as the plaque erected in his memory states – picked up the ball and ran with it. Unfortunately, the Ellis saga is a blatant fiction, perpetrated by an overly loyal gathering of Rugby Old Boys more than half a century later. As Thomas Hughes recalled, to run with the ball in the 1820s would have been a shortcut to suicide.

Hughes would have us believe, it was in spite of him rather than because of him. Not until the boys of his sixth forms had moved out into the world and taken up similar posts in the public school system did the idea of "muscular Christianity" blossom and football become a tool of the "new education." Since then, of course, sport – and football in particular – has remained on equal footing with the more studious school activities; indeed, in many American establishments, sport is now several clear steps ahead.

The football field – and, to a lesser degree, the boxing ring – was the ideal arena for playing out a moral life-or-damnation struggle. Lined up amid "the mud, the blood, the guts and the endless toil and fear of the playing field," as one survivor put it, a boy could prepare himself for what Arnold saw as life's battle against sin by fostering a whole range of manly qualities – bravery, chivalry, discipline and self-sacrifice. In the hands of Arnold's followers, football was no longer merely a game, but a force which shaped and tested the very depths of a boy's character. "A truly chivalrous football player was never yet guilty of lying, or deceit, or meanness, whether of word or action," opined the journal of one public school, *The Marlburian*, in 1867. It was a concept which many sports, particularly rugby, swallowed whole. As E.H.D. Sewell wrote earlier this century in his collection of rugby tales aptly titled *Rugger, the Man's Game:*

> No other game if it is played seriously in the highest company, equals Rugger in its combined call on its players for Courage, Self-Control, Stamina and Sticking-it. Why should this be so? Mainly, nay almost wholly, because of the Man-to-Man element in Rugger. To play Rugger well you must play it fiercely, and at the same time, and all the time, remember that while doing so that you are a gentleman.

Such opinions still occasionally emanate from the halls of the Rugby Union where the words *gentleman* and *amateur* are still breathed with almost religious reverence.

Another of Arnold's inadvertent legacies was the further intertwining of sport and war. What was learned on the playing fields of Eton reappeared in exactly the same form on the battlegrounds of the empire. "Play up, play up, and play the game!" was the rallying cry of the public school man, be it on a muddy acre of English turf or a bloodstained patch of desert sand in some far-off colony. The brotherhood of sport and war was another concept to endure in the public schools. "At my public school it was at once made clear to us that the best thing we could do was die in battle," recalled author John Le Carré in 1977. "We fought rugger wars almost literally to the death." One can only wonder what state football would have been in today without Arnold's influence; or, for that matter, warfare.

The upshot of all this was that, by mid-century, football had become respectable – even enviable. Play was openly encouraged by such head-masters as Hawtrey of Eton to help build stout characters and to rechannel the smoldering resentments which could at any time break out into insurrection. Instead of giving their souls to the devil or burning their masters' studies, boys now hurled themselves tooth and claw at each other on the playing fields, laying down if not their lives at least their front teeth for their house. Prefects goaded them on furiously from the sidelines, beating scrums with their umbrellas. Any boy who could talk after a match was ostracized for not having pulled his weight. Soon football had become the most popular recreation at school, supplanting even hunting and the other blood sports.

The growing mania for football led to a rush by students to bring some written order to what was still very much an undisciplined game. The resulting codes varied wildly: some schools attempted to regulate the more brutal aspects of mob football; others were content to take muscular Christianity at its most literal. The tougher codes could be very tough indeed. At Rugby, for instance, the state of play can be judged from those aspects the rule makers felt compelled to outlaw specifically by name:

Rule xiv. No hacking with the heel, unless below the knee is fair.

Rule xv. No-one wearing projecting nails or iron plates on the soles of or heels of his shoes or boots shall be allowed to play.

Rule xxii. A player standing up to another may hold one arm only, but he may hack him or knock the ball out of his hands if he attempts to kick it.

Eventually two distinct codes emerged: that played by Rugby, Marlborough and Cheltenham – destined to become rugby – which allowed the ball to be passed by hand; and "the dribbling game" – soccer – played by Eton, Harrow, Westminster and Charterhouse in which only the feet could be used.

This lack of uniformity made little difference to players as long as they remained at school, but as soon as they moved on to university and the proliferating Old Boy teams it became a major problem. The matter finally came to a head in 1863 when representatives of eleven schools and clubs met under the banner of the Football Association expressly to thrash out a common code. The meeting was not a success, foundering first on the question of handling and then, even more crucially, on the tolerable level of violence.

Although football *was* growing tamer, in theory at least – the year before the meeting, Blackheath, for example, had outlawed throttling in the scrums – many reformers could not bring themselves to legislate against hacking, the practice of stopping an opponent by kicking his shins. Hacking, they felt, was an integral part of the game's character building and any attempts to ban it "savoured far more of the feelings of those who liked their pipes and grog or Schnapps more than the manly game of football!" as Blackheath's representative thundered. Others, however, considered hacking far too brutal; permissible for schoolboys, perhaps, but lethal for adults. Unless it was stamped out, they warned, "men of business to whom it is of importance to take care of themselves" would turn their backs on the game.

The meeting finally collapsed in a welter of ill feeling and football continued to carry on under the two distinct codes. The Football Association played soccer; the others rugby with its handling and hacking. Ironically, it was only three years later that rugby also eliminated hacking.* But by then it was too late. The two games were irreconcilably divided, and were destined to remain so.

Although hacking had been excised from the Association game in theory, soccer remained a definite contact sport. Players took to the field protected by shin guards or with their legs swathed in rubber bandages. Hacking was defined as anything the referee saw, a philosophy condoned by the greatest of Old Boy players, even the legendary Hon. Arthur Kinnaird of Old Etonians.

"Look here, Kinnaird," complained one of his purple-legged opponents. "Are we going to play the game or are we going to have hacking?"

"Oh," came the reply, "let us have hacking by all means."

Charging the goalkeeper was also standard practice, and the Association's early history is ripe with reports of valiant goalies playing on with broken shoulders or collarbones, their arms hanging limply by their sides. It was certainly no game for women; during the 1870s when the mania for physical fitness was just beginning to bite, the headmistress of Wycombe Abbey, Miss Frances Dove, declared that the Association game was "quite out of the question" for her charges. The young ladies had to be content with a watered-down version of field hockey.

But the public schools and their Old Boy offshoots were not to remain the home of soccer. As early as 1857 ordinary working men had managed to form clubs despite the enormous restrictions of life faced by workers in the manufacturing belt. During the 1870s, when the tycoons of British industry

---

* Exactly why is still unclear; either it was because a player was killed during a practice match between Richmond and Blackheath, or because the two clubs found that they had to cancel a fixture, so many of their players being lame. The way the game was being played in those days, it could easily have been both reasons.

were forced to grant their overworked employees the luxury of a free Saturday afternoon, these clubs mushroomed. In 1878 Darwen, an unknown team of Lancashire mill workers, held their own in the Football Association Cup against the powerful Old Etonians. The match signaled the end of the Old Boy domination of football. Once more the game reverted to the common man, although it was vastly different from the game played in the free-wheeling preindustrial era. Much of the violence had gone, eliminated by the Association rules which reflected a more civilized approach to sport, and also by encroaching urban sprawl. There was simply no longer enough room for several hundred players to rampage across the landscape for a day. The basis of the game had become "controlled violence."

Which is not to say that the common man had become soft. When it came to sly hacking and hammering tackles, he was more than a match for Kinnaird and his Old Etonians. At Leicester Assizes in 1878, a player was charged with killing an opponent by striking him with his "protruding knee." Twenty years later a similar charge was laid against another player. In 1886 during an Association Cup match, Preston North End founded the long tradition of enmity between England and Scotland by beating Queens Park three goals to nil. They achieved their victory by literally kicking the Scots off the field. As the Queens Park players were stretchered away, fifteen thousand angry Scots poured down from the stands and invaded the pitch. The Scottish authorities were so disgusted by Preston's tactics that they withdrew into their own Scottish Football Association, sinking hopes of a British football league. Since then, Scottish teams and their supporters have approached football matches against the English with a purpose better suited to war than sport.

Rugby also aroused murderous sentiments among its players. Until the turn of the century tactics and skill had little business on a rugby pitch; the game was simply a matter of big men crashing through the ranks of their opponents. Cup ties in particular were notorious for their ferociousness, causing "warm partisanship to lead to ill-temper, and ill-temper to brutality," as the editor of *The Badminton Library* put it in 1888. "The present writer has seen various Rugby Union cup ties," he continued, "and never left such a match without feeling strongly that they are an abomination." Even more savage were the Home Internationals which provided a drama and pitch the loosely organized club matches lacked. In 1883 four Irish players were carried off the field, suffering broken ankles, butchered knees and concussions. Two years previously the same fixture had degenerated into what one writer described as "a spectacle of mass boxing."

Mob Ball Australian-Style

Rugby's inherent brutality did little to inhibit its spread throughout the empire; rather, the sport's zealous missionaries found a ready market for their rough trade in the "frontier" colonies of Australia, New Zealand and South Africa. Colonial players on their hard, sun-baked grounds learned their lessons well. Soon their teams were able to crush even the best of those sent out from Mother England.

In fact, only half of Australia was besotted by rugby. The southern states preferred their own code – Australian Rules – which had its roots in the Gaelic mob football brought to the gold towns of Bendigo and Ballarat by the Irish miners. By 1850 a local paper was able to report a game being played on the gold fields which was "a combination of many games, including football, wrestling and general roughhouse." In that year a former Rugby pupil, Tom Wills, set about bringing some semblance of order to this melee. What Wills was after was a game that cricketers could play in the winter months without risking injury; like the English Association, he considered rugby too dangerous for men charged with the responsibility of earning a living. It is, therefore, somewhat ironic that the game he produced became, for all its high-flying splendor, one of the hardest football codes ever to be devised, a game which would later number among its heroes such men as Jack Dyer – "Captain Blood" – who is credited with snapping the collarbones of a dozen opponents during his bruising career.

If rugby was a hooligan's game played by gentlemen, and soccer a gentleman's game played by hooligans, then Australian Rules could only be described as a hooligan's game played by hooligans. Wills's game contained exactly the right blend of skill and violence for a nation which liked to think of itself as engaged in a life–or–death struggle against the elements. By 1877 Australian Rules was the most popular outdoor sport in the state of Victoria, regularly drawing upwards of ten thousand spectators to a single match. The game's inherent roughness was reflected by the two-fisted exuberance of the onlookers, and from its earliest days the newspapers were filled with stories of fights, riots, attacks on players and assaults on umpires.

When it came to playing Rules, the young gentlemen of Victoria's public schools behaved equally as disgracefully as their adult counterparts. In 1905, after many years of simmering rivalry, a match between Melbourne Grammar and Wesley College erupted into a pitched battle involving players, officials and spectators. Finally the police had to be summoned to eject the pupils by force. The incident caused a public scandal which continued for months in the letters columns of the newspapers. However, it is a fair indication as to how Australians viewed their sport that a good 50 percent of the correspondents saw absolutely nothing wrong with such a riot. "It will be a poor look-out for the British Empire when its younger schoolboys do not behave roughly and even rudely at times," wrote one angry complainant who signed himself "Ex-school." "Nations are not made and sustained by milksops." Thomas Hughes could not have put it better.

The American Way

Like their Olmec cousins to the south, the Indian tribes of North America had become adept at a number of bruising ball sports long before the arrival of the first white settlers. Ball games were important facets of Indian culture on two counts: firstly as religious rituals and, more commonly, as a preparation for war. In both cases they were fast, hard and invariably bloody.

The Indians' principal ball game was *baggataway*, which the French settlers immediately dubbed *la crosse*. *Baggataway* was played with a ball and a hooked stick which, to European minds, closely resembled a bishop's crosier. Lacrosse was organized along roughly the same lines as English mob ball, with tribe set against tribe and village set against village. The sight of several hundred Indians gliding through the forest waterways in their canoes to attend a match was a familiar one to frontier dwellers; some European travelers of the seventeenth century reported seeing as many as several thousand Indians locked in combat on the North American plains. Such matches invariably left a trail of broken bones, bloodied heads and the occasional corpse in their wake.

How violently the game was played varied from tribe to tribe. Some tribes played with marked good humor, knowing only too well the dangers of a stick swung in anger. Any injuries they received they immediately shrugged off as simply the fortunes of war. Other tribes, however, found it difficult to keep their war games separate from the real thing. After witnessing a Choctaw match which left five players crippled (two of whom subsequently died), one observer noted that the injuries inflicted on a man were frequently avenged by his relatives.

Even worse was the game of shinny, an Indian version of field hockey. Edward Denig wrote of the Montana tribes that:

> When one of them, either intentionally or by accident, hurts another by a stroke with the play stick, a general shindy takes place, and the sticks are employed over each others' heads, which is followed by a rush for the stakes and a scramble. We have seen them, when this was the case, arm themselves and exchange some shots, when, a few being

wounded, the camps would separate and move away in different directions.

According to Dr. George A. Dorsey, a match among the Arikara tribe of Oklahoma in 1904 ended with the losing side murdering the winners.

Besides these stick-and-ball games, the Indians had also developed their own form of football – a strikingly similar and equally violent variation of the mob games of Derby, Chester and the other English footballing towns, with thirty or forty players on a side and goals a mile or so apart. "Before they come to this sport," wrote William Wood in 1634 of the Massachuset tribe, "they paint themselves, even as when they go to war, in policy to prevent mischief, because no man should know him that moved his patience, or accidentally hurt his person, taking away the occasion of studying revenge." The Micmac tribe favored tackling by the hair, a technique which mimicked the scalpings of a real war.

The Indian games provoked a mixed reaction on the part of the European immigrants. Lacrosse impressed them most, and early records mention matches played between the Indians and the French Canadians dating from the 1840s. By 1870 the game had become a major sporting fixture throughout Canada. Later it spread to the United States and even to the United Kingdom. Although the National Lacrosse Association of Canada tried on many occasions to stamp out rough play, echoes of *baggataway* still persisted. In 1870 the Montreal team refused to play against the Toronto Shamrocks after one of their players had been hit on the head with a brick.

The situation was greatly aggravated by the introduction of professional lacrosse leagues, and police were regularly forced to interrupt matches and restore order. Newspapers ran stories under such banner headlines as: "Lacrosse Is Featured by Many Fights – Boxing Is Considered Brutal but Go as Far as You Like in Lacrosse." On October 4, 1913, even the most hard-bitten supporters were shocked by the excesses of the New Westminster team. After winning the coveted Minto Cup, the team set upon a city alderman and beat him savagely in full view of the audience. "Not only are the fans disgusted with the Minto Cup men, but their officials have washed their hands of them," railed one newspaper. Another went a step further and, in an article bordered by black funeral columns, proclaimed the death of professional lacrosse. As it happened it was a rather prophetic proclamation. After World War I, although amateur lacrosse continued to flourish, the professional leagues found it difficult to enlist players and one by one disappeared.

Indian football, on the other hand, failed to bridge the gulf between native and settler. The colonists preferred their own mob ball, and early records are scattered with accounts of English immigrants kicking about air-filled bladders. In 1657 the Town of Boston issued this familiar edict:

> Forasmuch as sundry complaints are made that several persons have received hurt by boyes and young men playing at foot-ball in the streets; these are to Injoyne that none be found at that game in any of the Streets, Lanes and Inclosures of this Town, under the penalty of twenty shillings for every such offense.

In fact there was not much threat to public order; the colonists were far more interested in hunting game than in playing football. It wasn't until the football mania of the English public schools had filtered through to their North American counterparts that the game became anything like a feature of the American sporting scene.

The American colleges of the early nineteenth century – Yale, Princeton, Harvard and so on – were, like the public schools of England, extremely spartan establishments. Conditions were harsh and the discipline even harsher. "The professors are task-masters and police officers, the President is chief of the College police," complained an early *Atlantic Monthly*. It is not surprising then that American students also quickly developed a taste for rugged recreation. The first mention of football was in 1820 when the boys of Princeton at first punched, and then later kicked, a ball about in a game known as "ballown." At Yale during the same period, the first Monday of the fall term was set aside for a game which, at a stretch of the imagination, could perhaps be termed football. This was "Bloody Monday," so called because the sophomores, smeared with war paint and dressed like Indians, felt it their duty to kick the freshmen around the field until they drew blood. The ball would appear to have been an irrelevance.

By 1840 Bloody Monday had developed into a comparatively ordered interclass game. Freshmen, under the supervision of the upperclassmen, formed themselves into a huge phalanx with the ball carrier at the core and tried to storm their way through the ranks of the sophomores. In 1858 the New York *Evening Post* carried an account of a match: "Boys and young men knocked each other down, tore off each other's clothing. Eyes were bunged, faces blackened and bloody, and shirts and coats torn to rags." If the truth were to be told, commented the *Post*, the game would "make the same impression on the public mind as a bull fight." So often did these matches end in uproar that in 1860 the Yale and Harvard authorities banned them outright.

Of course both schools, like the kings of medieval England, soon discovered that bans had little effect on football. Just nine years later the first intercollegiate match took place with Rutgers at one end of the field and

Princeton at the other. This was the culmination of a long-standing tug-of-war over a Revolutionary War cannon; after Princeton had unsportingly cemented the offending gun inside its gate, the two colleges had settled on football as a means of continuing their rivalry. On the appointed day the chosen fifty players – twenty-five a side – stripped off and went at each other to the cheers of some two hundred spectators. One of the players later confessed that he had earned his place on the team purely because of his prowess at wrestling. After the schools had won one game each, the headmasters of both colleges cancelled any further battles in the interests of peace and student health. In that same year the students of Cornell played a forty-a-side match that proved so successful that the following year the numbers were doubled.

Judging from the reports of these early matches, one could be excused for believing them to be the forerunners of gridiron. In fact, what the colleges were playing was rudimentary soccer. It was not until Harvard switched to the rugby rules played by a neighboring secondary school that the dribbling game began to relinquish its grip on the college campuses in favor of an even more physical code. Although Harvard was initially shunned by its fellow Ivy Leaguers for changing to rugby and was forced to travel north of the border to McGill University for its games, by 1876 most of the other American colleges had followed suit. Within another decade American football had been born.

The father of the American game was Yale's Walter Camp. Taking rugby as his basis, he tinkered with the rules, adding some, discarding others, until he had created what was virtually an entirely new game. Fast, open, tactically challenging and, above all, irresistibly rough, Camp's brainchild was an impressive achievement, especially considering that its inventor had given up a career in medicine because he fainted at the sight of blood.

Camp's revised rugby perfectly suited college sporting tastes. It presented an ideal opportunity for the more muscular Christians on campus to show off their strength and daring, a game which, as one early witness recorded, permitted "both spectator and player to revert to aboriginal manners."

Not everyone, however, was willing to applaud the new game. In 1883 Harvard, appalled by the open slugging, warned that football had become "brutal, demoralizing to teams and spectators, and extremely dangerous" and threatened to pull out of all competition. The following year it did so, leaving the other colleges to deal with a mounting injury toll.

Harvard's departure made little difference to the style of play: if anything, the game got rougher. This was the heyday of the boxer-slugger, players who were capable of giving as much as they were forced to take. Recalled

John Heisman, of Heisman Trophy fame:

> The tackling wasn't clean cut . . . often it was wild, haphazard clutching. Arguments followed almost every decision the referee made. The whole team took part. Linemen lined up squarely against those who played the same position. Mostly they stood bolt upright and fought it out hammer and tongs, tooth and nail, fist and feet.

The fact was, added Heisman, that a player didn't stand much chance of even making the line unless he was a good wrestler and a fair boxer. "There's murder in that game!" whistled bare-knuckle champion John L. Sullivan in awe after attending his first match.

But murder notwithstanding, football ruled the campuses, its growing popularity impossible to ignore even by the staunchest of critics. "Even death on the playground is cheap if it educates boys in the characteristics that made the Anglo-Saxon race preeminent in history," urged one Harvard Club speaker, and in 1887 the college fell back into line and rejoined the fray. This time the Harvard coaches came prepared. Before the start of the season the whole team had been taught the art of self-defense by a professional instructor, and the linchpin of the attack was one Franklin Remington, the strongest man in the school. In its debut against Princeton, the team lived up to all its expectations; the match being recorded for posterity as "The Bloody Game." And the worst was still to come.

Murderous though they were, it was not the brutality of the individual players which was to cause the storm of outrage that soon enveloped football. Rather, it was the loopholes exposed by the game's inexorable shift away from rugby that came close to destroying football as a sporting entertainment. By 1887 the American game had already acquired considerably more sting than rugby: whereas in rugby the object was merely to stop the ball carrier, under American rules tacklers were required to slam him to the ground; in rugby only the ball carrier could be tackled, but on the American gridiron anybody was fair game. The change that eventually brought American football to the brink of suicide was the gradual whittling away of the rule which formed the basis of both rugby *and* soccer – the offside rule.

While rewriting much of the rugby rule book, Walter Camp, in his wisdom, had stopped short of tampering with the offside rule. Designed to eliminate interference in front of the ball carrier, the rule was a positive feature of the American game, allowing the ball carrier the opportunity to streak ahead of his teammates and weave his way through the enemy lines. As the game grew quicker and more complex, however, referees found it increasingly difficult to spot infringements, and the backs discovered that they could break the offside rule with impunity by edging forward and fending off tacklers *alongside* the ball carrier. From there it was only a short step before the backs were actually running ahead of the carrier, literally clearing a path for him. As the balance of the game veered sharply in favor of the attackers, the defenders began launching themselves in desperation at their opponents' knees, thus breaking the law which barred tackles below the waist. This too went unpenalized, and within a few seasons both tactics – although still technically illegal – had been absorbed into the fabric of the game.

The flouting of the offside rule opened the door to what became known as "mass plays," highly organized set pieces of group violence which took interference to ludicrous extremes. The first mass play was the work of Lehigh University – the "Lehigh V." At the kickoff, instead of booting the ball toward the opposition, Lehigh's kicker tapped it into his own hands, gathered his backs around him and headed off into enemy territory – men behind him, men beside him and men in front of him. Princeton, which had been working on the same tactic during roughly the same period, used a similar sort of "wedge" to defeat Pennsylvania in 1884. Two years later they thrashed Harvard 12–0 using the same formation.

But it was not until 1888 when Princeton unveiled its wedge against Yale that mass play finally came of age. As the Yale men watched in horror, the Princeton team locked arms around its ball carrier, fell into step, and thundered down the field toward the opposing goal. Only the quick thinking of the giant Yale guard William "Pudge" Heffelfinger halted the juggernaut and saved the day for Yale. Running full speed at the apex of the Princeton triangle, Heffelfinger launched himself over the heads of the leading blockers and crashed his two hundred pound bulk knees first onto the head of the unfortunate ball carrier. Years later Pudge was still crowing over the move which made him a college hero. "Stopping Princeton that day was my greatest thrill in football," he chortled.

Although it failed against Yale, Princeton's wedge caused a revolution. Each college coach went into seclusion to devise his own mass play and within the space of a few matches the game had been transformed by a rash of mass tactics bearing such names as the "shoving wedge," the "pushing wedge" and the "plough." The emphasis swung dramatically away from the man with the ball to those protecting him. Instead of a player weaving his way downfield, there was the dour spectacle of a tight pack of men edging goalward in a series of hiccupping confrontations with defenders who tore frantically at its fringes. Football became a chess game of brute force, the players reduced to the role of cannon fodder in the hands of the coaches. Play after play was devised and then discarded in the hope of gaining some slight advantage from the element of surprise. Each school had its own favorites; some conventional, others downright bizarre such as the "turtle back" in which the team crouched over in an oval shape and slowly revolved downfield. All were overwhelmingly brutal. "There is no 'sport' outside of a bullfight that presents the same degree of ferocity, danger and excitement as that shown in an ordinary intercollegiate game of football," opined the *New York Tribune* of 1890. It was not an exaggeration.

The rule makers could – and should – have wiped out mass play by simply instructing the referees to enforce the offside rule, thereby restoring to the game some of its original skill. Instead they capitulated, and in 1888, much to Walter Camp's disgust, mass play became legal. So began two of football's darkest decades.

Fittingly enough it was a chess master, Harvard's Lorin F. Deland, who perfected mass play. Using the simple formula of mass times momentum equals force, Deland reasoned that if wedges could be made to move forward with greater speed, they would be virtually unstoppable. In 1892, during Harvard's annual blood match against Yale, Deland unleashed his first "flying wedge." With the score locked at 0–0, the players took the field for the start of the second half, the unsuspecting Yale defense assembling as usual on the 55-yard line. The Harvard men, however, split into two groups and fell back to take up positions at opposite ends of the 25-yard line, leaving only the quarterback – the captain, Trafford – on the 45-yard line. At the beginning of play, Harvard's two units locked arms and charged diagonally across the field to converge on Trafford, who slipped quickly into the moving wedge of players and was crashed through the Yale defense. Only suicidal tackling from Yale's last-ditch line of defense halted the flying wedge a few yards from the goal line.

As with the mass play which preceded it, Deland's flying wedge caused a sensation. Overnight, "mass momentum" was the phrase on every coach's lips. Pennsylvania's George Woodruff positioned his guards behind the wedge and came up with the "guards back" formation; as the two units converged, the ball carrier was scooped up from behind and slammed bodily through the defense like a sack of potatoes. Amos Alonzo Stagg devised a system whereby his linemen could initiate a mass momentum play from the scrimmage rather than having to wait for the kickoff. Other coaches added similar refinements until eventually the tactics had reached ludicrous extremes. There were stories of players thundering down the field in perfect formation, each man gripping a suitcase handle which had been sewn into the trousers of the man in front. Ball carriers were fitted with handles on their shoulders so that if their colleagues behind failed to force them home through the gap, their teammates in front could haul them to safety like limp rag dolls.

As Deland had calculated, the flying wedge and its offshoots proved all but invincible. Coaches boasted that even if the opposing teams knew exactly where the wedge would strike their lines of defense, the information was still valueless. The only way to counter a wedge, advised Camp, was either to stove in its sides or lay down in its path and grab for the legs, a shortcut to certain suicide. Other coaches ordered defenders to hit the man at the apex of the triangle with the heel of their hand flush on the jaw. Another trick was to dive under the running mass in the hope that it would trip itself up. If you were built like Pudge Heffelfinger you simply ran at

---

DRESSED TO KILL

American footballers have always been slightly schizophrenic about protective equipment. Apart from shunning it for decades because it was a slur on their masculinity, when it did become accepted they were unsure whether to use it for protection or treat it as another weapon in their ever-expanding arsenal. Princeton's L. P. Smock was the first to foreshadow the future by pulling a canvas jacket over his sweater before a game in 1877. Significantly he did it not so much for protection, but hopefully to tear the fingernails out of tacklers' clawing hands.

Smock's embryonic armor did not, however, catch on. The game's he-man image required its players to sniff at anything that smacked of self-protection – horse-hair padding, quilted breeches and the like. Even at the height of mass play the only protective measure acceptable to Princeton men was to grow great shocks of hair to cushion the blows – a fashion which became popular on campus under the name of the "chrysanthemum look."

Mass momentum and the increasing brutality of the game forced players to look again at protection. Face masks in the form of bizarre beak-shaped nose guards began to appear, and by 1893 shin pads had become indispensable. Three years later even the hardest-headed player had come to accept the benefits of leather helmets. From this point onward, armor was to play a crucial role in the development of the game, freeing players from certain types of injury on the one hand and adding to the casualty list on the other. Today's game could not be played without armor, either defensively or offensively.

the leading man and hit him in the chest with your knees. In an era which scorned even the most rudimentary protective equipment as "unmanly," injury was rife.

To make matters worse, the game by this time had lost its last vestiges of sporting innocence. In 1889 the captains of Harvard, Yale, Princeton, Pennsylvania and Wesleyan had met and agreed to stamp out "slugging," but this was easier said than done. The unswerving momentum of the game toward greater and greater violence made frayed tempers and punch-ups almost inevitable. Both teams lined up eyeball to eyeball only inches apart, and the temptations were overwhelming. "There they stood, brow to brow, foot to foot, and carnage was the order of the day," recalled John Heisman. "Getting linemen that close to each other was to incite fighting, and fighting there was." Many a young college undergraduate had his features materially altered by a sly punch thrown during a football match. It was not until 1906 that a narrow strip of no-man's-land was introduced between the two lines, but by then slugging had become part of the game.

This escalating violence did not go unnoticed. Football had always had its detractors, and with the flying wedge storming across the campuses, these critics recoiled in loud horror. Surely, they cried, the purpose of a college education is to foster gentility, not to encourage the most physically gifted students to become thugs? "No father or mother worthy of the name would permit a son to associate with the set of Yale brutes" who comprised the Yale football team, railed the *New York Post*. People began to take notice.

Less than a year after the introduction of mass momentum there were strong moves to outlaw it, some of which were successful. Both West Point (Army) and Annapolis (Navy) banned flying wedges, and Cornell restricted its team to home games only. Both Yale and Princeton also leaned heavily toward prohibition. Against them, fighting to preserve the status quo, were Pennsylvania (now performing brilliantly under Woodcock, whose tactical preferences were reflected in his choice of halfback – Osgood, the American colleges' heavyweight champion for both boxing and wrestling) and Harvard. In 1894 representatives of the Big Four met to try and resolve their differences. After much heated discussion they voted to outlaw the Lehigh V, the Princeton wedge and the flying wedge, thus supposedly bringing an end to mass play. In fact, they had achieved very little; the rule changes they did adopt were, on close inspection, palpably no more than half-hearted compromise. It was to take many more such acrimonious meetings before mass play could be considered dead.

The trouble was that few of those associated with the game actually wanted to see the back of mass play. The coaches were anxious to retain every possible weapon which might assist them in their obsessional charge toward victory. The players were not complaining – besides anything else, it wouldn't have been considered manly – and nor were the fans, which suited the college elders who by now had seen the value of football as a means of gaining both revenue and prestige.

Even more important was the social climate of the times. America's "Gay Nineties" was a decade of brashness and bravado, an era in which the nation first began to flex its collective muscle and to feel its own strengths. Abroad there was the increasing military posturing and gunboat diplomacy which was to culminate in the marine invasion of Manila Harbor and the deaths on San Juan Hill of Roosevelt's Rough Riders. At home the ethos of Roosevelt's frontier life was taking root, soon to become an obsession affecting sportsmen from New Jersey to the Rocky Mountains. Sport became a substitute – a mirror, if you like – for the hardships of frontier living and the perils of the battlefield, and football was at its head, encapsulating perfectly the tough and aggressive mood of the nation. It is a depressing experience to read through the college records of the period and discover just how many college football heroes went straight from school into uniform to die on Spanish soil.

Throughout the decade the game progressed with giant strides in much the same way and for much the same reasons as professional football progressed during the last part of the '60s, the height of the Vietnam War. In 1888 sixty colleges were playing football; two years later the number had doubled. By the turn of the century big college matches were attracting upward of forty-five thousand spectators at a time. Why tamper with something so hugely successful? the game's rule makers asked themselves. Why indeed.

As if to emphasize the ineffectiveness of the new restrictions on mass play, the 1894 football season was one of the bloodiest on record. During the Harvard-Yale match alone, two tackles were knocked unconscious and the Harvard captain had his collarbone broken. In all, four players from each side were carried off. Other games recorded similar casualties. In that season the federal government stepped in and canceled the Army-Navy game to avert what it predicted would be "a bloodbath." Obviously something had to be done.

The following year the Big Four met again. This time they could agree on nothing and the meeting broke up in a turmoil, each college resolved to go its own separate way. It was the end of the Ivy League's domination. Soon after, the second-string Big Ten (comprised of such bush league colleges as Michigan, Minnesota and Wisconsin) attempted to achieve what their superiors had failed to do. This meeting, too, ended in stalemate, but the following year the Big Ten managed to thrash out a formula which satisfied even the giants of the Eastern Seaboard. What this formula did, in effect, was to make the lines stationary at the snap, thereby neutralizing the scrimmage.

The rules against mass momentum altered the pattern of the game, but they barely touched the level of violence. At the turn of the century, football was as tough as it had ever been – still, in the words of Michigan wonder coach Fielding Yost, "a man-to-man fight." At the first Rose Bowl game in 1901, Stanford was forced to request an early end to the match as it had run out of able-bodied players.

The critics renewed their assaults. Bills were introduced into several state legislatures outlawing the game, and were only narrowly defeated. Foreign newspapers carried reports of "the bloody American pastime." "One human life," thundered Syracuse Chancellor, James Day, "is too big a price for all the games of the season." Faced with this, some schools (California and Stanford) changed back to rugby or dropped football altogether (Columbia and Northwestern). Most, however, clung to the sport, not even bothering to alter the rules. For the first time in its brief history the game had become relatively stable, and its custodians were again loath to tinker. The only way injuries were reduced was by the devastatingly simple arrangement of playing less games. Soon some schools in the Midwest had reduced their playing season to a ludicrous five games.

That it took Theodore Roosevelt himself to force a change is ample proof of football's deterioration during the early years of the 1900s. A veteran of San Juan Hill and an almost pathological destroyer of wild animals, President Roosevelt was hardly a man to blanch at the sight of blood. Moreover, he was an avid enthusiast of rough contact sports, football in particular. "In life as in a football game," he declared in 1900, "the principle is: Hit the line hard; don't foul and don't shirk, but hit the line hard." By 1905, how-ever, even Roosevelt had reached the conclusion that perhaps the nation would be better off without football. In that season 18 college and high school students lost their lives and more than 159 were seriously injured on football fields around the country – a staggering toll considering the comparatively small numbers playing the game. What upset Roosevelt in particular was a single image – a newspaper photograph snapped during a Pennsylvania-Swarthmore game which showed the giant Swarthmore tackle Bob Maxwell stumbling toward the sidelines holding his bloody face in his hands. The president immediately summoned representatives of Yale, Princeton and Harvard and warned them that unless football mended its ways, he would ban it. "Brutality and foul play should receive the same summary punish-ment given to the man who cheats at cards," he remonstrated.

The upshot of this presidential ultimatum was the hasty formation of an Intercollegiate Rules Committee which, at its first meeting, finally severed American football's last obvious links with rugby by legalizing the forward pass. This move was in theory designed to open up the game and start players running again, thereby reducing the risk of a snapped neck on the line. But in practice, for the first few years at least, the forward pass was an unmitigated disaster so far as curtailing violence was concerned. Although it did succeed in opening up play, it had the unfortunate effect of critically weakening the defense without providing any compensatory restraints on the offense. As attacks ran riot, the defensive linemen found themselves on the chopping block, and injuries spiraled. In 1907 *Life* published a cartoon depicting a football field littered with brawling players and dismembered limbs. The caption read: "Football under the New Rule – showing how former rough play has been replaced by humane tactics and illustrating the impossibility of accident since the reforms have been instituted." The 1909 season was the worst ever, killing 33 and injuring 246 (73 severely). The most widely publicized death was that of star Army tackle Eugene A. Byrne, who was discovered under a pile of Harvard men with his spine broken. It was not until 1912 that a suitable balance between attack and defense was finally struck.

College football came of age amid the waving pennants, the raccoon coats and the bootleg hip flasks of the Roaring Twenties, an era which saw America fall headlong for sport. By then the game had become a spectacle, an entertainment attracting seventy and eighty thousand addled fans each weekend to the massive concrete stands which mushroomed across the country. By the end of the decade more than three-quarters of a million students were playing the game in some six hundred colleges and several thousand high schools.

It was this burgeoning popularity which finally overwhelmed the critics of football's brutality. By the beginning of the '20s, many of the more obvious opportunities for slaughter had been removed. There was no more interlocked interference or flying tackles, and seven men on the line of scrimmage had become the rule. More importantly, the forward pass had been absolved of its taint of cowardliness and had become a formidable weapon in the hands of such masters as Knute Rockne. But for all this cosmetic surgery, football remained essentially a game of shuddering blocks and arm-wrenching tackles. For every Red Grange streaking his way toward daylight, there was a George Pfann who "crept, crawled and ran on all fours with tackles draped around him." Injuries continued to escalate until in 1931 the game reaped its grimmest toll ever. In that season no less than forty players lost their lives, ranging from an eight-year-old killed in a street game to Fordham tackle Cornelius J. Murphy and Army end Richard B. Sheridan.

Only a few years before, such a body count would have come perilously close to destroying the game. Now, however, it was all but ignored. The game had become too big, too much of an established ritual to be jeopardized by a few deaths. Injury and death had become accepted as inevitable side effects of the game. They remain as such even today.

The Pros

By the end of the 1920s another equally popular and even more brutal game was looming ominously on the college horizon – professional football. The first truly professional club had made its appearance at the beginning of the decade in Canton, Ohio. The origins of the game were considerably older than that, however, dating back to the northern collieries and steel foundry towns of the late 1800s.

The professional clubs began life as local athletic clubs catering to a generation of youths whose upbringing amid the pits and the rolling mills effectively disbarred them from a college education. Like the college students, these sons of the American industrial revolution had also developed a fierce enthusiasm for hard competition. College football, in only slightly modified form, became an expression for this enthusiasm. Initially the clubs were wholly amateur. However, as rivalry intensified and football became increasingly ingrained in working-class leisure life, they began scouting for players capable of winning matches, be they foreigners or locals. Of course, outsiders were hardly likely to feel much filial affection for the small and grimy hamlets which housed the football clubs, and so cash payments to recruits became an accepted part of northern sporting life. Soon the gladiators of the college campuses were signing on as mercenaries for Pennsylvania's unlovely mining communities.

The first recorded professional football match was in 1895 when Latrobe, an obscure Pennsylvanian eyesore, beat its equally obscure neighbor Jeanette 12–0 with the help of a college quarterback hired for the day for $10 plus expenses. No description of the match survives, although if it was at all typical of the times it would have been a tough, undisciplined and devastatingly brutal contest. This was the period in which mass momentum was laying waste the college teams, and the embryonic professionals played to much the same rules. In fact, they were probably even rougher. Whereas college matches were tempered to some degree by the fraternal feelings of the participants, the professionals met head on, giving no quarter and expecting none in return. An opponent was an enemy from alien territory; more importantly he was a threat to your livelihood (still a common justification for no-holds-barred play among modern professionals).

The early history of the professional game is riddled with reports of fist fights, brawls and the dark deeds of such shadowy characters as Lawson Fiscus, an ogre Pennsylvanian mothers no doubt conjured up to silence their recalcitrant infants. Fiscus, an ex-Princeton halfback who was the first player ever to receive a weekly wage for playing football in America, had a fearsome reputation built largely on one particular incident. Prior to the turn of the century a ball carrier was not considered to have been downed until he had actually surrendered by shouting out "down." Refusal to surrender was the mark of a fool – a courageous fool, but a fool nonetheless. According to history, Fiscus was once confronted by just such a suicidally inclined fool. Drawing back his heavy boot he coolly kicked the man in the face and broke his jaw.

The spectators who turned out for these savage affrays were not much better behaved than the teams they supported. Although the game was far from widespread even in Pennsylvania, in those places that it did surface regularly it was supported by an enthusiasm bordering on hysteria. The two great rivals of the early years were the twin towns of Latrobe and Greensburg. When they met, every small-town patriot capable of landing a solid punch arrived to fight for the honor of his team. Invariably the match ended in a pitched brawl with players, spectators and officials all battling it out in the middle of the field. As the game spread farther afield – moving through Philadelphia, Chicago, upstate New York and Ohio – this fanatical support spread with it. In Ohio the Canton Bulldogs and the Massillon Tigers took on Latrobe/Greensburg's tattered mantle with even wilder results. Interestingly much of the hysteria surrounding these provincial stand-offs was purposely whipped up by the local newspapers of each town; even in those days violent rivalry was recognized as good for local business, the odd broken window notwithstanding.

The tactical balance of these early teams leaned solidly on the side of brute strength. Coaches chose players solely for their weight and muscle and were not above stacking their front ranks with professional wrestlers – giants such as the Chicago Tigers' 250-pound Marty Cutler, who was as expert in maiming an opponent with his cleats as he was in applying a hammerlock. Indeed it was one such strong man – the legendary Sac and Fox Indian Jim Thorpe – who did much to lift professional football out of its backwater and set it on the road to popular acceptance.

Thorpe had been the backbone of Glenn "Pop" Warner's sensational college team, the Carlisle Indian School, which had overrun the cream of the college circuit during the first decade of the century. In addition to Thorpe, the team had also boasted such acclaimed players as Indian Joe Guyon and

Pete Hauser, both of whom were more than competent all-in wrestlers. (Warner himself had been a heavyweight boxing champion at Cornell.) But it was Thorpe who was the undisputed star. He could run like the wind and slip under the very noses of would-be tacklers. More importantly, he could hit with the force of a small hurricane. Rumor had it that at the last moment before a game he would add a thin strip of rolled steel to his already heavily padded shoulders, such was the effect of his tackling. It was, recalled one of his former opponents, "like being hit with the blunt end of a telephone pole." During a college game of 1912, Dwight D. Eisenhower and another Army linebacker took the field with instructions to hit Thorpe with everything they had. In the third quarter they saw their chance and tackled him so hard that they both dazed themselves and had to be taken out of the game. Thorpe played on to the end. His college play made Thorpe a hero and when, in 1915, he signed with the Canton Bulldogs as playing coach, the professional game's stocks soared.

Even more important to the evolution of the professional game was the appearance of George Halas, a mediocre player with the unlamented Hammond Pros of Chicago, who discovered in 1920 that he possessed a particular flair for organizing football teams – and tough football teams at that. While Thorpe and his colleagues could provide the violence almost as easily as turning on a tap, it took a George Halas to direct it, package it and sell it to the public, which he did.

Halas began his coaching career by building a professional football team for an Illinois starch manufacturer. Offering the promise of a job at the starchworks and time off for practice, Halas was able to sign a formidable collection of college stars anxious to continue playing after graduation. To provide his new team with suitable competition, he petitioned the managers of the few other existing professional clubs, suggesting that they join forces and form a league, which is what they did.

For the next three decades Halas's team – first as the Decatur Staleys, after the starch manufacturer, and later as the Chicago Bears – overwhelmed all opposition. Their success was achieved largely by pursuing a philosophy of uncompromising violence. "It's true that the Bears were known for bruising people," confessed Halas to author Myron Cope in *The Game That Was* (1974), "but it was done in a legal manner, by hard-crashing blocks and tackles." Perhaps. But legal or not, the end result was the same. Halas himself was no stranger to football injury, having once played through a game with a broken jaw, and neither were his players nor their opponents: legs were broken, cleats sharpened to needlepoints, flesh gouged and teeth knocked out. Once when a quarterback had to be rushed to hospital with his eyeball hanging out on his cheek it excited only a passing comment in the local newspapers, so common had injury become.

The worst matches initially were against the Canton Bulldogs. Later the warfare moved north to the frost-bitten harbor town of Green Bay, where Curly Lambeau's Green Bay Packers ruled. According to those who played in them, matches between the Bears and the Packers were "always bloodbaths." Players such as the Bears' notorious Bulldog Turner would be lined up against men like Green Bay's Clarke Hinkle, who performed with such a maniacally fixed and glassy stare that he was often accused of taking drugs. "When you hit him," said one player of Hinkle, "it would just pop every joint all the way down to your toes." The star of this period was Bronco Nagurski, a giant who wrestled professionally during the off season. To further aggravate the violence the forward pass was a long time in finding acceptance on the professional circuit. "Only sissies throw the ball," declared Green Bay tackle Cal Hubbard, and that was that.

Back in 1920, though, the future of pro football remained very much in the balance. For the first few years of their existence the Decatur Staleys fought more against their own extinction than against opposing teams. In 1921, the year Halas moved from Decatur to Chicago, the end-of-season profit was a miserable $71.63. The next year, although attracting marginally better crowds, the club still barely managed to break even. Often Halas found that he literally could not give tickets away. As with the professional wrestling of the same period, the public sensed something distasteful about professional football. While it was acceptable for students to beat the life out of each other on a football field, for a grown man to make his living in the same fashion . . . well, that was something else again.

Halas, however, had faith in the game's ability to sell tickets. In 1924 he backed this faith by gambling everything he had in signing up the most talked about footballer the sports world had yet seen, Red Grange. Grange's defection from the ranks of college amateurs was a major breakthrough for Halas and the professional game, eclipsing even Thorpe's signing a decade before. The colleges still treated professional players as pariahs and there was massive pressure on Grange to reject any approaches. His college even promised to keep his jersey enshrined in perpetuity if he retired an amateur. Grange, however, had made up his mind. So the story goes, he slipped out of his dormitory window, scaled down the drain pipe and sped off in a waiting car to sign with Halas. It is easy enough to see what persuaded him: in exchange for his signature Grange received what are still the most favorable terms ever given an athlete – a full 50 percent of the club's total take.

Halas's generosity – or shrewd business sense, whichever you prefer – was rewarded. In his first appearance as a professional, Grange sold out Chicago's Wrigley Field. Immediately Halas launched him on a grueling coast-to-coast tour of the nation – eighteen games in two months; eight of them in just twelve days. For Grange, the tour was a nightmare: at the end of it he was an exhausted wreck, bearing the stamp of the game's ferocity across his body – a smashed mouth, a disabled arm and masses of bruises.

Although it crippled him, the tour made Grange an extraordinarily rich young man. Wherever he had played, crowds had flocked to see him in numbers surpassing even those of the most eagerly awaited college matches. In New York, where Grange was given a thorough going over by the Giants, 73,651 had managed to scramble through the turnstiles. Thousands more had been forced to remain outside. Grange finished the trip with several hundred thousand dollars in his pocket and a fist full of Hollywood offers, having given the pleasure seekers of the Jazz Age a new entertainment. From that moment on, Halas and his colleagues were certain that the most violent ball game ever devised was destined to prove very, very profitable.

Kill the Quarterback

Ever since the scholars of Rugby decided that to cripple a fellow's shins with an iron-clad boot was simply not cricket, the laws of football and the other contact ball sports have undergone countless revisions aimed at re-ducing their level of violence. No longer is it possible for a player to jump his opponent, shouting that he is making work for the surgeon – at least not if he wishes to remain in the game. Neither can a soccer player still leap feet first into a tackle from behind, or a wide receiver "crack back" on a lineman, or a hockey player spear his opponent with his stick. Unlike the situation in Rollerball, science fiction writer William Harrison's gory sport of the future which continually alters its rules to accommodate more bloodshed, it has been many decades since a rule was changed to make any of our ball sports purposely more violent.

On paper then, rugby, soccer, gridiron, ice hockey and lacrosse are all pale shadows of their former selves. In practice, however, they are not. Although to compare the memories of one era with the realities of another is always a dubious exercise, it is clear enough that the levels of violence in our most popular games have at best remained more or less constant, and at worst have escalated to a degree which would have appalled even a Lawson Fiscus.

❝ It's a violent game, sure, but it's just that kind of game! ❞

George Halas, owner of the Chicago Bears, 1977

> **❝ I've started daydreaming about Merlin Olsen. I see myself breaking his leg or knocking him unconscious, and then I see myself knocking out a couple of other guys, and then I see us scoring a touchdown and always, in my own dreams, I see myself as the hero.** ❞
>
> Jerry Kramer, former US pro football player, 1968

Take gridiron, the game which so shook Sullivan and which today is the single most popular sport in America. For all the tinkering and rule tightening which has gone on since the turn of the century, football has evolved into a sport of stupefying violence. Compared with the modern game, as Art Rooney, the veteran owner of the Pittsburgh Steelers once said, the early days of pro football with its Thorpes and Nagurskis and Hinkles was "just shoving and pushing." Even the college giants who propelled the flying wedges and who clawed at each other's "smocks" can only be classed as boys against the brutal sophistications of a Conrad Dobler or a Mean Joe Greene. As an example of institutionalized mass violence, modern football is in a league of its own. Each year it kills on average twenty-eight players and maims thousands more. It leaves everyone who reaches its higher levels with some form of lasting injury and, according to one medical report, cuts as much as twenty years off a professional player's life expectancy. Sometimes it even shocks the players themselves; as former Green Bay Packer star Jerry Kramer wrote in his 1968 bestseller *Instant Replay:*

> I don't really realize how brutal the game is until the off-season, when I go out to banquets and watch movies of our games. Then I see guys turned upside-down and backwards and hit from all angles, and I flinch. I'm amazed by how violent the game is, and I wonder about playing it myself.

"If a sane man stopped to think about American football," wrote English author Nicholas Mason, "he would never set foot on the field."

Testimonials to the game's monumental brutality such as Jerry Kramer's are not difficult to find, coming as they do from its every level of involvement. NFL player Jean Fugett:

> The game is *legalized* violence. Out in the real world you just can't go around beating on somebody's head the way we do. I can go into a game and just literally try to break somebody's neck.

Conrad Dobler, voted in 1978 the NFL's meanest player:

If you ever forget that football is a violent game, they'll catch you gazing at the stars and put your lights out.

Merlin Olsen, retired fourteen-year veteran of the Los Angeles Rams:

People ask, "You don't really hit that hard do you?" The answer is simply yes. The collisions are that violent, and the game itself is a very physical game. People who play for any length of time carry the scars for the rest of their lives. They may not be showing on the outside, but they'll have knees that are worn out, shoulders that don't work right, fingers that point in a different direction.

Robert Grant, associate professor of physical therapy at Ithaca College and a former college football trainer:

I would have to rate football as the most violent sport yet known. It's really almost undeclared war, and the way we play it in the professional game as well as in the high-pressure college games, it's just that – an organized, thoroughly campaigned and rigidly controlled game of outright violence.

Sports columnist and author Roger Kahn:

Football is terrifically violent. It's a game of impact, twisted knees and concussions. And whatever the mystique they try to put around it – that you have to be intelligent, that the scholar-athlete makes a good footballer – that's not really so. If you teach a gorilla to carry a football, he'd be the best running back in the history of the game.

A Game of Passion, an NFL publication:

Pro football is excessive. It's out of all proportion, beyond all bounds. It's an orgy of violence; an obsession with superiority; an excess of commitment, effort and discipline; a wallowing in flesh and will.

Psychiatrist Arnold Mandell, former football innocent seconded to the staff of the San Diego Chargers in 1972, after witnessing his first game from the sidelines:

The ground shook. Crunch . . . slap . . . snap . . . groan . . . scream . . . thud . . . Shit! Fuck! Motherfucker! I have to admit it, I closed my eyes. When I got up the courage to open them, I saw the result of my first on-the-field NFL play. Banaszack was down on his back in front of me. His mouth was twitching peculiarly. His eyes were closed. Rick Redman, our linebacker who got Banaszack, was down, too. On his right side and holding his left shoulder and whimpering quietly.

I was overwhelmed. I wanted to run away. . . . When I ran through the details of that encounter from the fleeting and cowardly glimpses I took, I became aware that they had actually accelerated into each other before the hit. Two hundred and twenty pounds hitting two hundred and twenty pounds while accelerating. Mass times speed equals kinetic energy. Kinetic energy is the force that dents cars on collision. My nervous system never really recovered from that first hit until close to the end of the game.

As Mandell discovered, football is not so much a contact sport as a collision sport. On each play, athletes chosen for their abnormal size and strength hurl themselves at each other with stunning force. In his book *A Thinking Man's Guide to Pro Football* (1972), Paul Zimmerman quotes a physicist who has determined that when a 240-pound lineman capable of running 100 yards in 11 seconds collides with a 240-pound back capable of covering the same distance in 10 seconds, the resultant kinetic energy is "enough to move 66,000 pounds, or 33 tons, one inch." When players stagger about the field mumbling to themselves after a play – "having your bell rung" in football parlance – the likelihood is that they have been hit on the helmet by a blow approaching 1,000 Gs (1,000 times the force of gravity). Astronauts on takeoff experience around 10 Gs and pilots tend to black out at about 20. Tests run on Detroit linebacker Joe Schmidt reportedly showed that he had to cope with blows which registered at 5,780 Gs.

Given this, it is hardly a source of wonder that football's injury statistics read like dispatches from the Crimea. According to the *Encyclopedia of Sport Sciences and Medicine* of 1971, from 1931 to 1965 there were 642 football fatalities (348 high school players, 54 college players and 72 professionals and semiprofessionals). A similar accounting by the National Collegiate Athletic Association determined that from 1931 to 1975 (excluding 1942) there were 821 fatalities directly related to football, with a further 400 or more indirectly related (the player collapses but does not die until at least four days later). Each season at least 50 and, according to one survey, as many as 86 out of every 100 high school players receive injuries serious enough to keep them off the field for more than a week. Another survey has estimated that each year 32 college and high school students become paraplegics as a result of playing football. Any boy who plays the game throughout both high school and college stands a 95 percent chance of a serious injury. Not so long ago, doctors at the University of Iowa examined 108 college freshmen recruits over a four-year period and discovered that more than a third of them had suffered unwitting neck and spinal injuries while playing high school football. Players at Ohio State University alone consume three thousand *miles* of surgical tape each season, mostly to pad and repair their injuries. According to the Occupational Safety and Health Administration, football players from all ranks – high school, college or pro – are two hundred times more likely to be injured than coalminers. As neurosurgeon R. C. Schneider wrote in 1973, "there is probably no better experimental or research laboratory for human trauma in the world than the football fields of our nation."

It is on the professional fields that this holds truest. There, with players dependent on sound bodies for their livelihood, the threat of serious injury hovers like an omnipresent gray cloud. In the end, nobody escapes unscathed. In the five years from 1969 to 1974 National Football League players suffered 5,110 injuries severe enough to sideline them for at least a day, at a cost to the clubs of some $17.6 million. The problem is increasing. In 1974 the injury count was 1,169, including 113 cases which required surgery – a 25 percent jump from the previous year. A year later it had risen to around 1,700. By the fourth week of the 1976–7 season, Miami's complete line-backing corps and secondary had been removed through injury, and by mid-season half the St. Louis Cardinals' starting defense had disappeared, all six Philadelphia running backs were on crutches and the quarterbacks of five other teams had been put out of commission for the year. It has been estimated that an NFL player now suffers 2.5 injuries every season. It has also been estimated that 4 out of every 22 players on the field are playing with a serious injury, and 5 out of every 22 are playing with an injury which would prevent any "normal" person from continuing his job. "In most clubs from around the tenth game on," veteran Los Angeles Ram Tom Mack told me, "80 percent are playing with some kind of injury, either minor pulls or bruises or a serious injury."

The average NFL career today lasts a mere 4.62 years – the shortest average in all professional sport. "And if you get hit solid game after game after game without learning how to absorb the hit," said NY Jet Clark Gaines, "you won't last two." For some positions, lasting two years would be considered quite an achievement for any player. For special team members – the "suicide squad" – wide open to blind-side tackles as they ferry the ball back down the field, injury runs at eight times the rate of other positions. In any given year there will only be eleven or twelve players in the entire NFL who are veterans of fifteen or more seasons. "I've spent my whole career watching fellas get injured, getting injured myself," NFL star Larry Csonka said without emotion. "Life expectancy is very short."

Statistics detailing the frequency of injury, of course, convey only the bare bones of football's violence. What must also be taken into account is the nature of these injuries. "I never saw such injuries, even in my intern years in the emergency rooms of inner-city hospitals," exclaimed Arnold Mandell. "Huge bruises spread over big slabs of the body." According to Dr. Alan Strizak, whose work at New York's Institute of Sports Medicine and Athletic Trauma brings him into close contact with several professional teams including the Jets, the toll pro football exacts on hands and head, although little publicized, is "enormous." "If you ever see a lineman, the first thing you'll probably notice is that his hands are totally deformed . . . broken fingers, dislocated fingers." Players such as Lloyd Voss, who retired in 1973: near the end of his career Voss took to taping up each individual fingertip because his fingernails kept getting torn out. "Concussions, too," said Strizak, "they happen a lot." As do shoulder separations, broken limbs and dislocated hips. Knee ligaments are especially vulnerable, collapsing under the strain of body blocks which, as one surgeon reported, "are comparable to the thrust of a railroad tie against the unsupported knee."

One week before the final game of the 1976–7 season, the Jets' training ground provided a stark illustration as to the rigors of pro football. After a grueling losing season, the number of crippled Jets far exceeded the healthy. Of the twenty-three defensive players on the roster, only ten were fit enough for action. In the medical room the rows of stainless steel beds were in constant use, with players lining up to take their turn under the heat lamps

---

RINGING THE BELL

Concussion is the common cold of football; for most players it is a seasonal experience. In *Instant Replay* Jerry Kramer confessed that after four or five concussions he was getting used to them. Many other players have suffered ten or more during the course of their career.

"The thing that scares me is the concussions," admitted Rams' quarterback Pat Haden, whose brief career has already included three "dings." "You kind of wonder how much a body can stand before you go punchy." According to one medical report published in 1952, Haden has already reached his limit. After studying seven thousand athletic injuries over a twenty-year period, Dr. A. Thorndyke outlined four circumstances which should preclude players from continuing contact sports for their own sake: loss of an eye, removal of the spleen or a kidney, and three or more cerebral concussions. If adopted, Dr. Thorndyke's proposals would effectively eliminate much of the NFL player pool.

---

and massage equipment. In among this assembly was quarterback Joe Namath, shortly to be traded to the warmer climes of California.

Even in the exacting world of NFL football, Namath's medical history has set him slightly apart from his colleagues. His particular cross has been his knees, which remain today as a pinnacle of surgical ingenuity. His knees severely battered during college, Namath was told by doctors that if they survived four years of professional football he could count himself fortunate. Up to that point, with the help of an unnerving number of operations, he had held them together for twelve, although, as he confessed, they were giving him a little trouble. By this Namath meant that he had difficulty stepping sideways or walking up a flight of stairs (a complaint he shared with another pro footballer, Leon Donahue, who was eventually forced to move out of his split-level home). The knee joint wasn't designed to be able to take a lateral blow or a medial blow, Namath explained. Whenever a big man hits you and has some power behind the hit, something's got to give. And with the object of the whole exercise being, in Namath's own words, to kill the quarterback, the blows have come painfully hard and fast.

But knees are only one episode in Namath's painful career. Worse still was the nerve injury in his leg which happened around the time of his first knee operation (the way in which Namath conjured up his past was interesting; whereas others dated incidents by the season or by the opposing team – "it was in my rookie year just after the Dallas game . . ." – his chronology revolved around major surgeries):

> I used to get a jolt from my foot up my body every five seconds or so. "It went on for about three weeks and almost drove me crazy. Medication wouldn't help it, morphine wouldn't help it. I lost thirty pounds. It was remarkable. One day I went into the doctor's office and I put the pills down and I said, "Doc, I can't take any more medicine. This stuff's killing me." Thirty pounds light! That was the roughest. Then I lost the feeling in my foot. The neurosurgeons all assured me that the feeling would come back, and it has. But it took more than three years.

Namath's other injuries included separations of both shoulders, a broken wrist, a broken cheek bone, a dislocated finger and a broken ankle. His current problem was a torn hamstring muscle.

"This one here," he said, pointing to what looked to be a heavily strapped thigh underneath his trousers. "It's balled up right there. I can't extend my leg like that more than two or three strides. Then it pulls up and you can't run on it."

I asked him if he had to wear the bandage all the time.

"There's no bandage," he grinned, grabbing my hand and running it over the bulge on the back of his leg.

What at first sight had appeared to be a bulky arrangement of pads and straps was in fact a solid knot of muscle the size of a half baseball.

"*Jesus Christ!*" I muttered.

"Yeah. The whole muscle just tore and rolled down. Looks like a damn grapefruit, don't it?"

"What will happen to it? You're just going to leave it like that?"

"They could fix it, but it's not necessary. It would take a major operation, and for what we do in everyday life it's fine. I just can't run at all."

"How long has it been like that?"

"Three years."

I looked at Namath in amazement and he grinned again. "This is a rough game," he said, "people *have* to get hurt. You can't keep track of the hits. When you come off the field it can be bad, but it's not as bad as it is that night or the next day. When you try to get out of the bed the next morning it's a bitch."

Although the name of the game may be quarterback killing – and indeed, one of the most enduring spectacles in American football is that of a quarterback disappearing under a welter of clawing bodies just as he releases the ball – everybody, said Namath, suffers. "Running backs . . . they want to jack 'em up and give 'em a good hard hit and if it puts them out of the game, well . . . that's a shame. When I see defensive linebackers and cornerbacks taking the kind of blows they take, I can't understand how they can get up and come back the next play. Every play they're getting hit from one side or another. As long as it's a good hard hit, that's the incentive. Make the guy not want to get up, not want to come back the next play."

Namath was phlegmatic about football's physical toll, a toll which, according to Dr. Ronnie Sue Stangler of the University of Washington, cuts twenty years off the life expectancy of NFL players.* Like many other NFL stars he was resigned to living with his injuries long after the cheering had stopped. He frankly admitted that by the age of 50 he fully expected to have difficulty merely putting one foot in front of the other, let alone negotiating a flight of stairs. Merlin Olsen, suffering through his last season with agonizing arthritis in both knees, was similarly aware of his fate. He

---

* A 1972 study of the comparative life span of professional athletes cited by reporter Clark Booth in the January 1977 issue of the Boston magazine *Mother Jones* found that half the pro football players had died before the age of 58. The age for boxers was 62; for baseball players, 65; for track and field athletes, 72.

talked about replacing his knees with artificial joints in a few years' time. "My shoulders and hands have also taken a real ripping and tearing," he added. "My body I am sure is full of calcium deposits."

The majority of pro football's unwanted souvenirs are generally less debilitating than either Olsen's joints or Namath's knees. They are more likely to be along the lines of the smashed thumb suffered by a Buffalo Sabre which, in retirement, fused rigid, or the scars – "from the top of my head to my ankles" – which earned Jerry Kramer the nickname "Zipper." But the fact remains that, as Merlin Olsen said earlier in this chapter, anybody who takes on pro football for any length of time can count on being marked for life. The game is a horse trade – high salaries, glory and a secure future in exchange for physical health. "A difficult thing to realize when you're 19 years old," remarked Dr. Alan Strizak.

Most players, it would seem, do not consider the price exorbitant. "It's not that one day I woke up and said, 'My God! Look what's happening to my body!' " said Merlin Olsen. "I knew this is the price to pay for being a pro. It's like the man who goes down the coal mine; he not only accepts the risks of the occupation, but also the side effects."

Yet even at the professional level where salaries average around $55,000, there are some doubts. Wayne Mulligan, a veteran pro center, was one of the casualties recuperating at the Jets' training ground in 1977. Three years earlier he had broken his arm, continued to play, and had broken it again. The doctors had inserted a plate in his arm to hold it together, but constant nerve pain forced its removal, leaving Mulligan with six screw holes drilled through his bones. "Is it worth it? That's a very good question. I don't know. I guess you have to pay a price for everything, and sometimes you only know if it's worth it when you're through. Right now, though, I just don't know."

At football's lower levels, the question is even more pertinent. Whereas the glory becomes far more fleeting and the material rewards are negligible, the price in terms of health remains the same.

Dave Meggyesy, former St. Louis Cardinal and author of the book *Out of Their League* (1971), on his college football career:

> During my four years, I accumulated a broken wrist, separations of both shoulders, an ankle torn up so badly it broke the arch of my foot, three major brain concussions, and an arm that almost had to be amputated because of improper treatment. And I was one of the lucky ones.

George Simpson, writing in a recent issue of *Sport* magazine:

... each time I put my arm around my girl, or sleep too long on either shoulder, or try to open a door with my left hand in wet weather, or make an awkward step and feel my ankle slide out of joint, I vividly remember my college football days. And it hurts.

Even more poignant was a letter which appeared in *Sport* following Simpson's article:

Last year I had my fourth knee operation. I can only bend my left leg about 60 degrees. I've had my left kneecap removed, my cartilage removed, my ligaments sewn back together three times. I had three blood clots that had to be surgically removed. The arthritis in my knees and other joints is getting worse and as a result, I probably take more aspirin than I should. My right knee has bone chips that cause my knee to lock and I often fall down when I'm walking. I've had eighteen casts on my legs and can't even count the number of times my legs have had to be drained of fluid. One doctor has recommended fusing my left leg perfectly straight and another wants to totally replace my left knee joint with some kind of metal joint. I already have enough metal in me to start a junkyard. I've been doing leg therapy for seven years now. *And I'm only 20 years old.*

From the perspective of the schoolyard, football's horse trade looks distinctly lopsided, a view held by former college coach John M. Barry. Throughout his coaching career, Barry was struck by the preponderance of injuries inherent in the game. Making the transition from high school to college teams, for instance, he could not believe the scars his new players were sporting. "So many athletes had zippers down the side of their knee, or knees; they thought nothing of it and called this or that a Band-Aid operation. I just kept looking at where the knife had cut and shaking my head. There were so many." In the end Barry quit coaching, haunted by the sight of a young opposition player lying helpless on the turf paralyzed from the neck down. "I looked at the boy's face," he recalled, "at the wonderment in it, and felt sick. Sick of football. It couldn't be worth it."

Few of those associated with football ever reach such a conclusion, even those who are closest to the bloodshed, let alone those on the fringes. Incredible though it might seem given the death and injury statistics, most Americans would not consider the game excessively violent. Hard and tough, maybe. But violent? Never! Consider this snippet from a recent interview with NFL commissioner Pete Rozelle. Defending the game against its critics, Rozelle snapped: "What we do object to is constant psychoanalysis. Football is warlike. Football is violent." What Rozelle was saying, in effect, was that the game is not warlike, is not violent. But how can a sport which pits a Conrad Dobler against a Merlin Olsen in what one player has called "a small, private war" possibly be considered as anything less than the epitome of violence?

The reasons for such an extraordinarily blinkered view of football's brutality are two-fold. Firstly, the game has reached such preeminence in American society that we see and enjoy its violence but don't recognize it as such. As James Michener concluded in his book *Sports in America* (1976):

> Football is the American form of violence, and whereas Spanish bull-fighting is pretty despicable – one practitioner killed about every four years – and Mexican cockfighting abominable – no men ever killed – our violent sport is neither, because we have given it our moral sanction.

Assaults which would be universally condemned if they occurred outside in the parking lot are lauded, applauded and accepted as being merely "part of the game" when they happen inside the stadium. Football violence has, in effect, been exempted from the condemnation heaped on other varieties of violence.

The second reason concerns the ways in which football is presented to its audience. The majority of paying spectators receive only a greatly diminished view of the game's violence. In the past when fans clustered on the sidelines, everybody was aware of the implications involved in two large athletes hurling themselves bodily at each other. Today, however, the giant stadiums which house the game across the country have divorced spectators from the realities of what goes on below them. The closest most fans now come to experiencing the sheer brutality of football is when the occasional crack of a plastic pad wafts up into the bleachers. In addition, the appearance of the players themselves, swathed in padding with their faces obscured by visored helmets, further diminishes the reality of violence; to the bleacher-bound eye the players appear impregnable, impervious to pain and something less than human beings.

And that is the game experienced live; even more fans take their football from a television set, a medium which can reduce the wildest prizefight to a seemingly painless exercise played out by 19-inch manikins. The violence of

---

❝ A defensive lineman can do just about anything. He can damn near haul an axe out of his jock and slash around with it before he'll be called for anything. ❞

Alex Karras, former US pro football star, 1976

---

televised football has all the unreality of a TV cop drama, slotted away as it is among the soap commercials. The language of the announcer further masks the brutality. "To jab a forearm into someone's throat is a poor show," said Roger Kahn. "But to *clothesline* a man, well . . . that's sport." The effects of the violence – the injured groaning on the sidelines – are never shown; it is violence without a conscience. As Kahn said, "You just don't hear the screams."

For these reasons, football's reputation for violence is considerably softer than the realities of the game would warrant. Certainly its image is far more demure than the broken-toothed aura which surrounds that other violent ball sport – or "puck sport" to be more precise – which has, over the last few decades, become a fully fledged American sporting institution: ice hockey. In modern sporting parlance, the word *hockey* is now more or less synonymous with violence.

Blood on the Rocks

Hockey was Canada's contribution to the manly arts. Probably derived from the children's game of shinny (so called because of the inevitability of bruised shins), it was first played in recognizable form by the British soldiers stationed beside the frozen wastes of Ontario's Kingston Harbor during the mid-1800s. The game suited Canadian tastes; by 1879 it had been codified and, a little over a decade later, more than a hundred hockey clubs had sprung up in Montreal alone.

From the start hockey was definitely a "man's game," a favorite of the lumberjacks of the frozen north who played it with the same violent abandon they used when attacking a forest. But even when played by the most genteel of Canadian high society, the game had a habit of bringing out the worst in its players. After a match at Toronto's prestigious Granite Club in 1890, the Toronto *Globe* reported:

> It is greatly to be regretted that in a game between amateur teams some
> players should forget themselves before such a number of spectators,
> a good proportion of whom on the occasion referred to being ladies, as
> to indulge in fisticuffs, and the action of some spectators in rushing on
> the ice is also to be deplored.

So much for the amateurs; and the professional leagues which followed were even worse. Faces were sliced open by skate blades, heads were cracked by whirring sticks (one early victim of a stick attack required twenty-two towels to staunch the flow of blood from his skull), shoulders were separated by slamming body checks in mid-rink, and fist fights, with the players hurling off their gauntlets and getting down to it with bare fists, were soon an integral part of the spectacle. Fans assaulted players and players assaulted fans, with sometimes whole teams invading the bleachers to administer some rough justice.

By 1907 the embryonic professionals of what was to become known as hockey's "prehistoric era" had claimed their first fatality – one Owen Mc-Court, who succumbed after a rap from his opponent Charlie Masson's stick.* In that same year a Montreal player almost died during a game which the Montreal *Star* called "an exhibition of brutality." In 1923, after a match between the Canadiens and the Ottowa Senators, Sir Arthur Currie, head of McGill University, was moved to remark: "I would rather every grandstand burned down rather than a repetition of the disgraceful scenes that took place in the Mount Royal Arena."

By the mid-'20s hockey had been embraced by other countries, especially the United States where, as the *American Pageant* coyly put it: "The sport's roughness was no deterrent to its popularity." The heroes of the period were the iron men – the "policemen" – whose job it was to "protect" the goal scorers on their team. These were men such as the Gleghorn brothers (Sprague and Odie); Billy Cotu, expelled from the league for hitting a referee; Bad Joe Hall and Newsy Lalonde, whose blood feuds were measured by the number of stitches they inflicted on each other; and the legendary Eddie Shore, hockey's archetypal strong man.

In an era which required players to brawl at least as well as they could play, if not better, Shore still stood out like a beacon. He is best remembered for the charging of Ace Bailey, a deed which earned him the wrath of fans of every persuasion. As Bailey bent over to catch his breath, Shore lifted him high into the air with a crunching body check and cartwheeled him back onto his head. The sickening smack reverberated throughout the auditorium. With Bailey lying prostrate on the ice, legs twitching uncontrollably, Shore made the mistake of allowing himself a grin, and in the best eye-for-an-eye tradition of hockey, was immediately coldcocked by one of Bailey's team-mates. After undergoing two brain operations, Bailey hovered on the brink of death for several weeks before finally recovering.

Shore's penchant for violence left its mark on his own frame as well. In a

---

* Interestingly enough, in light of the current controversy over police prosecutions for violence on the ice, Masson was arraigned on a murder charge which was only later reduced to manslaughter. He was ultimately acquitted because the judge could not determine which blow had actually killed McCourt – Masson's or a teammate's. Other arrests and convictions also occurred during hockey's formative years, but then sports as a whole had yet to be elevated above the law.

fourteen-season career with the Boston Bruins (1926–40), he accumulated a staggering number of injuries, including fractures to his hip, collarbone and back, a broken jaw (five times), a broken nose (fourteen times), an ear all but torn off and all his teeth knocked out. He boasted on his retirement a total of 978 stitches which had been sewn over some 80 lacerations – a record which still survives in a sport which has come to measure courage by a stitch count. (No doubt in deference to this ideal, Derek Sanderson's father has kept all his son's stitches in a bottle, which presumably holds pride of place on the Sanderson mantlepiece.)

Shore and his contemporaries set the style for much of hockey's future, drawing as they did large crowds eager for their particular brand of pugilism. (Shore himself is often referred to as the Babe Ruth of hockey in recognition of his work in popularizing the professional game.) Since then, hockey eras can be demarcated by whomever happens to have been ruling the ice at any given moment: Ted Lindsay, a plastic surgeon with his hockey stick; Leo Labine, who in the Eddy Shore tradition cut down the great Rocket Richard (himself no ice angel) as he was kneeling down unawares; Bill Ezinicki; Lou Fontinato; Larry Zeidel; John Ferguson. All of these men flourished in a game which, as a Canadian attorney was to later remark, encourages the use of physical intimidation *outside* the rules as a legitimate tactic.

For that is how hockey developed: somewhere along the line, it alone of all ball games (aside from its sister sport of box lacrosse) turned a blind eye to what in football terms is known as extracurricular violence. "Here was a game that could take us to the stars," lamented English sportwriter J. P. W. Mallalieu in 1953, "but by a process of suggestion we had come to want some other destination. This game was clean and godlike. But we wanted the Devil to play it because someone had told us it was better that way."

Whether or not hockey was ever godlike is highly debatable, but nevertheless Mallalieu's point remains: extracurricular violence had become a part of hockey's curriculum. It remains as such today. At the legislative level, few rules have ever been introduced to curtail charging, body slams into the boards, elbow work in the corners or a host of other violent tactics which in any other sport would have been heavily penalized long ago. It is only in recent seasons that the custodians of the game have made any real effort to reduce even fist fighting. Indeed, most still espouse the traditional hockey belief that fist fighting forms a sort of safety valve whereby players can release their frustrations and competitive excesses "harmlessly," a dubious prospect at best. While it is true that boxing on ice is potentially far less lethal than stick slashing, any argument which is based on the premise that, unlike other athletes, hockey players are demons unable to control

---

❝ I speared him, I pole-axed him and I cut him close to the eye. Things like that happen in the heat of the game I'm afraid. ❞

Bobby Clarke, captain of the Philadelphia Flyers, 1971

---

their behavior can only be regarded as highly suspect.

Following the owners' lead, hockey referees also acknowledge violence to be a strong part of the game, and coaches are so certain of violence's place in the scheme of things that they devise special drills specifically to promote it. Recently in Detroit it came to light that coach Larry Wilson had added two new workouts to his training program: one was the children's game of British Bulldog in which a player had to crash his way through a line of opponents; the other was boxing matches between teammates (an exercise which cost at least one player a tooth). Nick Fotiu, currently providing the muscle for New York's Rangers, used to hone his fighting skills on a speed bag strung up in the locker room.

As for the players themselves, the patterns of extracurricular violence are completely entrenched. The use of assault is regarded by players as "an occupational skill rather than an unsavory sin," according to sociologist Robert Faulkner who has conducted an extensive study of player attitudes to hockey violence. "The use of coercive violence is seen as totally unremarkable by all players; the presumption of assault is a most obvious and commonplace assumption," concluded Faulkner. "Not only do they approach their competition in this manner, and hold their colleagues to do likewise, they also expect to be treated in this way by their adversaries." More than that, the mayhem that has become the hallmark of hockey would hardly appear to be mayhem at all; it is, rather, in the majority of cases calculated violence applied for a specific purpose.

Judging by Faulkner's findings, the motivations for violence are both varied and deep. One of its basic uses is as a tool by which a player can establish his "character" and gain respect. Writes Faulkner: "Displays of violence, where something of consequence is at stake, serve as occasions for securing the appreciative evaluations of colleagues and the grudging deference of spectators." Like a fighting cock, a player is required to demonstrate his gameness; if he does so, he will be applauded – even by his opponents. A story told to me by Fred Shero, when he was still coach of the Philadelphia Flyers, illustrates the point:

I remember I knocked out Maurice Richard, illegally you might say.
He was coming in from the blue line, the puck was in the corner. He

was trying to get this pass and I hit him a split second before the pass, and I got away with it. I knocked him out cold. He got up and said, "Nice going, kid."

The converse of this violent character building is that players are constantly testing each other. "Intimidation and insult in the form of a deft forearm or elbow, butt end of the stick and fist are recommended procedures for finding out what others are about," writes Faulkner. The way a player responds to such probing is crucial. To back down is, in the eyes of most players, a heinous crime, far worse than incurring a penalty or being thrown out of the game. If a player earns the reputation of being a "chicken," it can bring his career to an abrupt halt. This holds especially true for rookies, whose first year in a major league is invariably a baptism of fire. "If a rookie backs down just once, he'll draw a crowd," said John Ferguson, erstwhile coach of the NY Rangers. "Enough guys'll want a piece of the kid to run him out of the league." Veterans, as one writer explained, seem to smell the blood of a rookie who won't retaliate. Not so long ago a Minnesota player pinned rookie Rick Middleton against the boards and set about hammering away at a half-healed eighteen-stitch gash on his mouth; soon after, another Minnesota player "checked" Middleton in full flight and broke his leg. "It's just like animals really, the strong against the weak," one player told Faulkner. Agreed another: "I would say that if ya give in you're just about doomed."

Besides this testing of self and opponent, hockey violence is also precipitated by an unwritten law which demands that, like soldiers under fire, a player must always support a teammate. When fighting erupts, a player is expected either to prevent members of the opposition from joining in, or to move in himself. As one of Faulkner's informants remarked:

You've got to help him. It's more or less just a policy with hockey players, you just do it. There's no question about it. You just drop your gloves and grab the guy and let the two guys fight it out, and when your teammate's losing this battle, you just get the other guy off. You just can't have a bunch of players standing around watching your teammate get his head beat in. And if you get in a fight and you're losing you can bet your last dollar there'll always be someone there to grab the guy and get him off of you. It's automatic, that's the way I look at it.

Failure to honor the "buddy code" can be disastrous, both for the player – his hockey character becomes "untrustworthy" – and for his team. As one man explained: "If somebody jumps you from behind you end up saying what the hell, I'm not going to risk my neck if nobody else's going to help

HANDS ACROSS THE WATER

The intimidation of players tested and found wanting was seen at its most ferocious during the 1973–74 season with the arrival of the first Swedes to be signed by North American clubs. As with the rest of Europe, Sweden has no tradition of extracurricular violence in its hockey – "The difference between North American and Swedish hockey? Look at the teeth!" said Lars-Erik Sjoberg on arrival – which earned the newcomers the nickname "Chicken Swedes." They became the focus for a concerted attack, aggravated by the Canadian players' fear that their jobs were in jeopardy. "I was prepared for the runs players took at me," Borje Salming told *Sports Illustrated*, "and I was ready for the spearing and so forth, but some of it was ridiculous." When Salming took to the ice against the Philadelphia Flyers during the 1976 Stanley Cup playoffs, for instance, he was immediately flattened by Bob Kelly's stick, hacked by Ed Van Impe and repeatedly punched by Dave Schultz. Eventually the attacks on Swedish players became so intense that veteran star Bobby Hull staged a one-game boycott in protest. Somebody, he said, was likely to get killed if things continued this way. As it turned out, the Swedes, although still basically nonpugilists, gave back enough violence to gain acceptance into the league. "I think in time I have earned my respect," said Salming a few seasons later. "I hit, I get hit."

me, so the hell with 'em. Your team morale can split like that." In other words, the team that fights together, stays together. How strongly this sentiment runs through hockey is emphasized by its surviving two major rule changes designed specifically to stop players intervening in brawls, either individually or *en masse* from the bench.

It was from such honorable intentions that the idea of designating specific players to look after a team's physical interests grew. Soon the policeman was fulfilling a crucial role, providing room for smaller or more skillful players to take their shots and boosting their confidence. "If you have a few good hitters," Faulkner was told, "you're not scared to do anything because you know that they will be right behind you if you get into trouble." Sometimes they can even inspire an entire team to victory. "I remember one night we were playing Boston in the play-offs," recalled Floyd Curry, a former Montreal Canadian who is still associated with the club. "Teddy Green, a big tough guy from Boston was on the ice at the time, and he and Ferguson got into a fight – the two tough guys from each team. I figured, if Ferguson loses this fight we could lose the series, because I knew it would give them a tremendous lift and just deflate us. Fergy beat him – heavily! I knew then we'd beaten Boston. No guy from Boston came in to help Green and their team just quit." *C'est la guerre.*

Today hockey violence is an extremely sensitive subject, especially along the corridors of the NHL. Depending on whom one talks to, the game is either as hard as ever and getting harder, or it is as clean as the driven ice and getting cleaner. On the one hand there are those like Ranger captain Phil Esposito who says that even during his career professional hockey has become tougher, with players resorting to illegal stick work "a helluva lot more." On the other there are people like Clarence Campbell (at that time president of the NHL): "Hell, it's a cakewalk now compared to then!" And: "The most violent thing that happens in the NHL these days is the language!"

Hockey's casualty sheets can be, and are, used to support either argument. It is, for instance, indisputable that hockey injuries are not in the same league as the injuries suffered by football players. There have been exceptions to this, of course: Ace Bailey, for example, and Minnesota North Stars' rookie Bill Masterton, who in 1968 cracked his skull on the ice following a body check and later died. There was also Red Sullivan, a victim of the "spearing" war of the 1950s, who was administered the last rites after a blow from a stick ruptured his spleen. Although he survived, the surgery left him with a 45-inch scar. And Bobby Orr, the Joe Namath of the ice rinks, whose knee after five operations in nine years looks, according to Stan Mikita, "like something horrible, something awful from outer space . . ." and to Bill White "like a bag of marbles." Yet compared with the victims of football's relentless carnage, hockey's wounded are generally in far better physical shape. "Football, that's got to be a brutal, brutal sport," whistled leading hockey strongman Dave Schultz. "They play one game a week and you just go in Monday morning to a team's dressing room and read the injury report for that one game. I mean, there's no comparison." "Fifteen, twenty deaths in football every fuckin' fall and nobody says a thing," snarled an embattled Fred Shero. "There's only been one death in the *history* of ice hockey!"

It is not through any lack of violence, however, that hockey injures less severely; it is merely that, unlike football players, a hockey player is not anchored to the turf by his boots and can therefore absorb far harder blows without being injured. A blind-side body check which would destroy the remaining ligaments in Joe Namath's knees and perhaps separate his shoulder into the bargain, merely leaves Bobby Clarke sliding harmlessly across the ice. Violence is still very much a part of the game; one has only to look at the number of injuries inflicted on the areas of the body which *are* vulnerable.

Take the eyes, for example. "From an opthalmologist's point of view," said Dr. Paul Vinger of Massachusetts in a recent issue of *Hockey*, "hockey is the most dangerous sport outside of boxing." Dr. Vinger was discussing junior amateur hockey, whose various leagues have long followed the professional model of violent play. During the 1974–5 season, thirty-seven juniors lost the sight of an eye while playing Canadian hockey. In that same season, a further seven youngsters lost eyes in Minnesota alone and forty-one suffered eye injuries. Equally disturbing is the number of concussions and head injuries suffered. "I think every kid before he reaches the age of 20, if he plays every year, is going to go through about five concussions," shrugged Fred Shero. Teeth, too: "If you go out on Long Island," said Dr. Strizak, "you'll see a great number of kids who have their teeth missing from hockey by the time they are fourteen." And the occasional bone: "The last team we played, they had a broken leg," one junior coach informed me. "A week before that a kid had a dislocated shoulder."

Mandatory helmets and face masks have now greatly reduced junior hockey's injuries, although during 1976 amateur players in the US suffered a staggering 25,000 facial injuries. At pro level, masks have also saved goalies' faces, as Madison Square Garden physician Gaetano Viti pointed out: "Compare the old time hockey players before the face mask with those after. They were just scar tissue." Goalkeeper George Gardiner remembers what it was like playing without a mask:

> I had nightmares before every game. I'd wake up in the middle of the night in a cold sweat, I'd see my teeth floating in a pool of blood, my eyes splattered on the wall of the room. It was hard to get back to sleep.

But in spite of their obvious advantages, neither masks nor helmets are popular among the great majority of professionals. Some of the players feel that head protection is liable to incite opponents to raise their sticks even higher. But mostly players simply do not want to be thought of as "sissies" in what is still an ultra-masculine sport.

Indeed, *machismo* requires players not only to disdain helmets but to shrug off injury with studied casualness. "It's part of the game, said former Boston Bruin "Terrible" Ted Green, explaining why he had played without a helmet following an operation that placed a plate in his skull. "It wasn't so much as skull fractures go," muttered player John McKenzie to reporters, "just a little bone where the nose hooked on to the forehead. It was un-hooked." The image of the hockey player charging back onto the ice with a needle and thread dangling from a half-sewn eyebrow is not so far wide of the mark. "I sew 'em up and send 'em back all the time, all the time," said Madison Square Garden's Dr. Viti.

Without full protection the "cosmetic" injuries suffered by major league players are harrowing. The NHL has estimated that each season an average of five thousand stitches are sewn into its performers. Anything from two to four hundred stitches is not uncommon in a career. The current claimant to Eddie Shore's stitch tally is Gordie Howe of the WHA, who reportedly has had more than five hundred sutured into his face alone. The game's violence is reflected best in the locker room after a tough match when players are busily examining their bruises and welts and reinserting their dentures. Visits to both the Rangers and Flyers locker rooms confirmed that few players manage to survive the game with more than just a few of their teeth still in their heads. Some lose only the front teeth; others, like Bobby Clarke, display mouths which collapse like umbrellas when they remove their dental plates.

Most players also bear the purple scars of multiple lacerations. "I'm not bad compared to some of the guys," grinned the toothless Clarke. "Rick MacLeish, he had thirty down here [pointing to his cheekbone] and twelve over here in two different games. Jimmy Watson got cut real bad, broken cheek and stuff." "Jimmy Watson!" exclaimed his former teammate Dave Schultz. "He got his jaw broke, he got stitches here and here – fifteen . . . ten up here. Then he got a stick in the eye and one eye is going to have impaired vision. Unbelievable!"

Many of these injuries are doubtless the accidents of a game which is pure, unrelieved intensity. Ice hockey is played in a frozen pit which affords no sanctuary from the checks and body slams of men moving at speeds of up to 30 mph. The players wield sticks which achieve a kinetic energy of 72 foot-pounds when slashed at full strength. They also skate with blades on the bottom of their boots, and the puck they play with travels at upwards of 120 mph. Accidents are inevitable. However, most injuries are the end results of a game which has adopted violent assault as its *modus operandi*. "In no other sport is it necessary to have such courage," said Fred Shero, brimming with pride. And although the professionals of bullfighting and motor racing might beg to differ, he does have a point.

5
THE WINNING EDGE

5 The Winning Edge

n late 1968, before what was to have been his last season, Vince Lombardi delivered the following speech to his Green Bay Packers:

I've never been with a loser, gentlemen, and I don't intend to start at this late date. You're here to play football, and I'm here to see you play as well as your God-given abilities will allow. And that means total dedication. I want total dedication from every man in this room, dedication to himself, to the team, and to winning. Winning is a habit, gentlemen. Winning isn't everything, it's the only thing. If you can shrug off a loss, you can't be a winner. The harder you work, the harder it is to lose. And I'm going to see that you work, I'm going to see that you execute, I'm going to push you and push you and push you because I get paid to win and so do you. Football is a violent game. To play you have to be tough. Physically tough and mentally tough. And you've got to have pride, because when two teams meet that are equal in ability and execution it's the team that has pride that wins. Gentlemen, let's be winners! There's nothing like it.*

As the current state of gridiron and hockey testifies, changing the rules of the game to reduce its quota of violence simply does not work. The reason for this lies with such visions of victory as expressed above by Lombardi and others like him. In their hands the competitive instinct has grown to engulf all other elements of play. Victory has become a religion, and "win at all costs" is its credo. The trouble is that winning at all costs now so often means exactly that.

"Kill, Kill, Kill!"

Contrary to popular belief, fixation with victory is not solely an aberration of twentieth-century man. An obsession with winners and winning has been an intermittent feature of sport since the ancient Olympics, and probably even farther back than that. "The pressure to *win* at the Olympics was awful," wrote sports historian Richard D. Mandell in *The Nazi Olympics*. Greek athletes were instilled with the unquestioning belief

---

* From *Coach: A Season with Lombardi* by Tom Dowling (New York: W. W. Norton & Company, Inc., 1970).

that they were fighting symbolic but supremely important battles for the honor of their communities. Those of them who won were feted and idolized, and their names were carved for posterity in the temples of their home towns. Consistent winners such as Theogenes of Thasos, who was reputed to have won more than 1,400 prizes, were elevated to the stature of semi-divinities. Losers, on the other hand, received nothing. "Significantly," wrote Mandell, "history has recorded almost no Greeks who took second place." It was literally winner take all.

Since then an obsession with victory has reappeared at regular intervals in sporting history. Whenever sport became a spectacle which catered not just to its participants but to spectators as well – the Regency prizefights, the dog- and cockfights of eighteenth-century England – winning became noticeably more important. The reason for this is simple enough. Denied the actual experience of playing the game, spectators turn to other means of participating in order to heighten the pleasure of the spectacle. To back a winner, either with money or without, is the most direct way for non-participants to include themselves in the action. While it probably mattered little to an eighteenth-century Derby mob-baller whether or not All Saints actually *beat* St. Peters – who, after all, kept score? – a favored pugilist only needed to even look like he was losing for his supporters to storm the ring. It is therefore not surprising that in the last few decades of the nineteenth century when sport once more became a spectacle, victory reasserted itself. Within a very short time, winning had become a virtue and winners virtual demigods.

It happened something like this. The legacy of mass production, which by then had effected the transformation of western society, was the creation of a vast pool of workers blessed with leisure time and a little money to spend on it, yet cursed by mundane, regimented and relentlessly boring jobs. Sport – and ball sports in particular, with their risk, daring and uncertainty, the very elements which industrialization had ironed out of most people's lives – offered an ideal escape. Almost overnight, society developed an enormous appetite for watching organized sport. Take, for example, the spectator explosion which centered around English soccer. In 1872 a bare

---

66 The cosmetic of going to a ball game, with its violence, skill and tactics, gives people a vehicle whereby they can break out of that drab and monotonous way of life they have – that job they truly dislike.   99

Allie Sherman, former New York Giants football coach

❝ I'd rather die a winner than live a loser. **❞**

Woody Hayes, Ohio State football coach, 1974

2,000 onlookers were present at the first Football Association final. Twenty-five years later 65,891 spectators turned out to see an ordinary interclub fixture (Aston Villa *vs.* Everton), and by 1910 no less than 110,000 were cramming Crystal Palace Stadium to watch Tottenham play Sheffield United. The pattern repeated itself in the United States with college football, and in other countries with sports such as cricket, ice hockey and Australian Rules. By the turn of the century, sport had become a service industry catering to perhaps the most demanding of all clients – the fan.

But it wasn't merely the spectacle which attracted crowds to the stadium. The rapid growth of new urban areas which occurred around the turn of the century had effectively shattered community spirit across wide areas, smothering the individual's sense of belonging to any group larger than the family. Again it was sport which filled the vacuum. Each Saturday afternoon provided instant community on the terraces or in the bleachers – thousands of people all fired with a common purpose: to urge their team on to victory. Supporters identified with their team, and a team's win/loss record – the only tangible result of sporting competition available to spectators – soon came to mean everything, especially to people born into a society which was already beginning to place its heaviest emphasis on success. "In a society that is preoccupied with competition, the average person needs something to latch onto that says, 'I'm really worthwhile, too,'" wrote psychologist Thomas Tutko and William Bruns in *Winning Is Everything and Other American Myths* (1976). "Winning can provide that boost, even if it means that a person is living vicariously through a team like the old Green Bay Packers or basking in the triumphs of a once-heroic Arnold Palmer."

When in 1908 the Bishop of Pennsylvania uttered his famous dictum – "The important thing in the Olympic Games is not winning but taking part; the essential thing in life is not conquering but fighting well" – his words were already years out of date. In American sports, and to a lesser degree throughout the rest of the world, all that mattered in the final analysis was the final analysis itself. If teams did not win, people simply did not watch. Conversely if a team was a winner, even a tiny frozen outpost like Green Bay could be thrust into the national limelight and prosper beyond its wildest dreams. These were facts lost on neither the college presidents of America who raised enormous stadiums to boost their finances and bring

---

“ What about winning? How about a good word for the ultimate reason any of us have for going into a competitive sport? As much as I enjoyed the physical and emotional dividends that college athletics brought me, I sincerely doubt if I ever suited up, put on my helmet . . . without the total commitment of going out there to win, not to get exercise, gold or glory, but simply to win.　　　**”**

Gerald Ford, former college football star
and president of the United States

---

prestige to their campuses, nor the sporting entrepreneurs who followed their lead. And with more and more money being poured into spectator sport, the pressure to win escalated.

By 1940 sport had a new catch cry, Vanderbilt coach Red Saunders's "Winning is not everything, it's the only thing!" – a line reiterated by John Wayne in the movie *Trouble along the Way*, immortalized by Vince Lombardi and rehashed by every subsequent coach who has taken his sport seriously. The game was no longer merely a game, as most of the major sporting figures of the past four decades were only too willing to point out:

Life without victory is tasteless –

Redskin coach GEORGE ALLEN

The only way I know how to keep football fun is to win –

Texas coach DARRELL ROYAL

In pro football, winning is all there is. If you don't win, you haven't done what the game is about –

Dallas quarterback ROGER STAUBACH

Today that pressure is immense. Spectator sports have become the national preoccupation of America – ninety million viewers tune into the Super Bowl alone each year; colleges now allocate football budgets of $10 and $11 million – and the fans identify with their chosen heroes with a passion bordering on dementia. The lighter aspects of this madness are the supporters who drive thousands of miles to attend games; paint their bathrooms, their living rooms and their entire houses in team colors; christen their unfortunate offspring with the first names of players from their favorite team; and, according to James Michener, purchase toilet paper dispensers fitted with pretuned radios so as never to be out of earshot of the local game.

It is the dark side by which the extremes of sports fanaticism are, however, better measured. Fans literally give up their lives – or take others – in the single-minded pursuit of team allegiance. During the 1930s when fan identification was really beginning to bite, a Dodger supporter went berserk with a gun after being taunted about a recent defeat. He shot two of his tormentors, killing one, and thereby beginning a pattern of violent tragedy which reasserts itself every season. In 1969 Frank Graddock of Queens landed a fatal blow on his wife's head when she had the temerity to switch channels during a Mets–Cubs game. In 1974 Paul Harris was shot to death by a friend following an argument over a disputed field goal during an Alabama–Auburn game. More recently, in late 1977 Richard Savage was gunned down by irate Denver Bronco fans when he insisted on turning up the juke box in a bar during the final minutes of a game. Two of Savage's friends were wounded. The bartender told reporters that those involved in the shooting were regulars who all knew each other. And it's not just the big games that stir dark waters. During a recent high school football match in Florida, an assistant principal was shot and killed by the opposing school's business manager.

The flip side of the coin are those fans who don't bother about other people but are content to take out their teams' losses on themselves. In 1973 a Broncos disciple attempted to blow his head off but missed. A suicide note later recovered by police read: "I have been a Broncos fan since the Broncos were first organized, and I can't stand their fumbling anymore." Whether or not he tried again after Denver's fumbling in the 1978 Super Bowl has as yet gone unrecorded.

But these are merely individual acts of commitment. The full power of the winning obsession is at its peak inside a stadium where fans are assembled *en masse*. When a crowd is repeatedly cheated of victory, it can become frighteningly destructive, turning with a vengeance against even the men who collectively make up its alter ego. In his book *The Nightmare Season* (1976), Arnold Mandell described walking out onto the field beside San Diego coach Harland Svare during the team's disastrous losing streak:

> A roar of disapproval rose like a suddenly released flock of ravens. It hovered in the center air, darkening the sky before dispersing. Barbarous screams, hoarse curses, foul censure. Fifty thousand people hurled their denunciation on the head of one man beneath them. I half expected to see a hungry lion emerge from the shadow of the opposing team's tunnel . . .

The return journey to the locker room after the anticipated loss was even more harrowing:

The rabble battalion above the tunnel had saved their ammunition. They fired pillows, paper cups full of Coke or beer, cans weighted with warm beer, javelins that had supported their hateful wrath. They slung obscenities with all the force of their wrath. The police were not much protection.

It was, Mandell later reflected, simply "win or be killed." Which is not so far fetched as it sounds. When Dan Devine, who succeeded Lombardi as Packer coach, failed to instantly measure up to the great man's mark, he was harrassed constantly by Packer fans, his family was spat on and insulted in the street and, eventually, his dog was shot dead. Most losing coaches are more fortunate; they are simply fired. From 1975 to the end of 1977, the NFL's twenty-eight teams had hired twenty-four new coaches, plus another four interim coaches. By January 1978 seven of those new coaches had already resigned or been fired. No coach is immune. In seven seasons with the Washington Redskins, coach George Allen won sixty-seven games, lost only thirty and tied one; he took his team to the playoffs five times and to the Super Bowl once. Yet when he failed to make the playoffs twice in three seasons, he was out of a job.

It is this overwhelming pressure to win at all costs that lies at the heart of the escalating level of violence within the games themselves. When the single-minded pursuit of victory is wedded to games of physical contact, violence is the inevitable result; and the greater the will to win, the greater the violence. Played amid the mania for victory which has engulfed American sport, it is hardly surprising that today's contact ball games are so incredibly ferocious.

Whereas in other sporting ages violence was a product of diverse, almost incidental, factors – the joy of hard knocks given and received while forcing a ball through a stream; the malicious delight of sinking an iron-clad boot into a junior-schoolboy's shin – violence has now become a tool in the pursuit of victory. "Kill, Kill, Kill! That is the litany of the training camp, the practice field, the game," wrote *San Francisco Examiner* columnist William Flynn. "A Terry Bradshaw's head driven into the turf is merely a symbol of the unquenchable desire of the participants to win at any costs." Or, as ice hockey star Derek Sanderson so succinctly put it: "I'll break a guy's leg to win."

Again it is American football that affords the perfect example, combining as it does a huge and committed fan following with the almost limitless opportunity for violence. Football is now a game of unnerving intensity played with the sole objective of winning. Under the relentless pressure to build a winning side season after season, coaches are locked into a never-ending search for the player who is, both physically and mentally, invincible.

> **We play our games with the same tenacious ferocity with which we fight a war in Vietnam and with as little reason or sense. We are taught from the cradle that we have never lost a war and that winning is everything, tying is like kissing your sister and losing is nothing.**
>
> Leonard Shechter, sports columnist

Brute strength is of paramount importance for all but a few positions, and now there is little room in the game for anyone who is not suffering at least partially from giantism. Men with a "killer instinct" are sought after as avidly as gold dust. "In football, the contract is either you hurt the opponent or he hurts you," said Harvard psychiatrist Chester M. Pierce. "The coach must have his men feeling that they not only *can* kill but that they *should* kill." A player is prized if he is a "vicious hitter" or if he "can knock a guy's head off." "I wish I had some headhunters," wailed Leo Cahill, manager of the Memphis Grizzlies. "A couple of guys who would run all around rolling their eyes and smacking people. I wish, I wish . . ."

Training for combat is as grueling as the combat itself. Before the first kickoff of the 1976–7 season, the Oakland Raiders had lost their entire defensive line through injuries received during training. Some years back *Sports Illustrated* investigated the training programs of several large colleges and what it discovered was nothing short of hair raising. Boys were urged to fight tooth and nail crouched underneath a low ceiling of chicken wire; others were encouraged to run full tilt into lightly padded cinder block walls; still others were harnessed back to back and forced to drag each other across the floor. These drills and others like them lasted for an hour each day; at one college at the end of that hour the rubbish bins in the gymnasium were filled with vomit. Not so long ago at Syracuse University a coach was quoted as saying that he never ended a practice session until he had seen blood.

It is not just the giants of pro and college football who indulge in such brutal toughening; the ethic of training players to withstand and inflict maximum physical violence reverberates the entire length of the football spectrum from the largest linebacker to the smallest peewee. Pop Warner and Peewee League coaches are just as violent about winning as Lombardi, Allen and the other professional generals – maybe even more so. "They want to win at any cost," said former Michigan All-American Chuck Ortmann on resigning as chairman of a football Little League. "They tell their players 'Go out there and break that guy's arm.' " In 1972 a neurosurgeon reported treating a 10-year-old peewee footballer for concussion suffered during a team workout. Apparently the coach had been "strengthening each player's head and neck" by having the boys line up six feet apart, charge each other and butt their heads together.

Tough bodies trained to ignore pain are not, however, enough to win football matches. What is also needed is the right mental approach to the game – the will to kill. Coaches strive mightily to send their boys trotting out onto the field in the correct bloodshot frame of mind to play winning football. One college coach reportedly includes footage of war films in his pre-game pep talks. Others prefer to smash locker-room doors, beat the walls and ruin their vocal chords. In early 1978 this story appeared on the wire services:

> Mr. Ian Sudder, a school football coach in Florida, has been accused of inviting his pupils to kick a chicken to death in order to put them in a fighting mood for a competition game. "He painted the chicken with gold and asked his team to think of it as an eagle," said Mr. Sam Foly of the American Humane Association. "Then he told them to see it as a member of the opposing team. The boys took him at his word, chased the chicken around the field, and kicked it to death." Mr. Sudder was also accused of biting the heads off frogs as part of his pre-game pep talks.

Whatever Mr. Sudder's crimes against nature, his only sin in footballing terms is that his techniques are perhaps a trifle unsophisticated. At the pro level such chicken-stomping hatred has become a prerequisite of the game. "There is nothing stokes the fire like hate," counseled Coach Lombardi.

Said Alex Karras, retired star of the Miami Dolphins:

> I hated everyone on the football field, and my personality would change drastically when I got out there. And that attitude was the only thing that kept me in the league. I'm not the biggest guy – I played at about 240, which is terribly light for a tackle – but I would hurt people. I had a license to kill for sixty minutes a week. My opponents were all fair game, and when I got off the field I had no regrets. It was like going totally insane. . . . Most linemen play it like that and most of them are very tough and very sadistic. In fact, the best linemen were all sadistic. They were like big docile dogs that were let loose on a football field and suddenly went crazy. Just like me.

Generally it is left to the individual players to generate their own frenzy. "It's something that can't be done just on Saturday and Sunday," explained Jerry Kramer in *Instant Replay* (1969). "It has to be done gradually, building

BREAKING THEIR NECKS TO WIN

In 1974 Blyth and Mueller published a report after a four-year study of 8,776 high school football players in North Carolina. Of the 4,287 injuries recorded, 12.9 percent were injuries to head and neck. In 1975 Dr. Joseph Torg reported that halfway through the season he had already seen within the Philadelphia vicinity one young player die from head injuries, another receive multiple fractures of the spine, and six others become quadraplegics.

The reason for this preponderance of head and neck injuries is linked to another set of statistics which Blyth and Mueller's study uncovered: of all injuries caused by a blow, 13.7 percent were the result of contact with the helmet or mask. What has happened is that since its introduction during the '60s the hard-shell plastic helmet has become an extremely lethal weapon to both attacker and victim. In 1973 R. C. Schneider reported a five-year study of 139 craniocerebral injuries resulting in 65 deaths and 78 spinal chord injuries resulting in 16 deaths. He attributed the primary cause of head and neck injuries to the use of the head as a weapon.

According to Tom Mack, for the past fifteen years players have been trained to hit with their helmets rather than with their shoulders or their bodies. They are taught to aim for the side, throat, knee or any other vulnerable area, a tactic known as "spearing." Although the spearer runs a serious risk of snapping his own neck, the ploy of hitting an opponent high on the chest with the helmet and then moving it up into his chin has become standard tackling practice. Each season Minnesota Viking Henry Tinglehoff's forehead would be distinguished by a permanent gash which, during the off-season, would become a ridge of calcium deposit. This was the result of his helmet being driven into his forehead each time he charged at the chest. Jerry Kramer once referred to his helmet as "probably the best weapon I've got."

Recently there has been a strong reaction against the use of the helmet and face mask as weapons, including calls for soft equipment. (High school football has now outlawed the practice.) However, as with the flying wedge, it would appear that coaches are unwilling to surrender any possible winning edge. As one physician put it: "Coaches think they need to hear the sound of hard helmets hitting together to make it sound like football."

up to the game. You work up an anger, then a hatred, and the feeling gets stronger and stronger until, on Sunday, you've got your emotion so high you're ready to explode." There are various ways of achieving this foam-flecked nirvana. "I think back on all the guys I know who have been injured," said former lineman Roger Brown, "and I say to myself those guys across the line are trying to do it to me. Well, they aren't *going* to do it." Former Boston defensive end Larry Eisenhauer preferred destroying the locker room before a game. Some players stop talking to people three or four days prior to taking the field, including their wives and families. Others deliberately put themselves in the way of a punch during training or at the very start of the game. And for those who find it difficult to raise their hatred week after week, either because of age or a naturally passive mental outlook, there is the easy way out through drugs.

High for the Game

It is one of life's smaller ironies that a game which has always prided itself on being the bastion of decency and clean living should have become so riddled with drug abuse. "When I got to the National Football League," wrote Dave Meggyesy in 1971, "I saw players taking . . . amphetamines and barbiturates at an astonishing rate. Most NFL trainers do more dealing in these drugs than the average junky." In that same year Chip Oliver wrote in *High for the Game:* "If Pete Rozelle, the commissioner of the National Football League, put a lock on the pill bottle, half the players would fall asleep in the third quarter." Since then several other players have testified to the inordinate amount of drugs consumed by footballers at all levels of the game, including even high school.

Several studies have been made which verify such statements. During the early '70s Mike Mohler, a Berkeley football player, polled his teammates and discovered that 48 percent took amphetamines. Other schools, he suggested, were probably even more involved in drug taking. The most potent study concerning NFL players was produced in 1972 by Lee Johnson, a Ph.D. in physical education at La Jolla, California. Deploying a network of personal contacts on several teams, he found, among other things, that 67 percent of NFL defensive players popped amphetamines. "It is likely that of the twenty-two players on the field at a given time," he concluded, "thirteen athletes are playing under the influence of amphetamines, a powerful and sometimes dangerous drug."

There are several reasons why players take amphetamines. One is that it staves off weariness (which explains its popularity amongst European long-distance bicycle riders). Another is that it deadens pain, an invaluable asset during a football game. But the primary reason is that it promotes aggression, giving players a violent – and, hopefully, winning – edge. "The violent and brutal player that television viewers marvel over on Saturdays and Sundays is often a synthetic product," wrote Meggyesy. When Houston Ridge filed suit against his former club, the San Diego Chargers, he did so alleging that he was given drugs "not for the purpose of treatment and cure, but for the purpose of stimulating mind and body so he would perform more violently as a professional." Ridge was eventually awarded $295,000. Similarly, Ken Gray's $3.5 million suit against the St. Louis Cardinals charged that he was administered "potent, illegal, and dangerous drugs . . . so that he would perform more violently." In football, drugs equal violence. As radical sports writer Jack Scott once remarked: "One way to measure the level of violence in football is the amount of drugs players take to be able to perform." It is no mere coincidence that special teams, the most violent position of all, are often referred to by players as "the Benny Squads."

Someone who has witnessed the effects of amphetamines on football players at first hand is Arnold Mandell. Prior to his season with the Chargers, drug consumption within the team had reached epidemic proportions. (One newspaper report revealed that in a single year the team had consumed ten thousand pills, many of them amphetamines.) Mandell found himself pitched into the middle of this wholesale drug consumption, and by the end of the season he had formed very definite conclusions about football violence. "The most important influence creating the violence in football – professional or college – is high-dose amphetamine," he told me. "You or I may take 5 or 10 mg, or the baseball player who has to be sharp will take 5 mg. Now that's a different business altogether." What Mandell's football players were regularly consuming amounted to massive dosages, dosages which research has shown led, effectively, to psychosis. "You actually become, for the peak effect of the drug, crazy," he said. "And it's the most murderous type of crazy that we know. It is the paranoid psychotic, the killer of presidents."

Every weekend the players would undergo a marked and rapid transformation before Mandell's eyes. On Sunday mornings they would arrive calm, sophisticated, relaxed – "a bright group of people." Then their personalities would start to disintegrate. Conversations would swing wildly from good-humored jocularity to loud, aggressive irritability. Players would storm about the locker room filling the air with obscenities. If Mandell happened to brush against a player accidentally, the latter might lash out in uncontrolled rage. He commented:

I have been in psychiatry for twenty years now, and I have never seen personality changes like that. The first few weekends I spent with the team I couldn't understand that. I know about getting up for something, getting uptight and tense and ready. But this was like Dr. Jekyll and Mr. Hyde; it's like their teeth grew longer almost. The up of football is not the up we know. It's the worst temper tantrum you have ever had in your life lasting for four hours. That's the state football is played in – murderous rage.

The continuing debate over whether or not pills actually *improve* a player's performance is, said Mandell, irrelevant. (Most researchers agree that they do not.) It is their psychological rather than their physical boost that counts, he told me:

> The question is, if you had to kill your mother, how would you get yourself to do that? Now that may sound like a far out example, but I'm not so far off. Joe Blow and Frank are going to play opposite each other in the line this Sunday. Last summer at the team union meeting they went and drank together and had dinner together and talked about each other's children and found they kind of liked each other and giggled and laughed and wrote to each other and their wives met each other and it's terrific. Sunday I'm going to break your leg. Okay, it's not your mother, but it's someone you like. I've got to hit you and knock you, I've got to spear your chest with my helmet and maybe if you're a quarterback I can smash your ribs. Now how do you do that? It's amphetamine. It's murderous out there – the effects are *horrible* – and I suspect that if I had to go out there I would have to take a lot of amphetamine.

The two defensive linemen that Mandell did manage to persuade to lower their dosage, were, he said, later cut for lack of aggression.

In 1973 following Houston Ridge's courtroom revelations and mounting concern in the press, the NFL moved against amphetamines. Notices appeared in locker rooms warning that "The use or distribution of 'pep pills' or 'diet pills' by members of this team is not condoned by the league or by the management of this club." "Official" lines of supply dried up.

How successful this operation has been is still largely a matter of conjecture. The NFL claims that the problem – never widespread – has been all but licked. Players of unquestioned integrity such as Merlin Olsen also insist that the numbers of drug users have dropped and that drug usage is now only marginal. There are less and less players "a little out of control" on the field, said Olsen, adding that the Chargers were a team beset by special problems and hardly representative of pro football as a whole.

Olsen's young quarterback Pat Haden agreed, saying that while he had seen a lot of drug usage at high school, at both the college and pro level it had been conspicuous by its absence. Haden did admit, however, that as a quarterback, a job whose requirement of clear thinking precluded the use of stimulants, he was not really in a position to say.

There are others who believe that the problem has barely been dented. "Amphetamine entered football in 1948 and it will never leave it," said Dr. Mandell. "It can't; it's a marriage, like the tranquilizer for the frustrated housewife. When a drug marries an activity to perfection, you can make it illegal but it will always come in under the counter. And football *is* amphetamine." Lee Johnson agreed: "I know enough players now to know that conditions are similar to what they were five or six years ago. If you know what to look for on TV, you know who's on pills – they're licking their lips, blinking their eyes. It's a big percentage of the defensive players."

In the December 1976 issue of *Sport*, reporter David Israel interviewed a collection of anonymous NFL players who stated that about half the players in the league resorted to some form of amphetamine before a game. Some players, they said, were so addicted that they had to dose up merely to practice. "One season I tried to go straight," one of the players told Israel. "But during a pre-game warm-up, I came out and saw the other team. Their eyes were huge, spit was flecking out of their mouths. It scared the crap out of me. I went back to the locker room and took my usual dosage."

Even more telling was this comment, which just about says it all:

If they say, "it's not whether you win or lose but how you play the game," then, fine, a lot less guys will use drugs. But they've never said that. And as long as winning is the name of the game, you have to take what you can."

Cheap Shots

Given the intense pressure, drugs and simmering hatred, it is no wonder that players are now increasingly overstepping the pencil-thin line which separates legalized violence from extracurricular assaults. For the first seven or eight years of his pro career, Tom Mack found football a "very clean game." However, over the past two or three years it has become, in his experience, progressively dirtier. Players cheat and their opponents retaliate with violence in an effort to make them follow the rules. "It's much more violent than people know," said Mack, "slugging, punching, people really trying to intimidate. There are not many fights, but a lot of intimidatory tactics, and most intimidation is violent." Violent intimidation includes such moves as hitting a receiver who runs a pass even though the ball is over his head, a lineman going after an opponent's legs with a leg whip and flattening him *after* the block, and quarterbacks being gratuitously sacked seconds after releasing the ball. "Happen much?" snorted Namath when I asked him about extracurricular violence. "Happens every game damn near. Guy running up behind another guy, man has his back to him and the fella just hauls off and hits him in the head. It's dangerous, super dangerous. We've seen licks this year that you wonder how guys survive."

The problem of extracurricular violence – "cheap shots," in player parlance – was brought sharply into focus during the opening game of the 1976–7 season when Oakland Raider George Atkinson cracked Pittsburgh's diminutive Lynn Swann over the helmet with his forearm when the play was on the other side of the field, giving Swann his fourth concussion. "I treat pass receivers the way you would treat a burglar in your home," an unruffled Atkinson later explained. During the attendant publicity, several multimillion dollar lawsuits exchanged hands and Atkinson became the bogey man of the league. One newspaper even ran a photograph of him with a gunsight superimposed on his helmet.

Out of this furor two differing views delineating the cause of cheap shots emerged. One camp held to the traditional belief that it was the individual player who was at fault, a "one-bad-apple-in-the-barrel" approach. "Something happens to some people when they get out on that field," drawled Namath. "They get out there and go crazy sometimes. You can't even talk to some guys they're so fired up out there. I think it's from way back. It's in a man and some things happen throughout his life. The football field just brings out the viciousness in him."

There is little doubt that in some cases cheap shots are the result of abnormally violent men playing a violent contact sport – men who, were they not pro footballers, would probably be standing at the shoulder of some Mafia boss sporting bulges under their armpits. However, the proliferation of extracurricular violence is far better explained by the theory expressed by many players that the cheap shot has now become an integral part of how the modern game is played. In other words, cheap shots are now a tactic.

❝ The harder I hit people the better I like it. When you hit a guy and he hits the ground hard and his eyeballs roll and you see it and he looks up at you and knows you see it, then you've conquered him. It's a great feeling.   ❞

Tim Rossovich, US pro football player, 1971

"When I first came into the league ten years ago you were always told to play by the rules," Detroit cornerback Lem Barney recently told *Black Sports*. "Nobody tells you that anymore. It's an every-man-for-himself thing. If you can get away with an elbow to the gut or a slap that'll get the ball loose, the feeling now is to go ahead and do it." "You get in a good lick around the head area, it rattles the man," explained former pro lineman Chris Hanburger. "You can beat a dazed man easier than an alert one. It's that simple." Said Conrad Dobler, an All-Pro guard credited by his opponents with a comprehensive array of extracurricular tactics including eye gouging, leg whipping, face-mask twisting and even biting, "I'll do anything to protect my quarterback."

Against this background an incident such as the Swann/Atkinson affair is just another tackle. As Atlanta defensive end Claude Humphrey remarked after the incident: "If you can get Lawrence McCutcheon or James Harris out of there when you play the Rams, then you've got a hell of a chance to win, and that's what it's all about. If Swann has a chance to catch a touchdown pass, why not hit him? It's just football."

The institutionalization of the cheap shot has still a long way to go before it reaches the level of ice hockey, with its endless round of fist fights and bench-clearing brawls. However, the writing is on the wall and has been so for quite some time. Following a Washington–St. Louis brawl in 1973, Redskin coach George Allen confessed that he had "loved the fight." "If we didn't go out there and fight I'd be worried," said Allen. "You go out there and protect your teammates. The guys who sit on the bench, they're the losers. That team's losing." A few years earlier, while coach of the Rams, he had even encouraged a free-for-all to "get 'em all going," he said. "Because unless you get 'em all together, unless you have that, you aren't going to be a winner. It's all part of winning."

Ice Wars

And what of hockey itself? The pressures involved in equating the figures on a scoreboard with the bottom line of a balance sheet have proved even more explosive on the ice than on the Astro-turf. "It's a high-pressure contact sport," said John Ferguson, then coach of the NY Rangers, "a sport where you play eighty games a year. And when you're driving for position – especially as a professional – you're in a pressurized pressure cooker. That's what spontaneous fighting comes from." In the past decade the lid has blown off more times than even the most dedicated NHL hardliner could care to remember.

Hockey's troubles began soon after the massive NHL expansion of 1967.

In a bid to broaden hockey's audience throughout the United States, the six existing NHL teams were suddenly doubled and then, on top of that, a further six teams were added. Fortunately for the NHL, this ambitious piece of planning was a success, adding millions of new fans to the game and establishing hockey in cities such as Miami and Los Angeles where hitherto the only ice to be found lay under a measure of bourbon.

Expansion, however, was not without its side effects, not least of which was an upsurge in the intensity of the game. Fans will persevere with a new sport only if their chosen team can produce a reasonable win/loss record in its first few seasons, a fact which several now-extinct hockey clubs soon discovered. To the fledgling teams, winning became a matter of survival, and they were willing to fight to survive. Another effect of expansion was that it spread the top players thinly around the country, leaving some of the new clubs decidedly short on talent and experience.

Combined, these two factors set the stage for the violence which was to follow – violence which was not merely the "spontaneous" outbursts of players driving for position, but rather a tactical instrument in the pursuit of victory. Burdened by the necessity of winning games with second-rate players, clubs resorted to what one writer labeled "a new martial art: selective, premeditated violence" rooted in the philosophy of "strike only when behind and always at the star." The role of the policeman was expanded into that of arch intimidator, whose job it was to slam the skills out of the opposition's goal scorers, frighten players off their game and, in the extreme, sacrifice himself by involving an opposing star in a penalty-earning brawl and taking him out of the game. "There were a lot of teams that were getting guys solely to fight with players who were better than them," recalled Bobby Clarke. "Players who never fought were having to fight guys who made their living at it, beating on various guys' heads."*

The tactics of winning through intimidation – or "goon hockey" as an increasingly scandalized press called it – were adopted most brazenly by Clarke's own team, the Philadelphia Flyers. Before the arrival of coach Fred Shero, the Flyers were a run-of-the-mill expansion team with little con-

---

* Bobby Clarke himself is certainly no "Chicken Swede." Although avoiding fist fights – "I'm like a rat . . . I only fight when I'm cornered" – his winning tactics have left scars on many opponents. His most infamous moment came in 1972 while playing for Team Canada against Russia. Trailing Soviet star Valery Kharlamoy, he decided that "something had to be done about this guy who was killing us," so he slashed the Russian across the ankles with his stick. The blow retired Kharlamoy, and Team Canada rallied to win the last three games and the series. "It's not something I'm really proud of," said Clarke later, "but I honestly can't say I was ashamed to do it."

fidence and even less fight. "They used to get the hell beat outa them," said Dave Schultz, the man who was to become the linchpin of Shero's strategy.

Shero changed all that. A feisty little man (he had been a formidable boxer in his younger days) with an unbroken record of coaching winning teams, he was appalled by the way in which the Flyers invariably left the ice with their tails between their legs. The nut of Shero's remedy was outlined in his book *Shero: The Man Behind the System* (1975). Although eschewing violence – "First thing I say to my teams at the start of every year," he told me, " 'If I ever ask you to start a fight, take this stick and break it over my head.' I'm perhaps the only coach in pro hockey who'll take a lie detector test on this" – Shero developed a strategy that was scarcely the work of a pacifist:

> One must realize that hockey is full of intimidations and often these attempts to terrorize do result in violence. If the opposition allows itself to be terrorized, for instance, it will lose the offensive edge and, finally, the game. Many a goal has been scored by dumping the star player . . .

Or, as he later put it, "If you keep the opposition on their butts, they don't score goals." With this strategy in mind, Shero picked his squad with a view to providing a solid wall of muscle behind his diminutive star, Bobby Clarke. "We want," he said frankly, "to put hitting back into hockey."

The results of a Columbia University study which discovered that consistent winners averaged more penalties than losers was also apparently not lost on Shero. During the 1972–3 season the Flyers were penalized a record 1,756 minutes – a full thirty games' worth, almost six hundred minutes more than the next most penalized team, the Boston Bruins. Included in this impressive tally were the two hundred penalty minutes each scored by four individual Flyers, led by rookie Dave Schultz with 259 minutes in the penalty box.* Suddenly the Fearful Flyers were the Broad Street Bullies. Players such as Bob "Hound Dog" Kelly became household names in Philadelphia. "They sure don't pay me to score goals," said Kelly, which was just as well, for in sixty-five games he scored only four times. Kelly did, however, have other talents; during the season he was involved in fifteen major brawls and only lost once. Dave Schultz became a star, notorious throughout the league. Brawling had become the Flyers' stock in trade.

It was Schultz who – fairly or unfairly – came to epitomize goon hockey.

---

* To give some idea as to the extent of Schultz's achievement, it should be measured against the earlier exploits of Barclay Plager of the St. Louis Blues. During the 1967–8 expansion season, Plager was hailed as an iron man in the Eddie Shore mold, yet at the season's end he had managed to tally only a mere 153 penalty minutes.

Nicknamed "The Hammer," to his embattled colleagues he was an invaluable asset, providing them with courage and confidence, especially on the road where these qualities were needed most. The home-town fans idolized him and would parade around the Philadelphia Spectrum wearing German army helmets with SCHULTZ painted on them in red lettering. His rendition of a pop song entitled "Penalty Box" became a hit in Philly. To opposing players he was a "goon" and a "head hunter" who couldn't skate to save his life, and they fought him savagely. On one occasion I was shown a picture of Schultz taken after a game; his face was covered in bite marks. "He should have been charged," snapped The Hammer when I broached the subject with him later. "Guy fights like a broad!" Whenever Schultz set foot inside a hostile stadium he was booed, abused and made the target of everything that wasn't nailed down, a reception which, incidentally, he remembers with considerable satisfaction.

Actually, as Schultz tells it, he began his hockey career as a straight-forward goal scorer. It was not until joining the minor leagues, first in Quebec and then in Virginia, that his true talent began to emerge. In one season with the Richmond Robins, he managed to amass a record-breaking 392 penalty minutes. "We had a real tough junior team," Schultz recalled. "I wasn't scared and the first game I got into a fight. The other players liked it, the fans liked it, the coach liked it." So too, apparently, did the scout from Philadelphia. According to Schultz:

> That's how I made the league, by fighting. And I've had to fight to stay here. I didn't have to be told that was why I was here. In my first year [with the Flyers] I only played two or three shifts a game. Whenever somebody was running our guys I would be put out there. Well, I knew what the hell to do. Not only did they want me to do it, I couldn't have played it otherwise. I would like to score goals. I'd *love* to score twenty-five goals. . . . Wouldn't care if I never fought again. But it's not my job, on this team or on any team.

His job, Schultz insisted, was merely that of the traditional hockey policeman. He vowed that he never went after opposing stars, and only fought players who were also willing to drop their gloves. "I go after the guy who's filling the same role as me, the goon or enforcer or whatever you want to call it." The famous quotes from those heady earlier days – quotes such as: "It makes sense to try and take out a guy who's more important to his team than I am to mine; if I take out Brad Park, that's not a bad trade is it?" – were "mistakes" which now "embarrassed" him.

Be that as it may (and it must be remembered that at the time of speaking he was rather half-heartedly trying to slough off his bruiser image), Schultz's interpretation of the policeman's role was considerably broader than that of his predecessors. The season following his record-breaking penalty-ridden rookie year, he scaled even greater heights – 348 minutes in the penalty box plus another 139 during the Stanley Cup playoffs. NHL president Campbell felt obliged to introduce three new rules, largely, it was said, as a result of Schultz's behavior. The changes barred head butting and the taping of fists, and forced penalized players to move directly to the penalty box without brawling on the way.

Schultz was hurt by the attention, which he felt was unwarranted. "I'm not that bad a guy," he said, managing to look miffed:

> I never want to hurt anybody, that's not what I'm here for. I mean, it hurts a little bit when you get punched in the face, but a couple of days later it feels all right. I hurt my hands worse; my hands are going to be crippled when I get done. After some games I used to take them and soak them in ice. [Ruefully he examined his gnarled fists.] I cracked this one a number of times and broke it ... pushed in my knuckles. This here was torn all the time. I don't swing with this one and this one here is in bad shape. I maybe should take up boxing to help me, but I think the best thing would be karate, you know, so you could move. I did talk to one guy who told me, "move in and just give 'em a little jab" because that hurts more than coming in like this [a haymaker is demonstrated].

How did Schultz feel about his chosen role? I asked. He had the off-ice reputation of being a "pussy cat" (his wife's words) whose hobby was building model ships. Did he actually enjoy brawling? After a moment's hesitation spent staring into his milkshake, he grinned evilly and nodded:

> You know, I haven't had a lot of good fights lately, and then last night I started swinging and ... it was *all right!* When you're winning, everything is great.
>
> I change on the ice. I don't know how. It's funny, I know lots of guys who never fight on the ice, but as soon as they get into a bar it's "You wanna fight?" I've never fought in bars. On the ice it's just a reaction. I'm not fighting for myself, it's for the team. Of course, at times I fight for the fans to a certain extent because they pay my salary. It's entertainment for them. But I'm not doing it just for them. If I feel I can help the team by fighting, I do it. I do it to win games.

He added as an afterthought that he was, after all, one of the highest paid ten-goal scorers in the NHL.

Whatever the ethics of Schultz's play or Shero's strategy, both certainly paid dividends. In 1974 the Flyers won the coveted Stanley Cup, the first-ever expansion team to do so. The following year they won it again. Philadelphia was beside itself with delight. The Spectrum was sold out night after night. Violence was obviously paying, and paying well.

Following the rags-to-riches transformation of the Flyers, there was a sudden scramble by other coaches to sign on strongmen. When John Ferguson took over the New York Rangers, he found the same lack of "backbone" that Shero had found in Philadelphia. One of his first signings was former boxer Nick Fotiu. "To be a winner," explained Ferguson, "a team, like an individual, must have some killer instinct." Toronto Maple Leafs president Harold Ballard, never a man to mince words, was even more blunt. Announcing that he was putting seven of his players on the trading block, he told reporters: "We've got to mold a lineup that can take on a bunch of goons. I'm looking for guys you toss raw meat to and they go wild." Commented *Sports Illustrated*: "The rationale seems to be something like this: if violence is what it takes to win these days, and winning violently is what makes the turnstiles sing, then bring on the raw meat." It was a philosophy which reverberated throughout hockey's entire structure, even down to infant level.

In 1973 a 16-year-old was convicted of manslaughter for kicking another boy to death during a Midget House League game. "At one time in sport, the losing team used to call for three cheers for the winners and the winning team reciprocated with three cheers for the losing team," said the judge presiding over the trial. "Do you remember those days?" The following year brawling reached such a pitch during a junior match between Hamilton and Bramlea (189 penalty minutes were given, which was light according to eyewitnesses) that the Ontario government ordered an inquiry into amateur hockey. QC William McMurtry, who conducted the investigation, reported a "substantial increase in violence" in amateur circles. Even more alarming, wrote McMurtry, was that the use of violence as a tactical weapon had filtered down to the bantam and peewee leagues. (Two years earlier another study had found that once a boy had reached bantam level his concepts of sportsmanship and fair play were virtual "dead letters.") Junior goons and peewee goons were appearing. Bobby Hull's young son arrived home after a game and proudly announced that his teammates had awarded him a new nickname for his aggressive play – "Dave Schultz." Hockey was being lost amid the muscle.

Public reaction was not long in coming. The influx of intimidatory violence arrived just as television coverage of the sport was getting into stride, and although many fans were enthusiastic about the brawling on their screens, others were appalled. Soon even the players themselves began

> ❝ When I see what's happening in hockey – tough kids jumping on other players' back to pound them – I doubt I want my son participating in such a game. ❞
>
> **Serge Savard, Montreal Canadien, 1976**

to voice their doubts, an event which is as rare in high-discipline professional sport as is a gracious word for a loser. "I always considered a hockey fight something that happened after a flare-up," said New York Ranger Brad Park, after a match in which he had been the subject of Dave Schultz's attention. "But with the Flyers, we find that fights are started deliberately." "The way things are going, someone is going to be killed," added Minnesota's Dennis Hextall. The most damning remark came from Montreal Canadien Serge Savard after the Canadiens – a "clean" team, as hockey teams go – had defeated the Flyers in the 1976 Stanley Cup final. "The Flyers were the worst thing that happened to hockey," growled Savard. "The way they fight, the way they set the example for the young kids. To sweep them, maybe we put an end to all the crap they stand for."

The greatest pressures against hockey violence, however, came not from within but from without – specifically from the courts, who resumed their role (long neglected in the face of sport's independence from the rest of twentieth-century society) as arbiters of hockey law and order. The first indication of what was in store came in 1970 with the separate trials of Ted Green and Wayne Maki following a near fatal stick-swinging incident during an Ottawa exhibition game. (Green suffered a fractured skull which required the insertion of an artificial plate.) Although both were found not guilty – with one judge commenting that "Hockey cannot be played without what normally are called assaults" – the district attorney had edged open the courtroom door. Three years later Bob Taylor of the Flyers was hauled into court and charged with breaking the law by "using obscene language and by fighting spectators with fists and by wielding hockey sticks." Taylor had been one of seven Flyers who had invaded the stands to settle a difference of opinion with the fans. This time the district attorney won a conviction; Taylor was given a thirty-day suspended sentence and fined $500, a landmark case despite the appeals court's overturning of the thirty-day sentence.

The 1974–5 season was a watershed year for hockey violence which saw players suspended for kicking, jaws broken by punches and "a massive gang brawl" involving the Flyers in Oakland. Even Clarence Campbell was forced to admit that "without doubt this has been our worst year ever for sheer violence on the ice."

It was also the season that the courtroom dramas began in earnest. The first to come to trial was the Dave Forbes–Henry Boucha case. During a Boston–Minnesota game, Forbes had hit Boucha in the eye with the butt of his stick and then grabbed his hair and ground his face into the ice. Boucha was left with a fractured eye cavity, twenty-five stitches and double vision, and Forbes was charged with aggravated assault. At the trial Forbes's attorney defended his client by charging that hockey was a "quest for violence" that taught players "from the age of four on, 'Don't let the other player intimidate you'" and "Win! Win! Win! at any cost." Boston coach Don Cherry admitted that he may have contributed to the violence. "The pressure was really on," he explained. "We'd been losing games. We really had to win." The trial resulted in a hung jury, in itself a fair indictment of the sport.

Later that year Detroit's Dan Maloney attacked Toronto's Brian Glennie from behind, knocking him senseless and beating his head on the ice several times. Ontario's attorney-general Roy McMurtry (brother of William) charged Maloney with assault. Although he was found not guilty, the jury took pains to point out that it did not condone such behavior.

The next year brought more of the same. Four Philadelphia players were charged with criminal assault after a Stanley Cup play-off game against Toronto which featured everything from flailing sticks and fisticuffs to spitting. In the NHL's rival league, the WHA, Calgary Cowboy Rick Jodzio was charged with "assault with intent to maim" when he attacked Quebec's Mark Tardif. "On the ambulance ride I thought I was going to be a young widow," said Tardif's young wife. Quebec's team president was similarly concerned, although for a slightly different reason: "We pay some players up to $225,000 a year. We're not going to have them chopped down by some stick-swinging maniac who earns $15,000." A judge in Kamloops, British Columbia, actually found a Western Canada Hockey League player guilty of assault. Although he gave him a conditional discharge, the judge did suspend the defendant from playing and warned that others would not be treated so leniently in the future.

The prosecution of hockey players caused intense bitterness in the game's higher echelons. Clarence Campbell was convinced that "political considerations" were behind it, that district attorneys were trying to make names for themselves. "It's ridiculous," snapped Fred Shero, who, when I spoke to him, had four of his Flyers awaiting trial:

The sport must handle itself. If we can't handle our sport *then* you bring in the law. I just watched a football game yesterday; they could have put *everybody* in jail with all the infractions. Same in baseball . . .

a guy comes into second base with his spikes high . . . a guy throws a ball at your head. . . . We've had sport since the time of the Romans, and even in those days when they had lions against the Christians the police weren't in the arena. [The thought that maybe they should have been did not seem to occur to Shero.] The athlete knows what he's facing and he's not complaining.

As for any spectators who might feel queasy about the violence, Shero had already made his position clear: "If it's pretty skating they want, let 'em go to the Ice Capades."

The pressure from players and the public in general eventually proved too great for the leagues to continue to ignore. In 1976 the NHL took what it considered to be a major step toward eliminating fisticuffs by introducing the "aggressor rule." Any player starting a fight was automatically liable to a five-minute penalty and could be thrown out of the game (although "spontaneous" outbursts were exempt). The Players' Association, after finding that even Lloyds of London would not insure them, had pressed for automatic game expulsions for both parties involved in a fight, but they had been defeated by the owners. The WHA similarly rejected players' demands for stiffer rules against fighting, settling instead for a special committee to study violence on the ice. It also reduced team rosters in an effort to prevent teams from carrying goons.

To date, the aggressor rule has proved a rather unsatisfactory means of curtailing violence. Riddled with loopholes, it places a heavy burden on the referees, a group of NHL employees not particularly well known for making decisions likely to antagonize owners. Although Bobby Clarke, after several months of the new rule, claimed that needless fighting had diminished, there is still enough bloodshed in hockey to satisfy even the most Roman of spectators. In a recent WHA game two dozen police were required on the ice to restore order after a stick attack, and in the Southwest League police had to use mace and nightsticks to separate players and fans. Former Canadien defenseman Jaques Lapierre quit his job as coach of the Montreal Juniors when in one game an aggressor was given only a minor penalty following a brawl, and in another the opposing team was penalized a total of 334 minutes. "By telling kids to fight, to intimidate, to concentrate on stuff like that, we are doing an injustice," said Lapierre. "We are not teaching hockey. We are creating goons."

In the NHL, the acknowledged standard bearer of hockey, after a brief lull in goon tactics, bloodshed is now enjoying a definite renaissance. At the beginning of the 1977–8 season, Detroit general manager Ted Lindsay issued his players with T-shirts reading "Aggressive hockey is back in town." Said Lindsay: "You've heard of *Star Wars*, well, this is going to be 'Ice Wars.' " *Sports Illustrated* reported of Detroit that "among the training camp survivors are some of hockey's best hatchet men."

An even more blatant call to arms was the signing of "Wild" Willie Trognitz by the WHA's Cincinnati Stingers. Trognitz was just another minor league policeman until on October 29, 1977, during a wild and bloody brawl he cracked his stick over an opponent's head and was banned for life by league president William Beagen. One week later he was signed by the Stingers. "We have a small, skating team and were getting pushed around," explained Stinger executive vice-president Bill DeWitt Jr. "We won't be intimidated anymore," vowed Stinger coach Jacques Demers. "Let's face it," said Stinger All-Star center Richie Leduc gloomily, "the goons are back."

Wild Willie, of course, was delighted. "Strange isn't it?" he crowed to *Sports Illustrated*. "Hockey's a game that condones fighting. Beagen tries to change that, and here I am smoking a buck-twenty-five cigar in the bigs." He was proud of his ability to throw a punch, he said. Although he didn't want to injure anybody, he did want opponents to be afraid of coming back, so it was his job to hurt them. "If gouging and scratching are necessary," he concluded, "I'll do it."

Unfortunately Trognitz's joy was shortlived. He proved adept enough at punching, but as one observer commented, "Wild Willie skates as if he's carrying a trunk through an airport, and he handles the puck as if it were a basketball." After a ten-game trial he was quietly dropped. Nevertheless the Stingers still had Bruce Greig, a 217-pound, 6-foot 4-inch rookie with a reputation almost, but not quite, as mean as Wild Willie's.

The fate of Philadelphia's much criticized Flyers no doubt loomed large in both Lindsay's and DeWitt's thoughts as they planned their Ice Wars campaigns. In the interim following the rule changes and court appearances, the Flyer management took steps to reconstruct the team's image, primarily with the shock trading of Dave Schultz to the Los Angeles Kings. "We've got the least violent team in hockey," crowed Fred Shero after Schultz's exit. "You put us in a box car with any other team, and the other team is coming out." This new pristine image, however, was to prove a disaster. The fans were furious with the club for trading their hero – when Schultz

---

❝ I broke a kid's nose in Juniors with a punch, and afterwards Lou Fontinato told me it was the hardest punch he'd ever seen. That was the biggest thrill I had as a kid. ❞

"Wild" Willie Trognitz, ice hockey enforcer, 1977

---

eventually did return to the Spectrum some months later he was given a standing ovation, despite his Kings' uniform. But even more crucially, the Flyers stopped winning games.

"Schultz won the Flyers two Stanley Cups," said John Ferguson:

> His participation in the club wasn't measured in goals, but it was sure as hell measured in backbone. And they've lost him. They traded him off to Los Angeles because, so the story goes, they made these rules to curb his actions. Whatever, they made a mistake by getting rid of him because when you went into the Spectrum, I don't care what kind of an athlete you are, you had to be thinking "There's Dave Schultz in there, and when I go into a corner to pick up a puck, he's going to hit me."

By the start of the 1977–8 season, Shero had learned his lesson. In a pre-season round-up, *Sports Illustrated* reported that the Flyers were to be "the Broad Street Bullies once again, led by pugilistic Paul Holmgren, a right wing whose best shot seems to be an overhand right from the blind side." The story ended on a reassuring note for the Philadelphia fans: "The Flyers initiated several bench-clearing brawls during the exhibition season, including a disgraceful donnybrook against Boston that spread to the corridors of the Spectrum." Come back, Dave Schultz, all is forgiven.

And what of Schultz, the king of hockey mayhem, exiled in Los Angeles? It came as no little surprise to learn that The Hammer was not quite the happy man one would have expected any player of his salary and splendid notoriety to be. It was not merely the bitterness of his being so callously and abruptly discarded by an ungrateful team which was bothering him; that had long since passed. No, Schultz's problem had surfaced well before the trade during his last season with the Flyers, and it was simply this: after so many years as a 30 MPH hired thug, Schultz had discovered that he preferred playing hockey. The trouble was that the Flyer coaches were not of the same opinion, and when Schultz attempted some plays which, unfortunately, did not come off, they told him so in no uncertain terms. In fact, he recalled miserably, "they gave me shit. They had three coaches and I was never helped by any of them. I was just there to fight." Unable to switch, Schultz continued fighting, which left him frustrated and depressed.

Then, out of the blue, he was no longer Flyer property. Although being traded had hurt, after the initial shock wore off he had begun to see the move in a more positive light. Perhaps, he had thought, it meant the beginnings of a new playing career. But this idea, too, was short-lived. The Kings had very definite views on what was required of Schultz, and they didn't include figure skating or shots on goal. "When I came here," he said, sadly poking a misshapen fist at the Kings' deserted training rink, "I thought I was going to start scoring goals. But I was just kidding myself."

The last view I had of Dave Schultz in action was of a man fully resigned to his fate. It came during a home game against the Washington Caps and, as hockey games go, this was a fine example of a back-alley gang brawl. At the center of the bloodshed and teeth breaking stood Schultz, charging head down after fleeing offenders, hurling off his gloves at the slightest provocation and flailing at the air with his disjointed fists like a man possessed. The Los Angeles fans were ecstatic. Each time he decked another opponent they leaped from their seats, beside themselves with delight. Each time he was led away to the penalty box, still mouthing threats, they hooted and stamped and chanted his name. One red-headed teenager several rows back kept shouting out the scores from what appeared to be another game – "4–1!", "5–2!" It was some minutes before I finally realized that he was counting fights, not goals.

During the course of the evening, Schultz earned two major (ten-minute) penalties and a slew of five-minute ones. He spent the entire last period in the penalty box, slamming its plywood sides with his stick and screaming dementedly at his enemies. When he was unpenned for the last time and skated off the ice, the ovation was deafening. In the locker room he was immediately surrounded by a swarm of reporters who thrust microphones in his face to learn why so-and-so deserved his split lip and why such-and-such had it coming. Schultz calmly gave them everything they wanted, as he had done all evening. Old soldiers never die. Some months later the Pittsburgh Penguins snapped him up for a fat fee that neither the Kings nor Schultz could refuse.

Beanballs and Broken Noses

Football and ice hockey by no means hold the monopoly on winning through violence. They are merely the brand leaders of an ethic which has now been embraced by the entire spectrum of mass-spectator ball sports. The use of violence as a tool varies widely from game to game, contingent as it is upon the opportunity for physical contact each game presents. However, there are few games – even those with minimal body contact – which have not been affected to some degree by win-at-all-costs violence.

Take baseball, the game pro football edged from its national pastime pedestal during the social violence and tension of the 1960s. Although in comparison with football's mass combat the opportunities for physical contact in baseball are far more limited, the game is certainly no wide-eyed innocent where violence is concerned, and has not been for generations.

TENNIS, ANYONE?

Perhaps it will be quite some time before the spectacle of two opponents jousting with each other across the center court net is a common feature of Wimbledon, but even such a noncontact sport as tennis is not immune to violent gamesmanship. Consider the recent advice of US tennis coach Art Hoppe. "The proper method of playing mixed doubles," counseled Hoppe, "is to hit the ball accidentally at the woman opponent as hard and as accurately as possible."

And if Hoppe's advice sounds less than serious, consider this report on the world amateur squash team championships which appeared in a recent issue of *Squash Monthly*. The trouble began when New Zealander Lilley met Saleem of Pakistan: "Saleem turned on almost every ball that hit the sidewall, and hit Lilley three times in the first game. Lilley threatened to stop play ..." Matters came to a head when Brownlee (NZ) took to the court against Maqsood Ahmed (Pakistan):

> Maqsood claims Brownlee started the elbows, but no matter who started it, it was clear to observers ... that both men were aiming at the opponent's legs, and that Brownlee finished it. It was twelve minutes into the third round when Brownlee mistook Maqsood's dark head for the ball. Knocked momentarily senseless, Ahmed tinned out the fourth game, 0–9.

In its earliest incarnations baseball was a close cousin of the mob ball of pre-industrial England. Played on the village green, it often served as little more than an excuse for a summer's afternoon free-for-all. Gloves remained for decades an unthought-of luxury, and the local youths counted it a sign of their manhood to continue playing despite bleeding or broken hands. Running between bases was particularly hazardous, with players being tagged by a ball aimed at any part of their anatomy.

Many of baseball's rougher edges were removed during the game's rapid transformation from village brawl to organized sport. (By the sport boom of the late 1800s, professional baseball was the most sophisticated ball game on the American continent, far ahead of pro football which was still wallowing in the slag heaps of Pennsylvania.) Remnants of baseball's bruising origins, however, did remain, although the motives behind the violence had changed considerably. Whereas before, as in mob ball, violence had been purely the product of a player's delight in raising a yelp from his opponent, by the 1870s the pressure on professional clubs to satisfy large crowds had already begun. Baseball had become a job, and that job was to win.

How attached those early crowds were to winning can be judged by their treatment of that universally unloved third party, the umpire. It is the nature of baseball that so much of the end result hinges on what one man sees – or thinks he sees. Given this, it is not surprising that from the Civil War onwards, as one early historian noted, "at all times, the lot of the umpire was a hard one." And when fans began flocking to the bleachers intent on seeing their team roll on to victory, the umpire's lot became not just hard but positively hazardous. "Mama, let me kill the umpire, let me hit him in the face," ran the opening line of one popular nineteenth-century ditty, a sentiment enshrined in baseball history by the 1888 classic *Casey at the Bat*:

From the benches, black with people, there went up a muffled roar,
Like the beating of the storm-waves on a stern and distant shore.
"Kill him! Kill the umpire!" shouted someone in the stand;
And it's likely they'd have killed him had not Casey raised his hand.

Casey, of course, was intended as a humorous parody, but on many occasions the catch cry "Kill the ump!" was delivered in deadly earnest. After "cheating" a home-town crowd of its rightful victory, an umpire's best friend was either a policeman or a pistol – and preferably both. In 1888, the year *Casey* first appeared, umpire Phil Power held a mob of enraged Philadelphia fans at bay with a loaded revolver until the police could muster up enough reinforcements to rescue him. Six years later in Milwaukee, another crowd beat umpire Jack Sheridan unconscious before the police could reach him. During the early 1900s the flamboyant New York manager John McGraw whipped up so much hatred against one particular umpire in the hope that he would be intimidated enough to make calls favorable to the home team, that at game's end the crowd gathered outside the changing room brandishing a noose. Steamboat Johnson, a minor league umpire of considerable repute, estimated that during his career he had been the target of some four thousand bottles, twenty of which had found their mark.

Caught up in this blood-in-the-eye desire for victory, it was not long before pitchers began to realize that they held in their hands a weapon which could be used to win games, either by intimidating or even retiring star opponents. By 1920 when Cleveland batter Ray Chapman was killed by a fast ball which split his skull before it ricocheted to third base, the "beanball" – a ball which, as its name implies, is aimed at the head – had become part of the game.

Today the urgency of winning is even more pronounced, with splenetic fans widening their attacks to include players as well as umpires. The most marked player of recent times is Cincinnati's Pete Rose, who has been hit with everything from chunks of ice to whiskey bottles. During the 1977 season fans pelted Yankee centerfield Mickey Rivers with cherry bombs, beer bottles, flashlight batteries and sundry other items. Even the great Hank Aaron could not escape being hit in the face by an orange in San Francisco. The worst incident, Cleveland's notorious Beer Night Brawl, occurred in 1972 when hundreds of drunken Indian fans invaded the field during the ninth inning of a tie-score game to "deal" with the Texas Rangers; four players and an umpire suffered injuries. "Before," sighed Bobby Thomson, hero of the 1951 "Coogan's Bluff" pennant, when I spoke to him in 1977, "young kids would toss stuff at you from the upper deck while you worked out – oranges or tomatoes or whatever. It wasn't mean stuff. But today it's just an unbelievable thing that people would go to a game and act this way."

Although it has now developed into a fine and subtle art, violence on the diamond has remained just as much a part of baseball's reality as the fans and their bottles. The most glaring example is the cleat slide as perfected by Ty Cobb, who reputedly was given to filing his spikes in the dugout as a warning to opposing basemen. "Playing second base, you're looking at two sets of razor-sharp studs coming at you face high," said one former Cleveland player, rolling up his shirt and turning his back to display the scars.

It is with the pitcher, however, that the real possibilities for violence still lie. There are several reasons why batters end up sprawled in the dirt from a ball which, over the twenty-odd yards it has to travel, can reach a speed approaching 90 MPH. There are some pitchers who simply enjoy the sound of rawhide connecting with a soft body – "We're not supposed to admit that," said Bobby Thomson, "but . . ." By general consensus, however, such a breed is rare. Injuries are more commonly the result of a pitcher's attempting to "brush back" players who crowd the plate. Then there is the pitcher as team "policeman" whose job it is to settle scores on behalf of his teammates. As in hockey, a pitcher's failure to even up the ante can have drastic effects both on his own standing among his colleagues and on team morale as a whole. "If one team is out-punishing the other team and the other team doesn't retaliate," explained Bobby Thomson, "they're just going to walk all over them," a view which any self-respecting hockey player would heartily endorse. (Another thing which baseball has in common with hockey is the wild, bench-clearing brawl prompted by one player's savage treatment – invariably the pitcher's – of another.)

But the most frequent use of the beanball is as a tactic of violent intimida-

---

❝ Getting hit is scary. The last thing you remember is collapsing over the plate, and the next thing you remember is riding in the ambulance. ❞

Roger Maris, retired baseball star, 1977

---

tion, designed either to soften up a player for a following pitch, or simply, in Bobby Thomson's words, "to put some fear into the batter." St. Louis Cardinal pitcher Al Hrabosky once recalled watching how batters shook visibly when veteran Bob Gibson, whose specialty was an under-the-chin fastball, pitched to them. "I learned my first lesson in the major leagues," said Hrabosky. "Be an intimidator!" Sometimes it is at the discretion of the pitcher whether or not he serves up a beanball; often it is ordered directly from the coach's bench. "I was once fined $250 for not throwing at a batter," said one pitcher. Others have reportedly been relegated to the minor leagues after refusing to throw beanballs. As one pitching coach told *Sports Illustrated*, ". . . you must use the weapons at your disposal."

Since Ray Chapman, no major league player has been killed by a beanball, thanks more to the introduction of the batter's helmet than to any decline in the art. However, there have been several near misses over the years. One Kansas City player was given a 50–50 chance of survival after being struck by a beanball. According to his manager, his head had an indentation "that looked like a deflated basketball." In 1970 Ken Tatum of the Angels was hit in the face by a beanball. "I put his nose back in place," reported the doctor, "but we'll probably have to operate just to set it. It was all over his face." "It's dangerous every time you step into the batter's box," Dave Cash of the Phillies told *Sports Illustrated*'s Mark Kram some years ago. "Your life is on the line. You're subject to getting killed. I hate to put it that way, but how else can you put it?"

Basketball, an avowed pacifist sport (at least as planned by its clergyman-creator Dr. James Naismith), also has its share of violence. Again, it is most noticeable at the higher levels of competition – college and pro – where the pressure to win is intense enough to leave a hard-bitten coach such as Bob Cousy doubled up with agonizing stomach pains before a game. As with other contemporary ball sports, the trouble stems not so much from the excesses of abnormally violent men, but from the way in which the game is played in these ultra-competitive times. "You used to get punched in the crotch, slugged in the mouth. Go up for a jumper and get kicked," star shooter Dave Cowens told *Sports Illustrated* recently. "We still got our cheap-shot artists but most of those fellas are gone now." But, added

Cowens, "you always try to intimidate. It's part of the game." Dr. Naismith, in his Christian innocence, believed that by eliminating tackling he would create a fast, safe, noncontact sport. Thoughts of intimidation probably never even entered his head.

It did not, however, take basketball long to change. In 1898, a bare seven years after the invention of the game, the *University Weekly* of Lawrence, Kansas, could report:

> Everyone who is at all interested in athletics is now talking basketball, yet it does not stop here. Those who hitherto have manifested no interest in any sport of skill and strength seem now to be enthusiastic over the new game.

What they were enthusiastic for was victory at all costs, as a despairing George Naismith recognized in 1914:

> So much stress is laid today on the winning of games that practically all else is lost sight of, and the fine elements of manliness and true sportsmanship are accorded a secondary place.

Today pressure to win has transformed the game. "Basketball a non-contact sport?" snorted Madison Square Garden physician Gaetano Viti, rolling his eyes to the Garden roof. "It's meant to be, but if you watch basketball out here – professional basketball – and you sit anywhere in the court-side area, you'll find out how much of a noncontact sport it really is. Under the basket it's survival. If a referee wanted to call fouls, you wouldn't have a sport at all." "There are violent blows struck out there," admitted Knicks' veteran Bill Bradley. "It's a very physical game, contact is a big part of it. It's a matter of establishing your territory out there. You have to be willing to defend your territory." There are shooters now in high school who are as good as the shooters in the pros, he continued, yet often as not when they reach the pros they fail, simply because they can't shoot straight in a rough-house. Bradley's teammate Phil Jackson, a self-confessed "physical" player, agreed. "The contact comes with forcing an arm in somebody's ribs," he said, "placing an elbow in the small of the back. It's done very subtly, but it's as crisp and hard as you can make it." Rebounds were the toughest. "That's the one time the ball is up for grabs. Whoever can get up there and get the ball comes away with it and there's a lot of fierce contact – elbows, a lot of body work."

The effects of this contact is written primarily on players' faces. With arms raised and faces unprotected, broken noses, split eyebrows, eye injuries such as detached retinas, and broken teeth are not infrequent. After suffering two serious eye injuries, NBA star Kareem Abdul-Jabbar has taken to wearing welders' goggles on the court. Jackson reeled off an impromptu casualty list of recent years which included Dave DeBusschere (nose broken three times), Willis Reed (nose broken five or six times) and Jerry West (". . . was it eight?"). For his part he had been fortunate, said Jackson, suffering only chipped teeth.

This physical harassment and intimidation has other repercussions besides injuries. With players in such close proximity to each other, there is a real temptation for a player to lash out at the opponent who is trying to knock him off his game. The most celebrated incident in recent seasons was when Abdul-Jabbar broke his fist on Kent Benson's head with a spectacular right-hand punch. Less frequent are the bench-clearing battles, but these too are certainly not unknown in basketball.

A more pressing problem is the increasingly violent reaction of basketball spectators. Unlike football, the fans are positioned only an arm's length from the players, almost on the court. Given the catalyst of a violent incident during the game – a demonstrative coach, a controversial refereeing decision or even just a neck-and-neck game – it is all too easy for a crowd to become part of the action. Phil Jackson remarked to me:

> I have seen fans come off their seats and kick officials in the pants. I have seen fans being ejected. I have seen lots of things thrown on the courts. And I think I've felt the fear of what crowd hysteria is – that mob kind of feeling. For years we played the Boston Celtics in the play-offs and it seemed we always beat them. I became their arch enemy because I put this type of pressure on them and harassed them defensively. So I was used to getting beer in the face and so on.

In such situations the role of the coach is crucial. Sandwiched on the sidelines between the players and the crowd, he serves as a highly visible link man between the two. A shrewd coach can orchestrate the emotions of a home-town crowd like a dance-band leader, slamming down his clipboard in a theatrical fit of pique, rolling his eyes in exaggerated despair at the fans, and barking abuse at both referee and opposition players. "Coaches control the crowds, they set the atmosphere," said Jim Howell, a former leading NCAA referee who resigned recently because of the behavior of the crowds. Much of the friction that occurred during the 1976 NBA championship between the Boston Celtics and the Phoenix Suns has been attributed to this coach/crowd relationship, namely to the Celtics' volatile coach Tom Heinsohn. In the fourth game of what was in any case an ill-tempered, foul-ridden series, *Sports Illustrated* reported that "Heinsohn set a new record for footage on the isolated TV camera as he complained, mocked, stormed, gestured, feigned bewilderment and conducted classes in sideline theater of the absurd." That was in Phoenix. During the next game, this time played on Heinsohn's own Boston turf, hundreds of alcohol-primed Celtic fans stormed the court, wrestled with the referee and assaulted the Suns' players. "It's a fortunate thing that one of the players did not wind up with a broken leg or a broken arm," said Suns' coach John MacLeod. Phoenix lost.

Heinsohn is generally regarded as being one of basketball's more driven coaches. After one close game during the play-offs, he staggered off court gray in the face and had to be revived by a doctor. Another inverterate winner is – or was – Bill Musselman, coach of the Minnesota Gophers. The story of what happend at the University of Minnesota in January 1972 has been told before, but it is worth retelling in that it provides the most glaring illustration in recent sporting history of how the willingness to win at any cost can explode into violence.

In 1971 the Minnesota Gophers were a less-than-mediocre Big Ten basketball team which had not won a title outright since 1919. Determined to reverse this losing streak, the Minnesota selection committee interviewed Bill Musselman, a coach who had compiled an impressive winning record at Ohio's Ashland College. When the committee asked Musselman how long it would take him to mold a winning team, he clinched his appointment with the reply: "We'll win right off. I don't believe in rebuilding years."

Musselman began his task by submerging the team in a winning environment. He introduced choreographed pre-game warm-ups to inspire both players and fans and intimidate the opposition. The walls of the locker room were plastered with Lombardi-isms, including one of his own: "Defeat is worse than death because you have to live with defeat." He also recruited several overtly aggressive players.

Musselman's strategies worked. Having won its first four games, the team was confident enough to anticipate victory against its next rival, the dauntingly strong Ohio State. As the game approached, emotions began to build. Luke Witte, Ohio's star center, was seen as the only stumbling block to victory. The talk a week before the game, recalled one faculty member, was "Stop Witte and you win the game."

The Gophers, however, failed to contain either Witte or Ohio State. With eleven minutes to go in the final period, Ohio scored ten straight points, putting the team in an invincible position. Although they fought hard, the Gophers could not bridge the gap, much to the displeasure of the fans who, as defeat became a certainty, hurled garbage and debris onto the court. Then, with only thirty-six seconds remaining, the Gophers erupted. Luke Witte was flattened, punched in the head as he went down by two Minnesota players. As he struggled to his feet, one of his assailants –

Corky Taylor – extended his hand as if to assist him, then kneed him viciously in the groin. Another player, Ron Behagen, leaped from the Gopher bench and stomped on Witte's neck and face as he lay semi-conscious. Several other Ohio players were attacked – both by the Gophers, who by this time had lost all control, and by Gopher fans who had invaded the court. When order had been restored, Witte and a teammate were out cold, Witte's face a bloody mess.

The incident, which was televised, caused a wave of public outrage. The governor of Ohio called it a "public mugging." *Sports Illustrated* described it as a "cold, brutal attack, governed by the law of the jungle." Taylor and Behagen were suspended for the rest of the season. Witte was never again quite the same basketball player.

The basketball powers were content to let the matter rest with the suspension of Taylor and Behagen, believing that the two players were to blame for the incident. But there were others – Luke Witte's father, for one – who felt that the cause of the riot lay not with the players but with the coach. As a professor of philosophy at Ashland College, Dr. Witte had been in a good position to view Musselman's tactics at first hand, and he had not been impressed. "As far as I'm concerned," he said, "the entire situation traces back to the coach, Bill Musselman. I'm not surprised. Musselman's intent seems to be to win at any cost. His players are brutalized and animalized to achieve that goal."

Musselman denied that he had in any way inflamed his players. Yet as *Sports Illustrated* pointed out, he had neither made any attempt to stop the riot nor later shown any remorse. Certainly the experience did not deter him from pursuing his "death before defeat" philosophy. A year later at an invitational tournament in New Mexico, an unabashed Musselman set a tournament record as the coach to be evicted earliest from a game.

Professional Foul

Bill Musselman's vision of sport has become common currency in a society which has come to judge its citizens and institutions almost solely in terms of winning and losing. But America's stadiums are by no means the sole preserve of violence in the cause of sporting victory; they merely host the extremes. In fact, "Winning is everything" is a philosophy which has, especially over the last few decades, developed almost universal appeal. Even in Britain, home of the public-school ideals of fair play and honorable conduct, the ethic of "playing the game" has, in most cases, been rudely supplanted by the tactic of "playing the man."

Britain's national obsession, which is shared to greater or lesser degree by some 150 other countries, is soccer. Ever since hacking was outlawed, soccer, like basketball, has officially laid claim to being virtually a non-contact – and certainly a noncombat – ball sport. Which, compared with rugby or gridiron or Australian Rules, it patently is. Indeed, it would be difficult to find on paper a less violent ball game than soccer. But again, paper and practice are two very different things.

By the 1920s and '30s, when soccer had become solidly entrenched as the favorite of the masses, every professional team worth its salt had learned to include at least one "iron man" in its starting line-up. As with ice hockey's policemen, it was the job of such players to provide their team with "back-bone" (although unlike their Canadian counterparts they usually performed their duties in a distinctly surreptitious fashion), be it with a boot, a body block or an elbow. "We always had what we called the Killers in the game," recalled former Wolverhampton manager Stan Cullis in Arthur Hopcraft's *The Football Man* (1968), "players who went deliberately over the ball to get the man." Players such as Frank Barson, whose rugged career left him with his nose broken four times.

It was the late '60s that were the crowning years of violence as a soccer strategy. By then soccer had fully adopted the American philosophy of winning, although in slightly revised form: instead of "Win at all costs," soccer's credo was the dour "Never lose." As a result, the emphasis swung from offensive soccer to defensive soccer – from inventive, positive football to hard, negative play. "We have to do what's necessary," explained Tottenham Hotspurs manager Bill Nicholson in Hunter Davies' 1972 book *The Glory Game*. "Supporters aren't interested in good teams that lose. This is professional football. The first rule in a manager's bible is 'Don't lose.' That's the way it is."

Against this background the role of the "killers" became crucial, for it was they who were pedaling a brand of soccer which was perfectly attuned to the new managerial philosophy. For every George Best threading his way goalwards there was a Norman Hunter or a Chopper Harris lurking one step behind waiting to bring him down with one stab of a heavy leather clog.

The most glaringly obvious feature of this pattern of play was a tactic known as the professional foul, in which a defender caught on the last line of defense elected to blatantly scythe down a striker and suffer the penalty or free kick rather than allow his opponent a shot on goal. As far back as 1937 *The Times* had railed against the professional foul. In an editorial entitled "Not Football," it had complained: "The unforgivable sin in any game is the cold-blooded and intentional foul, and it is unfortunately true that the modern game of professional football is all too full of it." But even by the beginning of the '60s the professional foul was still a fairly rare occurrence. By the end of the decade, however, it had become as common as violence on the terraces. Only the foolish ever admitted it; veteran England international Jack Charlton was heavily rapped over the knuckles in 1970 for confessing in front of television cameras that: "You do what is necessary in the circumstances. If I was playing in an international and saw someone getting away with the ball and I could not catch him, I would flatten him. My job is to stop a man scoring." Yet by then even the television commentators were openly talking about professional fouls, and although they tut-tutted their disapproval, they invariably added some comment such as "He had to do it, of course."

"Defenders were expected to chop opponents down as a rehearsed tactic," wrote referee Norman Burtenshaw in his autobiography *Whose Side Are You On, Ref?* "The philosophy that overtook football in England was simple: Win at all cost." Or as Ron Harris put it: "You don't get nothing for being second. Okay, you get your name taken, but if you save the game and win 1–0, you're a hero." In most cases even a draw was enough.

Ron Harris, for one, has carved out an enviable career for himself with such tactics, surviving seventeen years (including a period as captain) with Chelsea, London's glamor club. Somewhat surprisingly, like hockey's Dave Schultz he harbors few illusions about his role with Chelsea, often disarmingly referring to himself with the nickname most Chelsea fans know him by – "Chopper." "A few years back when I had a name for being a bit of a butcher and all that, it was accepted," he said. "If we were playing against Georgie Best or Jimmy Greaves or Dennis Law, these sort of people, 99 times out of 100 it was down to me to mark 'em, pick 'em up and do the best I could, whether it was a couple of sly elbows or something."

Harris's ability to bruise secured his place in the side, even though at one stage he was being booked by referees four and five times a season. Opposition stars gritted their teeth in anger at the mention of his name. Former Fulham idol Rodney Marsh refused point blank to discuss Ron; he said it would lower the tone of the conversation. "All Ronny Harris can do is kick," sneered Queens Park Rangers' goalscorer Stan Bowles. "He can't play so he goes around kicking people."

Today Ron is totally unabashed about his past record. After all, he is still playing when most of his erstwhile colleagues have long since been relegated to the Sunday kick-around leagues. "In any side you see people like myself," he told me. "You name a good side in the first or second division. I think it always helps to have that little bit of . . . *grit*. Maybe to let people know who's the guv'nor. It's nice to have somebody on your side who you know is capable of winning tackles, winning the ball, doing a *specific* job."

276

However, for all that, said Ron, the glory days of soccer's iron men have now faded. Although the Chelsea "Shed" still urges him on to vengeance, chanting "Chopper! Chopper! Do your job!" whenever a teammate is felled, the "hatchet men" (Ron's words) are now far less evident. Much of the reason for this can be traced to the general tightening-up of the rules relating to violence which began with the referees' campaign against "brutish" play in August 1971. In the first week of the "Referees' Revolution," 123 players were booked, and the game has never been quite the same since. According to Ron, such lethal tactics as the back tackle are now virtually things of the past. The opportunities for intimidation have now greatly diminished: "Before, the referee would give you a talking to and you'd say, 'Sorry, I won't do that again,' but by that time the feller's looking about thinking when are you going to come in again. Now, you're booked straight away."

An even more compelling reason, to Ron's way of thinking, is the increase in television coverage of matches. Under the unsparing eye of the camera, every "incident" is captured, magnified, slowed down and replayed over and over again to an audience of millions. To be the butt of such mass condemnation – "People look and say, 'Oh, no, that's a *diabolical* tackle!'" – is enough to curb even the most ruthless offender. Especially if, like Ron Harris, he earns much of his livelihood selling candy to children.

Other players, however, especially those on the receiving end, see little change in the overall level of tactical violence. "I know I am going to get smashed around by blokes twice as big as me," said Brighton goal scorer Peter Ward, "and though I don't like it I just accept it as part of my job.

Commented Queens Park Ranger Rachid Harkouk:

The game starts and a bloke comes over and tells me he is going to break my leg. Then he's going to smash my teeth or put an elbow in my mouth. Sometimes it gets so bad that I freeze when I get the chance to show some skill. I mean, what is the point in looking clever one second and the next getting whacked behind the leg. There seems to be too many players walking around with permanent limps these days.

A few seasons ago Fulham coach Bobby Campbell unveiled the shins of his then star attraction, George Best, to press scrutiny at the end of a par-

---

❝ It bothers me to have kids asking how they can be as mean as me. They write and say, 'I love the way you kill people.' ❞

Jack Lambert, US pro football player, 1976

---

ticularly vicious League Cup game. "They looked as if he had walked through barbed wire," reported one newsman. "He only has to move an inch before he takes a whack," said Campbell.

Best's erstwhile teammate Rodney Marsh feels that the referees' rule tightening has, instead of decreasing violence, merely spread it wider throughout each team:

> Twenty or thirty years ago everyone knew who the dirty players were. They were the arch villains, if you like – unshaven Saturday morning growth, blue shadow and all of that. The fans, the players, the referees all accepted it. It was part of the mechanics.

The referees's crackdown, however, changed all that:

> Instead of being open, it went underground. Now it is the cynical foul from players you don't expect it of. Today you don't know where it could come from. You could go into a tackle with a guy who looks innocuous and it ends up he's the one who's going to do you.

The days of strikers scoring thirty-five goals a season had now ended, he said, a direct result of the professional foul and other tactics of violence. "You can see for yourself," said Marsh, "there must be two hundred scars on my legs. Players now deliberately try to kick the stars off the field. It's very sad that you've got to live with this sort of stuff."

Marsh's analysis of the game is supported by the injury counts of recent years. According to Dr. Ian Adams, head of Britain's most successful sports clinic at Leeds, soccer injuries resulting from direct violence have been on the increase during the last decade. The statistics now stand at one injury (an injury necessitating at least three days off) for every thirteen player exposures at the professional level – in other words, an injury a match. According to Dr. Adams, the reason for this increase is simple – the difference in the style of play induced by a greater emphasis on winning. "The main thing is competitiveness," he said, "players playing harder to win."

That is English domestic soccer. The same pattern can be seen in many other soccer countries where the pressure to win and the resultant violence is, if anything, even more pronounced. In South America, where concrete moats and wire cages have now become a standard feature of most large grounds, referees are spirited away from stadiums disguised as women or policemen. In Italy, where committed supporters think nothing of traveling out to an airport in the early hours of the morning to pelt a losing side with fruit and rotten eggs on its homecoming, referees and officials are plucked from the clutches of irate crowds by helicopters. When the Portuguese side Benfica defeated its arch rival Portov in 1976, the referee had to be escorted from his dressing room in an armored car. In Turkey forty-two people died and four hundred were injured in a riot over an obscure second division match. In Tel Aviv the same year a 17-year-old fan was jailed for thirteen years for stabbing a player to death following a disputed decision. In France Corsican supporters beat up the Nice team, blew up its captain's sports shop and threatened to kill the club chairman prior to a Football Association cup semifinal. In Mexico a match between Otumba and a neighboring team was heading toward a 0–0 draw until in the closing minutes the 40-year-old referee awarded a penalty against the home team; the Otumba players stoned him to death. A month earlier a Viennese goal-keeper had been jailed for nine months for jumping on the neck of an opponent, leaving him paralyzed. In Guatemala City five persons were hacked to death when local fans, upset by a defeat, attacked the visiting team with machetes.

"This I call routine," said former Dutch soccer star Johann Cruyff in 1971, surveying the five fresh wounds he had suffered during a normal Dutch league match. "Once I had problems with my temper and hit back. Now I have learned to take the charges and do not do anything back. Sure, some-times I jump out of the way. It is not good for the team, my wife or anyone if I cannot play in the next game."

These are not merely isolated incidents; all, with the exception of Cruyff, occurred during the past three or four seasons, and no doubt there were many more equally as bad which went unreported. However, it is on the international field that soccer violence reaches its peak. When nationalistic hysteria, jingoism and overt political pressure are attached to a crowd's intrinsic support of one team over another, the will to win reaches a mur-derous level.

"Serious sport," wrote George Orwell, "has nothing to do with fair play. It is bound up with hatred, jealousy, boastfulness, disregard for all rules, and sadistic pleasure in witnessing violence: in other words, it is war minus the shooting." Too true. Whereas international sport was once (and in certain quarters still is) hailed as a lasting source of harmony between nations – a sort of sweaty bonding cement – it is now glaringly obvious that only in its most obscure forms does it escape Orwell's definition, which certainly does not include soccer. The surest way to foment ill will among nations, continued Orwell in a truly inspired flash of perception (it was, after all, still only the early 1940s), is to arrange a series of football matches between one hundred thousand spectators, which is exactly what happens every four years under the title of the World Cup. The results have been more or less as Orwell predicted.

As early as the 1920s, an amateur Czech team was sent storming off the field in protest against the tactics used by its Belgian opponents, thereby setting the scene for the next half century of international soccer conflict. The first World Cup, hosted by Uruguay in 1930, confirmed the trend. Although troops with fixed bayonets stationed inside the stadium dampened any immediate violence following Uruguay's victory against Argentina, across the border in Buenos Aires mobs of enraged Argentinians stormed and ransacked the Uruguayan embassy. A London Chelsea side which toured South America shortly afterwards was also accorded a hostile reception; players were pelted with fruit and physically assaulted by ugly crowds who so terrified the referees that they refused to call anything but home-town decisions. In the second World Cup it was Italy's turn to provide the fireworks. During its first match with Spain, the Italians, lashed into a patriotic frenzy by Mussolini, lost four men through injury and the Spaniards seven. Italy was eventually defeated by England in a final which became known as the "Battle of Highbury." After the Italian center-half suffered a broken toe in the opening minutes, the game rapidly degenerated into a war of sly kicks and behind-the-play punches. Four years later, with Europe on the brink of war and all sporting events a matter of intense nationalistic chest beating, Mussolini's Italians managed to win the Cup in equally vicious style. That year was also notable for the behavior of the Czechs and Brazilians; in their preliminary match three players were sent off after a series of violent injuries including broken arms and legs.

World War II cooled sporting hostilities for several years, but by 1954 the Brazilians were back at their opponents' throats – in this case the Hungarians. The "Battle of Berne" (the sporting press has recorded many World Cup "battles") was a particularly ill-tempered display on the part of both teams, but it was made even more memorable by the events which took place after the final whistle. As the players were filing off to their respective dressing rooms, a Hungarian player apparently hit his Brazilian counterpart in the face with a bottle (although some reports claimed it was a spectator who delivered the blow). The Brazilians immediately stormed the Hungarian dressing room, where there ensued the extraordinary spectacle of two dozen international players battering each other with boots and liniment bottles amid jock straps and dirty sweaters. The worst casualty was a Hungarian who had his cheek laid open.

The year 1962 was worse still, with the World Cup authorities forced to issue a public appeal imploring the teams to control themselves following a rash of bloody matches involving Argentina, Bulgaria, Germany, Chile and, of course, Italy. Two years later it was the fans' turn. At Lima Stadium on May 24, 1964, with two minutes remaining in a match between Peru and Argentina, the Uruguayan referee disallowed an equalizing goal scored by

Lobatón, the popular Peruvian winger. The crowd's reaction was so violent that the referee immediately abandoned the match, leading the players in a sprint to the steel-doored dressing rooms. In hot pursuit followed one Matias Rojas, a well-known local soccer fanatic nicknamed "The Bomb," who had managed to scale the high wire fence surrounding the pitch. When Rojas was roughly brought to ground by the police, the crowd went absolutely berserk, hurling bottles onto the pitch, setting fire to the stands and smashing through an iron fence onto the field. The police retaliated with tear gas and gunfire, killing at least four fans. The crowd panicked and stampeded toward the exit gates, which were locked. Three hundred and eighteen died in the ensuing crush and a further five hundred were injured. Later that night a mob marched on the Presidential Palace in Lima asking for justice. Their first demand was an inquiry into the police's handling of the riot. Their second demand was that the match be declared a draw.

By then the Argentinians had developed cynical fouling into a fine art. In 1966 they met England in the World Cup quarter-final and tripped, punched and pushed their way through the entire ninety minutes. At the end of the game England's manager Alf Ramsey, a man who rarely passed even the time of day with the press, was shaken enough to tell reporters that he hoped England's next opponents "would not act like animals," a judgment which Argentina has still yet to shake off completely. In 1969, following an even more deplorable display against Milan in the Intercontinental Championship, three Argentinian players were actually thrown in jail by the president of Argentina.

Five years after the Lima tragedy, George Orwell's gloomy prediction of international ill will finally reached its grimly inevitable conclusion with the South American "soccer war" of June 1969. After two bitter, riot-torn matches between El Salvador and neighboring Honduras, El Salvador launched a full-scale invasion, complete with tanks and air strikes. By the time a truce was arranged, the death toll had reached the thousands. Admittedly, soccer was not the sole cause of the trouble; relations between the two countries had long been strained by a number of contentious issues, notably land ownership and immigration policies. Soccer, however, was the spark which set the tanks rolling, and as a pretext for war, the choice of an international soccer match with its frenzied nationalism and hysterical patriotism can only be considered a stroke of military genius.

Since then the pattern of international soccer has continued pretty much along the same lines. In 1970 the great Pelé, who in 1966 had literally been kicked off the field by the Portuguese, was again a marked man, this time by the Italians. "I've come to accept that the life of a front-runner is a hard one," he said, "that he will suffer more injuries than most men and that many of these injuries will not be accidental." More recently, in his autobiography, Pelé recalled how he had been under constant assault by the Italians, particularly by the defender Betini:

> Betini was an artist in fouling a man without getting caught. Whenever he came close he managed to dig in the ribs, or put his fist in my stomach, or to kick me in the shins during a tackle . . . Betini was an artist, I must admit.

In 1973 Austrian fans rampaged through Budapest, and in Brazzaville, Cameroon soldiers invaded the field and beat up the entire Congolese national team. In Copenhagen a referee was clubbed into unconsciousness by a Turkish team which was defeated in the closing minutes of the game. During a game against the Ivory Coast in Mali, the Mali players went collectively berserk, attacking the referee, beating him to the ground and smashing his watch, and then, with the stands seething, forcing an Ivory Coast player to kneel at their feet and beg their pardon. Unlike the Olmecs, they stopped short of an actual beheading. One of the most spectacular incidents of recent times came during the African Games played midway through 1978 when the Libyan team descended on the victorious Egyptian team kicking, punching and wielding microphone stands.

And then, of course, there was the 1978 World Cup, perhaps not as spectacularly bloody as some of its predecessors, but nevertheless as depressingly cynical a series of games as there has ever been. The 1978 World Cup was the ultimate synthesis of soccer's winning ethos: foul-ridden, vicious, negative and ugly. It was the year that the professional foul came into its own. Forwards were automatically taking a dive as they approached the goals in the hope of tricking the referee into believing that they were scythed down, and hacking was so common in the penalty area that they often got away with it. A World Cup penalty box is a no-man's-land. Argentina – the eventual winners, their supporters baying at their backs at every match – set the pattern of play early on when they stopped the Hungarians with a full compliment of blatant – and largely unpenalized – fouls. Brazil, Italy, Peru and Holland soon followed suit. In almost every match there was an undercurrent of violence.

That there was no actual crowd violence in Argentina speaks far more for the soldiers, the guard dogs, the high steel fences and the water-filled moats which surrounded the grounds than for any lack of passion on the part of the spectators. Where crowds did have an opportunity to vent their spleen they used it to the fullest. One of the first televised moments of the Cup, taken during the qualifying matches, showed a glass bottle exploding in a halo of shards against a Spanish player's head. The Brazilians and the

Italians stoned their losing teams on their return – as they always do. When Germany lost to Austria a Kiel builder knocked out one of his 18-year-old son's teeth, and a nun belonging to the Merciful Sisters order leaped on a coach driver in an autobahn café near Frankfurt and half-strangled him when he cheered Austria's victory. In Aachen a bar owner drew a gun on three of his customers when they played the World Cup theme song on the jukebox following the defeat. Fortunately, they managed to flee. A Turkish lodger living in Germany was not so fortunate. He was stabbed to death by his 56-year-old German landlord when, with the score standing at 1–1, he scoffed: "There'll be worse to come for your lot."

"Perhaps in the twenty-first century things will be different," said English soccer manager John Bond of Norwich before the World Cup, "perhaps people won't want to see a winning side. Perhaps that will be good for football." Perhaps. But if Australian soccer is anything to go by, it is unlikely that we will ever have a chance to find out. In July 1978 an Australian coach R. Alagich hit on the idea of motivating his players before an important game by showing them films of Nazi atrocities. "I showed them twenty minutes of a film of Auschwitz," he later explained, "of the gassing and the shootings and told them to imagine they had a son, a wife or mother in the camp and to revenge their death." The team went out and smashed the opposition, who had previously beaten them heavily.

League of Gentlemen

For all its calculated cynicism and tactical savagery, soccer still remains the triumph of skill over brute force. Not so with that other British invention, rugby. The philosophy behind rugby is still more or less the same philosophy as that which was espoused by the men whose fondness for hacking split the Football Association more than a century ago. The game is still about courage, manliness and force; in other words it is still the direct descendant of the Arnoldian dream of "muscular Christianity." At least that is its popular image; in reality the "Christianity" aspect has now worn rather thin.

To the casual spectator – even to adherents of American gridiron – rugby invariably appears as a perfect instrument for sporting suicide. The game's terminology, with its "rucks," "mauls" and "scrums," provides a good taste of what actually occurs on the field. As with gridiron, a rugby team's backbone is its big men. It is they who bear the responsibility of forcing an advantage from the various set confrontations which are designed to put the ball back into play, confrontations which bear more than a passing resemblance to the wedges of the early gridiron game. The scrum in particular is a perfect example of mass play. The titans of each team lock themselves together in an inverted triangle using their limbs, bodies and heads, and then slam head down into the opposing triangle, trying to drive it back. Mired ankle-deep in the mud of an English winter pitch, the sight of a heaving, steaming scrum locked in combat is nothing short of awesome.

No less awesome is the game's tackling. As only the ball carrier is allowed to be tackled, the picture of a lone player being ambushed by three or four large opponents is replayed again and again during the course of a game. Until only recently the fashion was for "topping and tailing," a tactic whereby one tackler would launch himself at chest height from one direction while a teammate came in at the knees from another angle, thus twisting their victim like a corkscrew. It is this sort of assault, performed without any trace of protective armor, which appalls even Americans.

Rugby injuries, not surprisingly, can be devastating. Spines are particularly vulnerable, especially for the players in the front row of a scrum who are concertinaed between their opponents and their teammates. When a scrum collapses there is a massive shearing force exerted on the necks of the front-row players which can result in broken necks. It has been estimated that there are roughly twenty severe spinal injuries a year from rugby. In one Sydney hospital during a recent season, five players were admitted either as paraplegics or quadraplegics after having scrums collapse on them.

The most widely publicized injury of recent times was that suffered by British international Danny Hearne in 1967. Hearne had launched himself at a New Zealand opponent in a "crash tackle" which had misfired and broken his neck. "For some unknown reason I said, 'Don't stand me up,'" he recalled. "It probably saved my life." It was nine months before Hearne was discharged from the hospital. Now, more than a decade later, he is still almost totally paralyzed from the neck down. "Rugby," he said, speaking at the school where he now teaches, "is a very violent game and these things can happen. We nearly had a very severe accident here at the beginning of this term. In fact, they thought the boy had broken his back. He stopped breathing. Luckily it was only momentary spinal concussion."

Rugby also has its deaths. In mid-1977, 23-year-old Chris Sanderson died during a first division Rugby League match. A few months prior to that, a national television audience watched as trainers struggled to revive an Argentinian player with the kiss of life during a tour of Britain. The man had been crushed at the bottom of a maul, and by the time the trainers reached him he had stopped breathing.

In spite of this, the overall number of serious rugby casualties during a season is perhaps less than one might well expect. Although rugby statistics are all but nonexistent, it is clear that the game escapes the grisly toll reaped annually by American football.* The reasons for this are, ironically, largely those which cause American spectators to view rugby with shocked incredulity – the lack of "protective" padding and the gang tackling of individual players. Without protection there is no spearing or face-mask wrenching, and nor is there the host of armor-inflicted injuries now associated with gridiron. With only the ball carrier the target of tacklers, players are fully prepared to withstand assaults the moment they pick up the ball. The risk of "blind-siding" is greatly reduced.

All this is not to suggest, however, that rugby is played much less ferociously than its American cousin. On the contrary, deliberate violence – both legal and nonlegal – has become an increasing headache for rugby's various administrations.

There are two distinct rugby codes played throughout the world – the professional game of Rugby League, and Rugby Union, probably the most militantly amateur sport in existence. Ever since the two groups split in 1895 to go their own separate ways, the Rugby Union has regarded itself as the home of the gentleman sportsman – a bastion of chivalry and sporting honor where to play the game counts far more than the winning of it. To Union members, the opposition Rugby League game, distorted as it is by the forces of professionalism, is a disreputable, ill-tempered game and a sordid travesty of true Arnoldian rugby.

Although grossly exaggerated, the Union view of League rugby is not without some foundation. The game is, after all, a professional sport played in front of paying spectators who are just as keen on winning as any other body of sports fans. As such, violence in the course of duty is unavoidable. Arthur Machin, bruising protagonist of David Storey's *This Sporting Life* (1960) was a League man, and the way he played his sport had far more in common with Mean Joe Green than with Tom Brown:

> I waited three scrums, to make him feel relaxed and also to get the best opportunity. I kept my right arm loose. His face was upside down, his eyes straining, loose in their sockets, to catch a glimpse of the ball as it

---

* The most recent and complete rugby injury statistics were produced by France after the 1968–9 season. From among the 75,338 players included in the survey, 11,349 injuries were reported. Of these 16.29 percent involved the head, and a further 15.39 percent involved the neck, spine, pelvis, genitals or abdomen. The only other overall statistic comes from Japan which recorded a total of twenty deaths among rugby players over a ten-year period. Ten of these deaths resulted from head injuries and seven from broken necks. Some experts, however, view the Japanese figures as being unrepresentative of the game, claiming that Japan, a fledgling rugby nation, plays its rugby in much the same way as its kamikaze pilots flew airplanes.

came in. I watched it leave the scrumhalf's hands, and his head buckled under the forwards' heaving. I swung my right fist into the middle of his face. He cried out loud. I hit him again and saw the red pulp of his nose and lips as my hand came away. He was crying out really loud now, partly affected, professional pain, but most of it real. His language echoed all over the ground.

Machin is first and foremost a winner – he even swallows amphetamine pills before each game. And his real-life counterparts are also striving to be winners. Violence in such an atmosphere is simply another tool in getting the job done. As one Australian club captain wrote in 1969 after owning up to a variety of ungentlemanly tactics such as biting:

> Rugby League is for the tough. Outside the sideline is the only place for the chicken-hearted or the weak-bodied. It's violent for most of the time and, I'd say, a lot harder than professional boxing. The unwritten rule for this game is based on the word . . . SURVIVE.

It is not Rugby League, however, which has been responsible for the headlines concerning rugby violence that have become an increasingly common feature of British sports pages over the last decade or so. Rather, it is the amateur players of the Union who have earned the scrutiny of the press, and the press has been less than favorable. The inference is that the "League of Gentlemen" is no longer wholly comprised of gentlemen.

The first mutterings of Union violence came not surprisingly following an international series – the much-publicized British Lions tour of New Zealand in 1971. Although international rugby matches have always had the effect of turning players into warriors – in 1967 an Australian forward had been sent home in disgrace after biting off the lobe of an English opponent – 1971 proved something of a watershed year for rugby violence. During past tours the British Lions had always tended to turn the other cheek in the event of any dubious play by their colonial opponents. In 1971, however, they were determined to outface the New Zealanders. Their catch cries became "Get your retaliation in first!" and "Take no prisoners!" When one of their members was assaulted, a player shouted "Ninety-nine!" and the whole team would leap on the offender, confident that as no one player could be singled out, none would be sent off. As one Lion later recalled, victims of the "Ninety-nine" call "wouldn't perhaps be much alive at the end of it."

Conflict between the two sides reached a climax during the game at Canterbury. The New Zealanders, determined that they should be the first to get in their retaliation, tore into the Lions as soon as they stepped out of the dressing room. Barry John, the Lions' star who had been left out of the side through injury, remembers watching the game with clenched fists from the stands. "It was frightening, absolutely frightening," he told me, "thuggery hatched in the dressing room as a tactic, and a helluva tactic when you break somebody's jaw!" At half time the scene in the Lions' dressing room was "terrible," he said, with some players suffering appalling injuries. One, Sandy Carmichael, had one side of his face smashed by a blow. "Had Sandy been a boxer in the ring," wrote Barry John later, "no boxing referee would have let him carry on with the injuries he received at the hands of the Canterbury thugs." Carmichael and another Lions player were so badly mauled that they returned home before the end of the tour.

The following year during a New Zealand tour of Britain, the New Zealander Murdoch, a player notorious for violent behavior, was also sent home – for vicious play. Soon comparisons were being made with the "barbarians" of the League. "Which was worse," asked one *Guardian* writer, "Meade's assault upon the head of a Scottish halfback at Twickenham or the British revenge extracted by Mills when he trampled over the head of a prostrate New Zealander?"

The cause of the bloodshed in international rugby matches is obvious enough. As with any international sport – amateur or professional – the burden of nationalism heaped onto the willing shoulders of the players by their fans and a patriotic press is an almost inevitable cause of violence. Union fans in certain corners of the globe, notably Wales, are among the most committed sports fans in the world. As one writer put it, Welsh rugby teams are the expression of denied nationhood, the means by which a comparatively powerless province can exert its independence. "Against Scotland," commented one French rugby fan, "it is a battle. Playing Wales it is a war."

But what was even more disturbing to the press was that it had become increasingly apparent that international rugby was not the only source of Union violence. In the wake of the Lions' bloodbath, instances of club- and school-level violence began to surface with depressing regularity, the worst incident occurring in September 1974 when a player's ear was bitten off. The number of sendings-off – Union's ultimate disgrace – rose dramatically (in one case, four in one day) and there was growing concern as to the number of injuries which were being deliberately inflicted. Willful violence was seen to be an established tactic: players were being heavily tackled long after they had passed the ball; others had their heads kicked while they were trapped underneath a ruck; and others their faces smashed by the out-thrust forearm of a beaten opponent. The stiff-arm tackle – "an extended, stiffened arm swung simultaneously with a high tackle and making contact with the force of a baseball bat" – long a staple of Rugby League, was making its debut on Union fields. Worst of all, players were deliberately collapsing scrums – bad enough when accidental, but lethal when done on purpose.

In May 1976 the medical officer of the Bath rugby club, Dr. David Protheroe, fueled the controversy by disclosing in *The Sunday Times* a list of deliberate injuries he was having to deal with. Protheroe had played rugby as a student and for a year after graduating before he had drifted away from the game. Fifteen years later he accepted the Bath post and, even allowing for the occasional sly kick or punch, was shocked by the types of injuries players were now suffering: "I began treating gouges in and around the eyeballs," he told me. "I began treating scratch marks on the back. One player I treated had tramline scrapes from his buttock to his shoulders – five pairs of studs scraped across his back as he lay on the ground." Another player had displayed stud marks with "full rotation" which, said Dr. Protheroe, indicated somebody had trodden on him and twisted his boot back and forth as if stubbing a cigarette. Yet another man had had his lower lip deliberately torn to within a centimeter of the curve of his chin, an injury which required an hour's plastic surgery to repair. "I began to see people looking at a loose hand in a scrum and stamping on it. When the players' wives demanded that something be done, I decided to speak up."

Reaction to such violence was widespread. "Rugger," wrote one neurologist, "seems to have become a depraved and brutal sport, even in schools; the players punch each other freely and, of course, with bare fists, so they may well damage each other's brains as much as boxers do." An Edinburgh doctor complained: ". . . when I watch a game of rugby and afterwards survey the bruises beneath the shirts I am horrified. Without hesitation, if one of my sons, who both play rugby, were to show a preference toward amateur boxing, as a parent I would not object." A mother wrote to tell of her son's arriving home after a match with deliberate stud marks raked across his body: "I used to remonstrate him about this and was always assured that his school plays fair, the other side always starts it, and anyway 'everyone' does it." Commented sports writer Brian Glanville: "Rugby, which posed as the crucible of manliness, has degenerated into a savage contest of reciprocal violence."

Britain is not the only nation to suffer an escalation in violence. In France, where players have a decidedly less than pristine image, the lock forward of the Bezier club, Michael Palmie, was fined £165 and ordered to pay a massive £7,000 in damages for gouging an opponent's eye during the 1975 season. According to Colin Vaughan (the player mentioned in the Introduction who almost died as a result of an injury caused by a premeditated late tackle), in Australia perhaps a third of all injuries are the result of deliberate, cold-blooded violence. "In Union you just didn't get kicked deliberately in rucks," he said. "You'd always get a punch in the face in a game, but it was very rarely that you'd get kicked. Now when you go down on the ground you get up as quickly as possible because if you don't, you're finished."

Pinpointing the reasons for this accelerating violence has been the cause of much public agonizing by those connected with the Rugby Football Union. The traditional view is that of the "one bad apple," the "psychopath" who has thus far avoided being weeded out. "It's a physical game," said Colin Vaughan. "If a guy is the sort of guy who is aggressive in social situations – if he gets into brawls down at the pub or whatever – with rugby he has an avenue, a perfectly socially acceptable avenue, to go and beat the bloody Christ out of someone." But individual psychosis is, at best, only part of the problem, as is the violent example set for juniors by their elders in the widely televised international matches. A far more comprehensive reason is that Rugby Union has fallen victim to its own recent success.

Since the '60s, Rugby Union has been booming. Not only has the number of clubs in Britain doubled, but gates have soared and television coverage rocketed. As a result, the emphasis in rugby has switched by degrees from player to spectator. While still retaining its amateur status, the game has become big business – a feat which must surely rank as one of the seven wonders of the sporting world, given the universal demands by players for an increasing share of the profits. And with this transition has come the inevitable increased pressure on clubs, coaches and players to win.

Although the will to win has now touched all levels of Rugby Union, it is most noticeable at the top. Once it was Union policy that there was to be no end-of-season winner, no "league champion"; the closest thing to a Union "league ladder" was the informal lists kept by individual newspapers. Now there are not only knock-out cups but also a new Merit Table to sort out the winners from the losers. The monetary incentives for a club to succeed have, over the past couple of seasons, increased enormously, what with sponsorship and increased gate receipts. In turn the pressure on players from clubs eager to swell their finances with a win has also escalated, as have the demands of the crowds. Indeed, one of the first things which struck Dr. Protheroe on his return to rugby was the dramatic change in the attitude of the spectators. "Before, the crowds would exhort their team to better efforts," he told me. "Now they exhort their team to maim. Now you hear cries like 'Kill him! Sort him out! Fix him!' "

The fact is that Rugby Union has now become an amateur game played to professional standards. The commitment to winning is just as keen, the training just as rigorous and the chase after victory just as ruthless. In late 1976 Harlequins prop forward Terry Claxton was banned for fourteen weeks after allegedly throwing a punch during a match. When I asked him the cause of violence, he replied: "Team pride. After all the training and everything, teams go out there thinking they're never going to lose." Violence, as in the professional contact sports, has become a tactic to ensure they don't. "No coach is going to say, right, don't go out and slam anyone in the head, don't go out and kick them off the ball," said Colin Vaughan. "If a player can be dragged off injured, you've got a better chance of winning."

Even the "psychopaths" now have their place. "When you play against them you hate them and if you get a chance to kick them or belt them you do," said Vaughan. "But by the same token, we've got guys on our side who border on that incredibly violent mentality, and they're one of the boys. In the club they're a helluva guy. It's a complete double standard." "You know they are coming for you," said Barry John who, it should be said, believes that rugby violence is no worse than it was ten to fifteen years ago. "If you get hurt it's you're fault for getting bloody caught. You know what happens to the matador if he gets caught, the bloody bull gores him. I go to the stadium knowing that Joe Bloggs will be trying to mark me out; he couldn't play any other game. That's why they picked him."

But the most conclusive evidence of this trend comes from Leeds' Dr. Ian Adams. In his experience rugby's injury rate has increased by something like 25 percent within a decade. Besides the traditional afflictions of shoulder and knee damage, there has been a marked increase in the number of injuries caused by "violence around the head" (fractures, concussions and so on), the result of both fiercer physical contact and a rise in extracurricular violence. Injuries have become so widespread, said Dr. Adams, that the Rugby Football Union (RFU) has now introduced special medical courses for trainers. In Dr. Adams's view, the reason for these increases is simply a greater emphasis on winning. Players now play to win, he said, and Rugby Union is now a very different game to what it was because of it.

In mid-1976, shortly after Dr. Protheroe's revelations were published, the RFU issued a directive to its referees and disciplinary committees ordering them to clamp down harder on illegal tactics "in view of the publicity which has been given to increased violence and discipline on the field of play." As yet it is unclear how effective this campaign has been. According to the RFU it is already working well at club level. A punch which six years ago would have carned only a warning now means an automatic sending-off, said one official. It was, he added, proving a great deterrent. According to Dr. Protheroe, although he is still dealing with kicking injuries and hands which have been stamped upon, the situation has not got any worse and may have even slightly improved.

DAD'S GLADIATORS

One of the best indicators of winning pressure on a sport can be seen in the behavior of its Little Leagues. American Pop Warner football, for example, faithfully reflects the mania to win found in the college and pro games. In Florida a mob of parents attack the coaches of a winning team of 12-year-olds with pipes and clubs, cheering "He's dead!" when one of them is driven off unconscious in an ambulance. In Palm Beach the losing coach walks onto the field, extends his hand to the opposing junior star, and then punches him in the stomach. Somewhere else a coach injects amphetamine into his peewee club's pre-game oranges. There are countless other examples from an area of sport which one psychologist recently described as a "rat's nest of psychological horrors."

Now it is Little League rugby's turn. The boom in rugby has led to the establishment of a flourishing "mini rugby" league which, like its American counterparts, is as close to adult action as parent pressure can make it. Said Barry Barnet, an official with the Hendon rugby club:

> I went to watch a tournament last year and in the interval they had two games of mini rugby. The behavior of the spectators was disgusting – parents screaming at their boys "Kill 'im! Kill 'im!" It was just like watching gladiators in Rome. All they wanted was the opposition fed to the lions.

Halfway around the world in Sydney, youngsters are taught the joys of winning rugby in exactly the same fashion – parents running up and down the sidelines screaming, "Don't just run beside him, Brian, TACKLE! TACKLE! Get 'im by the ear and haul 'im down." One Sydney journalist overheard a coach telling his battle-weary gladiators: "I've got a dummy pacifier here for anyone that wants to cry and muck and you know what will happen if you run on the field with a dummy in your mouth; they'll laugh at you."

Australian rugby is a man's game – even when it is played by infants.

There are, however, plenty of less encouraging signs. At the international level, the game remains much the same. In 1976 television cameras captured a full close-up of a South African all but removing the right ear of a New Zealander with the cooly calculated swipe of a boot. (The New Zealander was, at the time, pinned helpless under a ruck.) The 1977 Lions tour of New Zealand was rife with stampings, late tackles and savage punch-ups. "I believe that it is a damned sight safer to go to war than to embark on a rugby tour of New Zealand," wrote the *Observer* correspondent. The 1978 Welsh tour of Australia was even worse. Welsh prop forward Graham Price had his jaw broken in two places by a blow from behind, and new player Alun Donovan was confined to a wheelchair. In South Africa during one month in mid-1978, fifty players from the Pretoria and Johannesburg areas alone were hospitalized by rugby injuries.

As for Britain's domestic game, reports of broken jaws and violent concussions still litter the sports pages of the press. Scrum collapsing, although outlawed, continues, as does charging in the scrums, another highly dangerous tactic. It was recently reported that the Welsh club Swansea had canceled all future fixtures with its rival Pontypool because of "punching, biting and stud raking." "You'd be very unlucky, in a sense, not to see a violent incident and a serious injury in any match nowadays," Doug Ibbotsan, long-standing rugby correspondent of the London *Evening News,* told me.

In the schools young players are still emulating their televised heroes. "Last weekend I watched a graceless, tasteless game of rugby between England Colts and Wales Youth," reported *Sunday Times* writer John Hopkins in mid-1977. "I saw butting, punching, raking and hair holding and I probably missed some other offenses." In two recent incidents a 14-year-old had his face trodden on twice after being tackled, and a 15-year-old was paralyzed by a kick aimed deliberately at his head after he had passed the ball. Sporting life has certainly changed since Tom Brown's schooldays, but whether or not it has improved is another matter.

In mid-1978 the chairman of the British Sports Council, Dickie Jeeps, invited sports administrators – including representatives of the RFU – "to see that players who don't wish to keep within the laws are stopped from playing." However rugby's administrators may soon find, as ice hockey's officials have done, that the responsibility for policing their game has moved out of their hands. Shortly before the Sports Council's invitation a Caerphilly rugby player was convicted at Newport Crown Court for inflicting grevious bodily harm following a punching incident during a game. Remarked the judge in his summing up: "Hereafter no one will be able to plead ignorance of the fact that violence of this sort on the rugby field is as much a criminal offense as it is off the field."

Not Cricket

Perhaps the saddest capitulation to the ethic of winning whatever the cost is that most "civilized" of English social conventions – cricket. Like baseball, cricket contains all the potential violence inherent in one man's hurling a hard ball at another. As early as 1751 Frederick, Prince of Wales, was killed when a cricket ball hit his head, and in 1825 William Hazlitt was writing in his essay "Merry England" of a cricketer named Long Robinson who "when two of the fingers of his right-hand were struck off by the violence of the ball, had a screw fastened to it to hold the bat."

Unlike baseball, however, the importance of winning a cricket match has rarely ever grossly exceeded the importance of "playing the game." Even with the most keenly followed international test matches, players have almost always strictly adhered to an unwritten but very real gentlemen's code. Batsmen were expected to leave the crease of their own volition, if they knew they were out, even before the umpire had given his decision. Both players and spectators always applauded successful opponents. Bowlers never bowled bouncers to tail-end batsmen. Only a decade or so ago Wes Hall, the whirlwind West Indian fast bowler, was ordered by his captain to publicly apologize to a tail-ender after he had hurled down a bouncer.

Until the mid-1970s there had been only one serious intentional breach of this gentlemen's agreement. The culprits were English captain Jardine and his fast bowler Harold Larwood, who devised a plan to neutralize Australia's batting sensation of the '30s, Donald Bradman. The plan was "leg theory" or, as it was more popularly called, "bodyline" bowling, which called for a relentless stream of short, rearing bouncers to be pitched at the leg stump. This had the effect of either forcing the batsman to concede a catch as he scrambled out of the ball's flight path, or of hitting him in the head. Needless to say, it was an extremely dangerous tactic, as Australian test cricketer Jack Fingleton recalled: "We knew if we got hit by one of those balls whistling by our head we'd either end up on a slab in the mortuary or be an imbecile for life." Another Australian cricketer, Dick Twining, had already been hit over the heart by a Larwood ball and knew exactly how it felt: "As I slowly woke up I saw the doctor moving to the door. I heard him say briskly, 'Well, I've done all I can.'"

Not only was bodyline bowling dangerous, it was also a clear breach of cricketing protocol. As such it was much resented by the Australian players and crowds when it was unveiled during the 1932–3 England tour of Australia. The controversy boiled over during the third test match when two Australian batsmen – captain Bill Woodfull and popular wicket keeper Bert Oldfield – were felled by Larwood deliveries. "There are two sides out

---

❝ I'm not ashamed of leaving a trail of fractures among the opposition – a finger, a thumb, a whole right hand and one foot on the latest count. After all, that's what I'm there for. Not to inflict deliberate injury, of course, but to rough up a batsman, make them apprehensive and destroy their confidence. I never let them forget the game is played with a very hard ball. ❞

John Snow, English fast bowler

---

there," declared Woodfull back in the dressing room. "One is playing cricket and the other is not." The Australian spectators were apoplectic and a riot seemed unavoidable until mounted police were called in. Cables threatening an end to friendly relations shuttled back and forth between the two cricketing authorities and some newspapers even talked of Australia's seceding from the Commonwealth.

It was a testament to the strength of cricket's sporting ethics that bodyline bowling did not survive. As a winning tactic it was wildly successful; England took the series four games to two and Larwood claimed a record number of wickets. By the time the England team had reached home, however, it had already been agreed by both sides that bodyline bowling must go. The tactic was banned, and Jardine and Larwood, winners though they were, never played against Australia again. Such behavior just wasn't cricket.

But that was 1933. Today the picture has changed dramatically. Now the bouncer is a major weapon in every captain's arsenal, employed over and over again innings after innings against all batsmen regardless of their position in the batting line-up. As West Indian captain Clive Lloyd remarked after one of his pace bowlers had injured an opposing tail-ender: "They are all batsmen. They all have to be got out." The same sentiments were also endorsed by Mike Brearley after *his* fast bowler had sent a Pakistani tail-end player stumbling back to the dressing room with blood pouring from his face. "We had tried everything," explained Brearley, "and he *had* batted for well over an hour." "Bowling to maim has now got out of hand," wrote veteran cricket commentator Robin Marlar. "Sport's got more aggressive," agreed England batsman David Steele. "More money is involved. There's more at stake. You must be a fool if you don't realize that people try deliberately to hurt."

The villains of cricket's new violence are fast bowlers such as Australia's notorious duo Dennis Lillee and Jeff Thomson, both of whom are capable of delivering balls at speeds of almost 100 mph (Thomson has been timed at 99 mph). Neither of them have any qualms about using violence as an intimidatory tactic, as Lillie's autobiography *Back to the Mark* (1976) shows:

> Batsmen are like thieves to me, desperately trying to steal from me the ascendancy I believe is mine. And I treat them like faceless, meaningless thieves. If you are a bowler you must strive for complete control over the situation. . . . Sometimes an opposing batsman will try to strike up a conversation with me out on the field, but I don't want to talk to him for a second. . . . I try to go the opposite way and find something about the faceless batsman that really annoys me, then I build on that until it becomes a sort of hatred that burns in my guts until I get him out.

Later on in his book Lillee added this piece of cricketing advice:

> I try to hit a batsman in the rib cage when I bowl a purposeful bouncer, and I want it to hurt so much that the batsman doesn't want to face me anymore . . . not many batsmen recover from a really good bouncer.

Lillee's erstwhile partner Thomson was even more candid. In a quote that would have ensured his place in cricketing history even if his bowling averages hadn't, "Thommo" confessed: "The sound of the ball hitting the batsman's skull was music to my ears."

That is a sound being heard more and more around the world's cricket grounds. In November 1975 Queensland first-class cricketer Martin Bedkober died after being struck over the heart by a rising fast ball. One month later a nineteen-year-old New Zealand player, Ewan Chatfield, "died" for several minutes after being struck by a bouncer. Since then there has been a rash of major injuries – broken jaws, fractured ribs, broken arms, split faces and bruised torsos. Several international batsmen, including England captain Mike Brearley, have now taken to wearing cumbersome crash helmets at the crease. "I'm amazed by the batsmen," one Australian cricket promoter told me. "They've got 0.4 of a second or something in which to decide what to do, and most of them are terrified."

But perhaps the saddest thing of all about cricket's capitulation is that the villains are no longer villains but heroes. Bouncers are now not only expected by crowds but are often greeted with cheers. The same crowds which jeered Larwood and Jardine have now made Lillee and Thomson sporting idols, cheering them on to greater injury and intimidation, chanting "Kill! Kill!" when another wicket is needed. "It's not easy to bat when people are baying for your blood," remarked Mike Brearley. Such behavior may not have been cricket half a century ago, but it certainly is today.

6
SOLDIERS FOR SPORT

6 Soldiers for Sport
Soccer Hooliganism and Other Spectator Sports

Bridgeton Cross is the name given to the tangle of road junctions which funnel travelers from the south into Glasgow's city center. For pure visual awfulness, it is a hard place to beat – a dismal landscape of unappealing bars, derelict warehouses and decaying acres of rubbish-strewn wasteland. As a place to live, it is a disaster area, the center of a rolling slum in which one adult in twenty is a chronic alcoholic, the infant mortality rate is the highest in Europe, and crime, vandalism and TB spiral ever upward. To quote from the Duke of Edinburgh's Commonwealth Study Conference on urban redevelopment, the life it encompasses "has no equal in Europe in terms of the horrifying statistics of multiple deprivation." In short, Bridgeton Cross is perhaps the worst urban sore on the continent. It is also the heart of Glasgow Rangers Football Club territory.

On Friday night, Michael Morrow is settling down to another evening of serious drinking in one of Bridgeton's ("Brig-e-don's") many bars. He is a thin, ferrety youth with a pale, pinched face and willfully neglected teeth, a true son of Glasgow. He claims to be 16 and is probably even younger, his hands barely reaching around his pint of bitter. Normally he would keep a weather eye cocked on the pub door, watching for the police who patrol the Cross collaring underage drinkers. Tonight, however, he doesn't bother; he knows no "polis" is going to be worrying about such trivial matters this Friday night. For this is the eve of that greatest of all possible sporting events, a Scottish Football Association Cup Final between Glasgow Rangers and Glasgow Celtic. The mere thought of the joys tomorrow holds in store sends a warm glow through Michael Morrow's undernourished frame, and he sinks down into the red vinyl seat with a thin smile on his lips. "Aye, it's going to be a great day," he murmurs.

Football – soccer – to Glasgow is the bright light at the end of a long and oftentimes exceedingly murky tunnel. Arising out of the grim realities of late nineteenth-century industrial Britain, it offered one of the few touches of color and excitement in an otherwise singularly gray and stupefying existence. As such it was adopted by the Glaswegian working man with an enthusiasm hitherto reserved only for strong drink (and indeed, the two were soon discovered to complement each other remarkably well). By the turn of the century, soccer had become the unofficial religion of Glasgow.

The problem was that it was a religion comprising two irreconcilable faiths, split firstly by a fanatical allegiance to team and secondly by the blunt instrument of sectarian hatred.

On the one hand were the predominantly Catholic Celtic, whose front-row seats were reserved for the priesthood and whose supporters massed under the Irish tricolor. On the other were the Protestant Rangers, a club whose affiliations with the Orange Lodge surpass those of King Billy himself. It is the Rangers' proud boast that in their 104-year history they have never signed a Catholic player. For well over half a century now, these two soccer tribes have been at each other's throats.

As early as 1909, a Rangers–Celtic match was the occasion for full-scale rioting. In that year the officials refused to allow overtime after a draw, and the ground became a battlefield. Clubhouse buildings were burned and when firemen arrived to fight the blaze, their hoses were cut and tossed into the flames. Hundreds were injured, including fifty-eight policemen. The simmering rivalry between the two clubs was not helped by the death of a Celtic goalkeeper in 1931 after an accidental kick from a Rangers' player. The incident sparked a long succession of vicious terrace wars astonishing in their ferocity. Less than thirty years ago, grown men were still beating each other over the head with bricks and being arrested for trying to smuggle hatchets through the turnstiles beneath their jackets. Until 1967, when the authorities belatedly canceled the fixture, the two teams met every New Year's Day in an alcoholic festival which filled the air above the terraces with a moving ceiling of flying bottles.

Today the brick-wielding adults of the postwar era have given way to a younger generation of front-line soldiers, namely Michael Morrow and his friends and sworn enemies. The violence, however, has remained constant. A Rangers-Celtic Cup Final is still the closest thing to open warfare sport has to offer.

"It'll start tomorra mornin' when the Celtic walk up through here from their area," says Michael with the absolute certainty born of long experience. He has been fighting these battles since the age of 10 or 11, his father urging him "tae get tore in" even as a child. "Usually they hide their scarves, but sometimes they don't and that means they're lookin' for trouble. For us it's when you get up to Hampden Park, havin' tae walk thru the lot of 'em – Celtic on all sides. That's when the bottles and cans come doon on you. Last year they were throwin' broken bottles. We just kept goin'."

According to Michael, it's broken glass that does the most damage nowadays. The cut-throat razor, once the Glasgow football soldier's inseparable companion, has waned in popularity over the last few years. Assault or breach of the peace usually carries only a fine and a thrashing in the cells from the screws, but if you get stopped carrying a blade it's instant jail, no questions asked. "Aye, it's mostly bottles now," says Michael, with perhaps a hint of regret. His mates, however, do not agree, and there is a brief argument as to the extent of "chubbing" on the terraces. It even transpires that one local figure carries a hatchet as his father may have once perhaps done; only last month he had buried it in a Catholic skull and then coolly stood on the boy's head with his boot to give him the necessary leverage to pull the weapon free. The move had obviously earned him much respect. "The guy was paralyzed . . . in the hospital for ages," recounts one of the lads breathlessly. Michael remains adamant. "*Sometimes* it's blades," he says, "but there's nae so many stabbings in Sco'land as there are in England." He lets that settle for a moment before adding, on reflection: "Then again, you keep it quiet if you get stabbed here, though, don't you? You just get ta'en away by the ambulance and don't say nothin'. If you do," he explains, "the guy will get you again. Sure to." After several run-ins with the police, Michael is loath to carry his blade tomorrow, although he thinks he might. Rangers are tipped to lose and he wants to be prepared.

The special buses laid on by the Glasgow Corporation to ferry the hard core of the Rangers' support to Hampden Park free of charge – no doubt in the faint hopes of limiting contact between them and "ordinary" citizens – leave from across the road outside the Cactus pub at 2 PM the next day. By midday the Cactus is a solid mass of blue-scarved supporters all busily priming themselves for the afternoon's entertainment. The badge of the Red Hand of Ulster is much in evidence, as are the Orange slogans tattooed on fists and forearms. The barman has the complete Rangers' crest covering an arm the size of a small ham. The entire pub is constantly erupting into the battle songs of the Orange Lodge – "I Was Born under the Union Jack," "No Surrender (to the IRA)" – and it is difficult to believe that it is a football match we are headed for and not a Paisley-ite rally across the water in Londonderry. An old man arrives carrying a large cardboard carton on his shoulder. Inside are 3-D plastic "portraits" of Queen Elizabeth, selling for a pound apiece. The old man does a brisk trade with his incongruous offerings. Some of his customers store their "portraits" behind the bar "for me mam." The rest elect to carry them along – something to wave at the Papist rebels.

As the buses fill up, the police move along the aisles frisking for bottles which have all long since been stashed away beneath the seats. Anyone who swears is ejected. A gang of English youths wearing cut-off denim jackets over bare chests arrive cursing all Catholics and the Pope in particular between swigs from a flask of whisky. They've been hitching all night from Liverpool, they say, and are here with the express intention of smashing the "Feenian bastids." This last revelation wins them hearty applause and as the convoy moves off through the thin drizzle, the songs and chants ring out, stopping the Glaswegian shoppers in their tracks:

> UDA all the way
> Fuck the Pope
> And the IRA
> UDA all the way

There are some tense moments on one of the approach roads to the park when two large groups of opposing supporters confront each other, taunting, jeering and hurling the inevitable bottles and cans. Inside the ground, though, all is relatively calm. The terracing has been divided in half – there are no innocent bystanders at a Rangers–Celtic Cup Final – and the two rival masses sway and chant at opposite ends of the ground, each penned in by high cyclone-wire fences. The game itself, fumbling and uninspired with neither side managing to gain any real advantage, also helps keep passions cooled. Then, in the closing moments, Celtic are awarded a disputed penalty and they score.

With a rising howl of fury, a wave of collective agony which reverberates around the terraces, the Ranger end erupts, its "cheated" hordes storming the fences at the foot of the stands and filling the air with flying glass. Some fans actually manage to scale the wire and hurl themselves at the police line which stands facing the terraces before they are hauled bodily to the exits. Far more are carried out bleeding or unconscious, victims of bottles hurled from higher up. As the game ends and the Celtic players begin an abbreviated half-lap of honor – they don't dare venture into the Ranger end – this aerial bombardment intensifies. Great holes appear in the crowd as the less committed fans rush to escape the missiles, and as those down below scramble back up the steps in a mad rush, the entire terrace takes on the appearance of a receding tidal wave. "It was like a mortar attack," one casualty was later to remark, and it is.

Eventually the Ranger army surrenders its end to the police and surges out into the suburban streets surrounding Hampden Park, hurling rocks, putting the boot into any remaining Celtic supporters and even wrecking several cars. The residents of the area watch wide-eyed in shock from their upstairs windows. By nightfall, a total of 139 fans have been arrested; the sound of anti-Catholic songs echoes clearly from the jail as I drive by. "Hail of Hate" is the following morning's front page headline. As Michael Morrow predicted, it has been a great day.

"It's Catholic against Protestant, it's as simple as that. That's what it's all about," one of Michael's friends had said in answer to the obvious question, why? "They sing 'Walk On' and we sing 'No Surrender.' Them showing the tricolor . . . aye, that's the cause of a lot of the trouble. The polis, they'll take the Union Jack off us, but they won't take the tricolor off the Celtic." Another had replied that it was more a matter of defending team honor; you held yourself back until the jeers and insults became too much to ignore, and then you retaliated. "You've got to support your team – it's as simple as that."

But for Michael, the joys of football represented something far more basic and less easily explained than that. "Sometimes . . . ," he had said, groping for words:

> sometimes you forget about Catholic and Protestant and it doesn't really matter what fans they are. You're just dyin' to get the boot in. You see 'em and you always want to fight 'em. Like when Sco'land play England, you get down to London and all you want to do is get hold of one of 'em. You can go all week wi'out thinkin' about it, about Catholic bastids and the rest of it. But then on Saturday you go down to the match and everything's *all there*, you know what I mean? When you're in a group and you get one or two of 'em alone and you get 'em down and get the boot in, it's . . . it's . . . *magic!*

By now his eyes were alight and he was emphasizing each sentence by slamming a bony fist into his open palm. "When you're 11 or 12 or somethin' and you get the boot in for the first time! Suddenly you're a big man, just like that, and you feel *great!* Such a *great* feelin' that is . . . *nothin'* can beat it . . . *nothin'* . . . not even *inta'cos!*" Sorry? "*Inta'cos* . . . you know, sexual *inta'cos*. Aye, straight up."

Some months later there was a small paragraph in one of the London papers reporting that a Celtic supporter had been stabbed to death on the terraces in Arbroath. He had just turned 17.

A Pattern of Violence

The Ranger–Celtic riots of twentieth-century Glasgow are by no means the worst crowd disturbances sport has had to suffer throughout its long history. In Pompeii around AD 70 an audience at one of the Games erupted into frenzied sword fighting among itself, and a number of citizens not listed for execution in the day's program were hacked to death. (Interestingly enough, after an investigation into the outburst, the Senate not only placed a ten-year ban on gladiatorial exhibitions but also exiled the promoters – a warning, perhaps, to modern sports impresarios, soccer directors in particular.) In AD 532 the Nika Riots which brought Constantinople to the brink of civil war, killing tens of thousands and almost toppling the emperor

Justinian, were also sparked by friction between rival chariot-racing factions – groups which bore an uncanny resemblance to modern soccer hooligans, even down to their adoption of outlandish styles of clothing.

There are many more examples. Crowd violence is not a new problem. What is new, however, is the sharp increase in the frequency of fan violence which now affects sport right across the board. If there is one point upon which sports promoters universally agree, it is that sports fans are becoming rapidly and increasingly more violent. Even in America where the fans are cushioned from many outside social pressures by their affluence, cosseted in luxurious stadiums and entertained every minute of the event, sport is now constantly faced with the prospect of violent disruption. "Sure it's increasing," said one NFL spokesman, whose sport has now come to accept bottle throwing as almost the norm. "It's a problem we're working on, but it's growing some." Basketball's crowd problems scaled new heights during the violent Suns–Celtics NBA playoffs, and they are unlikely to stop there. "If attitudes don't change," warned Dr. David Bachman, team physician of the Chicago Bulls, in 1977, "we're going to have to do what they do in South America: put up a fence and a moat to keep the fans away." So, too, with baseball; and as for ice hockey, even Clarence Campbell, a man hardly given to publicly airing his sport's problems, admitted that "there has been a tendency for fan intervention" over the past few seasons. (By "fan intervention" Campbell meant a variety of disorders ranging from the throwing of switchblades, darts, ball bearings and hot pennies onto the ice to savage assaults on individual players.) One sign of the times is the recent introduction of plexiglass backboards behind hockey penalty boxes to shield the occupants from the wrath of the fans.

"The only riots I read about at sports events before this era were at race tracks," sports columnist Roger Kahn told me. "Now I think we're going toward this wild South American soccer crowd type of thing, people who'll kill an official. We're moving that way. You can see it." The mechanics of crowd violence have been the subject of close observation by a number of social investigators over the past decade or so. What has now emerged is a broad behavior pattern which many sports crowds follow in their progression from enthusiastic support to violent disruption.

It should come as no surprise that many past crowd outbursts have been built on a foundation comprised of external social pressures totally divorced from the sporting spectacle at hand. Sport, of course, is not conducted in a vacuum, and it is therefore unavoidable that the spectators will bring with them the same social tensions, pressures and prejudices that influence them in their outside lives. What is surprising, however, is just how powerfully and directly these social pressures influence crowd behavior at sporting events. Without the bedrock religious bigotry which divides Glasgow, for example, it is unlikely that the Celtic–Ranger confrontations would be anywhere near as intense. It was a series of bitter territorial disputes which lay at the heart of the Honduras–El Salvador "Soccer War," and territorial rivalry which formed the backdrop to the protracted soccer riots which divided the two Italian cities of Bari and Taranto. Racial prejudices have caused even more "sports riots": in 1946 Vienna erupted when an Austrian police soccer club played Hakoah, a Jewish sports club; in the '60s, racial friction marred many sporting events in the US, several of which ended in stabbings; there is even evidence that race was one of the causes of the Minnesota–Ohio State basketball riot of 1971 in which Ohio star Luke Witte was savagely beaten. Other crowd disturbances can be traced back to underlying differences in class or economic advantage.

What sport does to these ever-present social tensions to make them erupt into open violence at sporting events rather than at rock concerts or the movies is to stretch them to breaking point by adding a new object of rivalry – victory. "When groups already in conflict meet in the sport setting in a vicarious struggle for a scarce commodity, victory," wrote York University researchers Alan Ingham and Michael D. Smith in their 1973 study *The Social Implications of the Interaction between Spectators and Athletes,* "it is not surprising that collective violence sometimes erupts."

These latent antagonisms are triggered into actual physical violence by one or a number of precipitative elements directly related to the game at hand. It could be a controversial refereeing decision (particularly if it confirms a general belief that the referee is in any way biased), or the exaggerated and provocative pantomimed anger of a losing coach. Violence on the field is particularly effective in igniting a crowd, especially if it confirms the belief that one of the teams is "dirty." In a study of seventeen soccer riots over a period of some years, Professor Smith discovered that in the majority of cases – almost three-quarters, in fact – "assaultive behavior" involving either police and fans, fans amongst themselves or, more frequently, player against player, preceded the collective crowd outburst.

"When a widespread hostile belief has crystallized around a precipitating incident, or series of incidents," wrote Smith, "the mobilization of the

❝ The old fan yelled, 'Kill the umpire!' The new fan tries to do it. ❞

Dr. Arnold Beisser, Los Angeles psychiatrist
and author of *The Madness in Sport*

participants for action begins." In some cases this mobilization is prompted by the actions of a leader, the lone charge of a Matias Rojas, for example. In others it is simply a spontaneous avalanche of spectators onto the field headed for the referee, the players or the police. When there are no human targets available, attentions are turned toward the stands. If the situation has been further aggravated by alcohol or overcrowding, the end result is only that much worse.

One of the best-documented examples of this sequence of events is the Washington, D.C., football riot of Thanksgiving Day, 1962. Set against the background of the bitter racial tension which characterized urban America during the '60s, the game drew a record 50,000 spectators to see Eastern High School, a school with only five white pupils out of a total enrollment of 2,400, play St. John's High School, a predominantly white, middle-class school. It was an important game, the final of the district football championships. The underlying tensions were glaringly obvious: black *vs.* white, rich *vs.* poor, a record crowd (80 percent of which was black), widespread teenage drinking and race riots on the television every night. It is little wonder that several spectators later confessed they had sensed trouble even before the starting gun had been fired.

In the first quarter, Eastern (the defending champions) scored a touchdown and appeared set to coast to an easy victory. In the second quarter, however, St. John's scored twice to take a commanding lead. The mood of many blacks in the crowd, denied their expectations, turned nasty and by half time there had already been a series of ugly confrontations, including several beatings and threatened stabbings. Fights began to break out around the stands as groups of young blacks invaded the expensive seats vacated by whites on their way to the refreshment counters. At the beginning of the second half, St. John's scored an immediate touchdown, and the violence escalated.

With six minutes to go and St. John's still well on top, an Eastern player angrily threatened his opponents, complaining that he had been roughly handled. The referee saw the incident and the Eastern boy was thrown out of the game. Eastern's coach stormed onto the field and acted out his violent displeasure in broad pantomime, gesturing repeatedly at the Eastern stands. Then the banished Eastern player lost his temper and charged back into the fray, punching wildly. He was finally overpowered, strapped to a stretcher and carried out of the stadium, but by this time dozens of young Eastern supporters had spilled from the stands onto the sidelines where they stood glowering at the St. John's players. When the game ended with the score 20–7 against Eastern, more than two thousand angry fans left their seats to invade first the field and then the St. John's stands. "It was like a moving

❝ The whole psychology of crowds – it's really wild. You can get them turned one way or the other and you never really know what's going to happen. Maybe I'm exaggerating a little, but I occasionally do fear physical harm when we do those games. ❞

Don Meredith, former US pro football star
and television sportscaster, 1978

tarpaulin about thirty or forty yards long," recalled one St. John's supporter. The violence was frenzied and savage, with people being beaten regardless of age or sex. By the time the police could restore order, a total of 512 spectators had been injured (all but 27 St. John's fans), the injuries including 13 broken noses, 16 knife wounds and 54 serious head injuries.

In this case the progression toward violence is clear: bedrock tension precipitated by alleged rough play, an "unjust" refereeing decision (the sending-off), the spectacle of player violence and the orchestrating efforts of the Eastern coach, plus a heavy and unexpected loss. Any one of these factors on their own could have sparked a riot; Eastern–St. John's had them all.

It is this pattern of behavior, then, or something very close to it, which lies behind many of today's "Sports Riot!" headlines – social tensions exacerbated by the atmosphere of the ball game. As columnist Leonard Shecter wrote, we play our ball games like wars, to win. We also watch them with the same driven intensity. When we lose – either the whole game or just an advantage – to an opponent we already have grave reservations about because of the color of his skin or his nationality or his hometown, we riot, especially if we feel the loss is unfair. It is a certain assumption that Matias Rojas was screaming the Spanish equivalent of "we wuz robbed" as he scaled the barricades in Lima.

And the more we *have* to win, the more we riot. It is no mere fluke of "Latin temperament" (although temperament probably does play a part) that many of the worst riots occur in South America. Rather, Latin sports riots are far more the products of South American supporters' burning desire for victory, a desire born out of the poverty and frustrations of everyday working life. As one sociologist remarked, "the need for success in sports is related to the degree of insecurity of the social structure of the community in which the game is played." The most striking example of committed support in recent years was the home-team crowds during the 1978 World Cup in Argentina, a country of police repression, raging inflation and very little else. What the Argentinian fans would have done had they lost to, say, their old rivals Brazil on a disputed penalty does not bear thinking about, moats or not. Similar tensions were behind the comparatively large number of racially inspired sports riots in America during the '60s. Deprived of legitimate means of proving that they were not inferior, many blacks turned to sporting competition. To have their team beaten, especially by a predominantly white team, was for many black fans more than they could bear. They *needed* victory, and rioted when it was denied them.

Sadly the one element of sport most capable of defusing such situations – sportsmanship – is now palpably absent from modern sporting contest, both professional and amateur. It is hard to envisage the Eastern–St. John's riot occurring if the players had shaken hands instead of fists, or if the coach had applauded an opposition move rather than abused the umpire. "These kids, they're playing for keeps," said Dr. Alan Strizak of the peewee hockey players whose wounds he attends. "It hardly teaches them sportsmanship, but it's like everything else, it's beyond a game." Or in the words of the great Leo Durocher: "Show me a sportsman, and I'll show you a player I'm willing to trade." It is worth reflecting that only now, when the sporting image of first-class rugby has become so irredeemably tarnished, are Rugby Union crowds yelling "Kill 'im."

War on the Terraces

One glaring area of crowd violence which this sociological pattern does not, however, satisfactorily explain is Britain's much-publicized "soccer hooliganism." British soccer has long suffered more than its fair share of spectator violence: Glasgow's interminable religious warfare; the bicycle-chain battles of the postwar London clubs; the missile throwing which by 1950 had forced the closure of the Millwall club three times. But although he shares much in common with the sporting terrors of the past, the "soccer hooligan" is a new and separate phenomenon.

Press reports identifying purposely disruptive "elements" among English soccer crowds first appeared in 1961 following a nationally televised pitch invasion at the Tottenham Hotspur's ground. However, it was not until the mid-1960s that the ever-increasing gangs of young supporters became recognized as an entity in their own right, something different to the usual run of football fans. By that time many of the older, more traditional supporters had already left the game, either moving away from the grounds into new redevelopment areas, or simply prefering a comfortable armchair and *Match of the Day* to the dubious pleasure of standing on a cold terrace in the rain. The young fans quickly filled the vacuum, massing together unrestrained by the presence of the older men. Within a few years they had entirely taken over whole sections of the ground, and by the beginning of the 1970s "hooligan," "bovver boy," "skinhead" and "aggro" had become as much a part of the soccer lexicon as "offside" and "handball."

These youngsters were the sons of the working class – of "low socio-economic status," as one government report described them. More often than not they were the products of the high-rise redevelopments which radically transformed many of England's urban working-class suburbs during the late 1950s. Their ages generally ranged between early and late teens (they have now dropped even lower), and they stood out from the mass of flat-capped and mufflered "ordinary" adult soccer supporters like chorus girls at a funeral. Their haircuts and clothing were in a constant state of flux, changing from season to season: crombie jackets and steel-toed Dr. Martin's boots ("bovver boots"); later, shaved heads and half-mast trousers; later still, denims and bare chests, long hair and scarves – always a scarf – knotted around the wrist or the neck or the forehead. They also managed to find enough money to travel *en masse* to away games by coach or, more popularly, by the British Rail "Football Specials," something which youngsters had never done before. Together they were like an army, bursting out of the "Football Specials" onto alien platforms and swaggering through the enemy streets escorted by phalanxes of police, stamping and chanting and hurling threats at the scurrying locals.

Once inside the grounds they grouped on the terraces directly behind the goals, "home" supporters at one end, "away" supporters at the other. Crammed into these "ends" (later penned in by steel barricades and cleared strips of no-man's-land which further isolated them from the "ordinary" spectators, thus increasing their sense of unity), they fostered an astonishing repertoire of songs, obscenities and chants. These were repeated over and over during the game to the accompaniment of waving scarves, gesturing hands and synchronized clapping. Some of these lyrics were paeans to club or team; more often, however, they were none-too-subtle threats directed at the enemy end:

> We'll take the Tottenham in half a minute
> We'll take the Arsenal and all that's in it,
> With hatchets and hammers,
> Carving knives and spanners,
> We'll show those Tottenham bastards how to fight!

And the simple but effective:

Stab stab stab the bastards!
Stab stab stab the bastards!

Swaying and chanting in their thousands under a massed banner of identical scarves, or swaggering through the city streets as if they owned them, they presented an unforgettable spectacle, as thrilling to the youngsters who flocked to join the "glamor" clubs – Manchester United, Liverpool, Chelsea – as they were chilling to the editorial writers of the Sunday press.

Despite their threats and posturings, the amount of actual havoc wreaked by soccer hooligans was considerably less than the press would have had its readers believe. Indeed, many observers now recognize press sensationalism – "The nightmare story of how soccer hooligans held a town in fear was revealed yesterday . . ." – as having assisted in the creation and perpetuation of the soccer hooligan phenomenon, attracting new recruits to the well-publicized "problem" clubs (often from towns hundreds of miles away), giving them an identity (Manchester's "Red Army") and encouraging them to live up to an overblown image. (In building this inflated image the press was assisted by the fans themselves who constantly embroidered their feats: "All right, fair enough, when we go away, I'll admit it, I do people in the eyes with ammonia. . . . There's no way I go away without that ammonia." "Where is it now, then?" "Today I haven't got it, right?") The bark of soccer hooliganism was – and is – far worse than its bite. No towns have ever been held to ransom and, indeed, few people outside the circle of home and away fans – innocent bystanders, if you like – have ever been assaulted.

Nonetheless, buried beneath the media's gleeful hysteria and the exaggerations of the hooligans themselves, there lay a solid and growing core of real violence. British Rail's football trains – the "Skinhead Specials," as they soon became known – were the first hooligan targets. On both the away and return journeys windows were broken, seats torn out and hundreds of light bulbs systematically smashed by fans. Some carriages were so badly damaged that they had to be scrapped. In 1975 the service was suspended after a gang of Liverpool fans looted the mailbags and used them to set their train alight. (Today the soccer specials are back in service, patrolled by police and, for a big match, by guard dogs.)

Soon the violence spread from the railways to the streets leading to and from the grounds, with visiting fans damaging houses and cars and sending ripples of panic through those in their path. In Derby, one of the hardest hit, home owners living adjacent to the ground would begin boarding up their windows the night before a match, and some would keep them boarded up all season. Women told of cowering under the kitchen table with their children as rampaging fans splintered their front doors. Their husbands bought shotguns and hired guard dogs. In 1977 they even applied to the courts to have the ground closed down, a tactic which was also adopted by harrassed residents living nearby London's tough Millwall ground.

By the early 1970s the British fans' reputation for destruction had spread abroad. In 1972 Glasgow Rangers fans charged through the streets of Barcelona, battling police and laying waste to the city's plate-glass windows. Two years later Tottenham fans outraged the citizens of Rotterdam by their behavior, and the year after that, Leeds supporters inflicted thousands of pounds' worth of damage on Paris shopkeepers. More recently the French city of St. Etienne was the site of a concerted English attack which left in its wake a reported £200,000 of damage.

But such demolition work is overshadowed by the more prevalent and far more disturbing damage the fans have inflicted on each other. Throughout the past decade, the face of English soccer has so often been that of a fan dressed in one set of colors kicking to insensibility a fan dressed in another. "For some unknown reason, football grounds have become the battlefield for youths who want to indulge in a good fight," said one London police commander whose district included three professional football clubs. It is a problem which has grown more pressing with each passing year, as the events of recent seasons have illustrated.

At the beginning of the 1976 season, the terrace wars claimed their first fatality, a teenager from Blackpool who was stabbed to death. The following year an 18-year-old Millwall fan died when he fell – or, as seems more likely, was pushed – from a train during a fight over scarves with rival West Ham supporters. In that same week a 21-year-old Charlton fan was beaten into a coma by West Ham supporters. The next month a 17-year-old was stabbed in the back and a policeman had his skull fractured when Glasgow Rangers played a "friendly" against Aston Villa; and the month after that two fans were stabbed during a brawl which halted a Notts Forest–Chelsea match. The season ended with an Arsenal supporter being hit in the eye with a dart thrown by a Middlesborough fan, a Manchester United fan stabbed on the terraces and a nationally televised riot at Norwich in which Manchester supporters cunningly outflanked the police and began demolishing the opposing stand. Viewers were treated to the spectacle of a Manchester fan plummeting forty feet headlong into the crowd. When ambulancemen tried to carry him away, he was dragged from the stretcher by Norwich supporters and savagely beaten. By the day's end thirty-six people had been injured, including a youth who was given seven pints of blood after being stabbed four times in the chest and another who needed ten stitches to close a stab wound. Later that month a Manchester supporter lost a kidney after being stabbed on the terraces at Sheffield.

The 1977–8 season began where the last one left off with the fatal stabbing of a Celtic supporter in Arbroath and the crippling of a 9-year-old boy in Liverpool who was thrown under a bus by rival fans. Two busloads of supporters, each returning from separate matches, made news when they fought each other across four lanes of motorway traffic leaving the road covered in bricks and broken glass. Manchester United's visit to St. Etienne left thirty-three people hospitalized, five of them with broken limbs. In the fighting that followed Scotland's win over Wales during the World Cup qualifying series in Liverpool, one fan died and fifty others were hospitalized with stab wounds, bottle lacerations and other injuries.

The larger ends have now been caged with steel barricades. Visiting supporters are isolated by wedges of empty terracing which are patroled by police. Routine vandalism, such as a mob of Tottenham supporters tearing out a row of picket fences to use as ammunition, now barely rates a mention in the press. Police talk of "only" twenty arrests at a game; often there are as many as eighty or ninety; MPs and football managers call for stiffer prison sentences, identity cards, reintroduction of flogging, electric shock treatment and in the words of one manager, "flame throwers to burn the bastards." The secretary of the Police Federation has recommended all League matches be suspended. Toward the end of the 1977–8 season the Sunday papers carried a photograph of a teenage fan stumbling from the terraces with a steel dart buried to the hilt between his eyes. Two weeks later another boy was pictured with a dart embedded two inches into his forehead. Only in Britain could a man (a Queens Park Rangers supporter, in fact) who was charged with stabbing his wife with a kitchen knife offer the defense that he had been dreaming of fighting off soccer hooligans . . . and be acquitted.

What is most disturbing to the press and public – and especially to those involved with the game, the players, managers and "traditional" supporters – is that soccer hooliganism is apparently completely divorced from the soccer itself. To most people it is as though an army of lunatics and psychopaths has suddenly and unaccountably battened onto the sport and is now engaged in a concerted effort to destroy it through mindless acts of random violence.

Certainly it is not impossible to view soccer hooliganism through the sociologists' pattern of behavior outlined earlier. In many instances of soccer violence this pattern does apply. Pitch invasions in particular are often related to an unexpected heavy defeat (Glasgow Rangers losing at Aston Villa in 1976; Millwall losing to Ipswich at home in 1977, the match at which flame throwers were first mooted). "Bad" refereeing and vicious play can also precipitate trouble. "No doubt about it,"said the police commander I spoke to. "If violence occurs on the field, if one player takes a swing at another, it's almost automatic that it starts up on the terraces. And if the referee gives a penalty against them which they don't think is fair and nor do the players, it really drives them into a frenzy." It is worth considering whether soccer hooliganism would ever have grown so large or so rapidly if it had not coincided with the rise of the professional foul. The surest guarantee of a soccer crowd riot would still be for a referee to award a bitterly disputed match-winning penalty to a known dirty player before a home-team crowd.

Most of soccer's hooliganism does not, however, come anywhere near to fitting an accepted chain of behavior. For a start, opposing soccer crowds are not social enemies outside the grounds. The ends are all of the same racial mix, the same nationality and the same socioeconomic background. Even Michael Morrow, the Glasgow Ranger front-liner supposedly engaged in a religious war against the hated Catholic, doesn't really mind whether it's a Catholic or an English or an Arbroath supporter's head he is kicking in, so long as it's a head. The aggro comes first, the religion a very poor second. Similarly, there is no history of territorial rivalry between, say, Manchester United and Norwich – that is, beyond the rivalry manufactured for the occasion by the hooligans themselves. More than this, much of the violence occurs without the precipitation of a trigger incident; in fact, many arrests are made long before the game has even started, sometimes a mile or more from the ground. The destruction of railway carriages and the throwing of 9-year-olds under municipal buses has precious little to do with bad refereeing or vicious tackling.

The fact is that most fans actually anticipate aggro and go to the game looking for it, as one Manchester United supporter quoted in a 1978 Sports Council study ("Public Disorder and Sporting Events") readily acknowledged:

> You know if it is a big day coming up. Everyone tends to get excited, like with Liverpool. They come down and they've had 7,500 tickets sent to them. We'll be thinking how many's coming down. Probably waiting for them or something. Getting ready.

Many fans now "get ready" by carrying a weapon, arriving at the turnstiles armed to the teeth like junior terrorists. In the days of the skinheads, weaponry was generally confined to knives, sharpened steel combs and steel-toed boots. (Great mounds of these confiscated boots would be piled outside the turnstiles, their owners forced to negotiate the terraces in stockinged feet.) Today the range of confiscated weapons is extraordinary – switch blades, sheath knives, kitchen knives, steel darts, belt buckles, concealed bricks, pepper. One fan was even caught carrying a snare wire with wooden handles at either end, presumably for use as a garotte should the occasion arise. Many of these weapons are undoubtedly purely for show, but some are not. Not so long ago an Arsenal supporter was stabbed through the abdomen with a bayonet. To date only one fan has been spotted with a handgun, a record attributable more to England's stringent gun control laws than to any lack of initiative on the part of the fans. "You'd be surprised at the number of things," one policeman told me. "Last Saturday we had a chap with a chain wrapped around his wrist. He had his mac [raincoat] covering it." "Everyone carries a tool. Straight!" confessed a Millwall supporter. And even if his claim is 50 percent exaggeration, it still represents a considerable cutting edge.

Given this, it is tempting to fall in with the popular belief that soccer's troubles are indeed the random and senseless acts of budding psychopaths, a temptation reinforced by many fans' expressed delight with administering violence – "It's more exciting if you hit someone, especially some Northern bastard. It's satisfying to hit someone. It feels good." However, several recent terrace studies have discovered that, far from being a world of random, unplanned and mindless violence, life in the ends is as structured and ordered almost as the game itself. Take Millwall, the subject of a recent television documentary and currently the most notorious club in the land. As one supporter proudly boasted: "People are frightened of us all over England." And they are.

End support at Millwall can be considered a career, with clearly defined levels of promotion and an acknowledged pecking order. As in all careers, life begins on the bottom rung, which in Millwall's case is a section of the ground known as the halfway line. It is here that the juniors congregate, youngsters aged from 8 or 9 to their early teens. They are beginners, novices, drawn by the excitement and danger and eager to learn from their elders. Mostly they generate far more noise than violence.

As they grow older, the fans graduate to the end proper, joining first Treatment and later, perhaps, F-Troop. Treatment members, distinguishable by the paper dishcloths they often wear over their heads, are the backbone of the Millwall end, chanting, taunting the opposition and urging on the team. They consider themselves true supporters, fighting only in retaliation against an enemy onslaught or an unbearable insult: "Any blokes that don't run when you're away from home, [who] stands there and has a good fight, is a good Millwall supporter." Life, for Treatment, is an unvaried diet of football, pub and bed. Their support is unwavering. "I'll do time," shrugged one member. "I don't really give a shit about it. It's easy, in'it. You come back out, support Millwall, have more punch-ups and go back in. Yeah. And that's that."

F-Troop are Millwall's hard men, an older (generally middle to late 20s), tougher brigade who are bent on "rucking" at every opportunity, even to the extent of attending games in which Millwall is not even playing. It is F-Troop which infiltrates the enemy end, either by guile – wearing enemy colors, cheering the enemy team, even talking in the enemy's accent – or by force. When they have gained a foothold on the rival terracing, they lash out, clearing a wide circle around them and sending visible ripples of panic through the tightly packed supporters. They are fearless – revered as "nutters" and "headbangers" by the other Millwall fans – and the sight of a dozen F-Troopers tackling a thousand enemy supporters is not uncommon. They have earned their position at the top of the Millwall pecking order with their fists, and violence is what they look for:

> I go to a match for one reason only: the aggro. It's an obsession, I can't give it up. I get so much pleasure when I'm having aggro that I nearly wet my pants – it's true. I go all over the country looking for it. I couldn't sleep all last night, I got so worked up looking forward to this match. My mother hid my shoes this morning.

Although F-Troopers are comparatively few – as are the members of Tottenham's Shelf Gang, Chelsea's North Stand and other similar groups – the violence they commit and incite is far in excess of their numbers. One recent study undertaken by Westhill College of Education in Birmingham found after interviewing 1,200 fans that roughly *one in four* males had participated in football violence.

In most clubs – even down to some of the smaller Third and Fourth Division sides – a similar sort of fan structure exists. Some may have different groupings which stand in different parts of the ground, or the average age may be a good deal younger than that of Treatment and F-Troop (Millwall's hardened docklands fans have been at it longer than most), but in general, a soccer End is a small society in itself. For several sociologists, life on the terraces suggests a "new tribalism," and with the identical uniforms, the colors, the chants and so on, it is perhaps as good a description as any. "It's . . . it's like a . . .*tribal* thing, y'know?" one Fourth Division fan explained to me. "Coming up into the woods, or out onto the veldt or somethin' and shoutin' at each other, like."

It is perhaps more helpful, however, to view the ends as a sort of overgrown sporting team. For that is what soccer spectatorship has become – violent sport. The action is no longer confined to the pitch, but has now made its way up into the terraces. Passive spectators have become active participants in a sport which, like the soccer match unfolding before them, is a simple struggle for territory. While the teams win points with a ball in the net, the fans win territory by dislodging the opposition, either by violence or sheer weight of numbers. "OUR MEN ARE THERE!" chant the ends when fights break out on the opposition terraces. "We've got the whole stand, in our hands," sing the fans when they've successfully edged out the enemy.

"Sure it's territory," said the Fourth Division supporter, whose wardrobe bulged with the visible record of countless raids – dozens upon dozens of captured scarves. "When you're away, you're tryin' to show that you're superior . . . your town's superior, your football team's superior. When you're at home, you're defendin'. It's a form of nationalism at its lowest . . . you know, the town, standing up for the town. It's our land, our piece of land. And if they come near, get 'em off!"

What soccer is now experiencing is, if you like, a "new spectator-ism," a way of watching a soccer match whereby the game itself is just a launching pad and the action on the field merely an occasional catalyst for the more exciting game of Terrace Warfare. To the ends, the soccer has become almost incidental; indeed, trapped in a sea of waving scarves, it is all but impossible to see, let alone appreciate. At one recent match where Millwall and Tottenham fans were divided by only a thin blue police line, the play was virtually ignored for the duration of the game as the two groups of supporters shouted and glowered at each other. A goal scored is merely an excuse to taunt the opposition; a goal missed just another club with which to beat the enemy head. English soccer has now reached the point where almost every weekend play at one match or another is halted with the players becoming spectators watching the fans lay into each other behind the goal mouth. The situation is best summed up by the old cartoon which shows two professional wrestlers leaning over the ropes arm in arm watching in amazement as a horde of little old ladies tear each other limb from limb.

Exactly why youths become hooligans has consumed more column inches in the British press than the entire George Best saga, girlfriends included. Is it society's fault? Is the soccer hooligan the end result of parental permissiveness? Or is it unemployment or boredom or bad housing? Is there too much violence on the field? Or too little? Alienation of the fans from their heroes? Working mothers? All these and more have been suggested as the cause of soccer hooliganism over the years. All of them may be valid, or none of them. Even the hooligans themselves are not much help in tracking down specific root causes. While one will blame the boredom of life in a country town ("It breaks t' monotony. I mean, there's no *outlet* here . . . no *intellectual* outlet. If there's nowhere to operate my mind on, why not operate physically?), another will describe it as an easy route to respect and recognition ("When you're at the top – just you and the other few – *everyone* looks up to you!"), and still another will grin and deliver a brief sermon on the joys of laying in the leather ("Magic!"). Again, all are no doubt honest confessions; soccer hooliganism is a dauntingly complex problem.

More easily answered is the question, Why soccer? For it is no fluke that today's youth has chosen the soccer ground as its venue for intertribal blood-letting (although most soccer officials would dispute this). As it is now organized, soccer in Britain provides a perfect setting for outbursts of mass aggression, ritual or otherwise. Not only is the game itself, like all team ball games, based on rivalry, but the opposing supporters, often in equal numbers, stand almost eyeball to eyeball, at the most only a few hundred yards apart.

More than this, the atmosphere in which soccer is played in Britain is a uniquely potent one which has been purposely made that way by its administrators, partly through greed and partly through innocence. Fans were encouraged to pack the ends long before the police forced them to do so, firstly because more of them could be squeezed in that way (half a dozen bodies stood shoulder to shoulder and belly to back can fit into the space required for just one seat), and secondly to provide "atmosphere" – a concept unique to British soccer, with the exception of Welsh rugby. While in other sports and in other countries the fans are regarded by promoters as passive consumers to be entertained in their seats, soccer, in the hopes of generating an attractive and *winning* atmosphere, has encouraged its supporters to become part of the entertainment. The "good supporter" is not simply the fan who pays for his position and leaves it at that, but the fan who is one of the ten thousand members of the Liverpool Kop, the greatest massed choir in history, singing "You'll Never Walk Alone." "No game in the world has the atmosphere of British soccer," is every British sports fan's boast. Unfortunately, no game in the world has quite the same degree of crowd violence either.

The trouble is that the line separating the clubs' idea of a "good supporter" and Treatment's idea of the same animal is thin to the point of invisibility. Just how *committed* should a fan be? How many slings and arrows should a good supporter take from opposing fans? When does "You'll Never Walk Alone" become "You'll Never Walk Again"? Such questions are difficult enough for a manager to define; a few years ago one manager gained considerable notoriety when he was accused of slipping money to youths who had just been ejected from the ground so that they could return to continue their support. For a boy caught up in the manufactured rivalries of the terrace such questions are all but impossible.

The fact is that soccer's vaunted atmosphere has now backfired miserably, as it was always destined to do. To gather two opposing armies a stone's throw from each other, pump them full of narrow-minded, blind allegiance expecting them to work it off by proxy through the struggles of a team which stands a fifty-fifty chance of defeat and which with each new season grows increasingly divorced from, and out of sympathy with, them (the bitterest critics of transgressing fans are players and, especially, managers) and then to send them home hoping that they will instantly deflate to normality and forget it all until 3 PM the next Saturday, is surely to court only disaster. "They build you up 'till you're fit to burst and then tell you to piss off out of it and they *know* there's nothing there!" Such was a "hooligan's" lament from a recent stage dramatization; fiction, but true nonetheless.

The Clockwork Orange Era

Although England and Scotland are unquestioned leaders of the sporting world when it comes to hooliganism, elsewhere there are also signs of a "new spectator-ism." "Incidents on the fringe of football matches, violent outrages by individual fanatics, bigger or smaller groups of rowdies on the way to the match and in the area of the stadium increased in recent months." That could have been any one of a dozen British chief constables issuing his monthly press statement on hooliganism. In fact, it was the president of the West German Football League. In Germany police stand on the sidelines with guard dogs, or sit before banks of sophisticated electronic equipment scanning the crowds. Marshalls search all teenage fans and all supporters are separated from the field by the high-wire fences. And *still* there are stabbings in the stands at Bremen. Italy has similar problems, as do several other European and South American countries. Perhaps only the USSR has hooliganism well in hand, although their methods are perhaps more than a little dubious. "We did have some trouble," said Soviet playwright Alexsei Arbuzov on a recent visit to London, "but they popped them into prison for three years and it stopped."

Other sports besides soccer are also now no longer immune. The English Rugby League recently had its first taste of hooliganism when a mob of some eight hundred youths stormed out of a ground and went on a "mindless" rampage, overturning a police car, hurling bottles at each other, assaulting police and jeering an injured officer as he was carried away. Later the police called for extra equipment to be used at future League matches, including riot shields and special protective helmets. "Violence, which is the national concomitant of Association Football matches, has spread to Rugby League," declared the Leeds prosecutor at the subsequent trial.

Sport in the United States has so far largely escaped the phenomenon, mainly because fans rarely travel to away matches with their teams. The country is simply too large to bother, especially when you can see the same game on TV more often than not, and so confrontations between sporting tribes do not occur. However, the signs of seemingly unrelated "mindless" crowd violence have already begun to appear.

One October evening in 1976 the New England Patriots faced the New York Jets in the rather sleepy suburban town of Foxboro, Massachusetts. The game itself was pretty uninspired, a home-town walkover 41–7 to the Patriots. However, the evening has earned itself a place in the football annals as the "Foxboro Riot." During the course of the night, thirty people were hospitalized with injuries suffered in the countless brawls and bottle-throwing incidents which turned the stadium into a combat zone. One man was stabbed in the parking lot, another was pushed from a high retaining wall. A policeman had his jaw broken, an elderly woman was hit over the head with a bottle and a young girl was maimed. Play was halted seven times by field invasions. When an ambulance man attempted to give artificial respiration to one of the injured, fans urinated on him. At the end of the game, fifty-one people had been arrested and another seventeen taken into what was termed "protective custody." "How can you figure things like this?" asked the stunned Foxboro police chief in despair.

How *do* you figure it? In exactly the same light as soccer views its hooliganism. (In the English press recently there was a report of a soccer match in the seaside town of Brighton which, two years later, was almost an instant replay of Foxboro: ninety-one arrests, one man stabbed in the chest before the start of play, a 17-year-old girl with her jaw broken by a brick, fourteen fans hospitalized, a fifteen-minute pitch invasion and dozens of missiles hurled through the air. The only difference was that the visiting fans arrived armed with metal rings covered in spikes.) At Foxboro, accepted social behavior patterns did not apply. The final score was hardly a cause for riot. There were no overtly violent "extracurricular" incidents along the lines of the Swann-Atkinson affair to rile the crowd, nor were there any controversial refereeing decisions. In Foxboro, as in England, the reports were filled with references to "mindless" violence, and one magazine even identified the troublemakers as "a *Clockwork Orange* subculture of sports freaks – brawling rowdies in their 20s – [who] terrorize in the seats much as the players do on the field."

It is too soon yet to tell whether America's sports crowds will follow the route of Britain's hooligans. Perhaps pro football, ice hockey, basketball and the rest of the big league ball sports will escape the consequences of hyped and manufactured rivalry. Then again perhaps the future is Foxboro, already at hand and hammering on the gates.

7

THE NEW ROME

7 The New Rome
Showsport

ANNOUNCER: Ladies and gentlemen. Live from the Chicago Amphitheater . . . Evel Knievel's *Death Defiers!* [Shot of a man staggering about helplessly in a snow-covered field. Smoke drifts slowly out of the picture behind him. He has just blown himself up with four sticks of dynamite.]

JILL ST. JOHN: Can you hear us?

TELLY SAVALAS: Orvil, are you all right? [Orvil stares blankly into the camera.]

JstJ: I don't think he can quite hear you . . . that was quite a blast. I don't think I'd hear for quite a while!

TS: Orvil, are you all right? [Orvil reels away from the camera hitting himself with his arms to keep out the cold.]

JstJ: It's amazing that he's only lost *fifty percent* of his hearing over the years!

TS: It's also amazing that he's still chilly after four sticks of dynamite! . . .

JstJ: Yep, ha ha . . .

TS: Are you all right Orvil?

JstJ: Speak to me, Orvil . . . say something . . . [Orvil remains mute.]

JstJ: I think we should see this again.

TS: Let's do it again, okay. Let's watch it on slow motion. Here we go . . .

[The staggering Orvil dissolves and is replaced by another Orvil standing poised, alert. The audience counts down – ten . . . nine . . . eight . . . Orvil explodes.]

TS: Oh! . . . Well, as you can see, when the countdown reached zero he touched off the dynamite with a battery. And although all we can see are clouds of snow, inside the clouds, remember, the blast is throwing Orvil *fifteen feet!*

JstJ: Orvil's body is taking the shock. His head is the most vulnerable, especially without any kind of protection. . . . How're you doin', Orvil? Can you hear us? [No reply.]

TS: ORVIL KISSABERG! Thank you for giving us the first chance to find out what a daredevil's all about!

JstJ: In-*credible!* [Wild applause.]

TS: Orvil made it, but now five men still wait for their chance to test the odds.

JstJ: As we told you, Evel has been injured in an attempt during rehearsal to jump his bike over the pool of sharks and we still have no word on his exact condition.

TS: While we wait for a report and also for Evel to come in, let's take time out with this pause. . . . [Commercial break.]

TS: Each of these daredevils has become a master of his craft. And I can't think of a better example than the man you are about to meet. He has tested almost every impossible hazard of the high wire. His career covers a span of over fifty years. Mr. KARL WALLENDA! [Applause.]

TS: Tonight, he walks the high wire outdoors and at night! Now when you consider Karl admits his eyesight and his coordination aren't what they used to be, the hazards far outweigh the chances of success. Karl's wife, Ellen Wallenda, has serious reservations about Karl's appearance here tonight. [Taped interview with Mrs. Wallenda expressing her reservations.]

KARL WALLENDA: I know what I can do . . . I have to do it. [Cut to the rafter of the Chicago Amphitheater where a man is perched on a tiny platform.]

TS: JUMPIN' JOE GERLACH! [Applause. Fanfare.]

TS: How're you feeling tonight, Joe?

JUMPIN' JOE GERLACH: Well, it's a little shaky here at the moment. There is a lot of confusion with all this activity, but, ah, I'm feeling fine enough to jump.

JstJ: Joe, you've jumped many times safely before, what's different about your jump tonight? . . . Joe?

JJG: Yeah?

JstJ: Can you tell me what's different about this jump tonight? Is there a difference in height? Or danger?

JJG: Well, I have jumped this high before, but the last time I did it, I had a little mistake and I overshot the end and I broke both my legs and the right hip and it was, ah, kinda an unfortunate jump.

JstJ: How long has it taken you to build up to this amazing height tonight of *eighty-four feet*?

JJG: Ah, let me answer this in a minute. [Joe waves instructions to his assistants below.]

JstJ: Joe, how big is that target? How big is that *sponge*?

JJG: Well, the problem with the sponge is that . . . [Silence.]

TS: Joe, can you hear us?

JJG: Yes, I can.

JstJ: That sponge must look pretty small from way up there eighty-four feet high on the ceiling!

TS: Joe . . . ?

JJG: Well, the target is a very small one and it's actually a sponge . . . it's very similar to what everyone has in their kitchen. And where I'm looking at it from it *is* about the size of your kitchen sponge! I need to adjust this sponge to exactly the right spot. Any deviation that I have up here and I could miss the sponge or land on the edge.

TS: Well, my friend, I know the concentration it must take. And I'm going to ask everyone here tonight to wish Jumpin' Joe Gerlach good luck. Let's give him a rousing send-off! [Applause.]

JstJ: Yaaay!

JJG: Well, I've decided I'm not going to use the helmet this time because it's a pretty high jump; it's a pretty tricky place with Evel's ramp under me. I need the control, the additional control, that I might not have with the helmet going over my head. Obviously my line is wrong so I need to move that sponge back over there . . . move it back . . . okay.

JstJ: Don't rush yourself.

JJG: Pull it out just there about a foot.

JstJ: You know, I've heard of daredevils, Telly, but I've never known anybody do any of the things we've got lined up here tonight!

JJG: Okay, it's about ready.

TS: Good luck, Joe, please . . .

JstJ: Good luck, Joe. [Joe jumps.]

JstJ: Oh . . . my goodness! How exciting! Is he all right?

TS: Yeah, he's moving.

JstJ: HE'S MOVING! HOORAAAY! [Wild applause.]

JJG: Like I said, all's well that ends well . . . Are you gonna play it back?

TS: Yes, we are!

JstJ: Play it back! . . . One . . . two . . . three . . . [Joe jumps in slow motion to the strains of orchestral music.]

TS: Keep your eye on the screen, Joe, and we'll get a playback on it.

JJG: Oh, there it is! O-*kay*! Oh boy, I almost missed that thing!

TS: Yes, you did!

JJG: Boy, I've never been quite this far out, ever! Jeez! There it is.

TS: There it is!

JJG: Oh, jeezus!

TS: Yeah.

JJG: Boy, that was a close one! Another flick to the left . . .

TS: Nice to have you, Joe Gerlach! [Applause.]

JJG: Thank you.

JstJ: You're a true daredevil!

TS: Another success by another man who did his homework – JUMPIN' JOE GERLACH! And thank you for sharing our incredible sponge plunge with us tonight. . . . Well, that's two out of seven. We've got five left to come.

jstj: Evel's attempt to jump the sharks has already become a nightmare for him. He's at the hospital at the moment, but he *is* alive.

ts: Well, Evel Knievel in his attempt for perfection, aside from being the daredevil, did the same jump that he was going to do here live tonight. We've captured it all on videotape, and in his, as I say, attempt for perfection, he got hurt. We hear that the breaks are all orthopedic, and the kind of guy he is, he's on his way here. Now, speaking of safety, Evel was very concerned about the welfare of his sharks. I want you to watch this . . . [Film of Evel's crew catching sharks humanely, followed by a commercial break.]

ts: There has been an accident in Evel's preparation to jump over the sharks. And while we await more news on the outcome, let's take you now live to the very top of the Fontainbleu Hotel in Miami Beach, some seventeen stories off the ground . . . [Cut to the hotel roof where a helicopter is circling a man.]

jstj: DAVID MERRIFIELD, who is awaiting his pickup by helicopter!

ts: It looks like Dave's pilot Jim Grogan is attempting to line up to make the pickup. But it also appears as though he may be having some kind of a problem. Dave's, ah, waving the chopper off. I guess he's aborting this pass. It looks like Jim Grogan is going to have to reposition himself for another pass. In any event Dave Merrifield needs a little more time to analyze his strategy. Meanwhile, let's take a closer look at the man and his mission . . . [Taped interview with David Merrifield.]

DAVID MERRIFIELD: I'm really concerned – nervous – about this show. We're going to be attempting something . . . working in areas that we've never worked in before and doing something we've never done before . . . a little out of the ordinary and the range of the act. And both Jim and I are, ah, a little tense about it. We hope it will come out well . . . [Cut to the hotel rooftop. The helicopter hovers into view, descends, and picks up David Merrifield by his teeth.]

jstj: I think it's just something a man's gotta do. Whether it's right or wrong, it's just something he's gotta do.

ts: I think it is!

jstj: We'll have a report on Evel's injuries right after this commercial . . .

Sitting in a motel room across town from the Michael Reese Hospital where Evel lay in state, I too was waiting anxiously for a report on the great man's condition. I had arranged an interview for the following day, and although I was uneasy about playing the ghoul, it had to be admitted that a recuperating Evel reflecting on his narrow escape was infinitely preferable to Evel the showbiz huckster beating the drum about such coming attractions as his

> **❝ I am the last gladiator in the New Rome. ❞**
>
> Evel Knievel

40,000-foot free-fall drop from a B29 bomber onto a haystack.

Unfortunately it was not to be. Evel never made it back to the show at the Chicago Amphitheater that night. His collarbone, forearm and several other lesser bones had been splintered by the crash, and he was confined incommunicado to his hospital bed for extensive rewiring throughout the next week. On his return to public life he was accorded the usual hero's reception. *Death Defiers* had scored near-record ratings and there would, he promised, be more challenges to conquer.

If so they will be conquered without the help of poor Karl Wallenda, the aging high-wire walker with the failing eyesight. After having seen many of his family plunge to their deaths in the name of showsport, one year later he too was dead, falling from a high wire strung between two apartment buildings in Puerto Rico. At least he did not die alone. The tragedy was, of course, captured in its entirety on videotape.

Blood for Fun and Profit

As Evel and his Death Defiers are only too happily aware, there is another, far uglier reason why violence has become so much a part of this sporting life, over and above its usefulness as a means of winning victories. It is this: for the vast majority of those who have made sport what it is today, violence makes for delicious entertainment. The brutal truth is that brutality thrills, violence is mesmerizing and bloodshed fascinating, just so long as it is someone else's blood that is being shed. It is no simple coincidence that so many of our most popular sports are essentially violent pleasures; we have the sports we have today because they are what we like.

Not surprisingly it was Vince Lombardi who voiced this most unequivocally, for whatever else he may have been, Lombardi was an unsparing realist. "This is a violent sport," he told his troops flatly. "That's why people love it." His troops no doubt all nodded in solemn agreement, as they still do today. Pro footballer Claude Humphrey, discussing the Swann/Atkinson cheap shot drama, commented: "It's just football. That's why it's the No. 1 sport. On a Sunday afternoon the fans get to screaming and they want to see somebody get hit." Tampa Bay's Ken Stone agreed. "It's all part of a violent game, and that's what people pay to see," he said. In *Out of Their League*, Dave Meggyesy wrote about the "violence and sadism," not so much on the part of the players, "but very much in the minds of the beholders – the millions of Americans who watch football every weekend in something approaching a sexual frenzy." Another player remarked on the subject of drug abuse: "I've often wondered how the public might react if we all didn't take anything. I think the public might not dig the game. It might be a little slow, a little dull."

Even in the halls of the NFL itself, this vision of the drooling fan is surprisingly deep-seated, as the League spokesman I talked to acknowledged:

> Why is pro football so popular? It's a physical contact sport. I think it's what society wants, they want to see contact sports. It's something that goes back to the gladiator days. Why did people go to the Colosseum in Rome to see the gladiators fight? Because it's a very physical thing. Instead of fighting with swords, we're fighting with padded bodies.

Such opinions are even more forthcoming around the ice rinks of the NHL. "There is no doubt in my mind that if the game wasn't physically violent I don't think it would have any appeal at all," Clarence Campbell, the former League commissioner once stated. When I visited the commissioner in his plush Montreal offices he had recently been to see two nonviolent Russian teams compete against each other. His verdict, as expressed to a congressional committee probing hockey violence, was less than favorable:

> I told them it's a great thing to look at once, but it's like a harness race – when you've seen one, you've seen 'em all. It's a mechanical process; a lovely thing to watch – I love to watch gymnastics – but I wouldn't want a steady diet of watching the same people do the same tricks all the time. *It won't win hockey games and it won't draw fans.*

Campbell, like Lombardi, is a pragmatist, and his erstwhile troops toe much the same line. "I think a lot of people like to see the game, but I think people also enjoy seeing a fight," said Bobby Clarke. "If there's a dog fight people will go to see it. If two guys want to fight, let 'em. Everybody enjoys a good fight. People *want* to see violence." Dave Schultz confessed that much of the time he engineered brawls simply to entertain the fans. "It's the

---

&& We're going to have to do something about all this violence or people are going to keep on buying tickets.   99

Conn Smythe, veteran ice hockey star

---

women," he said, shaking his head in awe. "I've talked to I dunno how many guys and they say that they take their wives to a football or baseball game and they just sit there. Take them to a hockey game, and they don't even know it's the same person sitting beside them. They go crazy – *Kill! Kill!*"

It's a repugnant thought that our stadiums are built on the same precepts as those which kept the Roman turnstiles clicking, and it is one which many fans are quick to dismiss. It is far more comforting to justify contact sports solely on the grounds of Joe Namath's aerial passes or Bobby Orr's lightning dashes across the ice, just as it leaves boxing fans feeling less guilty to talk about "scientists" rather than sluggers. But the conclusion that blood is a powerful attraction for the spectator is impossible to sidestep. Of the two dozen or so Minnesota Viking fans I talked with during a dinner dance on the eve of the 1977 Super Bowl, all said that they enjoyed football because of the "body contact," the "toughness," or, from the teenagers, the "brutality." "It's like the call of the wild," said one 16-year-old who had ruined both his knees playing high school football. "Like the dog when he hears those wild animals, back there deep in his ancestry. It's the same feeling when you hear that crunch . . . *crrrsssh* . . . you know. When it comes down to it, you *love* it!" His friends all nodded their solemn agreement. The hordes of hockey fans who crowded the exits of the Philadelphia Spectrum after a Flyers' game hoping for autographs were equally as adamant: "Fist fights? Neat!"

Yes, the Flyers; consider the meteoric rise of hockey's goon squad. "They used to have a team here called the Ramblers, but they weren't worth a nickle – maybe forty people in the crowd," one middle-aged female fan informed me as we sat in a Spectrum seething with fans. "Then came the Flyers!" In 1970 the Flyers were a lost box office cause; three years later at the height of their brawling they were setting attendance records in five NHL cities and had sold out the Spectrum for the entire season, not simply because they were winning games, but, more importantly, because of the *style* with which they won them. Consider Dave Schultz's elevation to the role of superstar. By his own admission a player who could neither skate nor score goals well enough to retain his place in the NHL, when the titular head of the Broad Street Bullies appeared on a Philadelphia phone-in program he received 84,194 phone calls – ten times the number received by the next most popular guest.

Other clubs who followed the Flyers' leap into violence also enjoyed similar box office success. The Pittsburgh Penguins were suffering severe attendance problems until they bought Steve Durbano and Battleship Kelly, both notorious hard men. Their home attendance immediately jumped by almost two thousand a game. When the Stingers acquired Wild Willie

---

❝ If the players were armed with guns, there wouldn't be stadiums large enough to hold the crowds. ❞

Irwin Shaw, novelist, on American football

Trognitz, owner Al Savill was quoted as saying: "Believe me, not only can't you win without an enforcer, it's hard to put people in your building if you don't have one."

Any lingering skepticism about the fans' desire for blood is quickly dispelled by a glance at the way seating prices are graded for contact sports. The best place to view the cut and thrust of a football or a hockey game is where the press boxes are – halfway up the stands. Yet the highest priced seats in the house are invariably those positioned smack on the sidelines where the only vision of the game possible is of hurtling bodies smashing into each other in a tangle of fists, arms and legs. Fight promoters, of course, have long been aware of the fans' desire to have their faces pressed hard against the bloodshed; ringside seats at major bouts now go for nothing short of a king's ransom. Before the Ali/Liston rematch when Ali received a number of threats on his life from anti-Muslims, one of the promoters was heard to remark wistfully: "If I could assure the people an assassination in the ring, I could sell a million tickets." And what price ringside!

Other promoters in other sports now also dream of assassinations. In their hands violence has become an asset in retailing sport, a situation which Los Angeles psychiatrist Arnold Beisser has labeled "a new use of violence." In Beisser's view, violence is now used "not as a means to an end, but for recreational purposes, for pleasure." It is, he says, "an end in itself." Other sports analysts have reached similar conclusions. Author and radical sports coach Jack Scott has accused owners of injecting violence into pro-fessional sports purposely to "titillate the fans." Even more forthright was Canadian ice hockey investigator William McMurtry, whose report to the Ontario government concluded that "the evidence strongly indicates that there is a conscious effort to sell the violence in hockey to enrich a small group of show-business entrepreneurs at the expense of a great sport (not to mention the corruption of an entire generation's concept of sport)."

Hockey owners especially have turned to violence as a means of filling the bleachers, a move undertaken with the blessings of commissioner Campbell who once stated that "insofar as [violence] is part of the show, certainly we sell it." This was seen most obviously during the expansion years when the NHL was striving to win over an entire stock of uninitiated spectators. To the inexperienced, the speed with which hockey is played often renders the game indecipherable. In order to prevent first-time fans switching off their sets in mid-game, viewers were treated to something they could both enjoy and readily understand – violence.

NBC began by promoting its hockey *Game of the Week* with a clip of a full-scale brawl. It then chose as one of its chief commentators the ubiquitous Ted Lindsay, one of the game's all-time great enforcers. Commented *Sports Illustrated:* " 'Terrible' Ted knew what he was there for and he delivered. His sensitive appraisal of one stick-swinging skirmish: 'That's layin' the ol' lumber on 'im! The hockey stick is the great equalizer!' " A cartoon series designed to educate the American public on the niceties of the game depicted players, in William McMurtry's words, "as brutal top heavy Neanderthal types who were shown demonstrating every conceivable type of foul with great gusto and relish." Another charge leveled by McMurtry concerned the rule change forcing players to proceed directly to the penalty box after being penalized. Apparently the network was concerned about the long delays caused by the interminable brawling. However, rather than reduce the fighting and risk affecting the ratings, the network and the NHL opted for the no-delay rule. Perhaps the most revealing piece of broadcast footage was a film produced by the North Stars which purported to depict the team "highlights" of one season. Of the twenty-six minutes of "highlights," no less than twenty were devoted to brawls.

Against this, Bobby Clarke's statement that "they [the owners] want us to fight" hardly comes as a revelation. Long before his first appearance with the Flyers, with expansion still four years away, the die had already been cast. "The big wheels of the NHL figure they have to have blood to fill the arenas," said Jack Mehlenbacher, a leading referee of that period. "I refereed for five years and that was all they were interested in."

The most damnable use of violence as a means of promoting hockey concerns the unpopularity of players' helmets. Given the high risk of head and facial injury inherent in the game, it seems ludicrous that helmets are not more widespread. The reasons usually given for this are that helmets are unmanly or uncomfortable or that the players feel they will invite high-sticking. However, when I asked Fred Shero why more of his players did not use headgear, he gave another reason. It was, he said, "because management don't want it." "They figure it's going to detract from the crowds," he explained. "They feel you lose your identity."

As I discovered later, Shero's belief that the management encourages players to leave themself vulnerable for the added enjoyment of the spectators was really nothing new. In his book *Slashing!* (1975), hockey pundit Stan Fischler had already covered the same ground. Hockey, he wrote:

is a specialized brand of entertainment, selling *machismo* as one of its three prime products along with skill and speed. Those who promote the NHL in the big money markets of television, radio and publishing stress the violent nature of the sport more than any other aspect of hockey. Its color and sense of adventure are all portrayed by these very same players. "If I had my way," says one NHL owner, "I'd toss every helmet in the trash can. I want my fans to see each of my players as a different personality. Violence is one of our assets, but you can't promise it as well when too many guys are wearing headgear."

It is a measure of hockey's romance with violence that Fischler, an otherwise sensible man, wholeheartedly supports such actions. "The point is simple," he wrote, "if big-league hockey players are so adventuresome, as they claim to be, and as tough as advertised, then a certain element of chance must be taken by them as part of their jobs." And Fischler does not stop at helmets; like some twentieth-century Emperor Claudius, he would order goalies to remove their facemasks as well: "Because of the mask, it's no longer fun to watch goalies. I do not want to see Tony Esposito's mask, I want to see his expression-filled face as the enemy threatens . . ."

Although no one has as yet suggested that footballers slough off their helmets and faceguards for the titillation of the fans, football too is guilty of selling itself on the promise of bloodshed and broken bones. Violence is the image that the NFL has chosen to project; "Kill the quarterback!" is the closest thing that the league has to a corporate logo. Mean Joe Greene not only wins games, he also fills stadiums.

In this, television has proved the NFL's perfect partner. Once the cameras would piously avert their lenses to the time clock during an "incident"; now they devour "incidents" like popcorn, spitting them out in endless instant replays.* *Sports Illustrated*: "Listen to Howard Cosell bleat with ill-concealed excitement after a defensive back has all but destroyed a wide receiver. Brutal contact is one thing pro football is selling . . ." Which is perhaps a little hard on Howard Cosell; there are far more dutiful sportscasters building football's image. In a recent Steelers/Baltimore game, the commentator delivered a gem which would have brought a blush even to

---

* Violent instant replay is not just an aberration of the American networks; in contact sports around the world – from soccer to motor racing – "incidents" are now given as much exposure as victories or goals. My most graphic memory of Australian Rules football is of an incident which became known as the "Peck/Sawley Incident," in which a famous full-forward dropped an opposing fullback with a perfect right to the jaw. Now, a decade and a half later, the image of Peck's fist whipping out and Sawley's head bouncing in slow motion on the turf is still crystal clear in my memory, the legacy of countless instant replays.

Ted Lindsay's scarred cheeks: "When you get someone down, stomp on him! It's an old cliché, but it sure applies!"

"They sell us pro football like they sold us the Second World War – the right films," said psychiatrist Arnold Mandell. "Rozelle – he's the genius of public relations, the genius of the field. He sold football to television and they are *exquisitely* aware of the image." It is an image which has now become totally accepted, and not just by sports fans. In all the furor over the effects of televised violence, not one voice to my knowledge has ever been raised against pro football.

The success which both football and hockey have enjoyed in selling themselves has induced other sports to exploit their violent sides. Some, one can't help thinking, live more in hope than in expectation. Tennis, for instance, which in America now advertises its professional matches like something out of *The Wild Bunch*: ". . . the ball crashing at close to one hundred miles an hour . . . real men slashing at the net . . . superb athletes ready for anything . . ." Ilie Nastase, ever-threatening to explode on court and savage a linesman, has proved a promoter's dream. In England recently a first-class tennis tournament was advertised by a series of huge bill-boards depicting Nastase and Jimmy Connors smashing each other over the head with their racquets.

Other sports have taken pro football's object lesson more seriously – American soccer, for example. American promoters have long been con-scious of the money to be made from the game if only players could be per-suaded to thump each other more. In 1967, with American soccer still in its struggling infancy, British author Paul Gardner recounted the story of a soccer club director from Atlanta who visited an English soccer game and chanced to witness a punch-up. "That's what this game needs," he crowed in delight. "This'll make the hockey men worry."

With soccer now making considerable inroads into American sport, the game is leaning more and more toward violence as a short cut to popular success. The "one-on-one" confrontation, much beloved of American sports commentators, is now a common term in soccer's promotional vocabulary, started by advertisements promising an all-out showdown between Pelé and George Best. When Pelé uncharacteristically punched an opponent during his final season, the replay was shown over and over, Pelé was elevated several notches on the ladder of sports heroes, and the pro-moters must have clapped until their hands hurt. "While record breaking attendance figures are lining pockets around the leagues, crowd titillating – and violent – episodes are on the increase," wrote soccer journalist Donald Edgington in an article which appeared in *Soccer Corner* headlined "A New and Violent Game." "The 'blood match' publicity hypes of pro hockey may be only a season or two away in soccer."

For some promoters a season or two is too long to wait. In 1978 a group of sporting entrepreneurs led by Jerry Saperstein, son of the Harlem Globetrotters' founder Abe, came up with a new twist to the game – Super Soccer, a bastardized form of field soccer played indoors. Super Soccer's similarities to hockey are unmistakable: the game is fast, hard and played in a pit, and even has a penalty box. "What we have is a product which is superior to soccer because it is tailored to *American tastes*," said Mr. Saperstein, unveiling his creation to the press. "The ball will be in play constantly. It will incorporate the traditional soccer skills, the excitement and speed of pro basketball, high scores and body contact."

If there were any lingering doubts in the minds of the assembled reporters as to what constituted "American taste," they were quickly dispelled by one of Mr. Saperstein's associates, Richard Ragone. "American players," said Ragone, "will fit into this game because even though they don't have quite the same skills as the Europeans, they are more *physical* and *aggressive*." Then, in the manner of all entrepreneurs trying to sell their souls without leaving a hole in their chests, Ragone hastily added: "I am not saying this will be a rough game. There may be a little shoving and a little kicking, but we won't allow it to get out of hand. The worst we'll have is a few broken legs." The wheel has now come full circle; one century after choosing skill in preference to brute force, soccer is back with hacking.

Crunch Crosscheck Meets the Roller Queen

Super Soccer is what remains after a promoter has debased a traditional sport by attempting to build gates with brutality. Wrestling becomes all-in pro wrestling, motorcycling turns into Evel Knievel, and so on. However, this century has seen the emergence of another set of sporting spectacles – games which have materialized out of thin air and been glued together solely by violence. They are inventions of violence, if you like – nothing more and nothing less, even though their inventors contrive to sugar the pill with talk of "athleticism" and "skill."

The first of these twentieth-century spectacles to emerge was the much-reviled and revered Roller Derby. The Derby was the invention of an American marathon dance promoter, Leo Seltzer, who, so the story goes, first outlined the game on a tablecloth in a Chicago restaurant in 1935. It was a simple enough sport – two teams whizzing around a banked track on rollerskates trying to lap each other – but it had two winning features: half of each team was female, and every move was made with outrageous violence.

As with pro wrestling, most of the Roller Derby's violence – the chair throwing, the hair pulling, the eye gouging, etc. – was purely theatrical with only occasional bursts of genuine malevolence showing through. No matter, the Derby barnstormed its way across America throughout the '40s in a blaze of publicity, delighting small town crowds wherever it played and in the big cities drawing tens of thousands of fans. Toward the end of the decade the bubble had burst and the game was faltering, the victim of a hostile press who refused to treat it as true sport. But Seltzer turned his attentions to television, and the boom began all over again. In New York the Derby was covered three nights a week in a prime time slot; then it was relayed all over the country. By 1950 it had topped the television ratings and become, in the words of the *New York Times*'s TV columnist, "an accepted way of life in pub and parlor." Again it was not to last. By the mid-'50s Roller Derby had become one of the first victims of television overexposure, and support dwindled.

Since then the game has come and gone, sometimes its coverage drawing more than pro football matches during a boom, at other times slipping back to obscure channels and late night slots. But it has never entirely disappeared. All the while its players have tirelessly criss-crossed America – and, indeed, the world – playing to audiences who love the sight of skaters careering across the track at 30 mph into a guard rail.

Today the Roller Derby still survives, although the days when it could draw 50,000 fans to Chicago's White Sox Park – as it did less than a decade ago – now seem well behind it. Metamorphosing as the Roller Game, it is now more or less confined to boxing promoter Aileen Eaton's scruffy Olympic auditorium in downtown Los Angeles. There once a week the "hometown" Thunderbirds take on one of three other "visiting" teams – the New York Bombers, the Texas Outlaws or the Chicago Hawks – which are all in fact based in Los Angeles and all owned by the same organization. Every Sunday night edited highlights of the game go out on a small local channel.

The game itself has changed not at all; the action is nonstop, half the players are still female, and it remains at first glance a painfully savage business. Without the violence, said veteran Ralphie Validerez, one of the game's most famous sons, "it would be like *Ben Hur* without the extras." The other players agreed. I spoke with Lenny Silverman, at 32 one of the current game's leading bad guys:

Lenny, tell me, how did you get into this business?

"Well, I watched it on TV and I just liked the way they were skating out there. There's a lot of violence which I've always felt I'd like to get into . . . the combat of one man against one man."

Is it really as tough as it looks?

"I've played everything," he said, "hockey, football, soccer, baseball, basketball, a little boxing, wrestling. The Roller Game's the most violent sport I've ever participated in. You don't have any protection compared to like football and hockey, and it's a contact sport on the same level, where you're hittin' a guy and he's hittin' you."

Do you get injured?

"I broke my nose eight or nine times, broke my ankle, got a set of broken shoulders . . . every conceivable injury a guy can have."

So you really try to hurt each other out there.

"You get so *violent* out there you lose control. You pick up an object and . . . you lose your temper real fast out there."

It's not just theatrics?

"It's not theatrics. I been hurt too many times for theatrics. It's like rugby or any of those. . . . It's the same thing. Those guys are going out for blood just like we are . . . tryin' to win."

To win? But doesn't the home side always just manage to squeak through by a single point or two?

"It's a very serious competitive business."

Some of that is no doubt true. "All the fellas," one of the girls told me, "have those huge knuckles because they get that . . . whaddya call it? Calcium? . . . from punching each other." And they do.

The fans are also just as they have always been: cheerfully gullible, bloodthirsty and strongly inclined toward taking matters into their own hands. It is these militantly "ordinary folks" – mums, dads, infants and grannies (many grannies) – who shout and scream abuse at the players, race up to the guard rails in a righteous fury after the corrupt referee unfairly penalizes the home team yet again, and shake their fists in the face of the visiting villain who turns with marvelous aplomb to give them the finger. I asked Bob Martin, a 20-year veteran, now retired, about his fans:

> Oh, they've tried to run me off the freeway, refused to serve me gas or food in restaurants, tore up my car, stuff like that. Once they tried to shoot me, here in the Olympic! Had a gun! The officer stopped it and nobody knew about it until after the game. It gets a little scary once in a while.

Yes, he added, the fans were still the same, perhaps even a little more so.

In fact, the only real change in the sport is that there are now less of them. Gates which once drew ten and fifteen thousand now average around three or four – on a good night possibly five. The television audience is not much better – a bare ten thousand. The Roller Game is once more scraping the bottom of the sports barrel, a depressing state of affairs for its chief, Bill Griffith, Sr. Mr. Griffith, a surprisingly articulate and polished man for the promoter of a sport which has so long been associated with Neanderthals on wheels, attributes much of the decline to the effects of the economic downturn on "the plain Sadie and Joe from average families . . . the sort of people the Roller Game attracts." Recession hits everybody hard, he said, but none quite so hard as those providing the working man's pleasures.

There was, however, a second and more interesting reason for the Roller Game's predicament. According to Mr. Griffith, football and ice hockey have now cornered the market on violence. As both have become more visibly violent, they have encroached upon what was once the sole preserve of pro wrestling and the Roller Game, a fact which greatly annoys Mr. Griffith:

I feel they have actually contrived a form of violence to attract the crowd and yet keep it on a very upper class level by rationalizing these acts as being feats of combat and athletic prowess. Then everyone feels that it's all right. But when Mr. and Mrs. America, or plain Molly and Joe get the same kicks out of watching this type of thing – excitement on a [roller] track or a wrestling ring – then the tendency is for the snobs to look down their noses. In other words, it's a double standard. In fact, there is no difference at all.

Was he bitter about this?

No, not bitter. I used to be, but you cannot be bitter about something you can't do anything about. I just feel a little sad that there are so many intellectual sheep being led down the primrose path kidding themselves that what they are watching and what they are doing is okay, but who don't let the little people – Mr. and Mrs. Average – have the same kicks. I guess it's like fornication: if dogs do it it's dirty, but if humans do it it's quite all right.

Mr. Griffith hoped that there was a Roller Game resurgence looming on the horizon, and he may well be right. At half time during the Roller Game, dozens of children, all perfectly dressed in official Roller Game helmets and leather shorts, take over the track to play a mini-game. Later I watched these infants practicing at their training rink and it was obvious that they had the game down pat – even to the extent of staging mock fist fights. However, just to be on the safe side, Bill Griffith had already begun to diversify. When I spoke to him his latest interest was Thai kick boxing, a "good sport," he said, with plenty of action. "I just hate to go watch a waltz for several rounds," he explained, "then some guy gets tired – I guess of holding the other guy up – and lets his guard down and *powie!* in comes the right, there goes the blood, and suddenly everyone is going out of their minds. But they don't stop to consider that probably for the first five or six rounds they were bored stiff because nothing happened. I think sports are entertaining and that they should be just that."

The Roller Game's true heir, however, is – or was – box lacrosse, or "boxla" as it was once known. It could be argued that box lacrosse was simply an offshoot from Canada's moribund professional field lacrosse leagues of the 1930s. But despite some similarities, the two games were so far removed from each other that box lacrosse could legitimately claim to be a sport invented from nothing solely for the purpose of retailing violence. From the beginning, boxla was a fearsome experience, and, not surprisingly, an instant success. First appearing in 1930, by 1931 a professional league had been formed and, a year after that, it had overtaken field lacrosse as the official lacrosse game of Canada.

So great was the Canadians' enthusiasm for their rough infant that concerted efforts were soon being made to follow ice hockey's successful migration across the border into the northern United States. Boxla's future seemed assured, as the New York *Herald Tribune* was grudgingly forced to concede: "There is no gainsaying the fact that we relish roughness in our sports." However, the expected support failed to materialize. Hockey had filled all new American sporting markets and boxla was ignored. Finally the league went bankrupt and the game returned to Canada where enthusiasm quickly dwindled. Then, forty years later with ice hockey's expansion teams brawling their way across the US behind Philadelphia's Flyers, somebody remembered boxla.

In March 1974 the blue-jawed warriors of the newly incorporated National Box Lacrosse League were unleashed upon an expectant American public. The NBLL was wholly dedicated to the premise that violence sells seats, and for weeks prior to the opening game it had waged a formidable advertising campaign which shamelessly promised sports fans nothing less than the chance of attending a ninety-minute public mugging. The league's principal ambassador of ill-will was a scarred, toothless cartoon character named Crunch Crosscheck, whose televised messages left as little to the imagination as his motto – "Ya gotta be *mean* ta play lacrosse!" The point was further driven home by a series of radio advertisements which featured "interviews" with various historical bogeymen – Attila the Hun, Genghis Khan – who all professed envy at the way box lacrosse organized its massacres. ("The meanest game in the woild!" whistled Attila.) Philadelphia fans were easier to sell; they were simply advised to think of box lacrosse as "hockey, where every team is the Philadelphia Flyers."

"Sure, we promoted violence," Andy Dolich, the former publicity director of the Maryland Arrows told me later. "We felt to get a mule's attention you have to punch it in the teeth. We had to get right in the public's face. We tried to get across to people that if you want a vicarious thrill for two hours, box lacrosse is the game."

In fact, what took place in the arenas was not so far short of what had been promised. The NBLL's laws allowed almost anything in the pursuit of player or ball. There was no off-side rule, and a thirty-second time limit on attacks kept the game moving at a frenetic pace. The players themselves were helmeted and heavily padded, and carried hefty sticks which they wielded clublike with abandon. Unlike in hockey their feet were firmly planted on the ground which made for crippling but undeniably spectacular collisions, with players flying ten feet or more through the air.

The majority of the athletes were genuine bruisers, semiprofessionals who knocked off work at the General Motors plant on Friday evening, climbed aboard a DC9, and flew across the border for a game later that same night. When the game finished they flew back home. Like their hockey brethren it was nothing for them to sustain a ten-inch gash, have it stitched at half-time and be back on the boards at the resumption of play. They were also under no illusions about what was required of them. Commented Sy Roseman, a former organizer with the Philadelphia Wings:

> When Philly went down to Washington to play the Maryland Arrows it was always a bloodbath – two very aggressive teams who didn't like each other. This guy, Doug Favell, sat down next to me before the match on one occasion and the way he talked! How he was going to maim people, break people's legs . . . I just looked at him. Crazy!

Unlike the Roller Game, box lacrosse promised its fans real violence, real bloodshed and real injury, and it delivered them.

Initially this push into the darker reaches of the American psyche was a resounding success. On opening day the Philadelphia Wings, riding blatantly on the Flyers' coat-tails, drew 12,841 fans to the Spectrum *after* the Flyers had won the Stanley Cup in the same stadium that same afternoon. A minimum of between seven thousand and eight thousand supporters could be expected at every Wings/Arrows confrontation, with the attendance often rising above the ten thousand mark. In their second season the Arrows were averaging six thousand spectators a match – by any sporting standards a reasonable turnout, and for an unknown game played by unknown people who left the country immediately after the final whistle, remarkable.

"It turned a lot of people off, especially the sports writers," Sy Roseman told me. "They wouldn't come to it. They thought they wanted to see sport rather than violence. But it sure turned the fans on. The crowds loved the violence, absolutely loved it!" "There *was* a section of the public who were turned off," agreed Andy Dolich. "But there were many more people who thought it was the greatest thing they'd ever seen."

Sadly for them, box lacrosse survived only two seasons – the summers of '74 and '75. It would be nice to think the game failed because it represented some sort of ultimate limit to the fans' appetite for sporting blood. But that is wishful thinking. The NBLL disintegrated through underfinancing and mismanagement, both Roseman and Dolich agreed. It was the owners in several of the marginal towns, greedy for quick returns and not prepared to nurture their investment, who brought the league crashing. Box lacrosse was not killed at the turnstiles, it simply committed suicide. Where the organization had been adequate, the game had flourished.

"Philly was doing just great," said a wistful Sy Roseman. "We'd sold 2,500 season's tickets when it stopped and we could have sold 5,000. We really had a great following. The people of Philly loved it. You'd have no trouble in bringing it back in Philadelphia tomorrow."

Deathrace 500

The Roller Game and box lacrosse, Crunch Crosscheck notwithstanding, are, however, small beer compared with some of the other violent sports invented over the past century, in particular those propelled by the internal combustion engine. Just as soon as engines were able to move wheels faster than 30 mph, motor sport became our most dangerous game, its history a history of accident, injury and fatalities.

The first official motor race was the Paris–Rouen Motor Trial of 1894. A bare four years later the first racing driver was killed. But it wasn't until the Paris–Madrid road race of 1903 that the full extent of the internal combustion engine's lethal capacities was witnessed; during the event at least five drivers and their mechanics and, although the figures were never officially released, probably more than a dozen spectators died. Since then death and motor racing have been inseparable. As cars became faster and lighter, and the number of top-level competitions increased (America's Vanderbilt Cup, founded in 1904; European Grand Prix racing, begun in 1906), the casualties soared. By 1908 Vanderbilt had been forced to move his Cup race from the open roads to an enclosed circuit, such were the number of tragedies. A year later the Indianapolis racetrack was unveiled – $2\frac{1}{2}$ miles of stone and asphalt. The first time the track was used it broke up, killing one driver, two mechanics and two spectators. Indy has been killing people indiscriminately ever since.

Motor racing is unique in that it kills its stars with just as much – and perhaps even more – enthusiasm as it kills its novices. Skill and experience afford scant protection; the higher up the ladder a driver climbs, the closer to the edge he drives, and consequently the more exposed he becomes. "The line between maximum speed and crashing is so thin, so thin," said Formula 1 veteran Wolfgang Von Trips a few hours before the 1961 Italian Grand Prix. "It could happen tomorrow. That's the thing about this business. You never know." Von Trips was killed later that afternoon. From 1946 to 1963, 175 competition car drivers died racing, 50 of whom were, like Von Trips, at the top of their profession. Since then Von Trips's line has become all but invisible. As Mario Andretti remarked in 1977: "The margin of error is nonexistent, and I mean nonexistent."

The names of many of those killed in recent years are sadly familiar: Jim Clark, who hit a tree at Hockenheim in 1968; Piers Courage and Jochen Rindt, killed while practicing for the 1970 Italian Grand Prix; Bruce McLaren, killed in that same year; Joseph Siffert, burned to death at Brands Hatch in 1971; 1972, Josephe Bonnier, killed at Le Mans; 1973, Roger Williamson; Francois Cevert, killed that same year while practicing for the US Grand Prix at Watkins Glen; 1974, Peter Revson and Helmut Koennigg; 1977, Tom Pryce, brained by a fire marshall's extinguisher; Ronnie Peterson, crushed at Monza in 1978. Barely a season passes without one or more of that elite coterie of Grand Prix drivers vanishing in a ball of fire. "When I hand over the car to a driver at the factory I cannot escape the thought that I may be going to his funeral in a few days," said Enzo Ferrari in 1956. "One by one I watched close friends die on the race track," said Jackie Stewart in 1973.

They are just Formula 1 names; not included in this grim list are the names of the famous killed at Indianapolis, nor any motorcycling deaths, nor the names of those killed attempting speed records. Neither is there any mention of spectator disasters, for motor racing is again unique in that it exacts almost as much of a levy on those watching as those participating. In Argentina in 1953 twelve spectators were killed according to the official figures, although the true number was undoubtedly much higher. At Le Mans in 1955 eighty-one fans died. During Italy's Mille Miglia of 1957 the Marquis de Portage and his co-driver Edward Nelson crashed their Ferrari into the crowd killing themselves and eleven others. In Cuba the following year another six spectators died. And at Monza in 1961 when Wolfgang Von Trips ploughed into the crowd at 150 mph he took fifteen onlookers with him. In these few races alone, at least 126 dead. Although the fans are now far better protected, tragedies such as the four spectators killed in the 1975 Spanish Grand Prix do still occur. After applauding the increased safety measures adopted by the Monte Carlo circuit in 1975, Jackie Stewart added: "I would be a hypocrite to deny that even here there is a possibility of something terrible happening." Death for a sport which now measures its speeds at over 200 mph has become an inevitability.

Motor racing's injuries are commensurate with its mortality rate. Madelaine Read, wife of British motorcycle veteran Phil Read, eight times world champion, attends every meeting carrying £1,000 in notes in her pocketbook. "You never know when your man will have an accident and you'll need to pay cash for a specialist or a private plane to get him home," she explained. During the course of his career her husband has suffered broken collarbones, back, pelvis, legs, arms, fingers and ankle. His long-time rival Barry Sheene has required even more medical attention, breaking both legs, his right ankle twice, his left ankle four times, two fingers, nine ribs, his right wrist once, his left wrist three times, both collarbones and a forearm. He has also suffered seven compression fractures of vertebrae and innumerable cuts, bruises and abrasions. His worst accident was falling off his bike at Daytona while traveling at close to 180 mph:

> I could feel the skin coming off my shoulder as I slid along. . . . Everything hurt. I could feel all this hot stuff running down my back. It was blood. I could see blood all around me on the ground. . . . I went to take off my glove and my wrist was bending three inches above where it should bend . . .

"It's tough to crash a car and come out of it without a scratch," one sprint car driver whose father had died racing told me. "No matter what kind of a crash it is – how easy it is – you come out of it sore. The centrifugal force is terrific. I've seen guys break their arms from just stoppin' . . . hittin' a wall and just stoppin'." Sprint cars are little more than guided missiles; a light frame with a 550 horsepower engine attached. But even the solid steel chariots of the stock car circuits, with their massive roll bars and heavy bumpers, afford little protection at 180 mph. "I had two bad ones last year," a young Florida driver told me. "One was a multiple roll over and it left me with bruised intestines and bruised internal organs and a couple of

---

If there is one driver who hasn't awoken in the middle of the night, fingers clutching a sweat stained pillow, eardrums bursting with shrieking tires, that man, I tell you, tumbled off another planet.

Juan Fangio, Argentinian motor-racing champion, 1961

> ** People would say it could have happened out on a highway or he could have gotten run over on the road, and I just kept thinking, well, it didn't happen that way. It happened in a race car, and if he hadn't been in the race car he'd be alive. **
>
>

Julie Horton, widow of a stock-car driver,
interviewed by **Mark Silber** in *Racing Stock* (1976)

broken ribs. Later on in the year I had a ninety to zero dead stop on a small track – I impaled the car right on the end of a concrete wall. The result was eleven different broken bones and forty stitches in my face and a lotta discomfort." After reeling off a list of broken bones suffered in a recent smash, Indianapolis champion Bobby Unser concluded with the throwaway line: "You always break your feet in a deal like that anyhow." As with bullfighters, few drivers and riders escape unscathed at the end of their careers. It is a cruel sport; one need only look at Niki Lauda's ruined face, burned as he frantically struggled with his seat belt at the Nürburgring in 1976, to know that:

> They showed me my face in a mirror. I could not believe it. I looked like some grotesque animal because my whole head and neck were swollen to three times the normal size. You would not believe this to be a human being. Everything was a mass of nothing.

Cruel as it is, motor racing is also extraordinarily popular. In the US fifty million auto racing tickets are sold each year – one million during the Indianapolis 500 week alone – making auto racing second only to horse racing in paid attendances. Millions around the world follow the Grand Prix circus each year. Crowds average over a hundred thousand at major motorcycle events throughout Britain and Europe. In England cinder track Speedway is second only to soccer in popularity. Then there are the sprint cars, midgets, motor cross races, hill climbs, enduros and the untold millions sitting glued to their televisions watching events which have become a staple of Saturday afternoon viewing.

There are a number of reasons why motor racing has grown so popular. Cars and motorcycles have become a major part of mid-twentieth-century living and racing machines – especially the recognizable stock models – offer irresistible possibilities for identification. Like modern hunting weapons they are also extremely alluring gadgets, thrilling toys for adults. Racing drivers and riders have themselves become personalities with their own fan followings. The spine-tingling fascination of pure speed (five million a year watch drag racing in America), the ear-shattering noise of powerful engines, the heavy charge of *machismo* which permeates the sport like the smell of butane fuel . . . all are powerful attractions.

But the biggest attraction is the delicious sense of danger which motor racing elicits. It is a risk sport and, although there are a number of others almost equally as risky (mountaineering, hang gliding, parachuting and so on), motor racing is so far the only one to have packaged its risks, promoted them and sold them to the public as violent thrills. It is the chance of witnessing the Formula 1 Ferrari cartwheeling through the fence which attracts the crowds, not the tedium of endless lap after endless lap around an oval circuit. It is the stock car driver locking door handles with an opponent, losing control and slamming through the rest of the field like a bowling ball hitting the pins which keeps everyone returning.

It is an ancient charge, this, and one which motor racing has long denied. Yet the evidence to support it is equally as ancient. The Greek and Roman version of motor sports was chariot racing, a sport viewed in much the same way as we regard our own motorized circuits – as violent spectacles. The chariots, sometimes forty or more at a time, ran the length of the Hippodrome or the Circus Maximus, circled a column and returned. The beginning of each race was just as hazardous as the start of an Indianapolis 500, with drivers jostling for position on the narrow circuit. The stretch of track around the turning post was even worse, allowing only a few fortunate drivers to pass by unscathed; the rest were jammed together in a grinding, splintering mass. Accidents occurred nonstop throughout the race, with many drivers being hurled from their chariots and dragged along the track by the reins which they traditionally wound around their waists. The Romans erected a barrier down the center of the track so as to minimize head-on collisions; the Greeks did not bother. There is also reason to believe that horses were purposely frightened when they reached the back straight of the Hippodrome, causing them to rear and upset their chariots. The mortality rate among charioteers was almost as high as that of the gladiators; most of the monuments unveiled to celebrate drivers' triumphs were erected by young widows. As is motor racing today, chariot racing in both Greece and Rome was an extremely popular pastime.

If our race circuits were pillars of safety with never so much as a fishtail or a spinout, it is a reasonable assumption that attendances would plummet. "Oh, I think there's a little element of that, yeah," said stock car star Bobby Allison when I asked him if accidents were a major attraction for the fans. "I think that people are excitable and that the idea of a crash is, ah . . . it keeps 'em, ah, *stirred up*." Few fans I spoke to agreed. As usual it was the younger spectators who were the least inhibited: "I like to see 'em wreck," said Scott, a 13-year-old Californian stock car fan. "Sometimes they go a whole race and don't wreck – only have a little spinout or something – and that's *boring*," added his friend Marty. Their parents shook their heads and talked of driving skills.

Yet it is the most violent events which attract the largest crowds – the locked door handle driving of the stock car circuit, the high-speed jeopardy of the Grand Prix and the Indy 500. "When cars start spinning and crashing, there's no place to hide at Indianapolis," said racing driver Peter Revson in 1974, and that is what makes Indianapolis great – wrecks. 1963, when rookie Dave MacDonald's car hit the barrier and exploded, killing him and another; 1966, which eliminated eleven cars and damaged another five before they had even reached the first turn; 1973, which killed Swede Savage; 1975 in which Tom Sneva destroyed his car so spectacularly – these are the races that are remembered, as the Indianapolis promoters are only too well aware. A few years back the Indy promoters took out a twelve-page advertisement in *Sports Illustrated* to herald the imminent arrival of that year's 500. The advertisement took the form of a panel of "experts" recalling "the most exciting and unusual moments at each given spot on the track." What the experts remembered was little more than great crashes of the past:

Turn One: 1956, when Paul Russo started eighth in the red and cream Novi, the car everybody loved, and was in first place by the end of nine laps. Holding the lead through the twentieth lap, he roared down the front straightaway and, just as he got to Turn One, he blew a tire and ran into the wall. The crash could be heard blocks away . . .

Turn Two: There would have been many arguments about this one until 1975 when Tom Sneva got sideways and began flipping as he came into Two. By the time he was halfway through the turn the car had slammed against the wall and ripped into a hundred pieces . . .

Turn Three: Again most of our experts agreed on this one – the Duke Nalon crash in 1949. Nalon had started on the pole and was really moving by Lap 23. He came down the back chute and backed off for Turn Three. But at that exact moment, the rear axle let go – the car spun around backwards and hit the wall. It burst into flames and, as it slid along the wall, it left a path of fire all through Three. The entire wall was engulfed in flame . . .

Turn Four: This seems to be the turn where most people disagree because so many accidents have happened there, many fatal . . .

Front Straightaway: Jack Turner . . . Turner's Offy-powered Kurtis cracked into the wall and began flipping end over end down the chute in front of terror-stricken, jam-packed bleachers . . .

This, remember, is an advertisement, presumably offering people what they want.

Do fans watch motor sports to see crashes? I asked Merv Wright, in 1977 the British manager of the world champion Suzuki works team. I had expected the stock denial; Wright's answer surprised me. "There's a lot of them do," he said, after a moment's hesitation:

> . . . a lot of them. I'd hate to hazard a guess just how many because I think I'd upset myself a bit. But there's no question that a great many people go to watch motor sports for crashes. It's fairly apparent the way people situate themselves at fairly well known "tricky" spots, shall we say, on the racetrack that that is what they are looking for. And it's curious that whenever there is a spectacular crash of any sort usually half the press photographers present just happen to be on the spot at that time and get it recorded on film. It's got to be a bit more than coincidence.

The media, and television in particular, is acutely aware of motor sport's violent attractions. The cartwheeling Ferrari is replayed over and over again in slow motion with perhaps an arrow superimposed to show where the driver – or a piece of him – is. (In one notorious press episode of recent times a leading New York newspaper actually arrowed a driver's clutching hand as he burned to death in his car.) It is the crashes which make the television commentators' voices catch in their throats with excitement. Film of Barry Sheene's Daytona crash was shown again and again on British television, far more than film of Sheene actually winning the event would have been. According to Merv Wright, although the continual repetition did not make Sheene a household name, "it certainly helped."

It is this awareness of the fans' appetite which has led the networks to throw their full sponsorship weight behind a number of motor sports which concentrate solely on destruction. The oldest and most widely known of these events is the Demolition Derby, invented in 1958 by one Larry Mendelsohn, a part-time stock car driver. Mendelsohn's career is an oily-rag-to-riches fable. While racing around a small circuit out on Long Island one night, Mendelsohn crashed his stock car through a fence and into the grandstand. As he climbed from the wreckage he noticed that far more spectators were interested in his crash than in the race. He immediately scraped together some money, bought the ailing circuit – Islip Raceway –

and devoted himself to promoting races dedicated solely to destruction. By placing advertisements in local newspapers reading "Wanted: 100 Men Not Afraid to Die," he recruited drivers willing to smash into each other. The last car left running at the end of the night was the winner.

The idea was a spectacular success. The Derby rapidly paid off both Mendelsohn's and Islip's debts and was soon a regular feature of ABC's *Wide World of Sports*. By the mid-1970s its ratings were among the highest for a televised sporting event – 25 million viewers in 1974. In 1975 CBS negotiated a five-year contract on the Derby, reputedly for $750,000.

Demolition Derby's success has spawned a number of imitators: Blackout Demolition, in which the winner is the last car with its lights still shining; Football Demolition, which uses a smaller car – usually a red Volkswagen – as a ball to be smashed over a goal line; and Figure 8 racing, which has stock cars criss-crossing from opposite directions at the center of a circuit in what amounts to a 50 mph game of "chicken." All of these events exist solely as a means of retailing traffic accidents, although it should be added that they look far worse than they really are; few Demolition Derby drivers ever die. Which is perhaps one of the reasons why the Derby and its offshoots, for all their millions of fans, are still confined to the motor racing basement.

Even among those willing to acknowledge that crashes are an integral part of motor sport's attraction, very few are likely to consider that the fans are interested in bloodshed and injury. The overwhelming consensus is that the highpoint of a race is the crash in which the driver walks away unscathed. As one race track proprietor interviewed by Jerry Bledsoe in *The World's Number One, Flat-out, All-Time Great, Stock Car Racing Book* (1974) put it:

> They's a certain amount that likes to see spinouts and wrecks and all. I'd say they'd preferably rather not see 'em git hurt, but they do like a certain amount. Why do people like football so well? Because of the body contact. And anytime you got a car spinning, or hit a wall, it seems like it does 'em a little good.

Other drivers and organizers I spoke to expressed similar beliefs. The possibility of physical harm being an attraction is one of the great unmentionables around race tracks. Yet that possibility is perhaps more real than most racing people would care to admit.

The most obvious evidence of this is the way in which crowds invariably surge toward a crash after it has occurred, the fans piling up against the wire fencing to witness the aftermath in much the same way as people slow down on freeways to get a closer look at accidents. When British driver Roger Williamson was killed during the 1973 Dutch Grand Prix, the chief of the

Zandfoort police, Mr. J. D. van Maris, defended his decision not to stop the race with the explanation: "If we stopped the race, fifty thousand people would have tried to get to the scene. It would have been impossible to control them and there would have been more danger."

Every Friday night at the Rugnis vegetable market on the outskirts of Paris, hundreds of young French motorcycle enthusiasts hold impromptu races, hurling their machines around a perilous circuit which has no marshalls and no safety precautions. The barriers are the spectators – two thousand and more on an average night. Over the past five years sixteen people have been killed at Rungis, and the injury toll now approaches four hundred. When there is an accident the spectators surge forward as one toward the noise. "That," commented the Paris newspaper *Liberation*, "is what they are there for."

In Britain the Isle of Man TT road race is one of the biggest events of the motorcycling year. The Isle of Man is a killer; in its seventy-four years of existence 124 riders have died, victims of a tortuous $37\frac{3}{4}$-mile circuit over mountains, through villages and past a lethal array of telephone poles, mailboxes and fences. As Barry Sheene, who refuses to ride there, once said: "All I could see everywhere was brick walls." In the era of 200 mph motorbikes, the TT is a savage anachronism. In 1978 five riders died – including three sidecar competitors killed in one crash – and two spectators. Death is omnipresent. "What on earth is all the fuss about?" snapped the circuit's press officer when reporters pressed him for details of the triple sidecar fatality. "We've had more than three in one day before." Nevertheless each year has seen bigger and bigger crowds at the TT. 1978 set another record, the fans congregating at the circuit's "danger spots" under the padded bridges and beside the blind curves. Skill is what Barry Sheene always believed racing fans were after. "But perhaps the people who go to the Isle of Man are looking for something a bit different," he said in 1978.

The scars of racing injury provide their own special fascination. One of the most heavily publicized features of the 1976 Grand Prix season was Niki Lauda's mutilated face. The frenzy with which press photographers and the racing public jostled to see what was left of Lauda shocked even long-term Grand Prix journalists. As Lauda lay on the verge of death in a Mannheim hospital after the crash, photographers burst into his room to snap close-ups "like hyenas on the prowl to bite off an image of disaster," as one correspondent wrote. On Lauda's return to racing he was followed constantly by a pack of "thrill seekers," as the press called them, thrusting Instamatics to within inches of his face. Lauda stared grimly ahead through it all. Eventually he fled to the seclusion of Spain.

"This is human nature, unfortunately," said Merv Wright. "There is always this morbid aspect. You will inevitably get a major race report on half a column on the third page of the sports section. But I guarantee that if anybody gets seriously injured or killed then it's headlines on the front page. That's what people want to read about."

Exactly why is difficult to say. Perhaps it is an attempt to reach out and touch mortality. Perhaps it is to reassure themselves that the sport really is as tough as it claims to be. Perhaps they are just thrilled by spilt blood – somebody else's, of course. Whatever the reason, it is not considered an entirely satisfactory year unless some well-known racer vanishes in a ball of flame. Drivers are meant to crash – how can they be giving everything if they don't? – and if a top driver retires at his peak unscathed there is a palapable feeling of disappointment underpinning his send-off testimonials. Drivers such as Jackie Stewart and Niki Lauda were, and are, despised for driving what the fans considered to be "carcful" races. When Lauda led a campaign for safer circuits the fans hung banners around the tracks which read "Niki the 20 km-an-hour driver, out!" When he pulled out of the Tokyo Grand Prix at the end of the 1976 season because of the hazardous weather conditions, he was branded by the press – headlines in Italy – and by many spectators as a coward. The aficionados of motor racing demand that, like bullfighters, their heroes lay their lives on the line every time they enter the arena. Nothing less will satisfy. When Argentina's legendary driver Juan Fangio retired, he retired an unpopular man. When asked why, he replied, "My only fault is being alive." Then, as if to underline the callous absurdity of his plight, he added, "It is a lonely fault among my generation of drivers."

The worst of motor racing's many disasters took place on June 12, 1955, during the twenty-four-hour Le Mans Endurance Race in France. It happened $2\frac{1}{2}$ hours into the race when the leading driver, Mike Hawthorn, pulled sharply into the pits causing fellow Briton Lance Macklin to swerve suddenly around him. Frenchman Pierre Levegh's Mercedes clipped the back of Macklin's Austin-Healey at 150 mph, rose fifteen feet, flew through the air and exploded "like a magnesium bomb" against the entrance of a concrete pedestrian tunnel. The impact tore the engine, front wheels and suspension from the car and hurled them into the packed public enclosure in front of the grandstand. Eighty-two people were killed amid scenes of appalling carnage.

Lance Macklin managed to wrestle his spinning Austin-Healey to a standstill several hundred yards further along the track. He climbed from the cockpit and began making his way back to the pits. In journalist Mark Kahn's book *Death Race* (1976), he recalled his thoughts:

As I walked along the earthern bank I could hear the exclamations from the crowd a few feet away: *"Quelle horreur!"* *"C'est affreux!"* How frightful! How ghastly! I had often found myself reacting against the crowds who thronged to motor races on the Continent. Not so much in England, where they went to see motor sport for the same reason that I was taking part in it, the fun and skill of it. Most of them on the Continent, it seemed to me were there only to see an accident. And when I heard them shouting how terrible it was, I felt like shouting back, "Well, that's why you came isn't it?" And in that moment I realized that I hated the crowd.

It was not until the next day when Macklin read the headlines that the full extent of the tragedy struck him. He returned to the circuit – the race was still in progress – to the spot where Levegh's engine and suspension had scythed through the spectators:

> The grass was soaked with blood and there was that awful smell of death you get in the air when there has been a lot of blood around. And the place was crowded. That same spot. I suppose they thought it must be a good place to be. Perhaps there would be another accident. . . . Even before this Le Mans, I rather disliked the crowds who went to motor races. . . . I always got the impression, especially in the Latin countries like Italy, or South America, that most of the crowd went there, as they went to a bullfight, hoping to see the matador gored to death. They went to motor racing hoping to see someone killed, or at any rate, have a bad crash. The car catches fire or goes end over end, and the driver is burned alive – that makes their motor-racing day. . . . They had come to see me die, or my friends die. And instead eighty of them had been killed. I knew it was terrible. And my mind was horrified. But I couldn't *feel* sorry.

Motor racing circuits are the true Colosseums of the twentieth century. They represent the modern arena of blood, courage, risk and violent death, in a form and on a scale which has not been seen since the days of Imperial Rome. Is it such an unreasonable contention, then, that motor racing's fans are separated from the Romans who once so enthusiastically packed the Colosseum by precious little more than just the passage of time?

Prime Time for Dying

The prince of motor sport is a man most racing drivers would contemptuously dismiss as a huckster and a carnival stuntman: the "legendary" Evel Knievel. Huckster, perhaps. But carnival stuntman? . . . no. There have been many "legendary" stuntmen in the past – Captain Joe Montford, who actually parachuted his motorcycle into the *real* Grand Canyon; Iron Man Irons; Speedy Babbs – all of whom performed equally spectacular and sometimes infinitely more daring stunts than Evel. Yet Evel has soared far above them all. Whereas they remained sideshow attractions, Evel is a star of the center ring, a modern American hero. Rich, idolized, revered, he has succeeded in insinuating himself into the folklore of the nation – quite an achievement for a "stuntman."

It seems to me that Evel Knievel has managed to assume such heroic proportions in the eyes of the American public for two basic reasons. The first is, oddly enough, that so many of Evel's daredevil projects actually fail. Evel's popularity stems not from the fact that he risks his neck, but that he breaks it. And not just once, but over and over again – almost every time, in fact, that he launches himself into space. Evel Knievel's career has been a history of expensive pratfalls. Consider his last few undertakings: in 1974 he attempted to jump the Snake River canyon and wound up plummeting to the bottom of the abyss; from there he moved to London to leap thirteen London buses which left him trapped beneath his bike with a fractured hand and a damaged spine after crashing on the landing ramp at 90 mph; from there he journeyed to the Chicago Amphitheater for his ill-fated flight across the shark tank which ended in the Michael Reese Hospital. Failures all of them, but all hugely successful.

Just how much failure means to Evel's success can be judged by the way in which he wears his ruptured heart on his ripped sleeve for all to see. Evel parades his injuries like badges of honor. "I can't keep track of my hospital time; it all sort of blurs together," he will tell one audience. "I've been on the operating table so many times that I count to twenty before I go under the anaesthetic," he will joke with another. When the Ideal Toy Company launched its "Evel Knievel Motorcycling Doll" in 1973, the selling line read: "It does everything that Evel does except go to the hospital." It seems that Evel is never happier than when he is discussing compressed vertebrae or fractured femurs.

As well he might be. For it is Knievel's willingness to sacrifice himself every time he jumps which has helped make his fortune. An Evel succeeding would be interesting; an Evel breaking his bones on the landing ramp at 90 mph is irresistible. The thrills of motor sport are danger, injury and death; Knievel offers two of these again and again, and in the minds of his adoring fans it must only be a matter of time before he delivers the third.

The second reason for Evel Knievel's extraordinary popularity is, of course, television. It is his good fortune to have been born into an age capable not only of broadcasting his daredevil exploits to the entire world if he so desired, but also of reproducing those feats in the minutest of slow-motion detail. When Captain Montford roared off the lip of the Grand Canyon he was probably watched by less than a handful of witnesses who saw little more than a puff of exhaust smoke and a flutter of parachute silk. When Evel Knievel was blasted into the blistering heat overhanging the Snake River, he was watched by millions, skewered for posterity on the lenses of a dozen strategically placed television cameras all eagerly recording every snapping bone and agonized grimace. Knievel uses television and television uses Knievel; so far the game has proved wonderfully beneficial for both parties.

According to the networks it is the public, not they, who are responsible for Evel Knievel's relentless media exposure. "Television is democratic," Kevin O'Malley, director of CBS's sports programs told me. "If Evel Knievel has a high-rated performance on one network, the tendency is for somebody to go and get Evel to do the same thing on our network. It is fair to say that we tend to follow an audience trend." There are many who would disagree, and with good cause. While it is true that television is a slave to its ratings, and ratings reflect the appetite of the viewing public, it would be naive in the extreme to believe that television is not at least partly responsible for building that appetite. Evel Knievel may be the prince of motor sports, but he is also the king of hype, a position which he has reached with the full collusion of the networks. Just one example: in the week before his Snake River leap, Knievel was the subject of two prime-time programs aired by the ABC network – a feature film and an in-depth documentary. By the day of the jump even the Eskimos must have been quivering in anticipation.

Just how culpable the networks are in molding public opinion is debatable. What is beyond debate is the fact that the public appetite for such displays is growing. "More people seem to be interested in watching somebody risk his neck, yes," said Kevin O'Malley:

> I really can say that people seem to respond to a larger element of violence in sports than they did even a couple of years ago. And the trend now seems to be increasing. I'll give you a perfect example, something they call full contact karate. That has become a viable sport for television exposure and I know that two years ago there was very little interest in it. Take *Evel Knievel's Death Defiers*, the ratings were extraordinarily good.

As public interest has increased, so too have the number of stuntmen willing to attempt bizarre and dangerous feats. "There's no question that you can in this day and age go out and find as many nuts as you want," said O'Malley. "The people I've had walk into this office! One guy wanted to hang himself. That's his particular schtick. Stands on a six-foot platform with a noose around his neck and jumps off it. The day after the Evel Knievel show a guy called me from England – still calls – who wanted to swim *through* the tank of sharks, not jump over it. I guess the definition of sports has gotten very fuzzy."

So with the public clamor for death sports and a long line of willing human sacrifices, just how far will television go? According to O'Malley, not much further. "There are people in television who have been made aware of the trend and there *is* a sensitivity. Even if the public's appetite for it becomes so great I don't think that television will just mindlessly feed that appetite. I suspect that the industry will draw its own line and that there is no way it will go over that line." He refused to program the hangman, for example. There was, he said, no chance of gladiators being televised live from Shea Stadium.

But hadn't there been talk of showing convicted murderer Gary Gilmore's execution on television?

"There *was* some talk of local stations carrying Gary Gilmore's execution. Somebody asked what percentage of television homes out there would watch it. I know I wouldn't and I mean that. But I think a sufficiently large number would watch it that we would all be very disappointed. It is an unfortunate side of people's fascination with danger and violence." O'Malley paused, staring down at his desk in silence. Then he sighed. "Look," he said, "I can't sit here and say nobody would ever put an execution on television. I know I wouldn't and I'm pretty sure nobody on this network ever would. But then again I've seen the standards change so much."

So how far off is sport from Rollerball, science fiction author William Harrison's gory motorized ball game of the future, with its armored motor-cycles, studded gauntlets and anything-goes rules? Perhaps not very far. The movie *Rollerball* was a box office smash, almost solely because of the game it was built around. At the close of shooting, the movie's stuntmen staged a mild version of the game in a 5,000-seat auditorium in Munich for their own amusement; 8,500 spectators showed up.

But the most telling reaction was that of a number of sports entrepreneurs. Following the film's release, producer Norman Jewison received more than half a dozen inquiries from both wealthy individuals and large corporations eager to purchase a Rollerball franchise. One organization presented meticulous plans for the game to be staged in the Houston Astrodrome; another had drawn up outlines for a Rollerball League. According to Jewison's publicity director, it was only Jewison's refusal to sell the rights to the game on moral grounds which has so far prevented science fiction from becoming contemporary sport.

8 SPORT AS CATHARSIS

THE MYTH EXPLODED

8 Sport as Catharsis
The Myth Exploded

Sport is the one sanctioned theater of real-life violence remaining in modern peacetime society. Only sport offers the opportunity of breaking a stranger's nose, destroying another man's knee ligaments or crashing an opponent against the boards without the threat of being thrown into prison as a homicidal maniac. Only sport offers the chance of taking a life solely for the pleasure of taking life, and being admired for it. Only sport offers the *spectacle* of all this – and more – for the price of a cheap ticket. Sport has it all: pain and injury, death and destruction, blood and guts, in ever-increasing doses. (War, of course, has much more, but war is abhorrent.)

Perhaps it will not always be so. Just as the Colosseum eventually withered and died, so too might our sporting entertainments grow less violent and less obsessed with winning. (Already several new "cooperative" games have surfaced in America over the last few years.) *New York Times* columnist Dave Anderson felt that sport was approaching a cutoff point after which the fans would turn away from violence. "People will watch violence only up to a point," he said. "But then they seem to realize what they're doing to themselves." Several other observers I spoke to expressed similar beliefs. "I don't think that what football really is is acceptable to the consciousness of America now," said psychiatrist Arnold Mandell. "It might have been in 1948, but now if the Marine Corps, say, mistreats its recruits, the recruits write their parents, the parents write their congressman and the congressman comes out here and cans the Marine sergeant. We just don't go for that anymore." Boxing, said Mandell, disappeared after enjoying enormous popularity during the 1940s because its violence was too naked. "I think football is also going to get too naked." Sports columnist Roger Kahn has suggested that the climate of post-Vietnam America would militate against the violent sports which boomed during the war years – football, ice hockey and so on. "Recently, in peacetime, hockey's ratings slumped and it lost its network television coverage," he said. "We've had our fill here of young men going off to a war that few of us believed in."

Such predictions, however, would appear to be more than a little optimistic, given the continuing popularity of sporting bloodshed. Even allowing for hockey's fluctuations (more the result of marketing greed than fan displeasure), violence moves from strength to strength: the Super Bowl is still the single biggest annual event in America, and the heavyweight boxing crown still the world's richest sporting prize. If anything is to upset the level of bloodshed it will have to come from outside – the spiraling cost of liability insurance prompted by generous court awards to the growing number of injured parties, for example – for within Sportsworld, violent sports are sacrosanct. The reason for this is not only that violence is entertaining, enjoyable or necessary for victory, but that violent competition is considered beneficial, even by those who are most aware of the pain, injury and death it now exacts.

On Aggression

It is the cherished belief of sport's vast constituency that violent sports represent one of the last safety valves for aggression left in our world. People need an avenue, so the argument goes, by which they can vent their hostilities and aggressions in a harmless and socially acceptable fashion. Without such an avenue, aggressions build up like a head of steam in a boiler until they burst out in antisocial directions – muggings, wife beating, warfare and other undesirable forms of behavior. By shooting a deer, boxing a few rounds or by watching a group of paid professionals locked in combat on a football field, people can relieve their pent-up hostilities, work out their aggressions and return home at the end of the day better for it. In other words, health through ventilation.

The theory of vented emotion – the catharsis theory – is by no means a modern discovery. It was first postulated by Aristotle (*catharsis* is derived from a Greek word meaning to purge emotion) who saw the dramatic stage as offering a means of dissipating "pity and fear." Later the theory was applied to sport. It is probable that the Roman rulers viewed the arena as a way of diverting the day-to-day hostilities of the public; certainly the Shrove Tuesday and Lammas Day sporting brawls of rural England were considered annual safety valves. There is also evidence that successive governments allowed the existence of the bare-knuckle prize ring in the hope of defusing the violence of the lower classes which on several occasions, such as the food riots of 1766 and the Gordon riots of 1780, had brought England perilously close to Continental-style revolution. Pierce

❝ What's wrong with a little good clean violence? ❞

Robert Timberlake, All-American quarterback, 1965

> **Would anyone sensibly suggest that the screaming crowds around the boxing ring are having implanted in them the fine qualities of pluck, endurance and restraint?**
>
> Dr. Edith Summerskill, 1960

Egan, for one, believed as much. "It is only from open and manly contests in England," he wrote,"that the desperate and fatal effects of human passion are in great measure, if not totally, prevented." It was not until the ring had already begun to destroy itself that the government turned against prize-fighting, recognizing it as a source, not a sublimation, of violence.

The passion for hunting big game which gripped the civilized world around the turn of this century was also seen as a healthy trend in certain quarters as this quotation from H. H. Munroe ("Saki") indicates:

> If he had unlimited money at his disposal he might go into the wilds somewhere and shoot big game. I never know what the big game have done to deserve it, but they do help to deflect the destructive energies of some of our social misfits.

The catharsis theory enjoyed a renaissance earlier in this century following the discoveries of Sigmund Freud. In an attempt to explain the horrors of World War I, Freud decided that mankind was cursed with an inherent aggressive drive, a "death instinct," which when turned inward led him to destroy himself and when turned outward drove him to destroy others. Other authors took up Freud's idea and developed it further, albeit along more optimistic lines. While acknowledging the existence of inherent aggression, they saw it as a potent drive, "not to be minimized, but to be dealt with; not to be denied, but to be converted; not to be hated, but to be harnessed" (Karl Menninger in *The Vital Balance*, 1963). One way of dealing with the build-up of aggression was by finding it an outlet. As early as 1948 Menninger's brother William was advocating that "competitive games provide an unusually satisfactory outlet for the instinctive aggressive drive." In his Reith Lectures of the same year, Bertrand Russell argued that there was a "savage" within each of us which must find expression through some means compatible with civilized life. He suggested sport, adding that what was wrong with society was that sporting competition played too small a part in the lives of ordinary men and women (a rather strange comment given that by then sport had become the religion of the working man).

It was the Nobel Prize-winning ethologist Konrad Lorenz who brought the catharsis theory to full popular bloom. After a lifetime spent studying the habits of birds and animals, Lorenz came to the conclusion in his celebrated book *On Aggression* (1963) that man was "a dangerously aggressive species" whose innate aggression, while winning him supremacy over his primeval competitors, now threatened him with violent destruction of the species. Man's aggression was an instinctive appetite for fighting, or at least deterring, rivals, he wrote. This appetite built up in the same way as hunger or the sex urge, but whereas an animal could discharge its hostility through fighting or ritual displays of aggression, man's sophisticated weaponry meant that his fights or ritual hostilities inevitably led to bloody conflict. In the age of the H-bomb, the consequences were annihilation. The only hope for mankind lay in redirecting this damned-up aggression into acceptable outlets. As before, it was sport which suggested the perfect solution.

". . . the main function of sport today," wrote Lorenz, "lies in the cathartic discharge of aggressive urge . . ." And there was more to come:

> The most important function of sport lies in furnishing a healthy safety valve for that most indispensable and, at the same time, most dangerous form of aggression that I have described . . . as collective militant enthusiasm. The Olympic Games are virtually the only occasion when the anthem of one nation can be played without arousing any hostility against another. This is so because the sportsman's dedication to the international social norms of his sport, to the ideals of chivalry and fair play, are equal to any national enthusiasm. The team spirit inherent in all international sport gives scope to a number of truly valuable patterns of social behavior which are essentially motivated by aggression and which, in all probability, have evolved under the selection pressure of tribal warfare at the very dawn of culture. The noble warrior's typical virtues, such as his readiness to sacrifice himself in the service of a common cause, disciplined submission to the rank order of the group, mutual aid in the face of deadly danger, and above all, a superlatively strong bond of friendship between men, were obviously indispensable if a small tribe of the type we have to assume for early man was to survive in competition with others. All these virtues are still desirable in modern man and still command our instinctive respect. It is undeniable that there is no situation in which all these virtues shine so brilliantly as they do in war, a fact which is dangerously liable to convince quite excellent but naive people that war, after all, cannot be the absolutely abhorrent thing it really is. Fortunately there are other ways in which the above-mentioned, admittedly valuable, virtues can be cultivated. The harder and more

dangerous forms of sport . . . all give scope for militant enthusiasm, allowing nations to fight each other in hard and dangerous competition without engendering national or political hatred.

It was not a new idea, but it was seductively simple and attractively put. After *On Aggression*, ethology became a popular science, Lorenz became famous, and catharsis – or "Drive Discharge" as it was now being called – became very fashionable. It was made even more appealing by Lorenz's disciples. "It is obvious that the encouragement of competiton in all possible fields is likely to diminish the kind of hostility which leads to war rather than to increase it," wrote British psychiatrist Anthony Storr in *Human Aggression* (1968); ". . . rivalry between nations in sport can do nothing but good." British MP Philip Goodhart and former athlete Chris Chataway wrote an entire book based on the catharsis theory (*War without Weapons*) which concluded:

> The contests will sometimes be far from peaceful. But sport is an outlet for the aggression that lurks beneath the surface in every society. . . . As the twentieth century devises yet more total means of mass destruction, it is not too fanciful to discern an instinct for self-preservation in the popular passion for representative sport. A kind of warfare perhaps. But war *without* the weapons.

More popular still were the works of Lorenzians Robert Ardrey and Desmond Morris. These were particularly warmly received by those already involved in sport; sport as the salvation of mankind was a very comforting thought. So widely accepted was Lorenz's doctrine of catharsis that even professional athletes fell under its spell. (One sports ethologist reported that pro football players had taken to reading Robert Ardrey's *African Genesis* in the locker room.) It tended to support what many sportsmen already knew – that after a tough physical game one "felt better."

Elsewhere, however, Lorenz's theory of an ever-expanding reservoir of aggression within man was being viewed with increasing skepticism. The trouble was that, as feasible as it sounded, this theory was supported by precious little actual empirical evidence. Shortly after the publication of

❝ There are enough real causes of trouble already, and we need not add to them by encouraging young men to kick each other on the shins amid the roars of infuriated spectators. ❞

George Orwell, 1945

On Aggression, Lorenz found himself under quite surprisingly virulent attack from several sides, notably from a group of psychologists who held that aggression was purely a learned behavior, reinforced by conditioning experienced during childhood, adolescence and adult life.

Since then the sources of aggression have been probed by many social scientists. The debate has been long, sometimes bitter and always . . . well, aggressive, with reputations being savaged and charge and countercharge flying from the presses. It still continues. At present, it would appear that Lorenz's detractors have the upper hand, especially with regards to catharsis. In academic circles at least, the drive discharge theory is now pretty much a dead letter. In the locker room, the press box, the bleachers and popular opinion, however, it is still hard currency.

"I think that if we could suit up the whole world in football uniforms," Pittsburgh Steeler Jack Lambert once said, "maybe we wouldn't have any more wars." It would seem that most athletes today would agree, perhaps not with Lambert's choice of sport, but certainly with the idea that athletic contest offers some form of therapy. Of all the sportsmen I spoke to, not one wholly rejected the idea of catharsis through sport, and many of them, from American pro football players to English fox hunters, considered it one of sport's major assets. "I think it's better for people to work out all their violence watching me smash into someone else rather than not to have this outlet and go home from the office and take it out on their families, beat their wives or something," said LA Ram Tom Mack. "[Hunting's] not a bad safety valve," said Master of Hounds Raymond Brooks-Ward. "I think it's catharsis – a way of letting off steam without doing damage to other people. You don't get much violence in the countryside."

In recent years the sporting press has heard many such utterances. When San Diego football coach Harland Svare was asked what he thought football was accomplishing for spectators after being howled off the field by a murderous crowd, he replied, "it's moving it from the front page to the sports page." "Football is the safety valve for these people," said Liverpool soccer manager Bill Shankly in 1971, gesturing at British soccer's problem children. "There would be far more violence without football, I'm sure of that." More recently Oxford psychologist Peter Marsh in his book *Aggro* (1978) warned that to suppress the comparatively harmless outlets of the football ends would only lead to hooliganism being expressed more violently elsewhere.

Catharsis is also a perennial favorite of those connected with boxing. Writing in a 1976 issue of *Amateur Boxing*, Dr. Max Novich, a member of the New Jersey Athletic Commission, attributed the rise in juvenile violence to the decline of organized boxing in schools. "We need more teaching of boxing as an alternative to the increasing amount of violence exhibited by youngsters who have turned to knives, sticks, stones, and bottles instead," he wrote. Boxing was, he felt, "a healthy sublimation of a boy's sadistic and aggressive tendencies," an opinion which was also recently expressed by Britain's minister for sport, Dennis Howell. According to Mr. Howell, boxing presented a perfect cure for soccer hooliganism, the same soccer hooliganism that others see as a perfect safety valve for youthful hostilities.

But the sport which dovetails most neatly with the catharsis theory is pro wrestling, and it has done so ever since the appearance during the late '40s of a New York psychiatrist named Dr. George Wagner, or "Georgeous George" as he was better known. It was Wagner's theory that the overt violence of professional wrestling could have possible therapeutic benefits for wrestling fans by acting as a catharsis. This catharsis, he reasoned, would be best achieved if the contest was between a recognizable "good guy" and an equally recognizable, rule-breaking "bad guy" – the classis struggle of good against evil. Wagner, who was himself a former Olympic wrestling gold medalist, took it upon himself to personify evil in the shape of Georgeous George, a repellently effeminate and vicious character. After letting his hair grow to his shoulders (this was the '40s, remember) and dying it gold, Wagner took to mincing around the ring dressed in gold lamé cloaks and velvet gowns blowing kisses to his apoplectic audiences. "The more spectators hate me," he wrote in his autobiography *Is There a Doctor in the Ring?*, "the more they will be free to love one another." And they hated him with a passion.

As the "man they love to hate," Wagner was a box office phenomenon, attracting huge crowds in the hope that he would be smeared around the ring by his opponent (a fact not lost on the young Cassius Clay, who was so impressed by George's arrogant performance on a TV chat show that he immediately adopted the same bad guy persona). Unfortunately the strain of keeping up dual careers proved too much for him (his psychiatric colleagues were unsympathetic to his theory, accusing him of "not playing with a full deck") and he eventually suffered a mental breakdown in the corridors of New York's Bellvue Hospital. After wrestling several security guards to the ground, he was finally straight-jacketed, sedated and led away into obscurity. He died a broken man in Los Angeles in 1963, the year that Lorenz's *On Aggression* linking sport and catharsis was first published.

Today Wagner's theory is still loudly expounded by wrestlers on both sides of the Atlantic. For British promoter Mike Judd, wrestling is the perfect avenue for working off aggression. "I think it's very good for people," he said. "Wrestling lets them get rid of all their emotions." American wrestler Butcher Vachon agreed: "They might be angry at their mother-

> ❝ I'd prefer those people got their aggressions out screaming at wrestlers than taking it out onto the street. I'm not a psychiatrist and I don't know if it's healthy to do it, but it's healthier for me if they do it in there. ❞
>
> Dick Schaap, *Sport* magazine, 1977

in-law or want to give hell to the boss, and they pay their four dollars and they come in here and it lets off steam." "Wrestling is number one sport for people," said Japanese star Professor Tanaka. "You know why? Many people so tense, must have some kind of let out. Wrestling is number one let out for everything in sight. People get let out, they go home and sleep that night. That is why they come to wrestling."

It may seem rather odd that the idea of catharsis is so popular with modern sportsmen considering that many of its exponents will, in the very next breath, acknowledge that violent games are ideal for inspiring militarism among players. One example of this double thinking is Major General Harry W. Brooks, Jr.'s "combat football," a bastard game in which two large teams of soldiers battle each other with neither armor nor rules. According to *Sports Illustrated* the general's aim in promoting such a violent game was first "to diminish racial and other tensions both within the division and between soldiers and the local community," and secondly "to sharpen his division to round-the-clock combat readiness." "It builds aggressiveness and a fighting heart," commented the general. "At the same time it burns off the kind of aggression that soldiers sometimes turn against local people when they are on duty." How sport could be so selective, increasing one form of aggression while diminishing others, the general did not explain. Yet despite such glaring contradictions, the beliefs that sports build warrior aggressions on the one hand while acting as a catharsis on the other sit happily enough in the minds of most sportsmen.

The trouble with the catharsis theory is that, like Lorenz's idea of the ever-widening well of aggression, there is very little evidence proving that it exists. Indeed, the fact is that almost all the research over the past few decades has pointed to exactly the opposite conclusion.

A Brutal Route to Nirvana

Those most likely to experience catharsis through sport would seem to be the players themselves, those athletes who confess to "feeling better" after a hard workout or a successful day's shooting. However, whether "feeling better" means in fact that the subject is less aggressive because of his sporting experience is highly doubtful, as laboratory tests have indicated. In one early experiment, subjects were given several minutes of strenuous nonviolent physical exercise (bicycle riding) and then tested for aggression. The subjects all showed heightened aggression when they were asked to administer punishment to a fellow student. This occurred regardless of whether or not they had previously been angered by the student, but those who had been angered displayed even more aggression. In other words, not only did the exercise not act as a catharsis, but it had the effect of strengthening aggressive inclinations. In a similar experiment an American psychologist, E. Dean Ryan, found that while physical activity produced no decrease in aggression, the subjects who were the most aggressive all said that they "felt better."

When active competition is added to violent physical exertion, the chance of players experiencing a catharsis becomes even more unlikely. In one 1971 laboratory study, after watching an adult playing aggressively, children were placed in either a competitive or a noncompetitive situation. The children who took part in the competition – whether they won or lost – were more likely to follow the adult's earlier aggressive behavior in their own play after the experiment. Competition, then, heightened rather than lessened the children's susceptibility to aggressive influence.

In an earlier experiment (1952), a class of nine-year-olds was divided into two groups. The first group was given a number of "constructive" activities to pursue – drawing murals, doing jigsaw puzzles. The researchers encouraged all forms of cooperation while discouraging aggressive behavior. Meanwhile the second group was given three highly competitive and aggressive games, and for them all aggressive tendencies were praised and encouraged. After seven ten-minute sessions, the children were finally placed in a free-play situation where they were then purposely frustrated. Those who had been given the competitive games behaved more aggressively than those who had experienced the cooperative activities. Another experiment has suggested that children who lose during competitive play are particularly likely to play aggressively afterwards.

One of the most famous experiments involving aggression and competition was the "Robber's Cave" experiment conducted by Muzafer and Carolyn Sherif in 1963. The subjects were 11- and 12-year-old boys at a summer camp. The boys were split into two groups and over the next few days took part in a tournament of competitive games – baseball, touch football, tug of war – which offered handsome prizes for the winning group and nothing for the losers. Although the tournament began in a spirit of good sportsmanship, it quickly degenerated into "vicious contests in which the sole aim was to win and in which the competitors became increasingly seen as a bunch of incorrigible cheats, quite outside the pale of that brand of humanity identified within one's group." Each group spent the day brooding over winning strategies; leaders or other previously respected boys who tried to modify the conflict were replaced; and acknowledged bullies who previously had been put in their place were now looked on as "heroes of combat." Hostile raids and other acts of aggression spilled over into areas outside the athletic competition, and the two groups took to hoarding caches of hard green apples to ward off attackers.

Life in the camp was becoming a war, as Carolyn Sherif recorded in *Social Problems in Athletics* (1976):

> Upon the victory of one group in the tournament, boys in each group possessed attitudes of extreme prejudice and hostility, universally condemning the individual characters of members of their rival group. In fact, each wanted nothing to do with the other group.

When the two groups were purposely brought together:

> they used these contact situations as opportunities for recriminations, for accusations of "who's to blame" for the existing state of affairs, for hurling invectives, and when food was present, for "garbage wars" that had to be stopped when the weapons changed from mashed potatoes and paper to forks and knives.

The results of the experiments showed, the Sherifs concluded, that "prolonged competition on a win-lose basis between groups of children had effects that extended far beyond the specific context of the games." It was only when the boys' attentions were diverted to a series of "subordinate goals" – a broken pipe supplying the camp's water, a damaged food supply truck – which required cooperative effort that the hostility diminished and, after a considerable period of time, friendship was restored.

These experiments are, of course, controlled experiments and as such

---

❝ Of the seventeen thousand fans in this place, I'll bet a thousand of them aren't all there. They let their emotions get to them, they spit on players, curse at them, throw things at them. Some night a guy is going to come in here with a loaded gun. ❞

Fred Shero, coach of the Philadelphia Flyers, 1977

---

are prone to a number of flaws and defects common to all situations divorced from complete reality. However, the similarities between the Sherifs' nightmare summer camp and much of modern sport are obvious, especially for games such as pro football and ice hockey (the USSR *vs.* Canada ice hockey series of 1972 which degenerated into bitter group brawling springs most immediately to mind). Like the summer camp, sport is dominated by an intense desire to win at the expense of an opponent, the spoils being the Super Bowl, money, adulation and fat contracts; it operates in an escalating atmosphere of hatred; and the violence and aggression of its participants is continually encouraged and applauded by coaches, spectators, owners and other players. Although interviews with sports bogey men usually follow a Jckyll-and-Hyde line – "He's really a pussycat off the ice," a Mrs. Dave Schultz will invariably tell the press – if the Sherif children did not manage to experience catharsis from their own limited conflict, there is even less to indicate that athletes who have usually been subjected to a continuing encouragement of aggression since their days in the Little League will do so. Indeed, it is hard not to believe that this constant reinforcement of aggression has a considerable impact on players' overall levels of aggression.

In the short term this was borne out by the observations of Dr. Max Novich, the passionate advocate of boxing as catharsis. According to Dr. Novich, new boys to his boxing classes became less passive and visibly more aggressive after even just a few sparring sessions:

> With patience, criticism, and concern, we have been able to develop many nonassertive boys into excellent boxers who exhibit appropriate aggressive responses as the situation calls for it. There are some boys who show a hesistancy to get involved. Those we let watch a few sessions with encouragement rather than prodding; we even managed to get them into the act.

Although there is little evidence either way, it is possible that violence and competition have a lasting effect on players. Of the 1,015 Wisconsin hunters polled throughout the state, only 36 percent considered that there was too much violence on television. Surveys of the total population in Wisconsin, however, showed that 64 percent thought that there was too much televised violence. In other words, only half as many hunters recognized violent television as did the rest of the population. This figure is, of course, open to several interpretations. But one of the foremost must surely be that hunting desensitizes its participants to violence.

In a game such as pro football, with its added burden of intense competition, the effects on players could be even more lasting. "Hatred causes mental illness, paranoia and depression," said Arnold Mandell:

And football players, because of the amount of rage they make a living with are that kind of person. So if they don't have it mobilized – going out – boy, are they a depressive lot! They tend to get depressed very easily, and the defensive team, which is the most rageful of the teams, can get *very* depressed. It's almost as if to feel well they have to be sticking it into somebody, and if it's not somebody else it's themselves.

In Dr. Mandell's view there should be halfway houses to help retired football players adjust to civilian life – not just to get them used to their lack of star status, but also to assist them in overcoming the need for a prolonged weekly bout of "orgiastic violence." It was the sudden absence of this dose of violence that often prompted players to take on a fringe drug life in retirement, he said. In his view, pro football was anything but a catharsis.

There are several well-known examples supporting Mandell's experiences, one of them being the celebrated Pittsburgh Steeler line of Mean Joe Greene, Jack Lambert and Ernie Holmes. While one moment Lambert was suiting up the whole world to end wars, the next he was detailing how his love of bar brawling had been abruptly curtailed by a whisky glass thrown at his head: "The blood was dripping in my eye and I couldn't see. I thought I was blind. That brought some realization. I've become more discreet since then." These are hardly the words of a man whose every aggression is drained each Sunday afternoon. Lambert's teammate Holmes is even less of an advertisement for the drive discharge theory. "I don't think I'm a violent person," he confessed on one occasion, "but sometimes at night when we're on a road trip, I look across at my roommate in bed, and I want to throw him against the wall." Ernie Holmes, it should be recalled, was the man who was driven to pick off trucks on the highway with his hunting rifle and who attempted to shoot a police helicopter out of the sky. "All my life I have had difficulty dealing with people," admitted Mean Joe Greene. As with his colleagues, it is unlikely that pro football has helped him with his aggression problems.

In late 1974 I spent a morning with Muhammad Ali sitting in the sunshine on the banks of the Zaire River. Less than five hours earlier Ali had reclaimed his heavyweight crown from George Foreman in a violent and bruising seven-round bout. If ever a man should have been drained of aggression it was Ali, and for a while, sitting peacefully with his camp followers, he was the perfect Lorenzian picture of catharsis. Suddenly a large African lizard scurried around the corner of the house and Ali leaped up and gave chase. As he caught up to it, the lizard froze and then frantically began to bury itself in the dirt. For a few seconds Ali watched it and then, with a wolfish grin, stamped it to death with several blows of his boot heel.

I left the camp shortly afterwards, and the picture I took with me was of the new world champion sitting on his verandah waving goodbye with one hand and with the other stabbing with his walking stick at the huge brilliant butterflies which clung to his wall. It was a bizarre sight, Ali savagely crushing the life out of butterflies, and one that spoke very little for catharsis.

Sport for the Fans – Release or Riot?

In their book *Sex, Violence and the Media* (1978), Professor H. J. Eysenck and Dr. D. K. B. Nias described the case of a patient whose wife had just left him for another man. The patient was advised by his doctor to take up football and pretend that the ball was the other man's head in order to relieve his hostility. The man ended up in court charged with smashing his rival over the head with a cosh. "Had the doctor been aware of the extremely tenuous nature of the evidence for catharsis," commented Eysenck and Nias, "he may have been inclined to offer a more effective form of advice." Still, however, the notion of catharsis still lingers. In another recent book (*Ectopia*) which has now gained considerable cult following in America, author Ernest Callenback suggests that in his visionary Utopia of the future, a twenty-hour work week will allow citizens time for "ritual war games designed to relieve aggressive tendencies." Not so much a brave new world, perhaps, as a foolish one.

Sport as it is played today awards participants only a bit part in the overall drama. Nowadays it is the fan who comprises the overwhelming bulk of sporting activity and it is on his shoulders that the theory of catharsis has come to rest most heavily. As indicated earlier, many sportsmen, especially those involved in violent sports, believe that they are fulfilling a higher purpose by releasing the hostilities of those in the stands. However, if sport is of dubious value as an outlet for players' aggressions, it is doubly questionable as a means of providing a cathartic experience for its spectators.

Much research has been done in recent years into the effects of viewing violence, not so much in relation to sport, but as part of the much-publicized debate over televised violence. To most people the results of this research probably appear inconclusive, with the television industry supporting the idea of catharsis through violence, and the critics arguing that watching violence only leads to more violence. However, as Eysenck and Nias have shown in their recent review of the experiments so far completed, the evidence is far from inconclusive. Of the 250 or so experiments which have been conducted, 200 showed violence to have a harmful effect on the viewer, 50 were borderline and only the merest handful supported the idea that televised violence had any sort of beneficial effect whatsoever. Although many of these experiments were severely flawed, it would seem evident that those football coaches who have taken to showing war footage to their teams before an important match are on strong psychological ground. "Whatever effect TV violence has is almost certainly in the direction of increasing rather than decreasing aggression," concluded Eysenck and Nias.

Television violence and sporting violence are, of course, two different things. As Dr. Nias told me, however, he would be very surprised if there was not a considerable overlap between the two. "Not only is it untenable to argue that 'the battle of Waterloo was won on the playing fields of Eton,' " he and Eysenck wrote, "it is also untenable to argue that wars can be prevented there." One of the experiments they cite in their book in fact dealt directly with watching sport. In 1971 American researchers J. H. Goldstein and R. L. Arms interviewed and assessed spectators before and after both a college football game (Army/Navy) and a gymnastics competition. The results found that hostility did not increase for the gymnastics spectators, but it did increase significantly among the football spectators. Interestingly enough, this rise was unaffected by whether or not the subject's team had won or lost; all the football fans experienced heightened aggression.

There have been several other studies involving sports spectators. In 1969 E. S. Turner examined the effects on college spectators of watching a football game, a basketball game and a wrestling match. Although there was no significant increase in aggression following the wrestling – a result Turner thought may possibly have been caused by the small crowd and the extreme one-sidedness of the contest – there was a significant rise in spectators' aggression following both the football and basketball games. "The results of the study do not support the cathartic or purge theory of aggression," Turner reported. Rather, he said, the results seemed to support the contention "that the viewing of violent or aggressive acts tends to increase the aggressiveness of the viewer."

Leonard Berkowitz has conducted several laboratory experiments using boxing footage from the film *The Champion*. He has found that the footage elicited aggression so long as the spectators believed that the fight was "aggressive" – in other words, that they thought one fighter was trying not merely to beat his opponent but to injure him as well. With the preponderance of "grudge" matches purposely manufactured to fill boxing and wrestling arenas, it is likely that many fans see bouts in exactly those terms. In 1966 Berkowitz and R. G. Geen showed the fight footage to one group of students and film of a track race to another group. Following the screening, neither group was more aggressive than the other. However, prior to seeing the film a number of the students had been angered by a researcher. After

---

**44 I think hockey and football will be more violent in the year
2000 because we may be such a sedentary society that we
need some release for our emotions. It'll be a matter of
psychological therapy to have violent sport. We may not
see men fighting to the death, but we could have animals
killing each other – cockfights, pit bulldogs, maybe even
piranhas eating each other to death on television.   77**

Lee Walburn, an executive of Atlanta's Omni group
which owns the NHL Flames and the NBA Hawks, 1975

---

the screening they were given their chance for revenge; those who had seen the boxing footage administered measurably more punishment than those who had seen the track film. According to Berkowitz, the combination of arousal and aggressive cues thrown up by sport increases rather than decreases the probability of open violence.

There are other such experiments on record, and now even Konrad Lorenz has qualified his views on sport as catharsis. In the April 1976 issue of *Psychology Today*, Lorenz stated that: "Nowadays I have strong doubts whether watching aggressive behavior even in the guise of sport has any cathartic effect at all."

The results of these experiments should come as no surprise to anyone who has sat in the bleachers or stood on the terraces over the past few years. To anyone who has kept half an eye cocked on sport over the last decade it should be blindingly obvious that sporting competition involving physical contact or, more particularly, a degree of violence, leads to spectator aggression on a depressingly frequent number of occasions. Instances of wives living in dread of their husbands' returning after Saturday's match looking to batter them have been reported from Melbourne to Manchester. (The wives have some cause for alarm for they are not without historical precedent: the emperor Nero, an inveterate chariot racing fan, once returned home from the circus and kicked his wife Poppaea to death.) Boxing matches have become notorious both in America and elsewhere for aggravating racial tensions into open hostility. Soccer riots, the endemic bottle throwing of American football, professional wrestling with its umbrellas and hatpins and bullets, none of these could by any stretch of the imagination truly be considered cathartic. Nor could the games which turned black high school students against white high school students in America during the '60s and early '70s.

Could the riots which erupted in the Pamplona bullring in 1978 have occurred at a tennis match? Was it merely a coincidence that they occurred during one of the most passionate and violent spectacles in existence? Is the soccer hooligan working out aggressions that would lead to a rise in muggings and social violence were they to go untapped? Or is he simply an average working-class youth who has his aggressions aroused every Saturday between the hours of three and five and who is then suddenly released into the street?

The international sporting scene is even more transparent. Regardless of its use as a political tool, international sport itself engenders its own hostilities all too readily. The classic example used to be the March 1969 defeat of the Russian ice hockey team at the hands of the Czechs. The match succeeded in uncovering all the ill-feeling implanted by the Soviet invasion of Czechoslovakia. However, instead of being satisfied with their victory, Czech supporters went on to ransack the Prague offices of the Russian airline.

The latest World Cup has provided an even more recent example. Neither Brazil nor Argentina had any cause for mutual ill feeling save that for many years they have been particularly intense soccer rivals. During the World Cup it was feared that this rivalry could spill over into international hostility. Quite early during the competition the Brazilians became, in the eyes of the Argentinian fans, the "hated Brazilians"; the Brazilians were booed and their opponents applauded. When it appeared that both teams might in fact reach the final, trouble was widely predicted – especially if Argentina lost. As it turned out, Brazil had to be content with third place. The nation's feelings on its defeat were best indicated by its sacking of the entire national team on its return home. Ill feeling between the two countries reportedly remained high months after the competition.

As George Orwell wrote in 1945 after an English tour by a Russian football team:

> Now that the brief visit of the Dynamo football team has come to an end, it is possible to say . . . that sport is an unfailing cause of ill-will and that if such a visit as this had any effect on Anglo-Soviet relations it could only be to make them slightly worse than before.

To date there has been little to contradict him.

War, not Peace

The most damning evidence refuting the idea of catharsis through sports comes from the investigations of American anthropologist Dr. Richard D. Sipes conducted in 1973. It was Dr. Sipes's intention to test both the drive discharge theory and the opposing "Cultural Pattern" – or learned aggression – model. He achieved this by the brilliantly obvious method of comparing the sports favored by different societies. If the drive discharge theory was correct, he reasoned, then societies which were most warlike would show a lower incidence of combative sports as they would have little need for other aggression outlets. Alternately, more peaceful societies, denied the outlet of warfare, would display a higher incidence of aggressive sports. On the other hand, if the learned-aggression theory was correct, it would mean that warlike societies would throw up warlike games and peaceful societies peaceful games.

Dr. Sipes selected at random ten warlike societies and ten peaceful societies. Of the ten warlike societies, he discovered, nine had combative sports and only one did not. Of the ten peaceful societies, only two had combative sports and eight did not. Further examining 130 different societies, Sipes found that there were only four exceptions to the rule that "where we find warlike behavior we typically find combative sports and where war is relatively rare combative sports tend to be absent." Catharsis, in Dr. Sipes's reckoning, was disproved. To further verify his findings, he examined the social history of the United States from 1920 to 1970, comparing the level of military activity for each year against the popularity of two combative sports (hunting and football) and two noncombative sports (betting and watching baseball). Again the drive discharge theory, which predicts a high incidence of milder sports during years of increased militarism, was disproved. In fact, the results indicated the exact opposite. Sports, Sipes concluded:

> especially combative team sports, do not serve as functional alternatives to other forms of aggression, such as warfare. Sports and war would appear to be components of a broader cultural pattern. The hope would seem dim of using sports to influence warfare, or any of the other forms of undesirable aggressive behavior. Attempting to siphon off aggressive tension by promulgating the observation of, or participation in, aggressive sports is more than a futile effort; to the degree that it had any effect at all, it most likely would raise the level of aggression in other social and individual behavior patterns. . . . My research would indicate that aggressive behavior is best reduced by eliminating combative or conflict-type sports.

Sipes's message is clear enough: combative sport is not merely aggressive entertainment; it is a violent curse.

We live in violent times – a cliché, but true nevertheless. In the decade from 1958 to 1968 (exactly the years during which pro football rose to unassailable popularity) violent crime in the United States increased by 100 percent. Since then it has continued to rise. Each year fifteen thousand Americans are murdered. In other western countries, although crime is generally on a far smaller scale, recent decades have also seen a marked tendency toward violence. In the United Kingdom the rate of indictable crime almost doubled during the years from 1960 to 1970, and over the quarter-century since 1951 violence against individuals increased ten-fold. As H. Rap Brown once said, "Violence is as American as apple pie." It is now fast becoming the national dish of other countries as well.

Against this background of rising social violence, the level of violence in sport has also increased dramatically until it has now, in many instances, reached Roman proportions. Under the dictates of our exploitive age we have turned great areas of play into theaters of blood, attracting an audience which is even more Roman than the Romans. Our sportsmen no longer purposely strive to slaughter each other, but we often attend in the hope that they will. We do not callously use "subhuman" slaves to entertain us with their blood, but we distance ourselves from our own gladiators through television so that they are deemed expendable, something less than human. We do not force athletes into blood sports against their will, but we have made the rewards so enticing that there are now any number of participants willing to risk their limbs and their lives for our benefit. Whether press-ganged or paid, they provide the same end result: violence and bloodshed for the delectation of others. Our sporting entertainments give the lie to the popular belief that blood spectacles are the sole prerogative of civilizations that are losing their grip. We the sophisticates of the modern age have become super connoisseurs of sporting violence.

It would be fatuous to blame our societies' violence on our violent sports, as fatuous as expecting sport to carry the burden of our private and national pride without its exploding in our faces. However, as Sipes and his colleagues have indicated, it is no longer just enough to excuse the brutality of sport by regarding it as merely a reflection of the violent society which surrounds it. The evidence seems overwhelming that the link between violent sport and violence in society is much greater than that of just a mirror and its image. Sport as catharsis is a myth; sport as another bullet in the chamber of social violence is a grave probability.

Which leads to the inevitable question: Can we afford to blithely follow the line of sporting violence without any regard for the consequences? Do we really need to perpetuate war games when the age in which wars were battles between athletes have long since passed? Can we, in view of the violence which so often stems from them, continue to risk violent sports?

In my opinion we can't.

Which does not mean that we should immediately reject our traditional games and throw ourselves wholeheartedly into frisbee. Some of our most overtly violent sports – football, ice hockey – seem to me to be eminently redeemable. The fault that they are so fearsomely brutal lies not with the games themselves, but with the burdens we have placed upon them – the wild-eyed craving for petty two-hour Saturday and Sunday afternoon victories; the demand for masculinity by proxy; the desire for blood. Stripped of these burdens they would still be fascinating and delightful games – skillfull, cooperative and as much a pleasure to watch as to play. They would also be infinitely less lethal.

Other sports, however, the ones whose only purpose in life is to provide a vehicle for merchandising violence, might be better discarded. Blood and pit sports – hunting, bullfighting, cockfighting and so on – besides being a callous waste of animal and human life, seem to me to be irrevocably brutal and brutalizing. Boxing, too, would have been better left to rust in the Colosseum along with the Christians' chains and the lion cages. I can see no possible good in encouraging young and invariably deprived men to literally scramble each other's brains in the name of sport. Does anybody seriously believe that Evel Knievel and the other motorized gladiators are desirable examples of twentieth-century Manhood?

These are, of course, the opinions of one man. They stand about as much chance of being implemented as of Vince Lombardi's rising from the grave to accept the Women's Guild's Good Sportsman award. The lessons of aggression, competitiveness, manliness and victory were drummed into us at childbirth, and we are now drumming them into successive generations with an even greater missionary zeal. We have been weaned onto violent sport at an early age, and our hard-edged visions are being constantly reinforced by an ever-growing superstructure of promoters, owners, coaches, players and media mouthpieces who all live off the proceeds of those visions and who all quote from the same sportsman's bible that to win is everything, to maim is manly, and to kill an animal glorious. Even the days of rule changing now seem past. When Darryl Stingley, a wide receiver for the New England

Patriots, broke his neck in a helmet-to-helmet confrontation in late 1978, one of the few NFL statements to emanate from what amounted to a virtual media blackout was this classic statement from Tex Schramm. "No one liked the assassination of President Kennedy," said Schramm, "but the world had to go on." We are now back to the days of the dilemma over the flying wedge, only this time there is no Roosevelt to force the issue. After all, who is going to tamper with a game which, over the next four seasons starting 1979–80, will receive 656 million dollars from television rights alone?

The future of violent sports seems assured. Games will grow harder and bloodier to feed the rising appetite of an audience which will grow both increasingly more jaded and sated with violence, and increasingly more violent itself, until, perhaps, something happens to bring it all crashing down. This time around, though, the likelihood is that it won't be the barbarian hordes outside banging on the gates which will destroy the Colosseum. This time the violence will be of sport's own making and will come from within the walls of the Colosseum itself.

Selected Bibliography

The literature of sport is inordinately large and to list all the books I have found useful during my research would require far more space than is available here. What follows is a list of contemporary books that have proved particularly valuable.

General

Butt, Dorcas Susan. *Psychology of Sport* New York: Van Nostrand Reinhold, 1976

Dunstan, Keith. *Sports* Australia: Cassell, 1973

Ford, John. *This Sporting Land* London: New English Library, 1977

Gardner, Paul. *Nice Guys Finish Last* London: Allen Lane, 1974

Lipsyte, Robert. *Sportsworld* New York: Quadrangle, 1975

McIntosh, P. C. *Sport in Society* London: C. A. Watts, 1971

Michener, James A. *Sports in America* New York: Random House, 1976

Roberts, Michael. *Fans!* Washington: New Republic, 1976

Scott, Jack *The Athletic Revolution* New York: Free Press, 1971

1 Call of the Wild

Amory, Cleveland. *Man Kind?* New York: Dell, 1974

Ardrey, Robert. *The Hunting Hypothesis* London: William Collins, 1976

Brander, Michael. *Hunting and Shooting* London: Weidenfeld & Nicholson, 1971

Caras, Roger A. *Death as a Way of Life* New York: Little, Brown, 1970

Elliot, J. G. *Field Sports in India* London: Gentry Books, 1973

Holman, Dennis. *Inside Safari Hunting* London: W. H. Allen, 1969

Morris, Desmond. *The Naked Ape* London: Jonathan Cape, 1967

Ortega y Gasset, José. *Meditations on Hunting* New York: Scribners, 1947

Ruark, Robert. *Use Enough Gun* London: Hamish Hamilton, 1967

Waterman, Charles F. *Hunting in America* New York: Holt, Rinehart and Winston, 1973

2 Give 'Em What They Want

Chesney, Kellow. *The Victorian Underworld* London: Maurice Temple Smith, 1970

Fulton, John. *Bullfighting* New York: The Dial Press, 1971

Schnell, Fred. *Rodeo! The Suicide Circuit* New York: Rand McNally, 1971

3 Blood and Canvas

Ford, John. *Prizefighting* Devon: David & Charles, 1971

Grant, Michael. *Gladiators* London: Pelican, 1971

Heller, Peter. *In This Corner!* New York: Dell, 1973

Reid, J. C. *Bucks and Bruisers* London: Routledge & Kegan Paul, 1971

Roberts, A. H. *Brain Damage in Boxers* London: Pitman Medical and Scientific, 1969

4 The Brawl Game

Cope, Myron. *The Game That Was* New York: Thomas Y. Crowell, 1974

Gitler, Ira. *Blood on the Ice* Chicago: Henry Regnery, 1974

Hoch, Paul. *Rip Off the Big Game* New York: Doubleday, 1972

Kaye, Ivan N. *Good Clean Violence* Philadelphia: Lippincott, 1973

Kramer, Jerry and Schaap, Dick. *Instant Replay* New York: Signet, 1969

Mandell, Arnold J. *The Nightmare Season* New York: Random House, 1976

Mason, Nicholas. *Football!* London: Maurice Temple Smith, 1974

Meggyesy, Dave. *Out of Their League* New York: Warner, 1971

Shero, Fred. *Shero: The Man Behind the System* Pennsylvania: Chilton, 1975

Zimmerman, Paul. *A Thinking Man's Guide to Pro Football* New York: Warner, 1972

5 The Winning Edge

Davies, Hunter. *The Glory Game* London: Weidenfeld and Nicholson, 1972

Hopcraft, Arthur. *The Football Man* London: Collins, 1968

Ralbovsky, Marty. *Lords of the Locker Room.* Peter H. Wyden, 1974

Tutko, Thomas and Bruns, William. *Winning Is Everything and Other American Myths* New York: Macmillan, 1976

Vinnai, Gerhard. *Football Mania* London: Ocean Books, 1973

6 Soldiers for Sport

Cohen, Stanley (Ed.). *Images of Deviance* Middlesex: Penguin, 1971

Ingham, Roger. *Football Hooliganism* London: Inter-Action Inprint, 1978

Robins, David and Cohen, Philip. *Knuckle Sandwich* Middlesex: Penguin, 1978

7 The New Rome

Fischler, Stan. *Slashing!* New York: Warner, 1975

Kahn, Mark. *Death Race* London: Barrie & Jenkins, 1976

Silber, Mark. *Racing Stock* New York: Dolphin, 1976

8 Sport as Catharsis – The Myth Exploded

Eysenck, H. J. and Nias, D. K. B. *Sex, Violence and the Media* London: Maurice Temple Smith, 1978

Goodhart, Philip and Chataway, Christopher. *War without Weapons* London: W. H. Allen, 1968

Lorenz, Konrad. *On Aggression* London: Methuen, 1966

Montagu, Ashley. *The Nature of Human Aggression* New York: Oxford University Press, 1976

Storr, Anthony. *Human Aggression* London: Allen Lane, 1968

Picture Credits

The author and publishers wish to acknowledge the following persons, agencies and institutions for permission to reproduce their material.

Camera Press: p. 322 (top and bottom)
Colorsport: pp. 186–7 (all)
CP Wirephoto: p. 125 (bottom)
Theo Ehret: p. 124
Richard Grona: pp. 14–15
Humane Society of the United States: p. 16 (bottom)
George Kalinsky: p. 126
Keystone Press: pp. 354–5
Los Angeles Rams: pp. 184–5
Ortiz: pp. 82–3
Photography, Inc.: p. 188

Rex Features: pp. 84, 320–1 (plus inset)
James Roark: pp. 8, 122–3, 238–9, 240, 374
Sports Illustrated: pp. 16 (bottom: photo by Eric Schweikardt), 298 (top and bottom: photos by Walter Ioos, Jr.). All photos copyright © 1978 Time, Inc.
Syndication International: pp. 296–7, 356
Wide World: p. 125 (top)

Index

Following is a comprehensive listing of names, places, sports and teams found in the text. Due to space limitations, however, it was necessary to exclude many of the minor historical figures who receive only passing mention.